The WTO after Hong Kong

After the World Trade Organisation's (WTO) critical December 2005 Hong Kong ministerial meeting, negotiations to implement the Doha Development Agenda (DDA) broke down completely in the summer of 2006. This book offers a detailed and critical evaluation of how and why the negotiations arrived at this point and what the future holds for the WTO. It brings together leading scholars in the field of trade from across the social sciences who address the key issues at stake, the principal players in the negotiations, the role of fairness and legitimacy in the Doha Round, and the prospects for the DDA's conclusion.

This is the most comprehensive account of the current state of the World Trade Organisation and will be of enormous interest to students of trade politics, international organisations, development, and international political economy.

Donna Lee is Senior Lecturer at the University of Birmingham, UK and author of *Middle Powers and Commercial Diplomacy: British Influence at the Kennedy Trade Round* (Palgrave, 1999), *The New Multilateralism in South African Diplomacy* (edited with Ian Taylor and Paul D. Williams) (Palgrave 2006), *Africa in the WTO* (forthcoming, Routledge), and *International Organisation: Global Governance* (with Rorden Wilkinson) (Oxford University Press, forthcoming).

Rorden Wilkinson is Professor of International Political Economy at the University of Manchester. He is author of *The WTO: Crisis and Governance of Global Trade* (Routledge, 2006) and *Multilateralism and the World Trade Organisation* (Routledge, 2000), editor of *The Global Governance Reader* (Routledge, 2005), and co-editor of *Global Governance: Critical Perspectives* (Routledge, 2002). He also co-edits the *RIPE Series in Global Political Economy* and the *Global Institutions Series* (both Routledge).

The WTO after Hong Kong

Progress in, and prospects for, the Doha Development Agenda

Edited by
Donna Lee and Rorden Wilkinson

Routledge
Taylor & Francis Group

LONDON AND NEW YORK

First published 2007
by Routledge
2 Park Square, Milton Park, Abingdon, Oxon OX14 4RN

Simultaneously published in the USA and Canada
by Routledge
270 Madison Avenue, New York, NY 10016

Routledge is an imprint of the Taylor & Francis Group, an informa business

© 2007 Donna Lee and Rorden Wilkinson

Typeset in Times New Roman by
Keystroke, 28 High Street, Tettenhall, Wolverhampton
Printed and bound in Great Britain by
Antony Rowe Ltd, Chippenham, Wiltshire

British Library Cataloguing in Publication Data
A catalogue record for this book is available from the British Library

Library of Congress Cataloging in Publication Data
A catalog record for this book has been requested

ISBN 10: 0–415–43194–8 (hbk)
ISBN 10: 0–415–43202–2 (pbk)
ISBN 10: 0–203–96109–9 (ebk)

ISBN 13: 978–0–415–43194–1 (hbk)
ISBN 13: 978–0–415–43202–3 (pbk)
ISBN 13: 978–0–203–96109–4 (ebk)

**For Robert and Katie
and for Claire**

Contents

Illustrations

Figures

Tables

Contributors

Jennifer Clapp is CIGI Chair in International Governance and Associate Professor in the Faculty of Environmental Studies at the University of Waterloo, Canada. Her books include (co-authored with Peter Dauvergne) *Paths to a Green World: The Political Economy of the Global Environment* (MIT Press, 2005), *Toxic Exports: The Transfer of Hazardous Wastes from Rich to Poor Countries* (Cornell, 2001), and *Adjustment and Agriculture in Africa: Farmers, the State and the World Bank in Guinea* (Macmillan, 1997).

Wyn Grant is Professor of Politics at the University of Warwick, UK. He has written extensively on agricultural policy and trade issues. He is the author of *The Common Agricultural Policy* (Palgrave, 1997), co-author of *Agriculture in the New Global Economy* (Edward Elgar, 1994), and co-editor of *The Politics of International Trade in the 21st Century* (Palgrave, 2005).

Bernard Hoekman is the manager of the international trade team of the Development Research Group of the World Bank. He has worked extensively on the Middle East and North Africa and economies in transition. Between 1988 and 1993 he was on the staff of the GATT Secretariat in Geneva. He is a graduate of the Erasmus University Rotterdam, holds a PhD in economics from the University of Michigan and is a research fellow of the London-based Centre for Economic Policy Research.

Donna Lee is Senior Lecturer at the University of Birmingham, UK, and author of *Middle Powers and Commercial Diplomacy: British Influence at the Kennedy Trade Round* (Palgrave, 1999), *The New Multilateralism in South African Diplomacy* (edited with Ian Taylor and Paul D. Williams) (Palgrave 2006), *Africa in the WTO* (forthcoming, Routledge), and *International Organisation: Global Governance* (with Rorden Wilkinson) (Oxford University Press, forthcoming).

Aaditya Mattoo is Lead Economist in the Development Research Group of the World Bank. Prior to joining the Bank in 1999 he was Economic Counsellor at the Trade in Services Division of the WTO. He also served as Economic Affairs Officer in the Economic Research and Analysis and Trade Policy Review Divisions of the WTO. He has lectured in economics at the University of Sussex and was lector at Churchill College, Cambridge University. He is co-editor of *Development, Trade and the WTO: A Handbook* (World Bank, 2002), *India and the WTO* (Oxford University Press and the World Bank, 2003), *Moving People to Deliver Services* (Oxford University Press and the World Bank, 2003), and *Domestic Regulation and Services Trade Liberalisation* (Oxford University Press and the World Bank, 2003).

Amrita Narlikar is University Lecturer in International Relations at the Centre for International Studies, University of Cambridge, UK, and Senior Research Associate at the Centre for International Studies, University of Oxford, UK. She is author of *International Trade and Developing Countries: Bargaining Coalitions in the GATT and WTO* (Routledge, 2003) and *The World Trade Organization: A Very Short Introduction* (Oxford University Press, 2005). She is currently working on a joint book project, *Pathways to Power: Brazil and India in International Regimes*, which is funded by the Nuffield Foundation.

Sylvia Ostry is Distinguished Research Fellow at the Centre for International Studies, University of Toronto, Canada. Her most recent publications include 'Between Feast and Famine: Fixing Global Trade', in Andrew Heintzman and Evan Solomon (eds), *Feeding the Future from Fat to Famine: How to Solve the World's Food Crises* (House of Anansi Press, 2004), and 'The Future of the World Trading System: Beyond Doha' in John J. Kirton and Michael Trebilcock (eds), *Hard Choices, Soft Law: Voluntary Standards in Global Trade, Environment and Social Governance* (Ashgate, 2004).

James Scott is a doctoral candidate at the Centre for International Politics, University of Manchester, UK, and a teaching assistant in the School of Social Sciences. He works primarily on international trade, the WTO, development, and institutional change.

Susan K. Sell is Professor of Political Science and International Affairs at George Washington University, US. Her books include *Intellectual Property Rights: A Critical History* (with Christopher May), *Private Power, Public Law: The Globalization of Intellectual Property Rights*, and *Power and Ideas: The North–South Politics of Intellectual Property and Antitrust*. She has published widely in political science and law journals and has contributed book chapters on globalisation, trade, and intellectual property.

Elizabeth Smythe is Professor of Political Science and teaches international relations at Concordia University College of Alberta in Edmonton, Alberta, Canada. Her research interests include the negotiation of international investment agreements and the role of transnational social movements in influencing trade and investment agreements. Her most recent article, co-authored with Peter J. Smith, was published in *Global Governance* in 2006 and dealt with the legitimacy and transparency of the World Trade Organisation.

Ian Taylor is Senior Lecturer at the School of International Relations, University of St Andrews, UK, and an Associate Professor at the University of Stellenbosch,

South Africa. He is also Visiting Lecturer to the Faculty of Development Studies, Mbarara University of Science and Technology, Uganda. He is the author of *China and Africa: Engagement and Compromise* (Routledge, 2006), *NEPAD: Towards Africa's Development or Another False Start?* (Lynne Rienner, 2005), and *Stuck in Middle GEAR: South Africa's Post-Apartheid Foreign Relations* (Praeger, 2001). He has also co-edited five books on various topics related to Africa's political economy, as well as numerous journal articles and book chapters.

Rorden Wilkinson is Professor of International Political Economy and Head of the Centre for International Politics at the University of Manchester, UK. He is author of, among other things, *The WTO: Crisis and the Governance of Global Trade* (Routledge, 2006) and *Multilateralism and the World Trade Organisation* (Routledge, 2000); editor of *The Global Governance Reader* (Routledge, 2005); co-editor of *Global Governance: Critical Perspectives* (Routledge, 2002); and co-editor of two book series: the *RIPE Series in Global Political Economy* (with Louise Amoore and Randall Germain) and the *Global Institutions Series* (with Thomas G. Weiss).

Gilbert R. Winham is Professor Emeritus of Political Science at Dalhousie University and a Fellow of the Royal Society of Canada. He has served frequently as a panellist on NAFTA dispute settlement panels, and as instructor on WTO trade policy courses for officials from developing countries. He has written and/or edited nine books on international trade and is author of more than 50 articles and chapters, including publications in *The World Economy*, the *Journal of World Trade*, the *International Journal*, the *Journal of Environment and Development*, *World Trade Review*, *Negotiation Journal*, the *Journal of World Trade Law*, *World Politics*, the *Journal of Conflict Resolution*, the *Journal of Peace Research*, the *American Political Science Review*, the *Journal of Politics*, and the *Canadian Journal of Political Science*. He is currently preparing a manuscript titled 'The Debate over Genetically Modified Foods: Implications for International Relations'.

Alasdair R. Young is Senior Lecturer in International Politics at the University of Glasgow, UK. He has written extensively on EU trade politics, including *Extending European Cooperation: The European Union and the 'New' International Trade Agenda* (Manchester University Press, 2002) and articles in the *Journal of Common Market Studies*, the *Journal of European Public Policy*, and *World Politics*. He is also co-editor of *Politics* and the *JCMS Annual Review of the European Union*.

Acknowledgements

The aim of this book is to evaluate progress in the Doha Development Agenda (DDA) beyond the World Trade Organisation's (WTO) critical December 2005 Hong Kong Ministerial meeting and the breakdown of the negotiations in the summer of 2006 in a manner that is helpful to understanding the dynamics of the Round as well as to the negotiators involved. Each of the chapters that follow is written by a leading expert or experts who generously gave up their time to participate in a specially convened conference – entitled 'End Game at the WTO: Reflections on the Doha Development Agenda' held at the University of Birmingham, UK, 11–12 November 2005. The papers presented at the conference were subject to intense scrutiny by the conference delegates and redrafted in light of those discussions as well as the Hong Kong Ministerial meeting itself and developments thereafter. In contributing to, as well as helping shape debate during the conference, we are particularly grateful to Simon Caney, Carolyn Deere, Matthew Eagleton-Pierce, John Kotsopoulos, Bernard Kuiten, Anna Lanoszka, Craig Murphy, and Geoffrey Pigman, as well as all those who attended the event. We would like to thank the Department of Political Science and International Studies, and the School of Social Science, both at the University of Birmingham, and the Centre for International Politics at the University of Manchester for generous funding towards the costs of the conference. We are also grateful to Claes Belfrage for his help with the smooth running of the conference. We appreciate the efforts of Craig Fowlie and his team at Routledge for their exemplary editorial and publication support throughout the production process. The editors are also grateful to Routledge for permission to reprint Rorden Wilkinson, 'The WTO in Hong Kong: What It Really Means for the Doha Development Agenda', *New Political Economy*, 11: 2 (June 2006), in Chapter 1 of this book.

Donna Lee and Rorden Wilkinson
Birmingham and Manchester
August 2006

Abbreviations

AB	Appellate Body
ACP	African, Caribbean and Pacific states
ACP/LDC/AU	African, Caribbean and Pacific/Least Developed Country/ African Union Group (also known as the G90)
ACWL	Advisory Centre on WTO Law
AD	anti-dumping
AGOA	African Growth and Opportunity Act (US)
AoA	Agreement on Agriculture
APEC	Asia-Pacific Economic Co-operation
AU	African Union
AVE	*ad valorem* equivalent
BATNA	best alternative to negotiated agreement
BPO	business process outsourcing
CAFTA	Central American Free Trade Area
CAP	Common Agricultural Policy
CBD	Convention on Biological Diversity
CCP	Common Commercial Policy
COMESA	Common Market for Eastern and Southern Africa
CTD	Committee on Trade and Development
DDA	Doha Development Agenda
DFID	Department for International Development (UK Government)
DG	Director-General
DSB	Dispute Settlement Body
DSM	Dispute Settlement Mechanism
DSU	Dispute Settlement Understanding
EBA	Everything But Arms (EU initiative)
EC	European Community
ECTEL	Eastern Caribbean Telecommunications Authority
EEC	European Economic Community
EU	European Union
FDI	foreign direct investment
FIP	Five Interested Parties
FTAA	Free Trade Agreement of the Americas

G6	Group of 6 key industrial and developing nations
G7	Group of 7 leading industrial states
G8	Group of 7 leading industrial states plus Russia
G9	Group of 9 developing countries (Doha Round)
G9	Group of 9 industrial countries (Uruguay Round)
G9/10	Group of 9/10 industrial net food-importing countries
G10	Group of 10 developing countries (Uruguay Round)
G22	Group of 22 developing countries (forerunner to the G20)
G20	Group of 20 developing countries
G33	Group of 33 developing countries (also known as the SPSSM alliance)
G90	Group of 90 developing countries (also known as the ACP/LDC/AU group)
G110	Group of 110 developing countries
GATS	General Agreement on Trade in Services
GATT	General Agreement on Tariffs and Trade
GC	General Council
GI	geographical indicators
GSP	Generalised System of Preferences
IATP	Institute for Agricultural Trade Policy
IBSA	India–Brazil–South Africa Dialogue Forum
ICAC	International Cotton Advisory Committee (US based)
ICTSD	International Centre for Trade and Sustainable Development
IF	Integrated Framework for Trade-Related Technical Assistance
IIBE&L	Institute for International Business, Economics and Law (University of Adelaide)
IMF	International Monetary Fund
ISI	import substitution industrialisation
ITC	International Trade Commission
ITO	International Trade Organisation
LDC	least developed country
LMG	Like Minded Group
MDGs	Millennium Development Goals
MFA	Multi-Fibre Agreement
MFN	most favoured nation
MTS	multilateral trading system
NAFTA	North American Free Trade Agreement
NAMA	non-agricultural market access
NFIDCs	net food-importing developing countries
NGO	non-governmental organisation
OECD	Organisation for Economic Co-operation and Development
OED	Operations Evaluation Department (World Bank)
PCCA	Plains Cotton Co-operative Association (US based)

PCIPD	Permanent Committee on Co-operation for Development Related to Intellectual Property
SAP	structural adjustment programme
SDT	special and differential treatment
SFPs	Single Farm Payments
SG	Secretary General
SPS	Sanitary and Phytosanitary Measures
SSM	Special Safeguard Mechanism
STEs	state trading enterprises
TBT	Technical Barriers to Trade
TDRC	Trade Deficit Review Commission (US)
TNC	Trade Negotiations Committee
TPO	Trade Promotion Authority (US)
TPRM	Trade Policy Review Mechanism
TRIMs	Trade-Related Investment Measures (Agreement on)
TRIPs	Trade-Related Aspects of Intellectual Property Rights (Agreement on)
UN	United Nations
UNCICT	United Nations Commission on International Commodity Trade
UNCTAD	United Nations Conference on Trade and Development
UNECA	United Nations Economic Commission for Africa
UNDP	United Nations Development Programme
UNEP	United Nations Environment Programme
UNHCR	United Nations High Commissioner for Refugees
US	United States
USTR	United States Trade Representative
VERs	voluntary export restraints
WIPO	World Intellectual Property Organisation
WTO	World Trade Organisation

Part I
Setting the scene

1 The WTO after Hong Kong[1]

Setting the scene for understanding the Round

Rorden Wilkinson and Donna Lee

In mid-December 2005 the World Trade Organisation's (WTO) primary decision-making body – the ministerial conference – met for only the sixth time since the organisation's creation just a decade earlier. The venue for this biennial meeting was Hong Kong; and the task at hand to inject energy into an increasingly delayed and periodically fractious Round of trade negotiations – the so-called Doha Development Agenda (DDA). Hong Kong was to be the first time trade ministers had gathered for a full conference since the collapse of the Cancún meeting a little over two years earlier; indeed, prior to the ministerial, two out of the WTO's first five ministerial conferences had broken down and, in the current Round, only the conference launching the DDA (in Doha in November 2001) had ended successfully. Given this backdrop it was understandable that many approached Hong Kong with some trepidation. Few relished a repeat of the heightened political contestation that caused the breakdown of the Seattle (1999) and Cancún meetings and the consequences that a collapse in Hong Kong might have on the DDA.

For all of the speculation, Hong Kong did not result in the breakdown feared by some (see Bergsten, 2005; Hills, 2005; *Financial Times*, 6 September 2005). It nevertheless failed to make sufficient progress to halt the Round's collapse seven months later (in July 2006). Indeed, despite the modest progress made in Hong Kong, signs that the negotiations were at serious risk of collapse were evident almost as the ink dried on the ministerial declaration. Bickering broke out between the US and EU over precisely which of them was at fault for the relative lack of progress in the Round ahead of the January 2006 Davos meeting of the World Economic Forum (WEF). A global trade opinion poll of 100 Geneva and capital-based negotiators, policymakers, and experts from developed and developing countries conducted in January 2006 by the University of Adelaide's Institute for International Business, Economics and Law (IIBE&L) reported that 63 per cent of respondents, and none of those based in Geneva, thought it likely that the Round would be concluded in 2006; and only 2 per cent all respondents thought that the April 2006 target for the agreement of modalities in agriculture would be met (IIBE&L, 2006a). Neither the Geneva preparatory meeting preceding nor the actual meeting of the Group of 6 (G6)[2] in London in March 2006 managed to bring members closer to agreement on agriculture or non-agricultural market access (NAMA) (*Bridges*, 15 March 2006; Elliott, 2006). The April 2006 deadline for the completion of full negotiating modalities (the means by which commitments to market openings are translated into actual liberalisation – usually in the form of formulas and other agreements) set at the Hong Kong meeting was missed as member states remained in their entrenched positions (despite near-universal rhetoric that all were willing to move). By June 2006 the number of respondents expressing pessimism about the capacity of members to conclude the round by the end of the year recorded by a second IIBE&L poll had risen 8 points to 71 per cent (IIBE&L, 2006b). And despite the furious efforts of the WTO Director-General (DG), Pascal Lamy, high-level caucusing among key member states during the 2006 St Petersburg Summit of the Group of 8 (G8), and intensive Geneva-based negotiations towards the end of July 2006, little progress was made in forging a consensus. The result was a breakdown in the negotiations and a resumption of EU/US finger-pointing (see Mandelson, 2006b, 2006c; USTR, 2006).

The collapse of the negotiations prompted Kamal Nath, India's Minister of Commerce, to comment that the Round is now somewhere between 'intensive care and the crematorium' (quoted in *Bridges*, 26 July 2006). While a complete breakdown of a Round is without historical precedent, and such an occurrence is unlikely given the amount of time and effort already expended in the negotiations as well as the potential gains on offer, little prospect now exists for serious negotiations to resume ahead of crucial presidential elections in France (2007) and the US (2008) or for the Round to be concluded much before the end of the decade. This book offers a detailed and critical evaluation of how and why the negotiations arrived at this point. It brings together leading scholars in the field of trade from across the social sciences in pursuit of a comprehensive account for the sources of contestation that have emerged during the Round and the likely shape of the bargain struck should the Round be concluded. In pursuit of its aims, the book focuses on four themes: (1) the key issues at stake, (2) the principal players in the negotiations, (3) the role of fairness and legitimacy in the Round, and (4) the prospects for the DDA's conclusion. These broad themes organise the remainder of the book. They exist, however, only for convenience of mind. Key issues and primary themes run throughout the book. We signal these issues and themes in the remainder of this chapter by setting out what happened in the run-up to and during the Hong Kong Ministerial. We then offer a survey of the contributions that follow, focusing on their place in the overall analysis provided here.

The run-up to Hong Kong

To understand why Hong Kong unfolded in the way it did as well as why it failed to make significant progress to halt a collapse of the negotiations in July 2006 we need to return briefly to the breakdown of the preceding Cancún Ministerial meeting. The collapse of the Cancún meeting revealed deep-seated tensions among WTO members over the shape and direction of the DDA. These tensions had been evident since attempts to launch a new round of trade negotiations first emerged in the mid- to late 1990s and had originally resulted in the collapse of the Seattle Ministerial meeting. However, the post-Seattle rehabilitation process, coupled with a conscious effort to show political unity among members of the international community in the wake of the 11 September 2001 terrorist attacks, proved sufficient to secure agreement to launch the DDA at the 2001 Doha Ministerial (see Wilkinson, 2002). Disagreements nevertheless remained.

The lack of an absolute consensus on the content of the DDA, however, had important ramifications for the Cancún meeting. A provision to begin negotiations should an explicit consensus be forthcoming on the contentious Singapore issues (investment, government procurement, trade facilitation, and competition policy) at the Cancún meeting pitted the industrial states against their developing counterparts. This combined with existing tensions over the liberalisation of agriculture, NAMA, the extension of geographical indicators under the Agreement on Trade-Related Intellectual Property Rights (TRIPs), the service negotiations, issues relating to the implementation of the Uruguay Round accords, and special and differential treatment for the least developed to produce an inflammatory situation.

The content of the DDA was not, however, the full extent of the problem. Tensions were exacerbated further by the way in which the negotiations were organised. Of particular concern was the continued use of Green Room meetings comprising 15–25 'key' states as the principal decision-making fora; the holding of meetings concurrently, thereby disadvantaging delegations (largely from the least developed) with limited numbers of personnel; the use of bilateral meetings between 'facilitators' (persons appointed by the Chair of the meeting to oversee negotiations in a particular area) and individual delegations to reveal the latter's bottom line (known as 'confessionals'); the introduction of draft texts as the basis upon which members negotiate but which were not widely agreed upon; the manner in which facilitators were selected and their (occasional) partisan behaviour; and the use of forum-plus tactics to cajole states into agreement such as placing telephone calls to capitals (thereby circumscribing and undermining delegations), or threatening to withdraw financial/humanitarian/military assistance, bilateral trade deals, or debt relief. It was unsurprising that the meeting collapsed.

The Cancún meeting was followed by a process of institutional and political readjustment (what has elsewhere been called a 'post-crisis politics' – see Wilkinson, 2006a) that resulted in the negotiation of an agreement during the July 2004 meeting of the WTO's General Council (GC) that took the negotiations forward (the so-called 'July Package', albeit it was actually concluded on 1 August). The package saw members agree to a framework agreement in agriculture and NAMA; movement forward in the service negotiations; a commitment to continue the consultation process on the extension of the TRIPs agreement; the commencement of negotiations on one of the Singapore issues (trade facilitation) and the ejection of the remaining three; and an extension in the timeframe of the overall negotiations with a view to their conclusion sometime after the Hong Kong meeting (WTO, 2004).

Importantly, the July 2004 package was brokered not by the Quad (the four leading industrial states of the US, EU, Japan and Canada), as was the established norm, but by a group comprising India, Brazil, and Australia as well as the US and EU (collectively known as the Five Interested Parties – FIP). This reflected both an acknowledgement of the significance of India and Brazil as leading developing countries and Australia as the most prominent industrialised agricultural producer outside of Europe and North America, and the need to bring into the fold leading members (in this case India and Brazil) of the most significant developing country coalition that emerged during the Cancún meeting – the Group of 20 (G20).[3]

Yet while the July package was sufficient to bring about a return to the negotiating table, it was far from a solution. Tensions among members remained much in evidence and progress in the negotiations thereafter proved frustratingly slow. In the agricultural talks concerns were raised by the Group of 10 net food-importing countries (G10)[4] and various least developed countries that the FIP were dominating proceedings and acting in just the same way as the Quad; significant divergences emerged in the way in which members interpreted the content of the July agreement on agriculture; least developed countries expressed anxiety about the potential for existing trade preferences to be eroded by commitments made in the DDA; the G10 and the EU expressed concerns about overly ambitious moves to reduce levels of agricultural domestic support; the agricultural negotiations were repeatedly deadlocked over a formula for converting specific duties into percentage base *ad valorem* equivalents (that is, moving from duties based on the volume of imports to ones based on their value); and the deadline of July 2005 for agreeing outline modalities for negotiations in agriculture was missed.

Beyond agriculture, matters appeared little better. A December 2004 Africa Group proposal amending the August 2003 decision on TRIPs and public health seeking to loosen the constraints placed upon members importing generic pharmaceuticals in times of national health crises was not well received, with particular opposition coming from Australia, Canada, the EU, Hong Kong, Japan, Korea, New Zealand, Norway, Switzerland, Taiwan, Turkey, and the US. By March 2005 – two years after the original deadline – offers were still outstanding in the services negotiations from more than 40 members (principally, though not exclsively, developing countries). The NAMA negotiations appeared in perpetual deadlock; members clashed on the structure of the discussions, the relative merits of pursuing single-sector (rather than cross-sector) negotiations, the tariff-cutting formula to be deployed (with the majority of the industrial states favouring the simple 'Swiss' formula – a method of cutting tariff levels across all sectors – while most developing countries pushed for 'less than reciprocity'), and the July 2005 deadline for agreement on the basic structure of the NAMA negotiations was missed.

Deadlines were also consistently missed in the Committee on Trade and Development (CTD) for proposing 'clear recommendations' to the GC on special and differential treatment. Little beyond a tacit acceptance that movement would be forthcoming only in the closing stages of the DDA occurred in negotiations on anti-dumping rules. Members divided on how to deal with the issue of fisheries subsidies. Little progress was made in the services negotiations; pressure by Australia, the EU, and the US to establish mandatory minimum market access commitments (so-called benchmarks) to increase the level of ambition in the services negotiations was strongly opposed by the majority of developing countries (with the notable exception of India); an Indian-led developing country push for improvements in industrial member commitments to the 'natural movement of persons' across state boundaries as service providers under 'mode 4' of the General Agreement on Trade in Services (GATS) yielded little; progress in all areas was hindered by a widespread reluctance to engage in meaningful negotiations without first knowing at least the outline of a deal in agriculture; and a statement by nine developing countries released just before the meeting sought to refocus attention on the Round's core purposes (i.e. development) and warned of the divide and rule tactics of 'some major developed countries' (G9 Developing Countries, 2005).

The run-up to the Hong Kong Ministerial was, nevertheless, qualitatively different from that which had preceded Seattle and Cancún. A willingness to keep moving forward with negotiations despite the persistence of significant differences was in evidence. In November 2005 the TRIPs negotiations saw members agree to exempt least developed countries (LDCs) from obligations to apply rules protecting patents, copyrights, and other intellectual property until 2012; and a 6 December 2005 decision saw members agree to a permanent solution to the issue of TRIPs and public health. In agriculture a formula for *ad valorem* conversion agreed at the 4 May 2005 Paris mini-ministerial (ad hoc gatherings of approximately 25–30 ministers deemed most important in caucusing agreement) was accepted by members as an acceptable way forward. Likewise, a G20 proposal on agricultural market access was agreed at the July 2005 Dalian mini-ministerial meeting as the basis for further discussions. In addition to market access commitments, on 10 October 2005 the US offered to make significant cuts in its domestic agricultural support regime contingent on EU and Japanese reciprocation. The EU made a counter-offer shortly thereafter and submitted a further 'new and improved' proposal on 28 October 2005. Proposals were also forthcoming from the G10, G20 and African, Caribbean, and Pacific (ACP) Group.

Crucially, when it became clear that members would be unable to bridge remaining differences ahead of the Hong Kong meeting and agree on full negotiating modalities at the ministerial, they agreed to scale back expectations, reflect upon the progress that had been made in the draft declaration, continue negotiations in the wake of Hong Kong with a view to agreeing full modalities in the early part of 2006, and shift the focus of the negotiations to reaching agreement on a package to assist the least developed. This package was to comprise, in addition to reaching a solution on the TRIPs and public health issue, duty-free and quota-free access for all products originating in LDCs; amendments to existing special and differential provisions in WTO agreements; and a strong Aid for Trade package designed to enable LDCs to take advantage of market-opening opportunities. The lowering of expectations and the focus on a development package proved instrumental in ensuring the ministerial's success.

The meeting itself

Inevitably, agriculture proved to be the principal fault line among members (and was seen as the key to the meeting's success), with development, NAMA, and services also figuring prominently. Despite efforts to emphasise that the drafting and redrafting of texts was a 'bottom-up' (that is, member-led) process, the DG,

Secretariat, and the facilitators[5] again came in for criticism for their role in shaping discussions. The pursuit of negotiating leverage encouraged grand coalition building as existing groups sought to bolster their strength by combining with others (as was the case with the coming together of the G20, the Group of 33 (G33), and the Group of 90 (G90) to form a self-styled but largely unconvincing Group of 110 – G110).[6] Ad hoc groupings of members emerged on specific issues, most notably the 'friends of ambition' and the NAMA 11 in the industrial goods negotiations.[7] And politics and grandstanding between key protagonists were played out during press briefings.

The negotiations followed a familiar pattern. Discussions began with intensity only on the third and fourth days and were concluded after the obligatory around-the-clock meetings. Green Room meetings continued to form the basis of negotiations – albeit that they were renamed gatherings of the 'chairman's consultative group'. The smallest and most vulnerable members continued to populate their delegations with foreign nationals (largely from the EU and US) in an effort to bolster their role within and understanding of trade issues. Translation facilities were variable and in some cases non-existent. More than one African delegation found access to information regarding the content and direction of the talks more freely available in the NGO centre than in the restricted 'delegates only' area. And vast differentials persisted in the number of personnel in each delegation.

Discussions during the meeting itself centred on improving the text that had been drawn up prior to the meeting. In what is now an established practice, the text was introduced on 7 December 2005 at the behest of Lamy and the Chair of the General Council (GC), Amina Chawahir Mohamed (WTO, 2005a). The text was itself a minor revision of two previous drafts incorporating agreed amendments.[8] In the case of the final and penultimate draft texts, the covering notes were at pains to point out that they reflected work in progress and were not agreed positions, thereby attempting to head off some of the criticism levelled at the process during previous ministerial meetings.

The meeting's unfolding reflected the concerted effort to produce a positive result. Negotiations were conducted, in the first instance, in only three areas reflecting those wherein significant tensions existed and where compromises were necessary to generate an agreement: agriculture, NAMA, and development. It was not until later in the ministerial that the negotiating group on services was convened (though informal discussions on services had been taking place between principal protagonists from the meeting's outset), while a fifth group put on call for the duration of the meeting was not operationalised.

Agriculture

In agriculture most of the discussion centred on the issue of a date for the phase-out of export subsidies. The meeting began with a widespread acknowledgement that 2010 would be reasonable and that, once this had been agreed, movement on the remainder of the outstanding issues would be 'pretty automatic'.[9] Even the EU – which was long held to be stalling on the issue – agreed during a 15 December press conference that 2010 was 'reasonable'. In the Green Room, discussions were, however, quite different. Behind the theatre played out for the benefit of the gathered press, which involved a three-way Punch-and-Judy show between the US, the EU, and the tag team of India and Brazil,[10] the EU consistently held off on agreeing to the proposed date. Robust exchanges also took place between the EU and Australia, New Zealand, and Canada, with the EU Trade Commissioner, Peter Mandelson, complaining that the latter were not interested in the complete elimination of export subsidies. The discussions were further complicated by a spate between the EU and US over 'food aid' – assistance given to the least developed in the form of food handouts by the US – which Mandelson deemed 'tantamount to an export subsidy' (*Bridges Daily Update*, 2005).

It was not until the very end of the meeting that Mandelson put forward a date of 2013. This appeared to be both part of a strategy to ensure that movement was forthcoming on services and NAMA (Khor, 2005) and a commitment that Mandelson could firmly make only after the 17 December 2006 agreement of the EU budget (at which the Common Agricultural Policy – CAP – was agreed). In the end, the members agreed to a date of 2013 on the understanding that a good proportion of the commitment would be realised by the 'end of the first half of the implementation period' (WTO, 2005c, paragraph 6). The agreement was, however, largely symbolic as most of the distortion to trade comes from subsidies given to support domestic production (on which there was almost no movement in Hong Kong).

The issue of cotton also figured prominently in the negotiations. However, much like the issue of export subsidies, what resulted was again more gesture than substance – though some notable political entanglements emerged along the way. Uganda in particular was unhappy that any initiative would focus solely on the four central African cotton producers (Benin, Burkina Faso, Chad, and Mali, collectively known as the C4) and sought to have it universalised to all African cotton producers. And matters were made more complicated by attempts by the US to get the EU to agree to movement in the rest of the agriculture negotiations before it would agree to anything on cotton – a move Mandelson described as 'taking tactical negotiating to a new level' (Mandelson, 2005).

The ministerial nevertheless resulted in an agreement to eliminate of all forms of cotton export subsidies by developed countries in 2006; duty-free and quota-free access for all cotton exports from LDCs; and an agreement to 'reduce more ambitiously than under whatever general formula is agreed' trade-distorting domestic subsidies for cotton 'over a shorter period of time than generally applicable' (WTO, 2005c, paragraph 11). The agreement was, however, as Joseph Stiglitz and Andrew Charlton point out, more symbolic than substantive. As they note, the US is the only industrial state to grant cotton subsidies; it was committed to removing cotton export subsidies following the outcome of a WTO dispute settlement case (the Uplands Cotton case brought by Brazil) anyway; US domestic cotton subsidies remain intact (and are by far the biggest distortion to trade in the sector); and US promises to reduce tariffs on cotton are of 'dubious value since America is a major cotton exporter' (Stiglitz and Charlton, 2006).

NAMA

From the outset it was clear that for the developing countries movement in NAMA was contingent on movement in the agricultural negotiations.[11] This was to serve as a frame for the NAMA discussions prohibiting significant movement in the area. There was, nevertheless, a broad measure of agreement on the tariff-cutting formula to be deployed in the Round, though not the precise coefficients to be agreed in the formula's application. This would be a non-linear formula (known as the Swiss formula) deployed with two coefficients (but which were not specified) to bring about deeper cuts in the tariffs of the industrial states than in their developing counterparts. That said, disagreements as to the relative gap between the coefficients prevailed (with, for example, Australia pressing for a small gap, while China and the Africa Group called for a much larger gap)[12] and were to remain key points of contention in the July 2006 collapse of the negotiations. Disagreements were also evident over calls for 'flexibilities' to be made available to developing countries during the negotiations as well as over what to do with unbound tariffs (that is, tariffs that are without a specified ceiling beyond which they cannot be raised). Some attempts at 'backsliding' from pre-meeting positions were also reported. And a group of newly acceded countries (which included China) pressed for special treatment in the discussions in recognition of the market-opening commitments they had only recently made as part of their accession negotiations.

Development

Discussions in the development group centred on four key issues: (1) a push by least developed countries for substantive commitments on the issue of duty-free and quota-free access; (2) a debate about entitlement to duty-free and quota-free access in which some (largely industrial) members were reluctant to extend such access to all LDCs; (3) resistance to 100 per cent duty-free and quota-free access on all products – largely in response to US reluctance to extend access to textiles and Canada's desire to continue protecting its diary markets; and (4) a debate about whether developing countries should provide duty-free and quota-free access to the least developed counterparts. Notably, the issue of implementation (relating to the problems arising from the implementation of the Uruguay Round accords – a key developing country concern and a stated focus of the DDA) figured very little in the discussions and appeared to have almost fallen from the agenda (Khor, 2006).

   Much of the discussions focused on the extension of duty-free and quota-free access to all products originating in LDCs. What was finally agreed was, however, not quite so impressive. While the EU took the high ground and was at pains to point out that it had already extended duty-free and quota-free access to products originating in LDCs under the 2001 'Everything But Arms' (EBA) initiative (albeit that bananas, sugar, and rice would be subject to longer phase-out periods), Japan, Canada, and the US agreed to extend access only to 97 per cent of their tariff lines (that is, the range of products imported). While the figure of 97 per cent appeared to be significant in that it extends duty-free and quota-free access to the vast majority of products imported by the industrial states (including, it should be noted, many that are not actually produced by the least developed), it does not open up Northern markets (particularly in the US and Japan) to imports of products of key economic importance to LDCs. The most obvious example is that it excludes imports of textiles and clothing from Bangladesh.

A second area of debate centred on Aid for Trade. The conference's first few days saw the US, EU, and Japan promise increased amounts of aid to assist least developed countries in addressing those supply-side factors preventing them from fully benefiting from market access commitments. These offers were designed (quite explicitly so) to grease the wheels of consensus-building by facilitating developing country agreement in return for financial largesse. The doubling of financial assistance by the big industrial three was, however, quickly denounced as (variously) recycled money, already announced but slightly repackaged bilateral assistance, and/or a naked attempt to buy off developing states (*Bridges Daily Update*, 14 December 2005). The result was a commitment to provide technical and financial assistance to enable LDCs to meet their obligations and commitments as well as to better realise the opportunities presented by trade liberalisation; and the establishment of a task force to provide recommendations to the GC by July 2006 (one of the rare deadlines established by the Hong Kong ministerial declaration that was actually met) on how Aid for Trade might contribute 'most effectively to the development dimension of the DDA' (WTO, 2005c, paragraph 57, also Annex F).

Services

Though development and agriculture inevitably grabbed the headlines, the discussions on services proved to be just as thorny. The primary fault line was between those members seeking a more ambitious commitment on service negotiations and those seeking to either weaken the text or secure its outright removal. A particular source of disagreement was the objectives for the services negotiations and the mandatory language set out in Annex C of the ministerial text. Here, debate centred on a proposal in paragraph 7 that members would be *obliged* to enter into negotiations with a group of members should a request to do so be forthcoming. The reference to a 'group of members' rather than a more WTO-normal (in cases when negotiations take place on a request-and-offer rather than a linear or across-the-board basis) bilateral format is known as 'plurilateral'. Many developing countries worried that such a system of negotiating would enable a greater degree of pressure to be exerted on them than would be the case during bilateral discussions. The response of the G90 was to submit an alternative annex to the ministerial text that, among other things, removed the obligation to enter into such negotiations, replacing it with the wording that plurilateral negotiations 'may also be pursued' (G90, 2005).

A second source of debate arose over mode 4. Many developing countries (including the G90 as supporters of a weakening of the text and India as a strong advocate of the original text) pushed for greater movement on mode 4. Such movement, they argued, would enable their nationals to provide services in other states (largely industrial members), which would, in turn, result in a proportion of earnings being returned to their countries of origin through either the sending of money home or repatriation at the end of a contract. As many have pointed out, while this might provide for marginal financial inflows in the short term, it is far from a sustainable development strategy.

Predictably, the services outcome satisfied few. Japan, the US, and the EU expressed their disappointment with the agreement, while India argued that it enabled the US to withhold meaningful movement on mode 4. What resulted was a modest weakening of the mandatory language of Annex C. In addition to an implicit acknowledgement that the services negotiations would take place in accordance with the principles of the GATS (and thus take account of members' varying levels of development) set out in the introduction (or chapeau – literally 'hat') to paragraph 7, it was revised to acknowledge explicitly the need to take account of the problems facing the least developed. Moreover, the obligation to enter into negotiations was removed and replaced with a commitment that members 'shall consider' requests to enter into negotiations on a plurilateral basis.

The role of this book

For WTO DG Lamy, Hong Kong moved the percentage of achievement in the Round forward from 55 to 60 per cent. As Mandelson noted, this was both 'pretty small' and 'very expensive . . . [i]f you consider how many people were in Hong Kong and how much it cost them to get there and stay' (Mandelson, 2006a). While it is probable that in the long run the Hong Kong meeting moved on only slightly the likelihood of the Round being completed, as quickly became evident, it did so in a fashion that failed to avert a collapse of the negotiations seven months later. Our purpose in this book is to get to the heart of what is going on in the negotiations. We set out to explore the key dynamics in the Round with a view to better understanding why the negotiations have ended up where they are as well as how they might move forward. Each of the chapters that follow focuses on a key aspect of the Round. Together they offer a comprehensive understanding of what is at stake in the DDA, why the negotiations have unfolded in the manner that they have, whether the Round is likely to be concluded, and what the consequences of such a conclusion will be for the further development of the multilateral trading system.

How the book unfolds

Sylvia Ostry begins the debate by locating the Hong Kong ministerial meeting and the DDA in the context of the transformation of the multilateral trading system that occurred with the conclusion of the Uruguay Round. Her aims are twofold: first, to detail the transformation brought about in the multilateral trading system by the conclusion of the Uruguay Round; and, second, to illustrate the consequences of that transformation for the DDA. Ostry argues that the conclusion of the Uruguay Round had a significant impact on the multilateral trading system in two ways. First, it extended trade rules into areas that had previously not been subject to the General Agreement on Tariffs and Trade (GATT) (largely services, intellectual property rights, and investment measures) or else had been subject to persistent and elaborate forms of protectionism (namely agriculture and textiles and clothing); and, second, it moved the focus of liberalisation beyond a concern with removing those impediments to trade that prevented goods and services flowing freely into foreign countries (that is, at the border measures) to those aspects of national legislation that had a trade-constraining effect (that is, behind the border measures). In detailing this transformation, Ostry argues that the Uruguay Round imbued the multilateral trading system with a structural asymmetry that served to disadvantage poor developing states. Of particular concern, she suggests, is the way in which the growing complexity and legalisation of the multilateral trading system has put a premium on knowledge and financial resources to the extent that the poorest are precluded from understanding, engaging with, and taking full advantage of trade rules. She further argues that once the consequences of the Uruguay 'Grand Bargain' (or 'Bum Deal' as Ostry terms it) became clear, a North/South divide emerged that obfuscated the capacity of trade negotiations to arrive at a successful conclusion. As Ostry points out, this divide underpinned the collapse of both the Seattle and Cancún ministerial meetings, and it played a role in both the Hong Kong meeting and the collapse of the Round in July 2006. Rorden Wilkinson explores the subject of asymmetry further and sets it within the longer historical context of the GATT in the last chapter of the book.

Ostry argues that only by attenuating a measure of this asymmetry will the negotiators be able to conclude the DDA successfully. And although she suggests that Hong Kong brought about some (albeit limited) breathing space for the Round, without a concerted effort to bridge the North/South divide the Round will not be concluded. To bridge this divide she proposes that the Aid for Trade deliberations consider enhancing the Integrated Framework for Trade-Related Technical Assistance (IF), and that WTO members look to correct those anomalies that exacerbate, as she puts it, 'rich/poor asymmetries' – the lack of an executive with legislative power in the WTO, the small size of the Organisation's Secretariat, and its peculiarly small budget – through the establishment of a policy forum with a financial capacity to pursue cutting-edge research designed to tackle the most thorny and troublesome of trade issues.

Key issues

Set against this background the following three chapters address the central negotiating issues and highlight what is at stake in the talks on agriculture, services, and TRIPs in the context of the more general development aims of the Doha Round. In Chapter 3 Jennifer Clapp focuses on what she sees as the 'central feature' of the Doha Round, the agricultural negotiations. Examining these negotiations in detail, Clapp suggests that there is little prospect of a meaningful agreement on this issue, largely as a result of the long-standing weakness of the strategic position of developing countries vis-à-vis the EU and the US (which have tended to dominate discussions of agricultural trade – see also Wyn Grant's chapter, Chapter 10). Clapp points to a number of interesting new developments in the agricultural talks during the Doha Round, perhaps the most significant of which is the increasing activism of what she refers to as the Global South. Developing countries have become increasingly assertive in the talks though the creation of like-minded as well as regional developing country alliances such as the G20 (discussed in detail in Ian Taylor's chapter, Chapter 9) and the Africa Group (discussed in detail in Donna Lee's chapter, Chapter 8). From 2000 the increased activism of the Global South was focused on the need to revise the 1994 Agreement on Agriculture (AoA). This agreement required developing countries to cut tariffs more deeply than industrialised countries and therefore produced gross inequities between industrialised countries and developing countries. While developing countries had been marginalised in the AoA negotiations, in 2000 they were determined to have more of a say and established negotiating groups on agriculture issues to ensure this happened. But, as Clapp points out, in the early phase of the negotiations the Global South continued to be ignored. Developing countries' views were not included in various ministerial texts, and throughout the talks the EU and US have continued to try to carve out agreements between themselves. As Clapp points out, by Cancún a fatal North–South confrontation on subsidies and tariff cuts brought the agricultural negotiations, and consequently the Doha Round, to a standstill.

As Clapp argues, the collapse of the Cancún meeting was to prove a watershed in the agriculture negotiations. Thereafter the dynamic of the talks changed. Developing countries had become key participants and forced important procedural and substantive changes. But, as Clapp concludes, as developing countries have become more involved, the diversity of their interests has become more visible and their coalitions have become more fragile. As Clapp notes, the diversity of agricultural interests within these developing country coalitions means that no single development deal can be struck that will satisfy equally the divergent needs of developing country members. So, despite greater activism on the part of bargaining alliances such as the Africa Group and the G20, and the emergence of what Clapp describes as a more consultative negotiating process in the WTO after the ill-fated Cancún Ministerial meeting, the options for developing countries in the agricultural negotiations remain limited to either accepting a deal largely thrashed out by the EU and the US or taking the nuclear option and walking out of those talks.

In Chapter 4 Susan Sell examines the negotiations on intellectual property, which, she argues, have been shaped by key public health concerns such as the HIV/AIDS pandemic, the 2001 anthrax attacks in the US, and the prospects of a global avian flu pandemic in 2005, with the latter having particular resonance in the run-up to the Hong Kong meeting. Given this backdrop, attention in the Doha Round negotiations has focused on the unfinished business in intellectual property, which promises to help in the global governance of these public health concerns. In particular, the following have been central to the Doha negotiations: the ability of developing countries to export generic drugs made under compulsory licence; the relationship of TRIPs to the Convention on Biological Diversity (CBD); provisions to provide protection from 'biopiracy'; issues relating to benefit-sharing arrangements; the problem of non-violation and situation complaints to TRIPs; implementation; and the expansion of geographical indications.

As with agriculture, Sell identifies a North–South confrontation in intellectual property over TRIPs. She argues that developing countries tend to see the TRIPs as a ceiling – a maximum standard of protection – whereas developed countries see it very much as a floor – a minimum standard of protection. Like Clapp, Sell also points to the increasing assertiveness and involvement of developing countries in the intellectual property negotiations. India, Peru, and Brazil have led a group of developing countries in a vigorous fight to amend TRIPs so that it will support the CBD, which they see as a more effective way of protecting them from biopiracy by the developed states. The Africa Group has been equally assertive in securing an amendment (which many NGOs see as too leaky) to the TRIPs agreement on the issue of compulsory licensing for HIV/AIDS drugs. While it seems that developing countries have secured important victories in intellectual property issues in the Doha Round, Sell cautions that they will need to be equally active in other international fora, most notably the World Intellectual Property Organisation (WIPO). It seems that the US and EU in particular, having been forced to accept compromises in the intellectual property negotiations in the WTO, have sought to shift their attention to the WIPO – an organisation dominated by firms which demand protection of their intellectual property and where there is little development agenda.[13] As such, the WIPO is considered to be more sympathetic to the mercantilist interests of industry than to the liberalising needs of citizens in developing countries. Sell argues that it is through the WIPO rather than the Doha negotiations that the US and the EU can get agreement to raise standards of intellectual property protection. Sell concludes that developing countries have the advantage that concerns about what some would see as the growing threat of health pandemics and biological terrorist attacks serve to push their liberalisation agenda forward and to offset the formidable protectionist pressures in the intellectual property negotiations in both the WTO and WIPO.

In Chapter 5 Bernard Hoekman and Aaditya Mattoo discuss the services negotiations in the DDA. They first highlight the importance of the reform of services for economic development, arguing that the gains to be made, especially for developing countries, are comparable to the potential gains from reform of trade in goods. The services negotiations also provide an opportunity for developing countries in particular to improve competitiveness. And, crucially, the services negotiations offer a useful bargaining tool in the Doha talks. Concessions can be offered in services to offset concessions offered in agriculture. Thus progress in services could be the key bargaining mechanism to achieve an overall agreement in the Doha Round.

Interestingly, although Hoekman and Mattoo argue that the WTO 'is not and should not become a development organisation', they see the services negotiations providing opportunities to address development issues if the talks can address issues beyond the traditional market access agenda. Services liberalisation offers the prospects of domestic policy reforms and the strengthening of service sectors in developing countries. For Hoekman and Mattoo both services trade liberalisation and Aid for Trade can play a major role in support of the domestic reform agenda. The point made is that connecting services liberalisation with tied aid programmes in the Doha talks could mobilise both liberalisation and assistance and, in so doing, encourage development, especially in the poorest countries, which have weak export interests in services outside of tourism.

Hoekman and Mattoo maintain that a change in negotiation approach and emphasis in the Round is required to realise the development agenda. They argue that a successful Round can be achieved only with a broad-based and multi-issue bargaining approach in the negotiations such that the services, goods, and agriculture talks lead to an overall balance of concessions and gains. They argue that the negotiations should shift from the existing bilateral approach, where members submit what tend to be highly ambitious requests and make minimalist offers, to a plurilateral formula approach. The goods and agriculture negotiations have been based upon a formula approach. It is seen to be more effective because it helps overcome the difficulty of achieving balanced concessions and significant exchanges between countries that have imperfect interests in each other's markets. Hoekman and Mattoo also call for an expanded and more prominent role for the WTO in services. This includes the provision of technical and financial assistance to poorer countries and the oversight of service-related domestic reforms to increase transparency and accountability in both developing and industrialised countries.

Principal players

Part II of the book examines the role of the principal players in the Doha negotiations. It begins with James Scott's chapter (Chapter 6) on the US. Scott provides an interesting and detailed analysis of trade politics – and in particular the fallout in Washington from US trade deficits and the effect this has had on the US's role and bargaining positions in trade negotiations. Scott's detailed illustration of the domestic politics of US trade examines the impact of the political economy of US trade deficits on the structure of bilateral and multilateral trade negotiations and the likely outcomes of the Doha talks in particular. In situations when the US is suffering trade deficits he finds that Washington is more inclined to actively seek trade agreements to address the deficit and, as such, is often the driving force in the launch of trade rounds and keen to provide leadership during negotiations to secure agreement. That said, the power and influence of Congress on US trade policy is such that any trade agreement negotiated – either bilaterally or multilaterally – will have to bring significant benefits to a range of constituencies and interests to secure Congressional approval. Trade agreements that exacerbate unfair trade practices from a Congressional perspective will be voted down on Capitol Hill. Thus, perhaps more than other key players, the US has to play a very fine balancing act in WTO negotiations. In the Doha Round, in sensitive areas such as agriculture the US is trying to hold fast to its domestic subsidy programmes and thus excluding significant development issues from the agreement. At the same time, Washington is pushing for tariff concessions in the NAMA and services negotiations in order to address what Congress sees as the main cause of the current trade deficit.

Scott's argument is that with a 'increasingly belligerent' Congress looking over its shoulder the US delegation has adopted a predominantly mercantilist position in the DDA – offering little to developing countries yet demanding a great deal in terms of open access to developing countries' markets (a charge also levelled at the US by the EU Trade Commission Peter Mandelson – see Mandelson, 2006b, 2006c). And as a result the DDA suffers a leadership vacuum, the result of which is stalemate and impasse. The chances of an agreement are slight, according to Scott, and, moreover, any agreement that might be reached will exclude any meaning-ful development content because the politics of the US trade deficit has so far managed to force development out of the DDA.

In Chapter 7 Alasdair R. Young examines the role of another dominant player in the DDA, the EU. As with the US – albeit for very different reasons – the EU's negotiating strategy in the DDA is dictated by the unique institutional politics of its 27-member customs union. The need to find convergence among the 27 members makes the EU an awkward and difficult negotiating partner, especially in the context of competition between member states and the EU Commission about who should direct trade policy. In his analysis of the Doha Round, Young finds that the driving motivation behind the EU's approach has been to secure an agreement wherein the overall bargain provides sufficient gains for a majority of members in order to offset the losses of the minority.

Young provides details of the EU's broad approach to the DDA in pursuit of concessions on NAMA and the so-called Singapore issues[14] (where the Europeans have been the principal advocate) in return for EU offers in agriculture (where, along with the US, the EU has been the main protagonist). Securing this agenda, however, is severely hampered not only by the EU's negotiating partners within the DDA but also by the extreme differences between EU members on key issues. As a result, Young argues, the EU's overall stance in the DDA is 'quite protec-tionist', but especially so in the agriculture talks. In pushing hard on the Singapore issues and vigorously defending European protectionism in agriculture, the EU usually finds itself in direct opposition to the developing countries in the DDA, though as the talks have gone on, it has proved to be flexible on the Singapore issues, offered minimal concessions in agriculture, and been supportive on issues such as TRIPs and 'Aid for Trade'. All in all, Young argues that the inability of the European Commission to offer further concessions in agriculture beyond those agreed by members in the 2007–13 budget talks means that Brussels has no more room for manoeuvre on agriculture. It is unlikely, therefore, that it can tempt the developing countries into offering more concessions in the NAMA and services negotiations. In this situation there are few reasons to expect a speedy completion of the DDA or one that results in significant agricultural market liberalisation.

Donna Lee's chapter discusses the role of the Africa Group in the DDA through a case study of the cotton negotiations. Lee finds strong evidence of a growing activism on the part of the African states in search of significant development content in the DDA. Countries such as South Africa, Uganda, Ghana, and Kenya have enjoyed significant involvement in the mini-ministerials and Green Room meetings in the Doha talks. Indeed, African agency was a contributing (and significant) factor in the collapse of the Cancún meeting. Yet as Lee argues, African agency in the DDA has had only minimal impact on the substance of agreements to date – particularly in the cotton talks. Although the Africa Group is one of the largest bargaining coalitions in the DDA, overshadowed only by the G90, it remains one of the weakest negotiators. The problems confronted by the African Group – problems shared by other developing country coalitions – prevent significant influence being exerted over the content of ministerial texts and agreements such as the Harbinson and Derbez texts as well as the July 2005 package. These problems include internal divisions within the Group as a result of divergent trade interests, vulnerability to the EU and US as a result of bilateral trade agreements and aid packages, and limited technical resources and skills. Lee argues that state-level factors within the Africa Group's major protagonists in the DDA also explain why the Group has found it virtually impossible to secure concessions, especially in the cotton talks. Affirming the observations made by Scott and Young in their chapters in this book, Lee finds that the political economy of cotton subsidies in the US and the EU prevents the American and European delegations from offering meaningful concessions to the Africans in these talks. The influence of the very powerful cotton lobby in the US forces a protectionist hand on the US delegation in the cotton talks, especially in the context of Presidential elections wherein the 'cotton states' in the US South and Delta are key battlegrounds. As cotton is the critical issue for the development of Central and West African states, but one on which there is likely to be very little meaningful movement, Lee concludes that the DDA is unlikely to deliver development for the WTO's poorest members.

Continuing the examination of developing country participation in the DDA, Ian Taylor's chapter focuses on the G20. As Taylor notes, the Group, led by the fast-developing countries Brazil and India, has become a highly significant vehicle for an assertive campaign by several developing countries for the implementation of the Uruguay agreements in market access and the dismantling of industrialised states' subsidies. Although the G20 has a slightly shifting membership, it is predominantly composed of the key proponents of greater liberalisation of agricultural trade and the elimination of the huge farm subsidies in the US and EU in particular. Taylor examines the reasons for the creation of the G20 in the run-up to the Cancún meeting and traces its emergence as a principal player in the DDA thereafter. Seen largely as an agricultural lobby in the first instance, the G20 has become the key voice for pushing the inclusion of development issues as an integral part of the DDA. These include special and differential treatment, greater agricultural market access, and the elimination of all forms of domestic and export subsidies. The G20 has not been afraid to adopt tough proactive negotiating positions in the DDA and it has shown enthusiasm for simply walking out of the talks to show displeasure at both the process and the content of the talks. Such an approach, as Taylor shows, is born out of frustration at what the G20 sees as the constant stubbornness and inflexibility of the US, EU, Japan, and Canada in the talks. At the Cancún ministerial the G20 led the developing country walk-out of the talks – sending a very clear and strong message to its negotiating partners that no deal was better than a bad deal for developing countries.

Taylor argues that at the Hong Kong meeting the G20 was successful at forging an even larger coalition with other developing country groups to create the G110 to advance the development content of the DDA – though the extent to which the G20 positioned itself as the leader of the developing world caused tensions with other developing country coalitions such as the G33 and the G90. Other dangers for the G20 include the tendency of its leading members to become co-opted into the WTO process and, in so doing, strengthening the liberalisation agenda at the expense of an alternative development strategy. Other dangers for the G20 include its tendency to splinter during ministerial meetings as members (notably from Central and South America) are teased away from the Group, or, like Venezuela, persuaded to soften their positions by the US and the EU through the negotiation of bilateral deals. Splintering also occurs, predictably, because of the divergent development interests of the G20, which, since it is composed of fast-developing countries as well as underdeveloped countries, finds it difficult to reach consensus positions, especially in the agricultural talks. Whether the G20 can achieve its objectives of reforming the global trade order in favour of a development agenda will, Taylor argues, depend, on the one hand, on how successfully it can foster a coherent developing world position in the DDA, and, on the other hand, how it might limit US and EU splintering strategies.

Wyn Grant's chapter takes a broader approach in our examination of the principal players. Through a detailed analysis of the agricultural talks, Grant identifies a key shift in the negotiating process in the DDA. This involves a realignment away from a predominantly two-player model of bargaining (what Grant calls a duopoly) which sees the US and the EU as the principal and sometimes exclusive protagonists towards a multi-player model (described as an oligopoly) involving a much larger and broader set of protagonists. This shift is driven by the dynamic development of a large number of bargaining coalitions in the agricultural talks. Grant begins his chapter by identifying these new bargaining coalitions and then goes on to examine the impact of these groups through a comprehensive discussion of the many turns that the agricultural talks have taken in the DDA. Grant provides an appealing account of trade negotiations structured around an oligopoly. He points out that in the oligopoly model he finds in the agricultural talks, the US and EU continue to be the most powerful players in the talks and remain key drivers of the negotiations. This reinforces their dominance but it does not exclude the influence of others, as the previous duopoly model had done. The EU and US are still forced to negotiate with a set of powerful coalitions, not least the G20, which, Grant argues, has been far more influential in the DDA than the Cairns Group was in the Uruguay talks. In tracing the increasing involvement of a greater number of principal players in the agricultural talks, Grant also provides a clear explanation of why agreement on this sector is so difficult to manufacture.

Fairness and legitimacy

The third part of the book includes two chapters that address normative issues rising from the DDA. In Chapter 11 Amrita Narlikar focuses on the impact that demands for fairer trade from members as well as civil society groups have had on the DDA negotiations. The concept of fairness she deploys has two elements: (1) a process-related element that focuses on the legitimacy of the negotiating process in the DDA; and (2) an equity-based element that focuses on distributive justice in terms of the substance and even-handedness of the outcomes of this process. Narlikar examines the trends in the fairness debate through the various stages of the DDA, placing particular attention on the contribution of Brazil and India in those debates. She provides a detailed historical account of the way developing countries have shifted away from the tendency to make equity-based fairness demands in the formative years of the GATT regime towards the more regular habit of negotiating on the basis of reciprocal trade concessions in the later phases of the GATT. Significantly, she shows that neither strategy proved particularly successful for the developing countries. In the DDA, however, developing countries have constructed a discourse of fairness that finds a balance between demands for fair process and outcomes.

Narlikar also argues that the way in which fairness is framed by developing countries impacts upon their capacity to sustain cohesiveness in coalitions. Given that there are many factors which cause divisiveness within developing country coalitions, as highlighted in the chapters by Lee and Taylor, Narlikar offers an alternative perspective and suggests that developing country coalitions have proved to be more united and long-lasting in the WTO than they were in the GATT. This, she argues, is because the fairness debate in the DDA combines legitimacy of process and equity of outcomes. In this situation, the larger developing countries – Brazil and India – are willing and able to make reciprocity concessions and bear the costs of providing greater equity of outcomes for the less developed countries. Thus, Narlikar suggests, current debates about fairness in the DDA facilitate agreement.

Both critics and supporters of the WTO are keenly aware that it faces a legitimacy threat from both internal and external forces that threatens its very existence. This threat has seemingly grown in the period of the DDA negotiations as member states within the institution and civil society groups outside point to both input and output legitimacy shortcomings in the DDA. The discussion of input legitimacy focuses on the argument that WTO decision-making and the negotiating process lack both internal and external transparency such that it has 'democratic deficit'. Elizabeth Smythe's chapter (Chapter 12) analyses the legitimacy debates in the DDA as well as the attempts the organisation has been making in recent years to respond to demands for greater openness. Smythe's chapter highlights the many incidences of unfairness in the negotiating process which lead to unjust outcomes, especially for developing countries, which, despite the fact that they have forged increasingly active bargaining coalitions, still lack the capacity to challenge the powerful industrialised countries. It is this asymmetry of negotiating capacity that enables the industrialised countries to ignore the demands of the majority of the WTO members for development trade policies.

Smythe also examines the WTO's attempts at internal reform. The Sutherland Report (Sutherland et al., 2004) marks the results of the first concerted effort to address the problem of the democratic deficit within the WTO. Although the Report recommended a number of procedural reforms, Smythe argues that these were designed primarily to improve the efficiency rather than the transparency of decision-making and negotiating processes. So disappointing was the Report that the WTO General Council failed to officially endorse it and it has been largely ignored by most members. Smythe also points out that the minimal steps the WTO has taken towards transparency have further exposed the inequity of the negotiating process. This raises the question, to what extent can the WTO claim that its outcomes are legitimate even if its processes are not? That is, are outputs not a more important criterion for judging the legitimacy of the WTO than its negotiating and/or decision-making procedures? Thus if, in the DDA, the process – however undemocratic – can deliver on its promise to place developing country needs and interests at the heart of the negotiations then this output legitimacy will override any lack of input legitimacy. Unfortunately, as Smythe points out, the DDA has secured only limited development outcomes and many now doubt whether the Round will achieve its stated development goals. For Smythe, the failure to deliver development commitments and the continued inequity in procedures can only increase the legitimacy challenge faced by the WTO.

Concluding the Round

In the final section of the book two chapters assess the likelihood of a conclusion to the DDA and the likely impact on the future development of the WTO should such a conclusion be forthcoming. In Chapter 13 Gilbert Winham begins by detailing the very complex nature of the Doha Round both substantively and procedurally. As he points out, the 2001 Doha Declaration launching the talks produced a very extensive and wide-reaching agenda. From the outset of the talks, 21 subjects were tabled for negotiation, with a further four – the Singapore issues – included at a later stage. However, because of developing country resistance to the inclusion of all four of the Singapore issues, in the end only one additional subject – trade facilitation – was included in the talks. Winham traces the gradual trimming of the Doha Agenda after the collapse of the Cancún meeting. Thereafter – as illustrated by the content of the July 2004 Package – a more nuanced approach to the negotiations emerged whereby what were seen as key subjects by the principal developing and industrialised countries would be singled out for priority attention. Thus, from July 2004 onwards the Doha Round had a trimmer substance, with talks in agriculture (including tagging cotton for special attention), NAMA, and, to a lesser degree, services taking precedence. This more focused agenda has, however, not led to any real significant progress in the talks and, while a minimum agreement emerged at the Hong Kong, the talks are now once again in crisis.

Although this stop–start pattern is not unique to the DDA, Winham argues that there are particular features that make him more pessimistic that this Round will not be concluded: an overly ambitious agenda (including the promise of a new set of development trade rules); an inconsistent set of objectives; a focus on tariffs; and the emergence of cohesive and active developing country coalitions enjoying far more power and influence in the Doha Round than in previous Rounds. To this complex set of obstacles we need to also add existing GATT/WTO problems of trying to forge consensus (particularly one that attempts to be a single undertaking). Combined, these features make agreement in the DDA a challenging prospect.

While Winham suggests that the WTO has the management tools to iron out the problems caused by the complex negotiating environment – such as small-group management of the talks by key players from developing and industrialised countries (as illustrated by the Group of 6 – G6)[15] – it is the substance of the DDA that is the key problem since this is more difficult for the WTO, as a member-driven institution, to manage. He argues that the failure of the negotiations to reach agreement will damage the WTO since it is, in essence, a 'negotiating machine'. The organisation was designed to be an improvement over the previous General Agreement on Tariffs and Trade (GATT) system. Yet while the GATT managed the successful completion of eight Rounds, the WTO has yet to complete one. Should the DDA fail, then questions will inevitably be raised about whether multilateral governance of trade is now possible, or even desirable. That said, Winham argues, the WTO remains relevant because it continues to offer trading nations the broadest possible base of trade rules backed by a judicial process for adjudicating trade disputes.

In Chapter 14 Rorden Wilkinson argues that apparent deadlocks in the negotiations are a well-established part of the WTO political milieu. Rather than being calamities that seriously threaten the completion of the Round, collapse and deadlock are often an essential stage in the negotiating process and 'merely punctuation marks in the general negotiating pattern'. For Wilkinson, the key issue is not whether the DDA will be concluded (since he is convinced that some form of agreement will emerge) but what form the agreement will take and the possible impact it will have on the institutional development of the WTO. Wilkinson argues that the DDA is unlikely to lead to development-boosting trade outcomes. The development content of the Doha Declaration has been so heavily pruned that what remains after the Hong Kong meeting is a few sweeteners such as the Aid for Trade package. Key development concerns such as reductions in American and European agricultural protectionism are unlikely to feature in the final agreement. It is far more likely that NAMA and services will be the only sectors where a measure of liberalisation will be achieved in the Round, and that the balance of potential benefits from a concluded DDA will disproportionately favour the interests of the industrialised countries.

Wilkinson argues that this lopsided outcome will, in turn, add to the existing asymmetries in the WTO system. Only an agreement that secures significantly greater gains for developing countries compared to industrialised countries, he argues, can begin to address the embedded imbalances in international trade regulation. Another Round that secures the opposite – by providing greater potential gains for the developed countries – not only will fail to achieve its stated primary objective of meeting the development needs of the poorest countries of the world but will, by increasing the imbalances in international trade regulation, consolidate their underdevelopment.

Wilkinson's chapter brings the analysis to a close. All the contributors offer cogent accounts that together point to more deeply rooted problems afflicting the Round than an inability of member states to adjust their negotiating strategies in pursuit of an agreement. Instead, the contributors suggest that the root of the problem lies in the manner in which the trade agenda has evolved. Yet while it might be the case that the Round eventually reaches some kind of conclusion, without a process of reform that addresses the substantive imbalance in that agenda, the DDA and any subsequent Rounds are likely to remain politically fraught and economically unbalanced affairs.

Notes

1 The first section of this chapter reproduces and updates Wilkinson (2006b).
2 The G6 comprises the EU, US, Japan, Australia, Brazil, and India.
3 Argentina, Bolivia, Brazil, China, Chile, Colombia, Costa Rica, Cuba, Ecuador, El Salvador, Guatemala, India, Mexico, Pakistan, Paraguay, the Philippines, Peru, Thailand, South Africa, and Venezuela.
4 Bulgaria, Chinese Taipei, Iceland, Israel, Japan, Korea, Liechtenstein, Mauritius, Norway, and Switzerland.
5 The facilitators in Hong Kong were (NAMA) Humayun Khan – Pakistan; (Agriculture) Mukhisa Kituyi – Kenya; (Development) Clement Rohee – Guyana; (Services) Hyun Chong Kim – Korea; (Rules) Jonas Støre – Norway; and (other issues) Ignacio Walker – Chile.
6 The G33 is a group of developing countries pressing for concessions on strategic products and a special safeguard mechanism in the DDA; the G90 brings together the least developed countries, with the African Union and the African Caribbean and Pacific states.
7 The friends of ambition comprised Australia, Canada, Chile, Costa Rica, the EU, Japan, Hong Kong, Korea, New Zealand, Norway, Singapore, Switzerland, and the US; while the NAMA 11 included Argentina, Brazil, China, Egypt, India, Indonesia, Namibia, Pakistan, the Philippines, Venezuela, and South Africa.
8 The three amendments were (1) the addition of brackets in paragraph 21 indicating the lack so far of agreement on an aspect of the services negotiations; (2) the removal of brackets in paragraph 53 indicating agreement to the accession of Tonga; and (3) the addition of 'and the Decision of the General Council of 6 December 2005 on an Amendment of the TRIPS Agreement' at the end of paragraph 34 dealing with TRIPs and Public Health.
9 Comments made during a press conference by the Indian Minister of Commerce and Industry, Kamal Nath, and the Brazilian Minister of External Relations, Celso Amorim, Hong Kong, 14 December 2005.
10 This was the Zambian Minister and Chair of the LDC group Deepak Patel's phrase to describe the press conference jockeying of USTR Portman and EU Commissioner Mandelson, though it also aptly applied to press conference pronouncements of the Indian Minister Nath and the Brazilian Minister Amorim.

11 See the text-based suggestions on the issues identified in NAMA submitted by Argentina, Brazil, India, Namibia, South Africa, the Philippines, and Venezuela on 15 December 2005; and the African position on NAMA submitted to the ministerial conference. See also the submission by Indonesia.
12 See Chinese and African Group positions on NAMA submitted to the ministerial conference.
13 For a more extensive discussion of the development agenda in the WIPO see May (2006).
14 Usually taken to be competition policy, investment, government procurement, and trade facilitation but which also include environmental protection and core labour standards.
15 The G6 comprises Australia, Brazil, the EU, India, Japan, and the US.

References

Bergsten, C. Fred (2005), 'Rescuing the Doha Round', *Foreign Affairs*, 84: 7 (December).
Elliott, Larry (2006), 'Blair Was Right, the Striptease Summit Was Embarrassing', *The Guardian*, 13 March.
Evenett, Simon J. (2006), 'The World Trade Organization Ministerial Conference in Hong Kong: What Next?', *Journal of World Trade*, 40: 2.
G9 Developing Countries (2005), Statement presented by South African Delegate Faizel Ismail, 28 November, paragraph 1. http://www.twnside.org.sg.
G90 (2005), Alternative services annexe, paragraph 6, submitted 16 December.
Hills, Carla A. (2005), 'The Stakes of Doha', *Foreign Affairs*, 84: 7 (December).
IIBE&L (2006a), 'Global Trade Opinion Poll Survey No. 12'. http://www.iit.adelaide.edu.au/docs/GTOP%2012%20Results.pdf.
IIBE&L (2006b), 'Global Trade Opinion Poll Survey No. 13'. http://www.iit.adelaide.edu.au/docs/GTOP%2013%20Results.pdf.
Khor, Martin (2005), 'Brief Assessment of the WTO's Hong Kong Ministerial Outcome', Third World Network (20 December).
Khor, Martin (2006), Comments to the joint Initiative for Policy Dialogue/Brooks World Poverty Institute task force on trade, 'An Assessment of the Doha Round after Hong Kong', University of Manchester, 3 February.
Lamy, Pascal (2006), Statement to the Informal Meeting of the TNC, JOB(06)/217, 1 July.
Mandelson, Peter (2005), Remarks during 15 December press conference.
Mandelson, Peter (2006a), Speech to the European Parliament, Strasbourg, 16 January.
Mandelson, Peter (2006b), Transcript of remarks following the suspension of the WTO Doha negotiations, 25 July. http://ec.europa.eu/comm/commission_barroso/mandelson/speeches_articles/mandelson_sptemplate.cfm?LangId=EN&temp=sppm110_en.
Mandelson, Peter (2006c), 'A Deal Can Still Be Salvaged from the Ashes of Doha', *Financial Times*, 31 July.
May, Christopher (2006), *The World Intellectual Property Organization: Resurgence and the Development Agenda* (London: Routledge).
Nath, Kamal (2005), Statement in Lok Sabha, 21 December, http://commerce.nic.in/dec05/index.htm.
Portman, Robert (2006), 'Keeping Doha Alive', *Washington Times*, 6 January.
Stiglitz, Joseph E., and Charlton, Andrew (2006), 'The Doha Round after Hong Kong: A Preliminary Evaluation of Progress Made at the Hong Kong Ministerial', background paper for the joint Initiative for Policy Dialogue/Brooks World Poverty Institute task force on trade, 'An Assessment of the Doha Round after Hong Kong', University of Manchester, 2–3 February.

Sutherland, Peter et al. (2004), *The Future of the WTO: Addressing Institutional Challenges in the New Millennium* (Geneva: WTO).

USTR (2006), Statement by the Office of the US Trade Representative, 25 July. http://www.ustr.gov/Document_Library/Press_Releases/2006/July/Statement_by_Office_of_the_US_Trade_Representative.html.

Wilkinson, Rorden (2002), 'The World Trade Organisation', *New Political Economy*, 7: 1 (March).

Wilkinson, Rorden (2006a), *The WTO: Crisis and the Governance of Global Trade* (London: Routledge).

Wilkinson, Rorden (2006b), 'The WTO in Hong Kong: What It Really Means for the Doha Development Agenda', *New Political Economy*, 11: 2 (June).

WTO (2001) *Doha Ministerial Declaration*, WT/MIN(01)/Dec/1, 20 November.

WTO (2004), 'Doha Work Programme: Decision Adopted by the General Council on 1 August 2004', WT/L/579, 2 August.

WTO (2005a), 'Covering Letter of 7 December from the General Council Chair and the DG to Secretary Tsang Transmitting the Draft Ministerial Text' and 'Doha Work Programme: Draft Ministerial Text', WT/MIN(05)/W/3.

WTO (2005b), Draft Ministerial Text, JOB(05)/298, 26 November, and Draft Ministerial Text (revision), JOB(05)/298/Rev.1.

WTO (2005c), Hong Kong ministerial declaration, 18 December, WT/MIN(05)/DEC.

2 Trade, development, and the Doha Development Agenda

Sylvia Ostry

Introduction

In this chapter I recount how the focus of the trading system shifted from trade to development or, rather, appeared to do so as exemplified by the Doha Development Agenda (DDA). The transformation of the multilateral trading system (MTS) was the result of the Uruguay Round, one of the unintended consequences of that negotiation being a serious asymmetry between North and South. This background is essential to a fuller understanding of the Doha negotiations and the uncertainty which prevailed at the Hong Kong Ministerial meeting in December 2005. The chapter concludes with some proposals for policy reform of the MTS since, whatever the outcome of the negotiations, the system must be strengthened.

Post-Uruguay multilateral trading system

The Uruguay Round was the eighth negotiation of the General Agreement on Tariffs and Trade (GATT). The GATT worked very well through the concept of reciprocity (denounced as mercantilist by trade purists) and because of rules and other arrangements to buffer or interface between the *international* objective of sustained liberalisation by a reduction of border barriers and the objects of *domestic* policy (mainly full employment and the postwar welfare state). This effective paradigm, termed 'embedded liberalism' by John Ruggie (Ruggie, 1982), was based on a consensus among the big players but it was certainly aided by the Cold War and the virtual exclusion of agriculture.

For all practical purposes agriculture was excluded from GATT disciplines almost from the outset. The US secured a GATT waiver for its support programmes in 1955. This was followed by the new European Community's (EC) Common Agricultural Policy (CAP) and its vast and growing subsidies. But since GATT rules for agriculture were looser than for other industries, many governments chose to ignore them – as, for example, did Japan in devising its wide range of restrictions. So agriculture was excluded for the first seven GATT negotiations. All that changed in the eighth negotiation, the Uruguay Round. The Americans had tolerated the CAP in its early days for political reasons (largely because of the Cold War alliance) but, as US exports to the EC diminished and as EC exports flourished and, indeed, penetrated the American market, anger at the 'unfair competition' of subsidised products exploded. All these factors had one cause – or so the US decided: the CAP. Agriculture became a central issue of the new negotiations.

From the 1960s the MTS was essentially managed by the EC and the US with other congenial members of the rich members' 'club'. The developing countries were largely ignored as players (although this began to alter in the 1970s as a consequence of the OPEC oil shock and the emergence of 'commodity power'). All that changed in the Uruguay Round. It was not just agriculture that made it unique. The endless foot-dragging by the EC to prevent a launch was reinforced by the opposition of a group of developing countries – tagged the G10 hardliners and led by Brazil and India – which wanted to prevent a trade round not because of agriculture but because of the so-called 'new issues' of services, intellectual property, and investment. They feared that these were essentially domestic policies and would constrict their industrial policy domain. But for the US the new issues were crucial in sustaining business support for multilateralism. American service industries were world leaders and the same was true in investment and technology. American multinationals controlled over 40 per cent of the world's stock of foreign investment at the outset of the 1980s and the American technology balance-of-payments surplus was well over $6 billion while every other Organisation for Economic Co-operation and Development (OECD) country was in deficit. The business advisory committees to the US Trade Representative (USTR) were very clear: without the new issues they would prefer a bilateral or regional approach. And they did not just talk the talk: they walked the walk. The US organised business lobbies in a range of other countries to pressure their governments to support the inclusion of the new issues. This probably helped in Europe to nudge the Commission to stop foot-dragging. In any event, the Uruguay Round was launched at Punte del Este, Uruguay, in September 1986 with the inclusion of agriculture, services, trade-related intellectual property (TRIPs), and, albeit in a more restricted scope than desired by the Americans, trade-related investment measures (TRIMs), as well as, of course, all the usual agenda items such as tariffs and rules.

The negotiations dragged on for over eight years as the transatlantic battle over agriculture continued and the negotiations came close to complete collapse at ministerial meetings in Montreal in 1988 and Brussels in 1990. Initiatives by Arthur Dunkel, the GATT Director-General, who prepared a draft of an agreement, plus threats of unilateralism by the US in the 1988 Trade and Competitiveness Act as well as regionalism in Asia (Asia-Pacific Economic Co-operation – APEC) all helped to keep the negotiations (barely) alive. In November 1992 an agreement on agriculture was reached between the EC and the US at Blair House in Washington (the so-called Blair House accord). The new GATT Director-General, Peter Sutherland, pushed hard to finish the job and the final agreement was signed in Marrakesh, Morocco, in April 1994, four years beyond the target date agreed at the launch. The Grand Bargain, as I have termed it, was essentially an implicit deal: the opening of OECD markets to agriculture and textiles and clothing in exchange for the 'new issues' (services, intellectual property rights, and investment measures). And, at the last minute, the creation of a new institution, the WTO, with the strongest dispute settlement system in the history of international law and virtually no executive or legislative authority (Ostry, 2002).

The Grand Bargain was quite different from GATT reciprocity. The Northern piece of the bargain consisted of some limited progress in agriculture; limited progress in textiles and clothing with a promise to end the Multi-Fibre Agreement (MFA) in 2005 with most of the restrictions to be eliminated later rather than sooner; a rather significant reduction in tariffs on goods in exchange for deeper cuts and more comprehensive bindings by developing countries; and virtual elimination of voluntary export restraints (VERs) most relevant to Japan. On the whole, not great; but in GATT terms not so bad even though the results were rather disappointing in agriculture and in textiles and clothing, with the MFA elimination more than offset by the impact of China. But this is not the whole story: the Southern piece of the deal was related not to the GATT but to a major transformation of the MTS.

The most significant feature of the transformation was the shift in policy focus from border barriers to domestic regulatory and legal systems: the institutional infrastructure of the economy. The barriers to access for service providers stem from laws, regulations, and administrative actions which impede cross-border trade and factor flows. Further, since these laws and administrative actions are, for the most part, 'invisible' to outsiders, a key element in any negotiation is *transparency*, that is, the publication of all relevant laws, regulations, and administrative procedures, as is common in OECD countries. Most important in this shift embodied in the services agreement is a move away from GATT *negative* regulation – what governments must not do – to *positive* regulation – what governments must do. In the case of intellectual property the move to positive regulation is more dramatic since the negotiations covered not only standards for domestic laws but also detailed provisions for enforcement procedures to ensure individual (corporation) property rights. In the area of social regulation (covering environmental issues, food safety, and the like) the positive regulatory approach is *procedural* rather than *substantive*. Thus the South side of the outcome involves major upgrading and change in the institutional infrastructure in most Southern countries, which takes time and costs money. Thus the Grand Bargain involved considerable investment with uncertain medium-term results. It is better described as a Bum Deal.

Finally, it must be emphasised that because of some clever legalistic juggling by the US and the EC in the end game (Steinberg, 2002) the Round was a 'single undertaking'. There were no opt-outs as in the Toyko Round. It was a take-it-or-leave-it deal. So the Southern countries took it but, it is safe to say, without a full comprehension of the transformative nature of the new system. As one of the Southern participants was reported to have said: 'TRIPs was part of a package in which we got agriculture' (Corner House, September 2004). There were a number of significant unintended consequences of the Uruguay Round. Among these was a serious North–South divide based on a consensus among the Southern countries, however varied in other respects, that the outcome was profoundly unbalanced.

The North–South divide was visible at the debacle of Seattle in 1999 when virtually all the developing countries walked out of the ministerial meeting. And then there was Doha. The main objective was to avoid another Seattle: thus its great success was that it did not fail. It is more than symbolic that the DDA term was coined. The Doha Declaration is replete with references to technical assistance and capacity-building (one cynic called this the new conditionality). And the Doha Declaration was a masterpiece of creative ambiguity. Too clever by half, alas, as was demonstrated by the failure at Cancún and the current state of the negotiations – to which we return below. First let us review one of the most serious legacies of the new system – asymmetry.

Asymmetry

If the Doha Round is to foster development then a major legacy of the Uruguay Round transformation will have to be confronted. While the idea of equity, in so far as it is included in WTO rules related to 'special and differential treatment' (SDT), is both weak and ambiguous, the concept of *structural asymmetry* has been completely ignored. While there is not the space here to describe these features of the MTS structure, let me just briefly review some aspects of the asymmetry.

Complexity

The first aspect of significance is *complexity*. The GATT focus on border barriers and its club-like management was relatively simple. The WTO is quite another story. The need for knowledge – advanced and sophisticated – is essential. Complexity requires knowledge and knowledge enhances power. The strong are stronger because of their store of knowledge and the weak are weaker because of their poverty of knowledge. So the system creates reinforced asymmetry. While we can debate whether or not there is a poverty trap, there clearly is a knowledge trap.

There are a growing number of case studies by the World Bank that demonstrate the capacity deficit (Finger and Schuler, 2000; Hoekman, 2002). There was very little participation by the African countries in the Uruguay Round because of their lack of representation in Geneva and the lack of co-ordination and expertise at home. Recent figures suggest nothing much has changed. And this situation is not confined to Africa. There is an institutional weakness in co-ordination mechanisms in many developing and transition economies.

The lack of capacity is of growing importance in agriculture, a key to development for poor countries. For example, the imposition of new standards for alleged (minor) health reasons cut African exports of nuts and greens by 60 per cent. This is one example of many of the impact of more and more complex standards imposed by the agreement on Sanitary and Phytosanitary Measures (SPS), as recent case studies by the Millennium Development Project have shown (UN Millennium Project, 2005: 146–165). The situation is likely to worsen as regulation for high-value-added products makes it more difficult for the small and medium enterprises that lack information about export markets to compete with Wal-Mart. The poor countries play no role in the setting of international standards because they cannot participate, lacking both money and human resources. Similar problems exist with Technical Barriers to Trade (TBT). While both the TBT and SPS were supposed to provide technical assistance, this has thus far been inadequate. Indeed, although a Working Group on Trade and Transfer of Technology was established at Doha, it has accomplished nothing and remains deadlocked. As a careful review of its operations concludes, this is because of the 'approaches of developed countries that favour pursuit of mere discussions without any substantive outcome that improve [*sic*] the transfer of technology to developing countries' (South Centre, October 2005: 29–30).

This is just the briefest of surveys of the knowledge trap. But there is another aspect of asymmetry which deserves mention. It is repeatedly stressed that the true jewel in the crown of the transformed multilateral trading system was the creation of the WTO and its Dispute Settlement Understanding (DSU). For the first time in international law a truly effective institutional constraint on the powerful has been achieved. So is the increased legalisation an offset to asymmetry? Alas, not exactly.

Legalisation

The WTO was not part of the Uruguay Round agenda. The Canadian proposal was not put forward until April 1990. It was soon endorsed by the EU (which had opposed stronger dispute settlement in the Tokyo Round) because of growing concerns about US unilateralism. It was deemed a useful device for the constraint of power. The US, dubious about the quality of legal expertise in the GATT Secretariat, insisted on the creation of an Appellate Body (AB) to review the legal aspects of panel reports. So a paradigm shift took place, as Weiler terms it: 'the juridification of the process, including not only the rule of law but the rule of lawyers' (Weiler, 2001: 339). Be that as it may, the main focus of concern in the context of asymmetry is whether the paradigm shift of juridification benefits the poorest countries. It is not possible to get any data on the number of legal experts in their Geneva missions or in their domestic ministries, but one can safely assume the numbers are very small or even non-existent. And there has been no participation as complainant or respondent by any of the poor African countries. This is asymmetry *writ large*.

One clear reason is very simple and straightforward – lack of money. The absence of government legal services either at home or in Geneva would require hiring private lawyers, which is far too expensive. An Advisory Centre on WTO Law (ACWL) was established in December 1999 and entered into force in July 2001 to provide some legal assistance for poor countries. It requires a membership fee based on per capita income and share of world trade. It is funded mainly by European governments plus Canada. The US refused to join or provide funding. While the ACWL is certainly a welcome initiative, it will require further funding and co-ordination with both enterprises and governments in developing countries as well as capabilities in economic research. The role of sophisticated econometric research and economic evidence in WTO dispute settlement is another example of the *reinforcement* of power by complexity in the mechanism designed to *constrain* power.

That said, the cost side of the cost–benefit model for dispute participation often includes more than money or legal service subsidies. Political costs – threats by richer countries to reduce development aid, or remove trade preferences – may also be very powerful deterrents to initiating a WTO dispute. An example of political deterrence is provided by a former US trade official who argued in an African capital that 'the U.S. might withdraw food aid were the country's Geneva representatives to press a WTO complaint' (Shaffer, 2006). More recently the Deputy US Secretary of State, Robert Zoellick, warned Brazil that the US might withdraw Generalised System of Preferences (GSP) privileges unless intellectual property rights protection was improved (*Inside US Trade*, 28 October 2005).

So asymmetry prevails. Indeed, there are other examples of problems with the DSU as a 'balancing mechanism' for poorer countries. Perhaps an increasing interest among legal scholars will lead to some feasible reform proposals. Let me turn to some of my own reform suggestions in conclusion.

Concluding comments: the road from Hong Kong

The avoidance of failure at Hong Kong has provided some breathing space – albeit not a great deal and certainly not enough to stave off a breakdown of negotiations in July 2006. The stakes are very high: what is at risk is not really a 'negotiation' but the survival of the rules-based system. The alternative is already evident. A fragmentation by an increasing proliferation of preferential agreements is being led by American 'competitive liberalisation' and shifts the system from one based on rules to one based on power and episodic ad hocery. These preferential agreements include 'WTO plus' agendas on TRIPs and investment and greatly increase the transaction costs for smaller countries and smaller companies because of the increasingly complex rules of origin.

The creation of the postwar international economic architecture depended not only on the role of the single hegemon but also on a broad consensus about a basic paradigm of international co-operation. That consensus no longer exists, even between the Big Two – Europe and the US. At Cancún a 'New Geography' became evident in coalitions of Southern countries. The G20 included the Big Three – Brazil, China, and India – as well as a number of other developing countries. Despite repeated efforts to eliminate it, the G20 has persisted and is playing a significant role in the trade negotiations. The other coalition at Cancún – the G90 of African and other poor countries – has also endured but its role in the trade games is not clear, although the G20 and G90 were introduced as the G110 in Hong Kong! So, one cannot deny the ongoing shift in the 'balance of power' engendered by the rise of China and India. The weakening of the transatlantic consensus is now joined by a wide disparity of views among the major players in the WTO. And we must add to this the views of the NGOs which are also players in the trade policy arena.

One real danger of the new geography is that it could result in transforming trade into a zero-sum game. By blocking consensus the G2 and the G3 can both exert power, but for what purpose? The G20 includes countries with considerable soft infrastructure and the proliferation of NGOs is able to provide knowledge and policy analysis. But so far there is no evidence of a significant effort to exploit the power shift by generating a coherent and flexible strategy.

Given the new breathing space and also the Aid for Trade project established in Hong Kong, perhaps the issue of structural asymmetry could be tackled. Perhaps it could consider enhancing an existing mechanism – the Integrated Framework for Trade-Related Technical Assistance (IF) established in 1997 and involving the WTO, the World Bank, the IMF, the United Nations Conference on Trade and Development (UNCTAD), the United Nations Development Programme (UNDP), and the International Trade Commission (ITC) as well as a number of bilateral donors. An evaluation of the programme in June 2000 was not very encouraging. Lack of clear priorities, ill-defined governance structure, and low levels of funding were among the problems cited. The heads of the six agencies then decided to revamp the IF. A new evaluation was undertaken in 2004 by the World Bank's Operations Evaluation Department (OED). While asserting that there had been some moderate improvement, the OED admits that radical reform is required if genuine results are to be achieved in mainstreaming trade into development (Agarwal and Cutura, 2004: xv).

The reasons for suggesting the IF is that it is probably safer to explore 'learning by doing' than to start from scratch. Innovation is a learning process, and mistakes are as important as a source of knowledge as are successes. There is no single formula for Aid for Trade and there will be different requirements for different countries and circumstances.

Finally, perhaps the road from Hong Kong could look at one other milestone. The WTO is a profoundly asymmetric institution without real executive or legislative power, a very small secretariat, and a very limited budget (about equal to the travel budget of the IMF). These structural deficiencies greatly exacerbate the rich–poor asymmetries. Perhaps most important at this juncture is that there is no policy forum in the WTO. There had been one in the GATT – the Consultative Group of 18 (CG18) involving senior officials from capitals. It was never officially terminated but meetings ceased at the end of the 1980s.

Establishing a WTO policy forum – recommended by the Sutherland Consultative Board among others – should be accompanied by an increase in research resources so that a new policy forum would be able to tackle the sticky and unsolved issue of trade and development inherited from the GATT and special and differential treatment (SDT). The negotiations have gone nowhere – not surprisingly, I think. The origins of SDT reflect the Cold War and the end of colonialism. The import substitution model of development is long since dead. But the idea of some form of industrial policy is in vigorous revival. The new term is 'policy space', concocted at UNCTAD XI (2004). While there is no nice, clear, shared definition of the requisites of 'policy space' there is certainly agreement that the impact of the Uruguay Round – especially TRIPs and TRIMs – has constricted many aspects of domestic policy related to growth and development. While SDT is a historic relic, surely it is essential to confront the issue of trade and development in analytic terms and aim for a new approach termed policy space (or whatever) (see Gallagher, 2005; also Ackerman, 2005, and Polaski, 2005). No wonderful econometric model generating estimates of how many jobs the Doha negotiations would generate can substitute. Because there is no consensus on the essential elements of a MTS today, surely there is a consensus that if Doha fails, a new world disorder threatens. A strengthening of the WTO legitimacy and capabilities and even a small step in the direction of tackling asymmetry and launching a new dialogue on trade and sustainable development should be considered a success, whatever the devil in the details of the final negotiations.

References

Ackerman, Frank (2005), *The Shrinking Gains from Trade: A Critical Assessment of Doha Round Projections*, Global Development and Environment Institute Working Paper No. 05–01, Tufts University (October).

Agarwal, Manmoham, and Cutura, Jozefina (2004), *Integrated Framework for Trade-Related Technical Assistance*, Case Study, World Bank Operations Evaluation Department, Washington, DC.

The Corner House (2004), *Who Owns the Knowledge Economy? Political Organising behind TRIPS*, The Corner House, Sturminster Newton, Dorset (September).

Finger, J. Michael, and Schuler, Philip (2000), 'Implementation of Uruguay Round Commitments: The Development Challenge', *World Economy*, 23: 4 (April).

Gallagher, Kevin P. (ed.) (2005), *Putting Development First: The Importance of Policy Space in the WTO and IFI's* (London: Zed Books).

Hoekman, Bernard (2002), *Economic Development and the World Trade Organization after Doha*, Policy Research Working Paper 2851, World Bank, Development Research Group (Trade) (June).

Inside US Trade (2005), 23: 43 (28 October).

Ostry, Sylvia (2002), 'The Uruguay Round North–South Grand Bargain: Implications for Future Negotiations', in Daniel M. Kennedy and James D. Southwick (eds), *The Political Economy of International Trade Law: Essays in Honour of Robert E. Hudec* (Cambridge: Cambridge University Press).

Polaski, Sandra (2005), 'In Agricultural Trade Talks, First Do No Harm', *Perspectives*, Trade, Equity and Development Project at the Carnegie Endowment, Washington, DC (Autumn).

Ruggie, John Gerard (1982), 'International Regimes, Transactions and Change: Embedded Liberalism in the Postwar Economic Order', *International Organization*, 36: 2 (Spring).

Shaffer, Gregory (2006), 'The Challenges of WTO Law: Strategies for Developing Country Adaptation', *World Trade Review*, 5: 2 (July).

South Centre (2005), *The Agenda for Transfer of Technology: The Working Group of the WTO on Trade and Transfer of Technology*, Geneva (October).

Steinberg, Richard H. (2002), 'In the Shadow of Law or Power? Consensus-Based Bargaining and Outcome in the GATT/WTO', *International Organization*, 56: 2 (Spring).

UN Millennium Project (2005), *Task Force on Trade*, London and Washington, DC.

Weiler, J. H. H. (2001), 'The Rule of Lawyers and the Ethos of Diplomatic Reflections on WTO Dispute Settlement', in Roger Porter et al. (eds), *Efficiency, Equity, Legitimacy* (Washington, DC: Brookings Institution).

Part II
Key issues

3   WTO agriculture negotiations and the Global South

Jennifer Clapp

The Doha Round of trade talks was christened a 'development' round. It was supposed to give special consideration to the needs and concerns of developing countries, which had felt that the Uruguay Round, and indeed all rounds that preceded it, reflected the agenda of the industrialised countries. It was widely assumed that the agriculture negotiations in the Doha Round would be where developing countries would make some of the most gains. Since the completion of the Uruguay Round, which was the first to address agricultural trade squarely, it has become apparent that the inequities in the agricultural trade system were not adequately addressed by the agreement. Agriculture is a highly distorted sector in the global economy. Total subsidies to agriculture in the OECD countries – both export subsidies and domestic support – average over $300 billion per year and depress global prices for agricultural commodities. Developing countries also face highly protectionist trade structures that limit their access to rich country markets, as tariff rates on the products they export remain high. Because agriculture plays such an important role in their economies, improvement in agricultural trade rules has been at the top of the agenda for most developing countries.

In light of the developing countries' disappointment with the Uruguay Round, the WTO membership endorsed the idea of a 'development round' at Doha. In the area of agriculture the Doha Declaration indicated that the WTO membership was committed to 'substantial improvements in market access, reduction of, with a view to phasing out, all forms of export subsidies, and substantial reductions in trade-distorting domestic support' (WTO, 2001). The Declaration went on to stress that special and differential treatment for developing countries would be integral to the agricultural negotiations.

In this chapter I analyse the politics of the Doha negotiations on agriculture. I focus in particular on the role of the Global South in the changing dynamic as well as the substance of the talks. I trace the rise of developing country groupings and outline their bargaining positions and impacts on the talks in relation to the US and the EU. Space does not permit an extensive analysis of the domestic political forces within each country which produced the positions, though this would provide a more complete picture. Space also does not permit an extensive discussion of the possibility of trade-offs between agriculture and other areas of the talks that might be found in a 'successful' development round should such an outcome be forthcoming. The aim of the chapter is to analyse the agriculture talks in particular, though I do recognise that this is only one aspect of the Doha Round.

My argument is that developing countries were instrumental in changing the dynamic of the agriculture talks, but that this change may not be enough to ensure that the content of the agreement is acceptable to all countries of the Global South. In the first two years of the talks the negotiation process was largely top-down. The key battles in agriculture were fought between the US and the EU, and the WTO produced texts without wide consultation or input. In this phase the Southern countries were yet again left on the sidelines, much as they had been during the Uruguay and previous Rounds. It was this dynamic that led the developing countries to put their foot down in Cancún, as they were angered in large part by the process as well as the substance with respect to the agriculture negotiations. Just prior to Cancún, several new groupings were formed – the Group of 20 on Agriculture (G20), the Group of 33 (G33) and the African Union/African Caribbean and Pacific/ Least Developed Countries (AU/ACP/LDC) group (the so-called Group of 90 – G90) – to add voice to the concerns of developing countries in the talks. Since these groups were formed, the developing countries, and the G20 in particular, have been key in changing the dynamic of the talks. Forming a loose coalition, these groups, though representing diverse interests, did have a sense of unity which gave them strength. Following the emergence of these groups, the agriculture talks in the post-Cancún period were less top-down and more consultative with developing countries.

As the nature of the talks changed, two of the leading countries of the G20 were brought into smaller core negotiating groups. While the composition of these core negotiating groups demonstrates recognition of the importance of the Global South for reaching a final agriculture deal, it has also been criticised by other countries – developing and industrialised alike – as being non-transparent and exclusive. While the developing countries have made a definite impact on process of the agricultural talks, it has become clear that their interests are indeed diverse, and it is likely that a single 'development' deal in the agricultural sector cannot be reached which addresses all of their interests to equal satisfaction. It remains to be seen if the countries of the Global South will be forced to concede any last-minute deals struck between the US and EU, or whether some will walk out if the deal is unsatisfactory to them. In either case it looks now as if any gains for developing countries will be marginal at best, and, while the groups have thus far maintained a significant degree of cohesion, there remains a risk that the varying interests amongst different groupings of these countries could break that cohesion when the final deals are brokered.

Limits to the 1994 Uruguay Round agreement on agriculture

Prior to the Uruguay Round, agricultural trade, though in theory covered by the original 1947 GATT agreement, was exempted from the GATT in practice (Braga, 2004: 1). This was the result of pressure by the US, which had demanded this exemption in the 1950s in order to maintain its complex system of agricultural protection (Jawara and Kwa, 2003: 26). The exemption was applied to all countries in practice, with the end result being that agriculture was not disciplined under the GATT. By the 1980s, however, the US and the EU found that the cost of protecting their agricultural sectors – primarily in the form of domestic farm supports in the case of the US and export subsidies in the case of the EU, as well as high tariffs on certain products in both cases – was getting out of hand, as one tried to out-compete the other. Other countries, such as Japan, also practised agricultural protectionism. By the mid-1980s OECD agricultural subsidies totalled some US$300 billion per year. The growing costs of maintaining the system of supports led the US to push the idea of including agriculture formally in the GATT.

The high level of agricultural protectionism in the OECD countries had especially harmful effects in the Global South. Years of excessive subsidies and other forms of protection drove down commodity prices for basic staples like rice, maize, and wheat, out-competing local production in developing countries, threatening local livelihoods and harming export income. Many developing countries, including most of Africa, became net food importers by the 1980s.

The 1994 Uruguay Round Agreement on Agriculture (AoA) was the result of intense negotiations (Balaam, 2004). The main provisions of the agreement cover the key aspects that were seen to be in need of liberalisation: market access, domestic support, and export subsidies. The AoA called for the conversion of quantitative restrictions on agricultural products to tariffs as well as their reduction. It also called for cuts to both domestic support subsidies and export subsidies. Developing countries had a more relaxed schedule of reductions and the least developed countries (LDCs) were exempt from these cuts.

Though the intention was to make radical steps toward liberalising agricultural trade, the end agreement took only the smallest of steps in that direction, some say that it even went backwards (Ritchie, 1996; Watkins, 1996). This is due, in large part, to some important exceptions to the rules, which have profoundly influenced their impact. These were largely negotiated between the US and the EU as part of what is now referred to as the 'Blair House accord', a bilateral agreement between the US and EU in 1992 which was seen to have broken the impasse between these major players and allowed for the completion of the AoA (see Jawara and Kwa, 2003).

The first exception has to do with the requirements to reduce domestic support. These subsidies were categorised into different 'boxes' according to their potential to distort trade. Those in the 'Amber Box' were seen to be highly trade-distorting because their level varied with production (such as price supports). These Amber Box subsidies were subject to reduction under the agreement, but countries were allowed to exempt *de minimis* amounts of them, up to 5 per cent of total agricultural production value and up to 5 per cent of the value of each supported product for industrialised countries (10 per cent under of each for developing countries). The 'Green Box' was another category of domestic subsidies which were deemed to have no or minimal distortions to trade (such as research and extension expenditures and income supports), and were exempted from the required cuts entirely, with no limits placed on them. A 'Blue Box' was also negotiated, which included those subsidies that normally would be in the Amber Box but which also required farmers to limit production, making them somewhat less trade-distorting. These subsidies were exempted from cuts and there was no limit placed on them. In addition, the US and EU insisted on a 'Peace Clause', which prohibited any challenges to subsidies levels until 1 January 2004, to give the members time to adjust their policies.

There were other important qualifications to the agreement, too. Although there were minimum cuts to the levels of tariffs which were to be reduced, the reductions were averaged, and in practice they were very different for each product. This meant that tariffs on some key products were reduced by very little in practice, especially where there were high tariff peaks to begin with. In addition, food aid was exempted from the export subsidy reductions. And finally the base period for the reduction of export and domestic support subsidies was set at 1986–90 and 1986–88 respectively, periods of historically high levels of subsidies. This meant that the cuts would bring subsidy levels down only minimally and in fact to levels that were higher than they were in the 1960s and 1970s. These various caveats to the deal created some significant loopholes in the agreement, which allowed the US and the EU to continue with many of the protectionist practices to which they had become accustomed.

The AoA has been criticised as reinforcing already unequal agricultural trade rules. Though subsidies were to have been dramatically reduced, they have in fact increased in the OECD countries since the mid-1980s, as around 60 per cent of OECD subsidies were, because of the exceptions, exempt from cuts (OECD, 2001: 8). The total of all agricultural support in OECD countries went from $271.2 billion in 1986–88 to $330.6 billion in 1998–2000 (Diakosawas, 2001: 10). The rise was due largely to the US and EU shifting their subsidies into the Green and Blue Boxes to save them from being cut. For example, Green Box subsidies more than doubled between 1986–88 and 1995–98 (Diakosawas, 2001: 24). In 2003 US agricultural exports sold for anywhere between 10 and 50 per cent below the cost of production (Murphy, Lilliston, and Lake, 2005). The EU similarly exports key commodities for less than the cost of production (Oxfam, 2002: 115). In 2001 prices received by OECD farmers were some 30 per cent over world prices (OECD, 2003: 4).

Developing countries were supposed to see a rising share of global agricultural exports as a result of the market access provisions. But their share of agricultural trade has remained steady at around 36 per cent since the agreement was implemented, and their share of agricultural exports to industrialised countries has remained at 22.4 per cent between 1990–91 and 2000–2001 (Ataman, 2005a: 22–23). Because the tariff reductions were averaged, industrialised countries were able to continue to discriminate against products exported by developing countries. Industrial countries have peaks in tariffs on certain products produced by developing countries. For example, tariffs on groundnuts, sugar, and meats are, in some cases, up to 500 per cent (Ataman, 2005b: 47–49; Josling and Hathaway, 2004: 2–3). Tariff escalation, the practice of applying higher tariff rates as the level of processing increases, has also been common with products exported by developing countries.

At the same time that their share in global agricultural exports failed to increase as expected, many developing countries experienced import surges, flooding their domestic markets with cheap, subsidised imported products from industrialised countries (FAO, 2003). Although both the North and the South were required to liberalise agricultural trade, many developing countries, especially the poorest ones, had already substantially liberalised their agricultural sectors under structural adjustment programmes (SAPs) in the 1980s. The liberalisation required under SAPs went much further than what is required by the industrial countries under the AoA. This has meant that even though the rich countries were required to make steeper tariff cuts than the developing countries, they started from a much higher level and it was not enough to eliminate the inequality. Under the AoA the depth of the tariff cuts made by developing countries was on average greater than that of the cuts made in industrialised countries (Anderson and Martin, 2005: 1303). The result was that developing countries were left much more vulnerable. Rather than levelling the playing field, the AoA made it more steeply stacked against developing countries. The effects on small peasant farmers, whose very livelihoods have been threatened by competition from cheap subsidised imports, have been particularly serious.

The early Doha talks: stalls and crashes prompt the Global South to organise

The problems with inequities in the 1994 AoA were recognised at the time that it was negotiated, and the agreement included a commitment to pursue further negotiations to begin in 2000. The need for revisions to the agreement was further reinforced at the 2001 Doha Ministerial, which highlighted the agriculture talks as a central feature. Revisions to the AoA were to include further liberalisation in each of the three pillars: export subsidies, market access, and domestic support. The negotiations on the modalities (broad parameters for the types of commitments) were to be completed by March 2003 and adopted at the Fifth Ministerial meeting (Cancún), to be held in September 2003. Neither of these deadlines was met, and the talks were plagued with disagreements over both content and process, with much discontent from the Global South.

The first phase of the negotiations, prior to the ministerial, saw rising frustration from the Global South. The US and the EU, meanwhile, continued to pursue the negotiations in the way to which they were accustomed – by assuming that any agreement would have to be the product of a deal amongst themselves first, usually as part of negotiations within the so-called 'Quad', in which Japan and Canada were also included, as was the case in the Uruguay Round. The WTO-appointed chair of the agriculture talks also worked in a top-down fashion as opposed to letting proposals emerge from the members. Both practices frustrated developing countries, which had made presentations on the issues of concern to them, but did not see their views reflected in the texts. Dissatisfaction with their exclusion prompted developing countries to finally take concrete action to form negotiating groups on agriculture issues to express their views. The collapse of the talks at Cancún in large part was a product of the developing countries' unwillingness to accept the 'business as usual' approach.

The timeline for the agriculture talks as outlined at Doha was highly ambitious. The developing countries were anxious about the negotiations and were vigilant about monitoring not just the content of the negotiations but also the process by which they were conducted. Little headway was made in the first year of the negotiations owing to the wide divergence in views amongst the members. Developing countries were focused on the need to incorporate special measures to enable them to protect rural livelihoods and food security. These were at first articulated as some sort of 'Development Box' or 'Food Security Box' (Murphy and Suppan, 2003). These concepts were later dropped in favour of a designation of Special Products which could be exempted from tariff cuts and a Special Safeguard Mechanism (SSM) to help protect against import surges (ICTSD, 2003a: 2). Developing countries also wanted to see a reduction in both domestic and export subsidies in the industrialised countries. The US was focused on tariff reduction in order to improve market access for its exports as well as a reduction of export subsidies practised by the EU. The EU's main aim was to see reductions in levels of domestic support which forms the bulk of US subsidies, as well as a widening of the pillar of 'export subsidies' to 'export competition', to incorporate what it considered to be hidden export subsidies in the form of export credits and food aid practised by the US.

With a lack of convergence on these issues, the chair of the agriculture committee, Stuart Harbinson, tabled a draft modalities text in February 2003 that contained a formula for tariff reductions and schedules for subsidy reductions. His aim was to arrive at a compromise text which could be approved in time for the 31 March deadline. The text was submitted in his personal capacity, as he had stressed that the gulf between the members was too wide and he had received very little guidance (ICTSD, 2003b).

The Harbinson paper was criticised from all sides. The US felt that it did not go far enough with respect to tariff cuts and export subsidies, while the EU and Japan felt that the proposals did not do enough to put disciplines on export credits and food aid. The developing countries felt that the text was heavily biased toward the concerns of the rich countries (ICTSD 2003c). That the South's concerns were not incorporated into the draft text was also echoed by several studies of the original draft text which estimated that the vast bulk of the gains from the proposal would accrue to the rich countries (for example, Danish Research Institute of Food Economics, 2003). It is not surprising that the deadline was missed. Harbinson vowed to continue to work toward an agreement in the run-up to Cancún in September 2003. But after the missed March deadline the talks were in jeopardy. Because of the inability to agree on concrete modalities, members decided to work toward a 'framework' for the modalities (for instance, general goals without specific numbers) as a first step (ICTSD, 2003d: 9).

In May 2003, when the overall talks were stalled, four West African countries – Benin, Burkina Faso, Chad, and Mali – submitted a paper to the WTO on the impact of cotton subsidies on their farmers and economies (WTO, 2003a). The paper called for recognition of cotton as a Special Product for developing countries and a complete phase-out of all cotton subsidies, as well as financial compensation for the least developed countries during the transition phase. Their aim was to raise attention to the issue, with the hope of having this addressed at Cancún. There was no precedent for a serious paper of this sort emanating from a group of the LDCs. The paper was extremely important in that it seemed to epitomise the problems faced by the poorest countries in the previous negotiations. While WTO members were forced to take note of this paper, little concrete action was taken.

In August 2003 a number of draft texts were put forward on agriculture in an effort to revive negotiations in time for the Cancún Ministerial. The US and the EU met privately and put forward a joint text. Two important features of this joint proposal were provisions for continued subsidies in the form of an amended Blue Box (rather than its elimination), as well as for a 'blended formula' for tariff reductions. This formula would combine different approaches to tariff cuts in different bands, some being linear cuts and some being cut under a more drastic 'Swiss formula', though which tariffs fell into which bands was to be self-selected. The document also called for a reduction, rather than elimination, of *de minimis* spending for the Amber Box. And it called for an extension of the Peace Clause. The document said little about special and differential treatment for developing countries, and noted that sectoral issues (such as cotton) were 'of interest but not agreed' (US–EU Joint Text, 2003).

The countries of the Global South were very disappointed with US–EU joint text, which paid little attention to their concerns. In response, a group of developing countries, led by Brazil, India, and China, formed a new coalition, the G20 Group on Agriculture, which aimed to be a developing country counter-force to the US and the EU in the negotiations. The G20 coalition[1] was an important development, as it brought together developing countries with different sets of interests with respect to agriculture, making it a wider-ranging coalition than, for example, the Cairns Group (which largely represents agricultural exporters, and which was an important counter-force to the US and the EU in the Uruguay negotiations). The G20 included some developing country members of the Cairns group, such as Brazil, Argentina, and Thailand, which have interests in improving market access for their own agricultural exports; but it also included other developing countries, such as India, Mexico, Bolivia, and Ecuador, which are mainly concerned about defending their own domestic markets from import surges (Narlikar and Wilkinson, 2004: 456).

The G20 put forward its own proposal in an attempt to avoid another 'Blair House accord' from emerging between the US and the EU. This proposal squarely reinserted provisions about special and differential treatment, and called for further subsidy cuts for industrialised countries. It also substantially modified the 'blended formula' for tariff reductions to better take into account different tariff structures in the North and the South and included special and differential treatment for the South. It further called for the identification of Special Products to be exempt from tariff cuts and a Special Safeguard Mechanism. In addition, it called for an elimination of the Blue Box, rather than its amendment, as well as spending caps on the Green Box. Such a substantial proposal from a new group representing over two-thirds of the world's population and led by three key emerging economies – Brazil, India, and China – brought it a degree of legitimacy that developing country coalitions in the past had not been able to muster. It had become clear that the G20 was an important negotiating group that the US and the EU would have to contend with (see Narlikar and Tussie, 2004).

Other proposals from developing countries also emerged around this time which echoed and amplified the G20 proposal. A joint text from the Dominican Republic, Kenya, Honduras, Nicaragua, Panama, and Sri Lanka also focused on Special Products and an SSM for developing countries and called for further measures for special and differential treatment for developing countries to be an integral part of the agreement (Dominican Republic et al., 2003). This group came to be known as the 'SP and SSM Alliance' and at times the 'Friends of the Special Safeguard Mechanism' and later the Group of 33 (G33), because it had a membership of 33 (which has since grown to 44[2]). A proposal from the African Union/LDC/ACP grouping (also sometimes referred to as the Group of 90 – G90) also put forward a proposal that called for yet further special and differential treatment for developing countries, particularly the LDCs. It highlighted the need to address the problem of tariff peaks and tariff escalation and also called for protection of existing trade preferences for these countries under other agreements (such as the Cotonou Agreement), or at the very least some sort of compensatory mechanism if these preferences are eroded by the tariff reductions (WTO, 2003b). Their main concern here was that if market access provisions required drastic cuts to tariffs, the special trade preferences they currently receive would be eroded.

The draft Ministerial Declaration attempted to incorporate these various positions. But the draft was highly controversial. It was widely seen that the draft did not represent all members' interests fairly, and in particular was inadequate with respect to developing country concerns (IFATPC, 2004). It was especially upsetting to those who supported the cotton initiative, as it only asked for further study on the impact of cotton subsidies and made no steps toward the demands of the African countries (ICTSD, 2003d: 29).

The Cancún Ministerial ended abruptly, ahead of schedule, owing to deep divisions expressed by members. Formally it was disagreement over the inclusion of the Singapore issues (investment, government procurement, competition policy, and trade facilitation) that brought the meeting down, but it was widely seen that agriculture was just as contentious even though the agriculture texts were not formally discussed. The emergence of the developing country groupings had energised many in the Global South. As Brazil's Foreign Minister, Celso Amorim, stated in his speech at Cancún, the G20's aim was to 'bring it [the world trading system] closer to the needs and aspirations of those who have been at its margins – indeed the vast majority – those who have not had the chance to reap the fruit of their toils. It is high time to change this reality' (cited in Bello and Kwa, 2004). And that reality did begin to change. One of the first signs of that change, and perhaps one of the more important outcomes of the failed Cancún talks with respect to agriculture, was the expiry of the Peace Clause on 31 December 2003.

A good deal of finger-pointing followed the failure at Cancún, with the US claiming that the G20 countries had been spoilers. Following pressure from the US to leave the group or forfeit the opportunity to engage in bilateral trade talks with the US, five of the G20 members – Columbia, Peru, Guatemala, El Salvador, and Costa Rica – dropped out of the group in the autumn of 2003 (ICTSD, 2003d: 37). The G20, however, expressed its willingness to continue the negotiations despite losing some of its members (it has since gained more members), though it wanted to ensure that the US and EU made genuine efforts to make compromises themselves before it came back to the table.

This early phase of the talks, then, was characterised by the frustration of the Global South countries, and their organisation into key groupings to voice developing country concerns. Their main impact in this period, culminating in the Cancún meeting, was to stand firm on their position in the talks as a way of raising awareness of their issues. Solidarity amongst the various groups – the G20, the G33, and the AU/ACP/LDC group – was high at Cancún, but this cohesion was fragile, as became apparent in the next phase of the talks.

A new start with the July 2004 Framework?

The second phase of the agriculture talks saw a consolidation of developing country positions, and a growing acceptance by the WTO members that the dynamics of the negotiations had to change. This prompted a change not just in content but also in process. But while the change showed the importance of the Global South as a force to be reckoned with, it also highlighted the fragility of the Global South as a single coalition. This was because only two countries, India and Brazil – leaders of the G20 – were chosen to represent them in the more exclusive meetings, and this contributed to discontent among other developing countries which were not always assured that their concerns would be given priority in the smaller group meetings.

By early 2004 the US was anxious to re-launch talks (Zoellick, 2004). The US Trade Representative (USTR) at the time, Robert Zoellick, travelled to the key developing countries in an attempt to win their support. In March the first formal talks since Cancún were held, with Tim Groser, WTO Ambassador from New Zealand, as the new chair of the agriculture negotiations. At these meetings a deadline of the end of July 2004 was set for an agreement on a framework to re-launch the negotiations which would then produce concrete modalities. At this time, however, the various groups of countries were still far apart on the three pillars, particularly on market access.

In addition to setting a deadline for the framework, the March 2004 meetings were significant for another reason. To avoid the North–South confrontation that had emerged at Cancún, the process for the agricultural talks shifted from one of presenting texts to the chair from various groups, and expecting the chair to come up with a text that members would have to decide whether to agree with, to having the various members and coalitions meet together in pairs as well as in larger groups (Yen, 2004). From the perspective of the developing countries, this new approach was an improvement in terms of increasing transparency, at least initially. Groser, as chair of the talks, vowed that he would not try to table a compromise draft on his own authority (Raghavan, 2004). It was out of this process that a new negotiating group emerged – which has come to be known as the Five Interested Parties (the FIP). This included the US and the EU, as key players, along with Brazil and India, representing the G20, and Australia, representing the Cairns Group. This new grouping was seen to be vital in reinvigorating the talks.

The framework negotiations were tense throughout the month of July as the deadline loomed. A consensus on the Framework was eventually reached in the early hours of 1 August 2004 (WTO, 2004). The adoption of the framework followed heavy pressure to reach a deal, despite the fact that countries had very little time to consider the document before the deadline because of delays in releasing the document, owing to last-minute wrangling by the FIPs.

The main debates on export competition in these talks were not so much over whether to phase out export subsidies, a goal which was widely agreed. But the EU, which has the highest export subsidies and thus would have to reduce them the most, wanted to ensure that the US also reduced the subsidy element of its export credits and food aid. It also stressed that it wanted to see food aid given only in grant form, and preferably in the form of cash. The US made some concessions on food aid, though it was quick to stress that only the subsidy element of such programmes would be reduced, and it would not commit to removing in-kind food aid (Clapp, 2004). Developing countries expressed their view that all forms of export subsidies should be ended, including the subsidy element of export credit programmes. Such practices are largely seen to be dumping of cheap food by the industrialised countries, which hurts the economies of most developing countries. They added, though, that they wish to see the special conditions and needs of the net food-importing developing countries (NFIDCs) and LDCs taken into account when disciplining export credits and food aid. It was agreed that export subsidies would be eliminated on a 'credible' schedule, with parallel elimination of export credit and export guarantee and insurance programmes that have repayment period of over 180 days. It was also agreed that food aid would be disciplined, with the aim of preventing commercial displacement. Consideration is to be given to reforming food aid to be on a fully grant basis only. New disciplines are also to be placed on the export subsidy elements of state trading enterprises. Developing countries are to be given a longer period to phase out export subsidies, and special attention is to be paid to the impact of the reforms on the LDCs and NFIDCs.

On domestic support, the US and the EU wrangled over specific rules on an amended Blue Box and reductions to *de minimis* spending in the Amber Box, while the G20 wanted to see both the Blue Box and *de minimis* spending in industrialised countries eliminated entirely. The G20 eventually gave in to the amendments to the Blue Box, provided there were disciplines placed on its use. There was immediate criticism of this move, even from within some of the G20 countries, including Brazil (Pruzin, 2004). The framework document calls for an overall reduction of support via a tiered approach, which would lead to steeper cuts for those countries that subsidise the most, with specific caps and cuts in each area. Major subsidisers are to make an immediate cut in domestic support as a 'down-payment'. The Blue Box will be redefined to include 'direct payments that do not require production', though other new criteria will be added to prevent box shifting. Blue Box spending will also be capped at 5 per cent of total agricultural production. *De minimis* spending under the Amber Box is also to be reduced for industrialised countries, and developing countries that allocate their *de minimis* spending to programmes for subsistence farmers are exempted from this provision. There is also to be a review of the Green Box to ensure that it remains non-trade-distorting.

The discussions on market access were perhaps the most contentious in the framework negotiations. There was much disagreement over the type of formula to adopt which would result in meaningful tariff reductions. The US and the EU had endorsed the idea of a 'blended' formula for reducing tariffs. But the G20 would not accept this approach because it did not take into account the different tariff structures in developed and developing countries. In practice, it would allow the US and the EU to maintain high tariffs on certain products, because they already have excessively high tariff peaks and would simply choose to apply a small linear cut rather than the steeper cut to those products. At the same time, because developing countries have a more homogeneous tariff structure, their cuts would be deeper on average than in the industrialised countries. The G20 favoured a tiered approach with steeper cuts for higher tariff levels, with developing countries having lesser cuts. The G33 and the G20 also wanted to ensure that Special Products of developing countries were recognised and exempted from tariff cuts. They also pressed for an SSM to help prevent import surges. The US and the EU would only accept this if they too could identify 'sensitive products' and make use of the SSM. In the end a tiered, progressive approach was adopted, based largely on the G20 proposal, and the developing countries are to have some sort of special treatment, most likely as a percentage cut of the industrialised countries, with the least developed countries exempted from these cuts. A specific formula on how to achieve the tariff cuts, however, was not articulated in the framework. All countries can identify an appropriate number of sensitive products, though the number and how they will be chosen was not specified. Developing countries, however, are to be given more flexibility in terms of identifying Special Products based on livelihood and food security considerations as well as rural development needs, and they will be allowed to use an SSM (for details on all three pillars see WTO, 2004; ICTSD, 2005a).

The July Framework was just that, a framework, and the detailed specifics of the commitments and how they are to be achieved were to be hammered out in subsequent negotiations, with a view to adopting full modalities on each of the three pillars at the Hong Kong Ministerial in December 2005. Though the developing countries did make some major concessions in the July Framework process, such as giving in to the revised Blue Box, they also were able to secure a Special Safeguard Mechanism and Special Products for the developing countries, a tiered formula for tariff reductions, lower cuts and a longer timeframe to cut their own tariffs, and the ability to keep *de minimis* spending for developing countries that was earmarked to support subsistence farmers. Given the pressures at the time, it may have seemed to be the best they could do. But the bargain may come back to haunt the developing countries. Some critics have complained that India and Brazil were co-opted by the US and the EU, being brought into the FIPs only to be neutralised (Bello and Kwa, 2004). The acceptance of the Framework deal on the part of these countries then could serve to drive a wedge between the G20 and other developing country groups.

The rocky road to Hong Kong

Remarkably little in terms of concrete progress on defining the modalities was made until just a few months before the Hong Kong meeting, and even then it was largely seen to be too little, too late for the agriculture modalities to be adopted at the ministerial. The lack of progress was linked in part to two important rulings handed down from WTO dispute panels in 2004 with respect to complaints about agricultural subsidies, both of which have relevance for the agriculture negotiations. Both cases involve a complaint about subsidies brought by Brazil. In one case Brazil launched a dispute against the US with respect to its subsidies to cotton producers, claiming that what the US counted as Green Box subsidies to cotton producers had the effect of depressing global prices, and as such they were trade-distorting. The WTO ruled in favour of Brazil, accepting the argument that the Peace Clause had expired and thus Brazil was free to raise the case. The US appealed but was turned down and is currently attempting to work out a way to comply with the ruling (ICTSD, 2005b). In the other case Brazil, Thailand, and Australia complained that the EU dumped sugar, subsidised beyond what is allowed under WTO rules. Again the WTO ruled in favour of the complainants. The EU appealed and lost (ICTSD, 2005c). Before the WTO was established, following the completion of the Uruguay Round, binding decisions on international trade disputes were not possible, and weaker trading partners had little recourse. With the new WTO dispute resolution process, the decisions have real impacts on the members involved in them. Both the US and the EU are probably nervous about future litigation of this type.

While these rulings were being deliberated and released, the agriculture talks got off to a very slow start. The G20 restated its preferences, but waited for specific proposals from the US and the EU, as it felt that it was up to these players to make the first move (Yerkey, 2005: 1537; G20, 2005). But the US and the EU were still far apart from each other, particularly on market access. In addition a new chair of the agriculture talks, Crawford Falconer, was brought in at this time. As a result, little headway was made in the summer months and the target for the first approximations of the modalities was not met.

In an attempt to restart the talks the EU put forward a proposal in late September 2005 to guide the negotiations at the Hong Kong Ministerial. It called for cuts to domestic support in four tiers, according to a country's level of subsidisation, with cuts ranging from 30 to 65 per cent. On market access, it offered tariff cuts of between 20 and 50 per cent in four bands, with a cap on tariffs of 100 per cent for developed countries. Under this formula developing countries would have two-thirds of the developed country cuts, and a cap on tariffs of 150 per cent. It also asked for 10 per cent of its tariff lines to be designated as sensitive products to be exempted from the tariff cuts. The EU committed to the elimination of export subsidies, but did not specify a date (Pruzin, 2005a, 2005b). The EU could not go further than this offer, as France refused to make any further concessions, and in fact argued that the EU commissioner had already overstepped his bounds in making the offer that he did (Kirwin, 2005).

The US was disappointed with the EU proposal. Its own proposal called for the elimination of export subsidies by 2010, as well as elimination of trade-distorting domestic support by 2023. The proposal also called for cuts to domestic support in three tiers, ranging from 37 to 83 per cent. It proposed a cap on the Blue Box of 2.5 per cent (lower than what was agreed in the July Framework), and a 50 per cent reduction of the *de minimis* cap to 2.5 per cent. In an interesting move it called for a new Peace Clause. These measures were made conditional on substantive progress on market access. On this front the US proposal was aggressive, calling for tariff cuts of between 55 and 90 per cent in four bands, with sensitive products being only 1 per cent of tariff lines (Pruzin, 2005c).

The developing countries were not impressed with either proposal. The G20 was disappointed with the EU, and very sceptical of the US. It claimed that the US proposal with respect to domestic support was merely box-shifting, and that spending under its proposal could actually increase (IATP, 2005). The G20 was also not happy with the suggestion of a new Peace Clause, which it saw as a bid to avoid future litigation of the kind Brazil was able to bring forward at the WTO. With respect to the EU proposal, it thought the designation of 10 per cent of tariff lines as sensitive was far too high, and that tariff cuts were too low. In its own proposals the G20 called for additional disciplines on the Blue Box (beyond spending the cap of 2.5 per cent), such as product-specific caps, and limits to the use of counter-cyclical payments. Its proposal on tariffs calls for cuts of between 45 and 75 per cent across four bands, with a maximum tariff of 100 per cent. Developing countries would face tariff cuts of between 25 and 45 per cent and lower thresholds on the tiers, and a maximum tariff of 150 per cent. It also proposed that developed countries could designate only 1 per cent of their tariff lines as sensitive products, while for developing countries it would be 1.5 per cent. Further, it wants to see more overall cuts in domestic support than offered by either the US or the EU (Pruzin, 2005d).

Other developing country groupings, including the G33 and the ACP group, also put forward statements. The G33 stressed again the importance of the Special Safeguard Mechanism and Special Product (SP) designation for developing countries (G33, 2005). The ACP submission reinforced the SSM and SP issues, as well as the need for more attention to special and differential treatment in all the pillars of the agreement. It further states that the group cannot join a consensus on modalities unless the issue of preference erosion is taken into account. In this respect it was not critical of the EU's lack of commitment to steeper tariff cuts. Taking this position put it in direct conflict with the G20 position on market access. The ACP submission also stressed the importance of incorporating specific modalities with respect to the elimination of cotton subsidies (ACP, 2005). Neither the US nor the EU proposals mentioned the cotton issue. The West African countries warned that without specific measures to address it, they could not join any consensus on an agreement on the agriculture modalities (Lam, 2005).

Although all these proposals and statements were issued within a very short period of time, it was widely seen that the EU's position was the biggest stumbling block that would prevent any meaningful deal from being reached in Hong Kong. With threats in late October that the Hong Kong Ministerial might be cancelled if the EU did not come up with a better offer on agriculture, the EU put forward a revised proposal. But this 'revised' proposal hardly made any movement on market access. On export competition it called for a gradual move to untied and cash-only food aid. And while it called for slightly more of a cut to domestic support than it had earlier, there was a significant catch. The EU tied its new proposal to significant movement on other areas in the trade talks, specifically non-agricultural market access (NAMA) and services (Khor, 2005a). The US, the G20, and most developing countries expressed dismay at the EU offer. The US said it did not go far enough on market access, and developing countries resented having the offer, which did not even go as far as the G20 proposal, tied to the non-agricultural talks. Further, the cuts to tariffs that the EU demanded that developing countries make on NAMA were much deeper than the EU was willing to take on agriculture. It was widely seen that the EU made this move to deflect blame if the agriculture talks fail to reach an agreement (Khor, 2005b).

Expectations for Hong Kong were lowered following the EU's revised proposal on agriculture. Several high-level meetings of ministers, including India, Brazil, the US, and the EU (dubbed by some as the 'new Quad'), were held in November, but little progress was made. The negotiating positions on agriculture did not change much at all going into Hong Kong, nor during the conference. The main objective of the WTO seemed to be to adopt a Ministerial Declaration that contained at least some further agreement on agriculture beyond the July Framework. It became clear that the one area where agreement on agriculture might be possible was on an end-date for agricultural export subsidies. But throughout the week little progress was made even on this issue. The EU indicated that it would prefer 2015, while the US and the G20 pressed for an end-date of 2010. But the EU held out on the later date, with little support from any other members. This stubborn position on the part of the EU angered many developing country delegates.

The lack of real progress on development issues, especially in agriculture, prompted the various developing country groups to hold a joint press conference, with India and Brazil taking key roles. The meeting was dubbed as 'historic' by many, being the first joint meeting of the ministers from the G20, G33, the ACP Group and the African Group (the G90), and the Small Economies (collectively dubbed the G110). The group stressed its solidarity on key issues, including the 2010 end-date for export subsidies, helping to ease the adjustment of those countries affected by preference erosion and support for duty-free and quota-free market access for the LDCs, as well as the need to address the cotton issue (see ICTSD, 2005d). Although these groups had some differences among them in terms of which issues they saw as most important in the agriculture talks, they were able to reach agreement on supporting each other's goals at this stage.

After long negotiating sessions in which the EU refused to move up its offer of a 2015 end-date for export subsidies, the EU finally offered an end-date of 2013 in the last hours of the final day of the conference, which other members finally accepted. The main reason the EU could bring the end-date up to 2013 is that the 2003 reform of the Common Agricultural Policy (CAP) would see the end to most export subsidies by that date anyway. The Ministerial Declaration that was adopted the following day, however, called for efforts to ensure that the bulk of the reductions be completed within the first few years of its implementation. The Declaration also set 30 April 2006 as a deadline for completing the modalities on the other aspects of the agriculture agreement. It reiterated many of the points in the July Framework, such as working toward disciplines on in-kind food aid, though it also added provisions for the creation of a 'safe box' to ensure that there were no constraints on genuine food aid in emergency situations. With respect to domestic support, in order to cut down on the opportunities for box-shifting, the Declaration calls for cuts in this area to be at least as large as the total sum of reductions in all the boxes and *de minimis* levels. But the Declaration did not place any specific constraints on the Blue Box (see WTO, 2005).

Although the WTO and the media portrayed the decision on the end-date to export subsidies as major progress made at Hong Kong, in reality it was a tiny step, with a long list of other modalities on agriculture which have yet to be decided. The details in many areas were left very vague, and the impact will be fully understood only when final details are hammered out and agreed upon. Analysis by some groups of the proposals on the table already shows that they will not make much impact in practice. On domestic support it looks as if the redefinition of the Blue Box will enable the US to immediately shift some $10 billion into it, subsidies that are currently in its Amber Box. Meanwhile the EU is also shifting major portions of its Blue and Amber box payments into the Green Box. According to Oxfam, the EU and the US will be able to increase their trade-distorting domestic support by $35 billion and $7.9 billion respectively by the end of the implementation period, and there is also scope for both to increase their export subsidies before they are eventually eliminated (Oxfam, 2005: 36). Moreover, the sensitive products designation for the industrialised countries could make the tariff reduction formula ineffective.

Conclusion

The developing countries of the Global South have made an important imprint on the Doha agricultural negotiations. After being systematically ignored in the early years of the Doha Round, developing countries took steps to influence both the process and the substance of the negotiations. The emergence of key groupings of developing countries just prior to the Cancún Ministerial, including the G20, the G33, and the AU/ACP/LDC, were products of their frustrations over the talks. These groups were able to voice their concerns through formal proposals and put pressure on the other key players, primarily the US and the EU, to incorporate their views or face the consequences. They had forced a change of dynamic. This new dynamic was very apparent at Cancún, when the talks collapsed, in part because of the lack of incorporation of the South's concerns on agriculture in the official text. The turn taken at Cancún was not transitory, as the developing country groupings, the G20 in particular, have become key participants. Because it has a unique mix of countries with diverse interests and has attempted to reach out to other developing country groupings, the G20 had gained the support and respect of most of the countries of the Global South.

The G20 has worked hard to show solidarity with other developing country groups, but the cohesion of the Global South on the agriculture talks is fragile. While India and Brazil's membership of the FIPs is significant for the Global South in that it demonstrates the importance of incorporating the voice of developing countries, it has also drawn criticism. It was a demand for a more transparent process and incorporation of developing country views that spawned the G20 and other groups in the first place, but bringing India and Brazil into the elite group of negotiating countries only sparked new complaints about lack of transparency and inclusiveness on the part of other developing countries. The G20 is aware of this tension with other developing country groups, and took efforts at Hong Kong to reinvigorate the cohesion of all the developing country groups by focusing on their points of agreement on broad issues. But because there are still so many details of the modalities that have yet to be decided upon (which itself was made problematic by the collapse of the negotiations in July 2006), it is not clear that this cohesion will last. Indeed, it appears highly likely that whatever deal emerges will result in meagre gains and an uneven impact across the Global South. Recent estimates indicate a significant drop in the expected economic gains for developing countries from the Doha Round. Whereas early in the Round some were predicting around $500 billion in gains to the Global South, new estimates indicate that figure to be more like $16 billion. Moreover, the new estimates indicate that about half of the gains for developing countries resulting from the Round will go to just a handful of countries, including most importantly Brazil, India, China, and Mexico (Wise, 2006).

In this context it is ironic that the shifts in the negotiation process to include more developing country representatives may lead to a weakening solidarity in the Global South on agricultural trade issues, as it has become clear that there is no one 'development' deal that will bring significant gains to all developing countries. With the global agricultural trading system already so unevenly stacked against the Global South, particularly the poorest countries, this outcome would be unfortunate.

Notes

I would like to thank the Social Science and Humanities Research Council of Canada for financial support for this research, the Centre for International Governance Innovation for research support, and Jason May for research assistance. I would also like to thank Gerry

Helleiner, Sylvia Ostry, Rorden Wilkinson, and Robert Wolfe for helpful comments on an earlier draft of this chapter.

1 The original members of the G20 were Argentina, Bolivia, Brazil, Chile, China, Columbia, Costa Rica, Cuba, Ecuador, El Salvador, Guatemala, India, Mexico, Pakistan, Paraguay, Peru, the Philippines, South Africa, Thailand, and Venezuela. The G20 was briefly was called the G22 in September 2003 because Kenya and Egypt had joined after the initial text was put forward. As of autumn 2005 the membership of the G20 included Argentina, Bolivia, Brazil, Chile, China, Cuba, Egypt, Guatemala, India, Indonesia, Mexico, Nigeria, Pakistan, Paraguay, the Philippines, South Africa, Thailand, Tanzania, Uruguay, Venezuela, and Zimbabwe.

2 Ahead of the Hong Kong Ministerial (December 2005), the group's members included Antigua and Barbuda, Barbados, Belize, Benin, Botswana, China, Côte d'Ivoire, Congo, Cuba, Dominican Republic, El Salvador, Grenada, Guatemala, Guyana, Haiti, Honduras, India, Indonesia, Jamaica, Kenya, Korea, Madagascar, Mauritius, Mongolia, Mozambique, Nicaragua, Nigeria, Pakistan, Panama, the Philippines, Peru, Saint Kitts, Saint Lucia, Saint Vincent and the Grenadines, Senegal, Sri Lanka, Suriname, Tanzania, Trinidad and Tobago, Turkey, Uganda, Venezuela, Zambia, and Zimbabwe.

References

ACP (2005), 'ACP Proposal on Market Access in Agriculture' (October). www.agtrade policy.org/output/resource/ACP-MarketAccess_.pdf.

Anderson, Kym, and Martin, Will (2005), 'Agricultural Trade Reform and the Doha Agenda', *The World Economy*, 28: 9.

Ataman, Aksoy M. (2005a), 'Global Agricultural Trade Policies', in Aksoy M. Ataman and John C. Beghin (eds), *Global Agricultural Trade and Developing Countries* (Washington, DC: World Bank).

Ataman, Aksoy M. (2005b), 'The Evolution of Agricultural Trade Flows', in Aksoy M. Ataman and John C. Beghin (eds) *Global Agricultural Trade and Developing Countries* (Washington, DC: World Bank).

Balaam, David (2004), 'Agricultural Trade Policy', in B. Hocking and S. McGuire (eds), *Trade Politics* (London: Routledge).

Bello, Walden, and Kwa, Aileen (2004), 'G20 Leaders Succumb to Divide-and-Rule Tactics: The Story behind Washington's Triumph in Geneva', Focus on the Global South. www.focusweb.org.

Braga, Carlos Primo (2004), 'Agricultural Negotiations: Recent Developments in the Doha Round', *Trade Note 19* (Washington, DC: World Bank).

Clapp, Jennifer (2004), 'Agricultural Trade Battles and Food Aid', *Third World Quarterly*, 25: 8.

Danish Research Institute of Food Economics (2003), *Note on the Harbinson Draft on Modalities in the WTO Agriculture Negotiations*. www.ictsd.org/issarea/atsd/Resources/docs/note_harbinson.pdf.

Diakosawas, Dimitris (2001), 'The Uruguay Round Agreement on Agriculture in Practice: How Open Are OECD Markets?' (Paris: OECD). www.oecd.org./dataoecd/54/61/2540717.pdf.

Dominican Republic et al. (2003), 'Negotiations on Agriculture: Joint Text by Dominican Republic, Honduras, Kenya, Nicaragua, Panama and Sri Lanka for the Cancún Ministerial Declaration', 19 August. www.agtradepolicy.org/output/resource/LMG%20Joint%20Text2.pdf.

FAO (2003), *WTO Agreement on Agriculture: The Implementation Experience: Developing Country Case Studies* (Rome: FAO).

G20 (2005), 'New Delhi Declaration' (March). www.agtradepolicy.org/output/resource/G20_delhi_declaration.pdf.

G33 (2005), 'G-33 Press Statement', Geneva, 11 October. www.agtradepolicy.org/output/resource/G33StatementOct05.pdf.

IATP (2005), 'The U.S. WTO Agriculture Proposal of October 10' (Minneapolis: IATP). www.tradeobservatory.org/library.cfm?refid=77195.

ICTSD (2003a), 'Agriculture', *Doha Round Briefing Series: Cancún Update*, 2: 2 (August).

ICTSD (2003b), 'Agriculture: Harbinson Circulates First Modalities Draft', *Bridges Weekly*, 7: 5 (12 February). www.ictsd.org/weekly/03-02-13/story1.htm.

ICTSD (2003c), 'Agriculture: Harbinson's Modalities Draft Receives Mixed Reactions', *Bridges Weekly*, 7: 6 (19 February). www.ictsd.org/weekly/03-02-19/story2.htm.

ICTSD (2003d), *Agriculture Negotiations at the WTO: Post-Cancún Outlook Report* (Geneva: ICTSD).

ICTSD (2005a), *Agriculture Negotiations at the WTO: The July Package and Beyond*, Quarterly Intelligence Report No. 12 (Geneva: ICTSD) (April).

ICTSD (2005b), 'Brazil: WTO Cotton Victory against US Reaffirmed: Pressures on EU Sugar', *Bridges Weekly*, 8: 9 (9 March).

ICTSD (2005c), 'EU Sugar Dispute: WTO Appellate Body Confirms Brazil's Win', *Bridges Weekly*, 15: 9 (4 May).

ICTSD (2005d), 'Revised Ministerial Draft to Be Issued Today', *Bridges Daily Update on the 6th WTO Ministerial Conference*, Issue 5 (17 December).

International Food and Agricultural Trade Policy Council (2004), *Twenty-five Ways to Improve the Derbez Draft on Agriculture* (Washington, DC: IFATPC). www.agritrade.org/Doha/Derbez/Derbez.htm.

Jawara, Fatoumata, and Kwa, Aileen (2003), *Behind the Scenes at the WTO: The Real World of International Trade Negotiations* (London: Zed).

Josling, Tim, and Hathaway, Dale (2004), 'This Far and No Farther? Nudging Agricultural Reform Forward', *International Economics Policy Briefs*, No. PB04-1 (Washington, DC: IIE).

Khor, Martin (2005a), 'EU Agriculture Proposal Shifts Burden to South in NAMA, Services', *SUNS*, No. 5905 (31 October).

Khor, Martin (2005b), 'Reactions to EU Proposal Range from "Disappointing" to "Unacceptable"', *SUNS*, No. 5906 (1 November).

Kirwin, Joe (2005), 'EC Retains Doha Negotiating Mandate as French Plan to Monitor Offers Fails', *International Trade Reporter*, 22: 41 (20 October).

Lam, Esther (2005) 'West African Cotton Producing Nations Warn of Failure in Hong Kong unless Needs Met', *International Trade Reporter*, 22: 41.

Murphy, Sophia, Lilliston, Ben, and Lake, Mary Beth (2005), *WTO Agreement on Agriculture: A Decade of Dumping* (Minneapolis: IATP).

Murphy, Sophia, and Suppan, Steve (2003), 'Introduction to the Development Box' (Winnipeg: IISD).

Narlikar, Amrita, and Tussie, Diana (2004), 'The G20 at the Cancún Ministerial: Developing Countries and Their Evolving Coalitions in the WTO', *The World Economy*, 27: 7.

Narlikar, Amrita, and Wilkinson, Rorden (2004), 'Collapse at the WTO: A Cancún Post-Mortem', *Third World Quarterly*, 25: 3.

OECD (2001), *The Uruguay Round Agreement on Agriculture: An Evaluation of Its*

Implementation in OECD Countries (Paris: OECD). www.oecd.org/dataoecd/50/55/1912374.pdf.

OECD (2003), *Agriculture Policies in OECD Countries: Monitoring and Evaluation* (Paris: OECD), www.oecd.org/dataoecd/25/63/2956135.pdf.

Oxfam (2002), *Rigged Rules and Double Standards: Trade, Globalisation and the Fight against Poverty* (Oxford: Oxfam). www.maketradefair.com/en/index.php?file=2603 2002105549.htm.

Oxfam (2005), *A Round for Free: How Rich Countries Are Getting a Free Ride on Agricultural Subsidies at the WTO*, Oxfam Briefing Paper 76 (Oxford: Oxfam) (June). www.oxfam.org.uk/what_we_do/issues/trade/bp76_modalities_and_dumping.htm.

Pruzin, Daniel (2004), 'Former Brazilian Ag Official Criticizes Brazil/G-20 Concession on Blue Box Support', *International Trade Reporter*, 21: 21 (20 May).

Pruzin, Daniel (2005a), 'EU Signals Movement on Domestic Support, Seeks Significant Cuts from United States', *International Trade Reporter*, 22: 38 (29 September).

Pruzin, Daniel (2005b), 'EU Tweaks WTO Farm Subsidy Proposal, Offers 70% Cut in Amber Box Support', *International Trade Reporter*, 22: 40 (13 October).

Pruzin, Daniel (2005c), 'U.S. Unveils Ag Subsidy Proposal for WTO, Would Cut U.S. Amber Box Support by 60%', *International Trade Reporter*, 22: 40 (13 October).

Pruzin, Daniel (2005d), 'G-20 Offers Tariff, Domestic Support Proposals for WTO Farm Trade Negotiations', *International Trade Reporter*, 22: 40 (13 October).

Raghavan, Chakravarthi (2004), 'Agriculture Negotiators Resume Efforts for July Framework', *SUNS*, No. 5600 (24 June).

Ritchie, Mark (1996), 'Control of Trade by Multinationals: Impact of the Uruguay Round of GATT on Sustainable Food Security', *Development*, No. 4.

US–EU Joint Text (2003). www.agtradepolicy.org/output/resource/EC-US_joint_text_13_Aug_2003.pdf.

Watkins, Kevin (1996), 'Free Trade and Farm Fallacies: From the Uruguay Round to the World Food Summit', *The Ecologist*, 26: 6.

Wise, Timothy (2006), 'The WTO's Development Crumbs', *Foreign Policy in Focus*, 23 January.

WTO (2001), *Doha Declaration*. www.wto.org/english/thewto_e/minist_e?minol_e/mincecl_e.htm.

WTO (2003a), *WTO Negotiations on Agriculture – Poverty Reduction: Sectoral Initiative in Favour of Cotton*, Joint Proposal by Benin, Burkina Faso, Chad and Mali, TN/AG/GEN/4. www.agtradepolicy.org/output/resource/CottonSubmissionWTO.pdf.

WTO (2003b), *Consolidated African Union/ACP/LDC Position on Agriculture*, WT/MIN(03)/W/17 (September).

WTO (2004), *Doha Work Programme: Decision Adopted by the General Council August 1, 2004*, WT/L/579. www.wto.org/english/tratop_e/dda_e/ddadraft_31jul04_e.pdf.

WTO (2005), *Doha Work Programme: Draft Ministerial Declaration, 18 December, 2005*.

Yen, Goh Chien (2004), 'Members Still in a Listening Mode: Report on the Agriculture Week of Negotiations in WTO, 22–26 March 2004' (Penang: Third World Network) (4 April). www.twnside.org.sg/title2/twninfo111.htm.

Yerkey, Gary (2005), 'Brazilian Minister Says WTO Waiting for U.S., EU to Move First in Trade Talks', *International Trade Reporter*, 22: 38 (29 September).

Zoellick, Robert (2004), 'A Strategic Opportunity for Trade', speech given at the French Institute of International Relations, 13 May.

4 Intellectual property and the Doha Development Agenda

Susan K. Sell

Ever since the Uruguay Round ended, a number of World Trade Organisation (WTO) members have pressed for clarifications of the Agreement on Trade-Related Aspects of Intellectual Property Rights (TRIPs). Developing country members have engaged in sharply pitched battles with developed country governments over broken promises and unfinished business.

TRIPs requires all WTO members to increase protection and enforcement of intellectual property rights. When negotiating parties agreed to TRIPs it was part of a quid pro quo in which developing countries agreed to high-standard intellectual property protections in exchange for access to developed countries' agricultural markets and the liberalisation of developed countries' agricultural sectors. In the wake of the Uruguay Round, developed countries have failed to make good on their promises to cut domestic supports for agriculture, while they aggressively pursued WTO action against developing countries for failure to implement intellectual property policies. They also have pursued a vigorous campaign of bilateral and regional investment and trade agreements that incorporate 'TRIPs-plus'[1] standards of intellectual property protection. However, Brazil successfully challenged the US over its cotton subsidies; the WTO ruled in Brazil's favour in May 2004 (ICTSD 2004: 7). Brazil is considering placing sanctions on US-held intellectual property (cross-retaliation) if the US does not meet its deadline to cut cotton subsidies.

The unfinished business in intellectual property includes the ability of developing countries to export generic drugs made under compulsory licence; the relationship of TRIPs to the Convention on Biological Diversity (CBD); provisions to protect plants and genetic material located in developing countries from 'biopiracy' (Shiva, 1997); benefit-sharing arrangements; the inapplicability of non-violation and situation complaints to TRIPs; implementation; and the expansion of geographical indications. All but the last item are central to the Doha Development Agenda (DDA), although the EU is pushing hard to expand geographical indications. The acrimonious ending to the Cancún Ministerial in August 2003 has put the negotiating spotlight on agriculture, but intellectual property issues received extra attention in October 2005 in the face of a global threat of an avian flu pandemic.

The first section of the chapter provides some background on the key events shaping the intellectual property agenda. In the second section I discuss the intellectual property issues in this Round of trade talks. The third addresses forum shifting and the strategic use of international organisations that threatens the development agenda. The resurgence of the World Intellectual Property Organisation (WIPO) and the proliferation of regional and bilateral trade and investment agreements are particularly noteworthy in this regard. Finally, the chapter offers some conclusions about the challenges ahead for the development agenda in intellectual property.

The road to Hong Kong

Public health issues and fights: AIDS, anthrax, and avian flu

Public health issues have animated the sharpest controversies over the WTO's intellectual property rules. They also have provided interesting opportunities to promote the development agenda. WTO negotiations over intellectual property have been shaped directly by the HIV/AIDS pandemic, the appearance of anthrax in the US just after the terrorist attacks of 11 September 2001, and the spectre of an impending global avian flu pandemic in late 2005. The HIV/AIDS pandemic sparked demands for clarification of TRIPs flexibilities for the protection of public health. The American anthrax episode immediately before the WTO Ministerial meeting in Doha, Qatar, facilitated agreement on a Doha Declaration on the TRIPs Agreement and Public Health (WTO, November 2001). Finally, the very real threat of a global avian flu pandemic reinvigorated the debate over patents and public health on the eve of the WTO's Hong Kong Ministerial meeting.

In the late 1990s Africa and Asia grappled with a still-ongoing and quite horrific HIV/AIDS pandemic. Afflicted countries desperately needed to obtain life-saving antiretroviral drugs to reduce the shocking death rate. Brazil had pioneered a public health programme that provided HIV/AIDS drugs to all afflicted persons. Brazil negotiated steep price discounts for non-generic pharmaceuticals by threatening to issue compulsory licences (seising the patents to allow someone else to produce the product or to use the patented process without the patent owner's consent). In its post-TRIPs 1996 industrial property law Brazil had strengthened its intellectual property protections as required by TRIPs, but retained a provision that 'local working' of the patent is required for the patent holder to enjoy patent rights in Brazil. 'Brazil's law permits it to issue compulsory licenses for goods that are not manufactured locally within three years of receiving patent protection; mere importation does not "count"' (Sell, 2003: 137). South Africa passed a Medicines Act in 1997 that permitted the health minister to revoke patents on medicines and to allow for broad-based compulsory licensing to manufacture generic versions of HIV/AIDS drugs. Article 15(c) permitted parallel importing so that South Africa could take advantage of discriminatory pricing policies and import the cheapest available patented medicines. However, the United States Trade Representative (USTR), at the behest of its non-generic pharmaceutical firms, pursued aggressive action against both South Africa and Brazil. The USTR pressured South Africa to revoke the offending provisions of its law, threatening South Africa with trade sanctions and suspending its Generalised System of Preferences (GSP) benefits in

1998 (Bond, 1999: 771). Only after HIV/AIDS activists disrupted then US Vice President Albert Gore's presidential campaign appearances in September 1999 did the government remove South Africa from the USTR watch list (Gellman, 2000; Vick, 1999: A18). In 2000 the US initiated a WTO case against Brazil, maintaining that Brazil's working requirement violated Article 27(1) of TRIPs. Non-generic pharmaceutical companies insisted that under Article 27(1) importation satisfied the 'working' requirement and thus Brazil's provision violated TRIPs.

The South African and Brazilian cases animated a concerted effort, led by the African group, Brazil, and India and supported by a number of NGOs (for example, Médecins sans Frontières, Consumer Project on Technology, ACT-UP, Third World Network), to obtain clarifications of what flexibilities were permissible under TRIPs for addressing public health emergencies. In November 1999, on the eve of the WTO's Seattle Ministerial meeting, a group of NGO activists issued the Amsterdam Statement addressed to WTO members (MSF, HAI, CPT, 1996). This statement called for the WTO to create a working group on access to medicines, to endorse compulsory licensing of patents under Article 31, and to allow exceptions to patent rights under Article 30 for production of medicines for export markets when the medicine is imported into a country with a compulsory licence. This latter exception would help countries without manufacturing capacity to obtain generic drugs. At the Seattle WTO Ministerial meeting President William Clinton announced a major shift in US policy by supporting African access to HIV/AIDS drugs. In May 2000 Clinton issued an Executive Order that stated that 'the United States shall not seek, through negotiation or otherwise, the revocation or revision of any intellectual property law or policy of a beneficiary sub-Saharan African country, as determined by the president, that regulates HIV/AIDS pharmaceuticals or medical technologies' (Executive Order No. 13,155, 65 Federal Register 30,251: 2000). Additionally, the order endorsed no TRIPs-plus for HIV/AIDS in Africa.

The non-generic pharmaceutical industry faced mounting public pressure to reduce prices and make life-saving HIV/AIDS drugs available to afflicted developing countries. In March 2001 the non-generic pharmaceutical industry withdrew its private lawsuit against South Africa, and in June of that year the USTR officially withdrew its WTO case against Brazil. Meanwhile the African group exercised leadership by requesting a special TRIPs Council session on access to medicines. Chaired by Ambassador Boniface Chidyausiku of Zimbabwe, the June 2001 TRIPs Council session focused on access to medicines. Developing countries sought official confirmation that measures to protect public health would not make them subject to dispute settlement procedures in the WTO. The Brazilian delegation highlighted Brazil's successful approach to providing HIV/AIDS medicines. Discussions continued throughout the summer in the run-up to the November 2001 Doha WTO Ministerial meeting (Odell and Sell, 2006).

On 11 September 2001 terrorists attacked the United States using gas-filled passenger planes as bombs, hitting the World Trade Center's Twin Towers, the Pentagon, and a field in Pennsylvania. The next month some media and postal workers in the US died from exposure to anthrax spores sent through the mail. In the shaken and uncertain climate of late 2001 American policymakers feared that the anthrax incidents heralded the launch of a major bio-terror attack. Both the Canadians and the Americans threatened to issue compulsory licences to seize Bayer's patents on Cipro to ensure adequate stockpiles of the most effective drug for treating anthrax. Ultimately neither Canada nor the US followed through on the threat, but, just as Brazil had done in the past, they both negotiated deep price discounts with Bayer.

On the eve of the November 2001 Doha meeting everyone was well aware of the irony that the US had done precisely that for which it had criticised the Brazilians and harassed the South Africans. Led by the African group and Brazil, a coalition of developing countries stuck together and insisted that without clarification of the public health flexibilities in TRIPs and reassurances of immunity from prosecution there would be nothing to discuss at Doha. Their threat to walk away from the negotiations was credible, and since the developed countries were so eager to launch a new, more liberalising Round, the parties quickly reached agreement on the Doha Declaration on TRIPs and Public Health (Odell and Sell, 2006). While various stakeholders had different assessments of the significance of this declaration, developing countries saw it as a significant victory for their position that TRIPs must not stand in the way of providing medicines in public health emergencies (Sell, 2003: 161–162). Paragraph 6 of the Declaration left unresolved the ability of countries with little or no manufacturing capacity to make effective use of TRIPs compulsory licensing provisions (Abbott, 2002). The African group and its supporters sought clarification that nothing in TRIPs should prevent countries from exporting generic drugs to poor countries. The Declaration instructed the TRIPs Council to resolve the issue by the end of 2002.

The Paragraph 6 deadline came and went without resolution. Just before the September 2003 Cancún WTO Ministerial meeting, negotiators struck a deal in the TRIPs Council to implement the Doha Declaration's Paragraph 6. The deal authorised any member state lacking sufficient pharmaceutical manufacturing capacity to import necessary medicines from any other member state. This waiver of TRIPs Article 31(f) (restricting compulsory licensing only to supply one's domestic market) included procedural safeguards to prevent diversion of cheap medicines to rich countries' markets (WTO Council on TRIPs 2003; Matthews, 2004a). Therefore, according to the 30 August 2003 deal, generic copies of drugs made under compulsory licence can be exported to countries lacking production capacity (WTO, 2003). The 30 August 2003 decision also included a Chairman's Statement, emphasising the 'Members' "shared understanding" that the Decision will be interpreted and implemented on a "good faith" basis in order to deal with public health problems and not for industrial or commercial policy objectives' and their agreement to take steps to prevent drug diversion to third markets (Matthews, 2004b: 11). According to James Love, Director of the Consumer Project on Technology, the Chairman's Statement was approved by Pfizer CEO Hank McKinnell and the office of Karl Rove, President Bush's Deputy Chief of Staff in charge of policy (Love, 2005). The Decision also includes a list of 23 countries that agreed to opt out of the system as importers, 11 awaiting accession to the

EU pledging to use the waiver only in cases of 'extreme emergency' until such time as they gain membership and then to opt out completely, and finally a group of 13 additional countries that pledged to use the waiver only in cases of extreme emergency (WTO, WT/GC/M/82, 13 November 2003: 7, para. 29). Many of these countries are concerned about whether they can 'opt back in' in the event of an avian flu pandemic (IP-Watch, 2005: 25 October). In the US, Senator Charles Schumer called for the compulsory licensing of Roche's Tamiflu to ensure adequate supplies (Ip-health, 2005: 18 October, Message 15).

TRIPs and the CBD, biopiracy, and traditional knowledge

As early as 1993, when the TRIPs negotiations were still under way, hundreds of thousands of Indian farmers demonstrated against TRIPs proposals, claiming that their right to save, reproduce, and modify seeds could be jeopardised by the required implementing legislation (Sutherland, 1998: 293). Vandana Shiva, an Indian activist, helped to mobilise a campaign against 'biopiracy' (Shiva, 1997). Biopiracy is seen as a new form of Western imperialism in which global seed and pharmaceutical corporations plunder the biodiversity and traditional knowledge of the developing world. Biopiracy is the unauthorised and uncompensated expropriation of genetic resources and traditional knowledge. According to this argument, corporations alter these 'discoveries' with science, patent them, then resell the derived products or processes at exorbitant rates to the very people from whom they stole them in the first place.[2]

Since the 1980 US Supreme Court decision in *Diamond v. Chakrabaty* that genetically modified organisms could be patented, the scope of patentable materials has grown considerably to include substances that previously had been regarded as natural and outside of the realm of intellectual property (May and Sell, 2006: 190). Article 27.3(b) of TRIPs allows plants and animals, as well as 'essential biological processes', to be excluded from patentability but does require some form of protection for plant varieties. Article 27.3(b) requires that members provide protection for plant varieties either by patents or an effective *sui generis* system. However, there is little consensus on what a *sui generis* system should include. The US has pressed for the Convention for the Protection of New Varieties of Plants (UPOV) 1991 as a model for implementing 27.3(b); this convention is quite generous to the corporate plant breeder and restricts farmers' traditional practices of seed saving and curtails farmers' rights. By contrast, a number of developing countries have favoured a *sui generis* approach that protects them from biopiracy and explicitly honours farmers' rights. Laurence Helfer has analysed developing countries' options under 27.3(b) to assess how much policymaking discretion follows from each option (Helfer, 2002). States that adopt TRIPs *and* ratify or accede to UPOV91 have the least policy flexibility (Helfer, 2002: 37). States wishing to retain maximum flexibility and discretion to serve the needs of smallholder agriculture would be well advised to adopt TRIPs *only*. As John Barton suggests, poor nations are best off adopting minimum compliance with TRIPs (Barton, 2003: 12).

A number of high-profile controversies sparked developing countries' interest in resolving the relationship between TRIPs Article 27.3(b) and the UN Convention on Biological Diversity (CBD). For example, in the 1990s foreigners obtained patents on Indian turmeric as a healing agent and neem tree seed extracts for pesticides. Both uses were traditional practices in India. Assigning patents to researchers isolating these qualities in a laboratory demonstrated that Western patent systems had no protections for innovations that are passed down from generation to generation. They recognise only 'individual innovations which were "scientifically" achieved, the typically communal "folk" knowledge of developing countries is excluded' (Marden, 1999: 292).

The CBD differs from TRIPs in two important ways. It highlights the principle of national sovereignty over the use and exploitation of natural resources, and incorporates the idea of communal knowledge. The concept of communal knowledge is at odds with the Western conception of individual ownership embodied in TRIPs. Article 8j concerns the need to respect and preserve communal knowledge resources to ensure the sanctity of traditional practices and also 'to promote their wider application with the approval and involvement of the holders of such knowledge'.

India was the first to call for the primacy of the CBD over TRIPs Article 27.3(b) and argued that TRIPs should be amended to comply with the CBD (Tejera, 1999: 981). Participants negotiating TRIPs agreed to revisit Article 27.3(b) four years after the date of entry into force (1999). Since 1998 the TRIPs Council has engaged in discussions to address the relationship between the CBD and TRIPs Article 27.3(b). Jonathan Hepburn has argued that the Article 27.3(b) review process in the TRIPs Council has been important in building developing country negotiators' confidence and issue-specific knowledge (2002). At first, discussions focused on the mandate of the review process, but broadened to include acknowledgement of diverse *sui generis* approaches to plant variety protection, concerns about indigenous peoples, and the relationship between TRIPs and the CBD (Hepburn, 2002). India, Brazil, and the African group submitted papers to the TRIPs Council, and delegations also began to acknowledge the relevance of the CBD and the international treaty of the Food and Agriculture Organisation (FAO) (Hepburn, 2002). Developing countries succeeded in incorporating these issues into the formal negotiating mandate of the Doha Ministerial Declaration.

The intellectual property issues

The most pressing intellectual property issues in the Doha Development Agenda address public health, biopiracy, indigenous people, and traditional knowledge. The first issue revolves around the legal status of the 30 August 2003 waiver of 31(f) of TRIPs that allows countries to import generic drugs produced under compulsory licence. The next three issues are addressed in the discussions of the relationship between TRIPs and the CBD, the review of TRIPs Article 27.3(b), and the introduction of disclosure of origin requirements and benefit sharing. I will discuss each of these in turn.

By the end of the Doha negotiations, member states needed to decide upon the status of the Paragraph 6 agreement on compulsory licensing and access to medicines. The 30 August 2003 Decision was a temporary measure pending final agreement. The questions that dominated the negotiations over Paragraph 6 on the eve of the Hong Kong Ministerial were: (1) whether the 30 August 2003 decision should be included in Article 31 of TRIPs; and (2) what the relationship is between the Statement of the Chairman of the General Counsel and the 30 August 2003 decision (that is, what is its legal status?).

The African group of countries proposed that the 30 August 2003 Decision be incorporated into Article 31 as an amendment to TRIPs, but recommended that both the Chairman's Statement and the annexe of the Decision that details 'best practices' regarding packaging and manufacturing drugs to prevent diversion of low-cost medicines to high-income markets should be excluded. The African Group argued that the Chairman's Statement should not be part of the amendment as it was not part of the 30 August 2003 Decision, and opposed any elevation of the statement's legal status (WTO, 2005b, IP/C/W/440). The African group suggested that certain measures recommended in the annexe on drug diversion would be costly (Matthews, 2004b: 7). The African group's proposal received 'a fairly hostile response from developed countries' (South Centre and CIEL, 2004: 5). In 2004 Mozambique, Zimbabwe, and Zambia issued compulsory licences for selected antiretroviral drugs, which helps to underscore the African group's desire for an enduring solution (South Centre and CIEL, 2004: 11). Kenya had tried to issue compulsory licences for HIV/AIDS drugs under the waiver, but two European pharmaceutical companies holding the patents stopped them and offered voluntary licences instead (IP-Watch, 2005: 6 December). The EU and US have insisted that the Chairman's Statement and the annexe should be retained in any amendment. This reflects their concerns about drug diversion.

Informal discussions between the African Group, the US, and the European Community (with the TRIPs Council Chair, Ambassador Choi Hyuck of Korea, present) angered a number of developing countries. Argentina, Brazil, and India protested against their exclusion from and the lack of transparency in these deliberations (IP-health, 2005: 28 October). Ultimately the African Group and the US worked out a compromise. In the end delegates voted to adopt the waiver as an amendment to TRIPs that includes Article 31*bis*, the waiver, one annexe on terms and conditions, and an appendix on the assessment of pharmaceutical manufacturing capabilities (IP-Watch, 2005: 6 December). In a rather elaborate compromise arrangement ('choreography') the Chairman's Statement was read aloud and adopted, and the developing countries that in 2003 had agreed to opt out of the waiver except in cases of national emergency had to restate their commitment. During the process no one was allowed to embellish his or her remarks in any way.

Even though the final agreement did not mirror the original African Group proposal, a number of African delegations were pleased with the outcome. One delegate expressed relief that the uncertainty generated by the waiver was resolved as it is now a permanent part of TRIPs (IP-Watch, 2005: 6 December). Another developing country delegate said that 'political pressure' had led the Africans to soften their stance and that 'the deal was a matter of "not losing what you already have"' (IP-Watch, 2005: 6 December). While the US did not succeed in having the Chairman's Statement incorporated as a footnote to the text (which would have elevated its legal status), USTR Rob Portman hailed the agreement as a 'landmark achievement' and took credit for making it happen (IP-Watch, 2005: 6 December). Non-generic pharmaceutical companies 'welcomed the agreement to maintain "anti-diversion measures and other aspects of the "chairman's statement"' (IP-Watch, 2005: 7 December).

As a number of public health activists and NGOs immediately stressed, the amendment is disappointing for those advocating easy access to generic medicines. It comes with numerous conditions that make it difficult to use; this is one reason why not one country has availed itself of the August 2003 waiver (Doctors Without Borders, 2005: 10 December). The CPTech Director, James Love, stated that 'big pharmaceutical companies and the EU' bullied developing country negotiators into accepting the deal; he referred to this 'awful decision' as being 'anti-consumer, anti-competition and anti-free trade' (CPTech, 2005: 6 December). Many NGOs suspected that developing countries were pressured into the deal so that WTO members would have something to show after four years of talks; they further presumed that the US and EU were desperate for a deal to 'deflect attention from their lack of movement in agriculture and their anti-development proposals in NAMA and Services' (CPTech, 2005: 3 December).

Additionally, members agreed to grant least developed countries an extension until July 2013 before they are required to comply with TRIPs. Zambia had proposed an extension until 2020 against the US, Japanese, and Swiss preference for reviewing extensions on a case-by-case basis. The 2013 deadline represents a compromise between these two approaches. In the meantime, least developed countries may not roll back any existing intellectual property laws unless they are already more stringent than TRIPs. Significantly, this decision came about one week before the 6 December 2005 TRIPs amendment agreement. According to one proponent of high standards of IP protection, this was a strategic move designed to provide *some* results to make the WTO process seem valuable, especially given the fact that no one expected movement on agriculture. Furthermore, he maintains that this decision took 'a lot of hot air out of the activists [*sic*] balloon' and lessened 'the risk of a disastrous weakening of TRIPs in Hong Kong' (IP Blog, 2005: 29 November).

The Doha Ministerial Declaration instructed the TRIPs Council to examine the relationship between TRIPs and the CBD. This relationship has yet to be resolved. Developing countries have been keen to amend TRIPs so that it will support the objectives of the CBD (South Centre and CIEL, 2005a: 1). Seventeen countries have formed the Group of Like-Minded Megadiverse Countries, representing between 60 and 70 per cent of the biodiversity of the planet (South Centre and CIEL, 2005a: 2).[3] So-called megadiverse countries want to halt unauthorised and uncompensated commercialisation of their biological and traditional know-ledge resources. They have pressed for TRIPs amendments that would require member states to disclose the source and country of origin of biological resources and traditional knowledge and to provide evidence of prior informed consent and benefit sharing. Their proposals came out of the work of the CBD's Conference of the Parties committee of experts that led to the adoption of the Bonn Guidelines in 2002. These guidelines stipulated that applicants for intellectual property rights should disclose the origin of any genetic resources or related knowledge relevant to the subject matter. Such disclosures are meant to facilitate monitoring whether applicants have received informed prior consent of the country of origin and complied with the country's conditions of access (Helfer, 2004: 29). While states could adopt these policies in national patent systems, developing countries have argued that without an *international* agreement, national-level laws would do little to stop biopiracy (South Centre and CIEL, 2005a: 8). By contrast the US prefers contract law to more global regulation. Alan Oxley, chairman of the Australian Asia-Pacific Economic Co-operation Study Centre, commented on his Centre's PhRMA-funded study championing a free market approach and argued that India and Brazil sought a 'new regime of control' and 'unnecessary regulation' (IP-Watch, 2005: 13 December). Susan Finston, former PhRMA lobbyist and executive director of the American BioIndustry Alliance, expressed objections to Peru's efforts to regulate biopiracy and said that it had set up a 'bio-piracy Gestapo' (IP-Watch, 2005: 15 December).

While implementing a disclosure requirement would not stop all misappropriations of biological and traditional knowledge resources, it could help to improve the patent examination process regarding prior art. A September 2004 submission from Brazil, India, Pakistan, Peru, Thailand, and Venezuela highlighted that, beyond prior art, disclosure requirements would also 'be useful in cases relating to challenges to patent grants or disputes on inventorship or entitlement to a claimed invention as well as infringement cases' (WTO, 2004: para. 5). This would help reduce the prevalence of patents that lack novelty or an inventive step. While this is not a panacea, a number of costly and time-consuming cases of litigation could have been avoided with the disclosure requirements.[4]

Developing countries would prefer a binding requirement that contains non-compliance penalties through the WTO Dispute Settlement Mechanism, whereas the European Union has been sympathetic as long as 'non-compliance with the requirement does not affect the validity or enforceability of the granted patent' (Correa, 2005: 6). This would seem to undercut the purpose of curtailing biopiracy. As Graham Dutfield argues,

> to be truly effective, the legal means should be made available to allow governments to challenge the patent's legality in the jurisdiction in which it was granted if they consider a foreign patent they were not notified about may have been for an invention resulting from resources or traditional knowledge acquired under their ABS [access and benefit sharing] regulations.
>
> (Dutfield, 2005: 4)

Therefore, Dutfield recommends a higher standard than either voluntary or mandatory disclosure. A third way would be to require 'proof of legal acquisition' to connect the patent system more strongly to the CBD's access and benefit-sharing provisions, especially for those countries directly providing the resources (Dutfield, 2005: 2).

Dutfield argues that both mandatory disclosure and legal proof of acquisition might work very well in the context of pharmaceuticals. The non-generic pharmaceutical industry opposes mandatory disclosure and has favoured contractual arrangements for bio-prospecting such as the deal between Costa Rica's INBIO and Merck (Reid et al., 1993).

At the Hong Kong Ministerial, Brazil, India, and Peru negotiated aggressively to include provisions in the final ministerial text exhorting the Director-General to intensify consultations on outstanding implementation issues – specifically on the TRIPs–CBD relationship. India argued that without addressing the disclosure of origin of material in patent applications there would be no development package (IP-Watch, 2005: 15 December). The US, and global pharmaceutical and biotechnology companies, strongly resisted agreeing to negotiate the disclosure issue (IP-Watch, 2005: 17 December).

Peru's efforts to take a strong position on disclosure seemed to be ironic in light of the fact that it had just signed a bilateral deal with the US that incorporated the US's preferred contractual approach to the issue. The US–Peru bilateral free trade agreement is TRIPs-plus and endorses the utilisation of contracts for protecting biodiversity. The US had been negotiating a broader Andean FTA but Colombia and Ecuador broke off negotiations in November 2005 over TRIPs-plus provisions. The US–Peru FTA disclosure requirements appear in a 'side letter' to the agreement stating that access to genetic resources and benefit sharing 'can be adequately addressed through contracts' (IP-Watch, 2005: 17 December). Some sources at the WTO meeting argued that Peru had sold out and feared that the contract provisions meant that 'companies could negotiate contracts with indigenous communities without any transparency and in this case without any requirements to disclose . . . from whom and where they obtained their resources' (IP Watch, 2005: 17 December). Furthermore, the unequal bargaining power of the parties does not bode well for equitable deals. While Peru had been prominent in pushing for TRIPs–CBD linkage, critics blamed the US for its strategy of dividing coalitions through bilateral deals.

The Hong Kong text called for the WTO General Council to review progress and 'take any appropriate action' by 31 July 2006 on implementation issues. The final text altered the earlier language urging the Director-General to 'continue with' his consultative process on implementation issues, such as CBD and geographical indications; the new text urges him to 'intensify' his consultative process. The Indian Minister of Commerce and Industry, Kamal Nath, was pleased with the new language and with the deadline for review (IP-Watch, 2005: 18 December), though the collapse of the negotiations at the same time as the General Council review called the process into question.

The Europeans and the Swiss may attempt to link support for disclosure of origin to progress on geographical indications (South Centre and CIEL, 2004: 10). The Europeans have been increasingly adamant about progress on geographical indications (IP-Watch, 2005: 28 October). The EU is seeking the establishment of a multilateral registration and notification system of geographical indications for wines and spirits (for example, Champagne, Bordeaux) and the extension of protection of geographical indications for products other than wines and spirits (South Centre and CIEL, 2004: 13). Some observers have suggested that supporters of the TRIPs–CBD linkage and geographical indications may join forces to achieve their desired outcomes. The US opposes both positions.

Powerful US-based industry lobbyists are mobilising to prevent any amendment to TRIPs that would require disclosure of origin and benefit-sharing arrangements. The newly formed American BioIndustry Alliance, representing Merck, Pfizer, Bristol-Myers-Squibb, Eli Lily, General Electric, and Procter & Gamble, is launching a campaign to persuade developing countries that such an amendment will reduce foreign investment and is embarking upon an alliance-building initiative to get Indian biotech industries to join forces with them to oppose such an amendment (IP-Watch, 2006: 6 January).

The threat of forum-shifting

One of the most important assets for developing country negotiators in the WTO will be peripheral vision. The biggest threat to any gains that developing countries may bargain for, or even achieve, in this Round of trade negotiations lies outside of the WTO. At the end of the Uruguay Round, negotiators did not share consensual assessments of TRIPs. Negotiators from the US and the European Union tended to see TRIPs as a floor – a minimum baseline for intellectual property protection. By contrast, developing country negotiators saw it more as a ceiling – a maximum standard of protection beyond which they were unwilling and/or unable to go.

Given this perspective, it should come as no surprise that the US and the EU have been aggressively pursuing efforts to ratchet up TRIPs standards, to eliminate TRIPs flexibilities, and to close TRIPs loopholes. They have been busy negotiating bilateral and regional trade agreements that incorporate TRIPs-plus standards of protection (Drahos, 2001; Abbott, 2004). Playing a multi-level, multi-forum governance game, countries like the US have been able to extract a high price from economically more vulnerable parties eager to gain access to large, affluent markets. TRIPs-plus standards dramatically reduce policymaking autonomy for developing countries to incorporate intellectual property into broader public policy goals. In recent years developing countries have begun to challenge this discrepancy between the multilateral rules and the TRIPs-plus standards proposed in regional and bilateral agreements. As mentioned earlier, Ecuador and Colombia broke off talks with the US over TRIPs-plus issues and have refused to agree to TRIPs-plus standards. Russia currently is engaged in negotiations for its accession to the WTO as well as in bilateral discussions with the United States about TRIPs-plus standards. Russia's lead negotiator on WTO accession, Maxim Medvedkov, has endorsed TRIPs but is balking at the TRIPs-plus demands; he stated that 'I think we have to draw a line between WTO and bilateral issues' (IP-Watch, 2005: 24 October). This reflects Russia's view of TRIPs as a ceiling.

The US and the EU also have been engaging in forum-shifting by taking some of their unmet concerns to the World Intellectual Property Organisation (WIPO) (Musungu, 2005). This latter move is particularly intriguing given their audacious shifting of many intellectual property issues *out of* the WIPO and *into* the GATT in 1986 at the outset of the Uruguay Round (Sell, 1998; Braithwaite and Drahos, 2000). At the time, the US expressed frustration that the WIPO was too focused on North–South issues and sought an alternative forum in which the US had more leverage. Industry leaders welcomed the intellectual property–trade linkage as being more effective in realising their interest in higher standards of intellectual property protection. Now that intellectual property issues have received so much unwelcome attention in the WTO, the US and EU are turning their attention to the WIPO.

The resurgence of the WIPO troubles many supporters of a development agenda. Sisule Musungu notes that WIPO reflects 'a build up of significant bias against latecomers to the intellectual property field' (Musungu, 2005: 4). As administrator of the Patent Cooperation Treaty, the WIPO derives about 80 per cent of its operating budget from PCT users. These users overwhelmingly are global firms that promote a high-protection approach to intellectual property. The WIPO is now regarded as being much more sympathetic to industry interests than it had been in the past. Ongoing WIPO negotiations on a Substantive Patent Law Treaty have reflected a TRIPs-plus approach to harmonisation (May and Sell, 2006: 213). Furthermore, developing country WIPO delegates come from intellectual property offices that are socialised to favour protection (Drahos, 2002: 785); the professional camaraderie among intellectual property lawyers from both North and South means that discussions are far less adversarial than is the case in the WTO.[5]

In 2004 a group of developing countries (Group of Friends for Development) proposed a development agenda for the WIPO.[6] The US objected, arguing that the WIPO is not a development agency but an organisation specialising in intellectual property (Musungu, 2005: 4; WIPO document IIM/1/2). The General Assembly created an intergovernmental process to discuss the proposal, which has met three times (in April, June, and July 2005). At the end of the July meeting the group was unable to reach a consensus on continuing the process owing to the opposition of the US and Japan (Musungu, 2005: 4). In closed informal meetings, delegations argued over whether discussions should continue in the high-level intergovernmental meetings that report directly to the General Assembly, or be consigned to a minor technical body, the Permanent Committee on Co-operation for Development Related to Intellectual Property (PCIPD) (ICTSD, 2005: 22). 'For the first time, the Friends, led by Brazil, expressly linked the development agenda to the Substantive Patent Law Treaty under elaboration at WIPO, refusing to discuss the latter in the absence of progress on the former' (ICTSD, 2005: 22). The PCIPD has been dissolved in the meantime, and negotiators compromised by creating a 'provisional committee' to conduct two one-week sessions on the development agenda. The committee's status remains unclear.

Developing countries have pressed for disclosure of origin and benefit-sharing systems within the WIPO. The WIPO even established an Intergovernmental Committee on Intellectual Property and Genetic Resources, Traditional Knowledge and Folklore; its mandate has been extended until 2007 (South Centre and CIEL, 2005a: 16). The WIPO is institutionally constrained from pressing very far on issues that its main constituency (users of the PCT) opposes. It has worked hard to get back into the good graces of the OECD since 1986, and it seems unlikely that the WIPO would jeopardise its position by directly challenging the high protectionist agenda (May and Sell, 2006: 214). Indeed, playing on this very sensitivity, the US delegate warned the WIPO not to pursue a substantive development agenda; he said: 'we support WIPO. We would not want to change WIPO in a direction that would diminish that support' (IP-Watch, 2005: 11 April). A number of industry representatives, including former US Patent and Trademark Office official Bruce Lehman and civil society groups sympathetic to the US position, issued a letter urging the WIPO not to be diverted from its mission by a 'so-called development agenda' (IP-Watch, 2005: 14 April). At the November 2004 WIPO General Assembly, industry lobbyists showed up to express their opposition to a development agenda. As reported in *IP-Watch*, 'one industry source said they were there for an "anti-development agenda"' (IP-Watch, 2005: 4 November).

Concluding thoughts

Developing countries face a tough challenge in achieving their intellectual property goals. Many critics argued that the meagre results in intellectual property at the Hong Kong Ministerial were overblown to make it appear as if something important had been achieved as a 'smoke screen' for the broader failure of the talks. One of the biggest challenges for developing countries is to stay abreast of the proliferation of intellectual property policymaking in diverse institutional settings. The US and the EU have been able to exploit resource disparities and shift forums whenever it suits their interests. This holds true of the shift from WIPO to WTO and back again, as well as the shifts from multilateral and bilateral negotiations. Referring to the development agenda at the WIPO, Eric Smith, head of the International Intellectual Property Alliance (a very powerful US-based copyright lobbying organisation), stated that the development agenda was 'revisionist' and that if its proponents 'can convince the rest of the world to change it, good for them. But they won't' (IP-Watch, 2005: 4 November). While asymmetrical power relations and the political influence of global high-technology industry in OECD decision-making continue to shape intellectual property policy, developing countries may be able to take advantage of situations like the looming avian flu pandemic to push their issues forward. The recent massive public protests in Argentina and Thailand against Free Trade Agreements may portend a less compliant approach to globalisation in general and development issues in particular.

Notes

1 TRIPs-plus refers to standards that either are more extensive than TRIPs standards or eliminate options under TRIPs standards (Drahos, 2001: 793).
2 Paragraph from Sell (2003: 140).
3 Bolivia, Brazil, China, Colombia, Costa Rica, the Democratic Republic of Congo,

Ecuador, India, Indonesia, Kenya, Madagascar, Malaysia, Mexico, Peru, the Philippines, South Africa, and Venezuela.

4 For example, turmeric and camu camu, but not ayahuasca. See Correa (2005: 3); IP-Watch (2005: 28 October). Also see Dutfield (2005: 5–8) for a sceptical view.

5 One glaring example of this can be found in the WIPO publication entitled 'Striking a Balance: Patents and Access to Drugs and Health Care' at http://www.wipo.int/about-ip/en/studies/publications/health_care.htm in which WIPO, 'despite the adoption of the Doha Declaration on the TRIPS Agreement and Public Health in November 2001 . . . essentially labels all the concerns that developing countries have raised with regard to TRIPS and public health as "myths" four years later' (Musungu, 2005: 7 and at note 43).

6 Argentina and Brazil presented the proposal to WIPO's General Assembly. The proposal was co-sponsored by Bolivia, Cuba, the Dominican Republic, Ecuador, Egypt, Iran, Kenya, Peru, Sierra Leone, South Africa, Tanzania, and Venezuela. WIPO document WO/GA/31/11 (September/October 2004).

References

Abbott, Frederick (2002), 'Compulsory Licensing for Public Health Needs: The TRIPS Agenda at the WTO after the Doha Declaration on Public Health', Occasional Paper 9 (February) (Geneva: Quaker United Nations Office). http://www.afsc.org/quno.htm.

Abbott, Frederick (2004), 'The Doha Declaration on the TRIPS Agreement and Public Health and the Contradictory Trend in Bilateral and Regional Free Trade Agreements', Occasional Paper 14 (April) (Geneva: Quaker United Nations Office). http://www.quno.org.

Barton, John (2003), 'Nutrition and Technology Transfer Policies', UNTAD/ICTSD Capacity Building Project on Intellectual Property and Sustainable Development (August). http://www.iprsonline.

Bond, Patrick (1999), 'Globalization, Pharmaceutical Pricing, and South African Health Policy: Managing Confrontation with U.S. Firms and Politicians', *International Journal of Health Services*, 29: 4.

Braithwaite, John, and Drahos, Peter (2000), *Global Business Regulation* (Cambridge: Cambridge University Press).

Consumer Project on Technology (2005), 'WTO Members Should Reject Bad Deal on Medicines: Joint Statement by NGOs on TRIPS and Public Health', 3 December. http://www.cptech.org/ip/wto/p6/ngos12032005.html.

Consumer Project on Technology (2005), 'Statement of CPTech on TRIPS Amendment', 6 December. http://www.cptech.org/ip/wto/p6/cptech12062005.html.

Correa, Carlos (2005), 'The Politics and Practicalities of a Disclosure of Origin Obligation', Occasional Paper 16 (January) (Geneva: Quaker United Nations Office). http://www.geneva.quno.org.

Doctors Without Borders (2005), 'The Second Wave of the Access Crisis: Unaffordable AIDS Drug Prices Again', 10 December. http://www.doctorswithoutborders.org/news/hiv-aids/briefing_doc_12-10-2005.

Drahos, Peter (2001), 'BITS and BIPS: Bilateralism in Intellectual Property', *Journal of World Intellectual Property Law*, 4: 6 (November).

Drahos, Peter (2002), 'Developing Countries and Intellectual Property Standard-Setting', *Journal of World Intellectual Property*, No. 5.

Dutfield, Graham (2005), 'Thinking Aloud on Disclosure of Origin', Occasional Paper 18 (October) (Geneva: Quaker United Nations Office).

Gellman, Barton (2000), 'Gore in Conflict for Health and Profit', *The Washington Post*, 21 May. http://www.washingtonpost.c...rticle&nodecontentID=A41297-2000May20.

Helfer, Laurence (2002), 'Intellectual Property Rights in Plant Varieties: An Overview with Options for National Government', *FAO Legal Papers Online*. http://www.fao.org/Legal/pub-e.htm.

Helfer, Laurence (2004), 'Regime Shifting: The TRIPs Agreement and New Dynamics of International Intellectual Property Lawmaking', *Yale Journal of International Law*, 1: 71.

Hepburn, Jonathan (2002), 'Negotiating Intellectual Property: Mandates and Options in the Doha Work Program', Occasional Paper 10 (Geneva: Quaker United Nations Office). http://www.quno.org.

International Centre for Trade and Sustainable Development (2004), 'Brazil Wins Landmark Cotton Dispute', *Bridges*, May.

International Centre for Trade and Sustainable Development (2005), 'WIPO Development Agenda Status Unclear', *Bridges*, No. 9 (September/October).

IP Blog (2005), 'WTO Extends Deadline for Poor Countries to Implement TRIPS by Seven Years', 29 November. http://www.ipblog.org/blog/IPBlog.nsf/dx/wto-extends-deadline-for-poor-countries-to-imp.

Ip-health (2005), 'Deadlock on TRIPS and Public Health Deliberations on a "Permanent Solution"', 28 October. http://lists.essential.org/pipermail/ip-health/2005-October/008531.html.

IP-Watch (2005), 'Nations Clash on Future of WIPO Development Agenda', 11 April. http://www.ip-watch.org.

IP-Watch (2005), 'Non-Profits, Industry Offer Views on WIPO Development Agenda', 14 April. http://www.ip-watch.org.

IP-Watch (2005), 'IP Issues Reappear on Agenda of WTO Talks', 14 October. http://www.ip-watch.org.

IP-Watch (2005), 'Official: In WTO Talks, US Pushes Russia to Restrictive TRIPS Standard', 24 October. http://www.ip-watch.org.

IP-Watch (2005), 'Avian Flu Issues Could Arise at TRIPS Council Meeting', 25 October. http://www.ip-watch.org.

IP-Watch (2005), 'Pandemic Fears Raise Questions about WTO Health Waiver Opt-Out', 27 October. http://www.ip-watch.org.

IP-Watch (2005), 'TRIPS Council Issues Still Alive for WTO Ministerial', 28 October. http://www.ip-watch.org.

IP-Watch (2005), 'EU Elevates Geographical Indications as Priority for Hong Kong', 28 October. http://www.ip-watch.org.

IP-Watch (2005), 'Interview with Eric Smith, President, International Intellectual Property Alliance', 4 November. http://www.ip-watch.org.

IP-Watch (2005), 'Industry Concerned about Development Agenda at WTO', 4 November. http://www.ip-watch.org.

IP-Watch (2005), 'African Countries Ready to Accept TRIPS and Public Health Deal', 6 December 12:36am. http://www.ip-watch.org.

IP-Watch (2005), 'WTO Strikes Agreement on TRIPS and Public Health on Eve of Ministerial', 6 December, 10:53pm. http://www.ip-watch.org.

IP-Watch (2005), 'TRIPS Health Amendment Evokes Harsh NGO Reaction, Industry Caution', 7 December. http://www.ip-watch.org.

IP-Watch (2005), 'Experts Debate IP Issues as Hong Kong WTO Ministerial Opens', 13 December. http://www.ip-watch.org.

IP-Watch (2005), 'TRIPS Public Health Announcement Questioned; China Implements Decision', 14 December. http://www.ip-watch.org.

IP-Watch (2005), 'India, Brazil Tie Biodiversity Negotiations to Doha Development Package', 15 December. http://www.ip-watch.org.

IP-Watch (2005), 'Peru Attempts Strong WTO Position on Disclosure despite Weaker US Deal', 17 December. http://www.ip-watch.org.

IP-Watch (2005), 'Latest WTO Ministerial Draft Urges Discussion on IP Issues to Intensify, Adds Review Date', 18 December, 11:51am. http://www.ip-watch.org.

IP-Watch (2006), 'Biotech Firms Form Alliance to Fight Off Possible TRIPS Amendments', 6 January. http://www.ip-watch.org.

Love, James (2005), 'No Gift to the Poor: Strategies Used by US and EC to Protect Big Pharma in WTO TRIPS Negotiations', 1 December, *Working Agenda*. http://working agenda.blogspot.com/2005/12/no-gift-to-poor-strategies-used-by-us.html.

Marden, Emily (1999), 'The Neem Tree Patent: International Conflict over the Commodification of Life', *Boston College Environmental Affairs Law Review*, 22.

Matthews, Duncan (2004a), 'WTO Decision on Implementation of Paragraph 6 of the Doha Declaration on the TRIPS Agreement and Public Health: A Solution to the Access to Essential Medicines Problem?', *Journal of International Economic Law*, 7: 1.

Matthews, Duncan (2004b), 'Is History Repeating Itself? Outcome of the Negotiations on Access to Medicines, the HIV/AIDS Pandemic and Intellectual Property Rights in the World Trade Organisation', *Electronic Law Journal*, LGD 1. http://www2.warwick.ac.uk/fac/soc/law/elj/lgd/2004_1/matthews/.

May, Christopher and Sell, Susan K. (2006), *Intellectual Property Rights: A Critical History* (Boulder: Lynne Rienner Publishers).

Médecins sans Frontières, Health Action International, and Consumer Project on Technology (1996), 'Amsterdam Statement', 25–26 November. http://www.cptech.org/ip/health/amsterdamstatement/html.

Musungu, Sisule (2005), 'Rethinking Innovation, Development and Intellectual Property in the UN: WIPO and Beyond', TRIPS Issues Papers 5 (Quaker International Affairs Programme, Ottawa, Canada).

Odell, John, and Sell, Susan K. (2006), 'Reframing the Issue: The WTO Coalition on Intellectual Property and Public Health, 2001', in John Odell (ed.), *Negotiating Trade* (Cambridge: Cambridge University Press).

Reid, W., and Laird, S., Meyer, C., Gamez, R., Sittenfeld, A., Janzen, D., Gollin, M., and Juma, C. (1993), *Biodiversity Prospecting: Using Genetic Resources for Sustainable Development* (Washington, DC: World Resources Institute).

Sell, Susan K. (1998), *North–South Politics of Intellectual Property and Antitrust* (Albany: State University of New York Press).

Sell, Susan K. (2003), *Private Power, Public Law: The Globalisation of Intellectual Property Rights* (Cambridge: Cambridge University Press).

Shiva, Vandana (1997), *Biopiracy: The Plunder of Nature and Knowledge* (Cambridge, MA: South End Press).

South Centre and Center for International Environmental Law (2004), *South Centre and CIEL IP Quarterly Update: Fourth Quarter, 2004* (Geneva: South Centre).

South Centre and Centre for International Environmental Law (2005a), *South Centre and CIEL IP Quarterly Update: Third Quarter 2005* (Geneva: South Centre).

South Centre and Centre for International Environmental Law (2005b), *South Centre and CIEL IP Quarterly Update: Second Quarter, 2005* (Geneva: South Centre).

Sutherland, Johanna (1998), 'TRIPS, Cultural Politics and Law Reform', *Prometheus*, 16: 3.

Tejera, Valentina (1999), 'Tripping over Property Rights: Is It Possible to Reconcile the Convention on Biological Diversity with Article 27 of the TRIPS Agreement?', *New England Law Review*, 33 (Summer).

Vick, Karl (1999), 'African AIDS Victims Losers of a Drug War', *The Washington Post*, 4 December.

WIPO (2005), 'Proposal by the United States of America for the Establishment of a Partnership Program in WIPO', WIPO Document IIM/1/2 (18 March).

WTO (2001), 'Declaration on the TRIPS Agreement and Public Health', WT/MIN(01)/DEC/2,20 (November). http://www.wto.org/english/thewto_e/minist_e/min01/mindecl) trips_e.htm.

WTO Council on TRIPS (2003), 'WTO Decision on Implementation of Paragraph 6 of the Doha Declaration on the TRIPS Agreement and Public Health', IP/C/405.

WTO (2003), 'Implementation of Paragraph 6 of the Doha declaration on the TRIPS Agreement and Public Health', 2 September, WT/L/540. http://docsonline.wto.org.

WTO (2004), 'Elements of the Obligation to Disclose the Source and Country of Origin of Biological Resource and/or Traditional Knowledge Used in an Invention – Submission from Brazil, India, Pakistan, Peru, Thailand and Venezuela', WTO Document IP/C/W/429 (21 September).

WTO (2005a), 'Compulsory Licensing of Pharmaceuticals and TRIPS', October. TRIPS and Health: FAQs. http://www.wto.org/english/tratop_e/trips_e/public_health_faq_e.htm.

WTO (2005b), 'Legal Arguments to Support the African Group Proposal on the Implementation of Paragraph 11 of the 30 August 2003 Decision', IP/C/W/440 (1 March).

5 Services, economic development, and the Doha Round

Exploiting the comparative advantage of the WTO

Bernard Hoekman and Aaditya Mattoo

Introduction

Recent research demonstrates that deep global trade reforms would be good for the world economy as a whole and enhance economic welfare in most developing countries.[1] Although national interests differ, and not all countries might gain, numerous models suggest that a key area for multilateral liberalisation is Organisation for Economic Co-operation and Development (OECD) countries' agricultural policies. These severely distort world markets for products in which many developing countries have a comparative advantage. It is appropriate therefore that agriculture has attracted most of the attention of negotiators in the Doha Round. However, the emphasis on agriculture has led unfortunately to a relative neglect of services.

The neglect of services matters for several reasons. First, the potential direct gains from reform of services trade for most WTO members are likely to be at least as large as those from goods trade reform. These gains are hard to quantify because services trade and the barriers to such trade are hard to measure. But the potential is evident when we consider that liberalisation could lead to improved financial, communications, transport, education, health, and a variety of business services through increased cross-border trade, foreign direct investment in services, and the temporary movement of individual service providers.

Second, services reform is needed to enable developing countries to take advantage of the new opportunities that arise from goods trade liberalisation. Many poor countries lack trade capacity and competitiveness, reducing the ability of their firms to benefit from access to export markets or to compete with imports. Improving competitiveness is largely a service agenda: fully exploiting trade opportunities requires access to efficient and competitively priced transport, distribution, and many other services. For example, sub-Saharan African exporters today pay transport costs that are at least five times greater than the tariffs they face in industrial country markets, but neither international maritime nor air transport services figure seriously on the WTO agenda.

Finally, the WTO negotiating process requires countries that seek market access concessions to offer concessions in turn. Thus, greater ambition in terms of global liberalisation of agriculture will require greater opening in services, an area of export interest to the OECD countries that protect their agriculture sectors.

A major impediment to making progress on services is the complexity of the underlying policy issues. In the case of both agriculture and manufactures, the negotiating agenda is well understood, and numerous analyses have informed negotiators and interest groups on the determinants of the value of alternative outcomes – the number of sensitive products that are not liberalised, the level at which tariffs are capped, the coefficients determining the depth of cuts in tariff bindings, and so on. The challenge in services is to define meaningful commitments in the WTO that will be beneficial to the countries that undertake them *and* be of value from a mercantilist negotiating perspective. In this chapter we suggest certain elements that would satisfy these requirements at least for the industrial and larger developing countries. These elements include locking in the existing openness of cross-border trade in services, eliminating barriers to foreign investment where there is adequate regulatory preparedness, and facilitating the freer movement of at least some categories of natural persons.

Identifying desirable goals is one thing, getting there another. Fortunately, there is increasing recognition that moving the negotiations forward requires those WTO members that are large enough to play the mercantilist game to engage each other. The 2005 WTO Hong Kong Ministerial declaration's inclusion of 'plurilateral' negotiations that are limited to a subset of the WTO membership therefore offers a way forward, based on reciprocal commitments by the larger players (OECD and Group of 20 – G20) that are extended to all members through the MFN rule.

Beyond the traditional market access agenda we need to determine what the WTO can do to support domestic policy reforms and strengthen service sectors in developing countries, particularly the poorest countries, which are at serious risk of marginalisation from global services trade. These countries have weak export interests in services outside of tourism, which is mostly free of restrictions, and unskilled labour services, which face high barriers that are unlikely to be lowered through multilateral negotiations. Furthermore, successful liberalisation in these countries will require substantial strengthening of domestic regulatory institutions and infrastructure. Aid for trade can play a major role in ensuring that these requirements are satisfied. By adding an additional instrument – development assistance – to the table, the General Agreement on Trade in Services (GATS)/WTO could become much more relevant as a mechanism not just to promote services liberalisation but, more importantly, to bolster and improve domestic reform in services.

There is an emerging view that additional dedicated 'aid for trade' is needed to make the WTO more relevant from a development perspective (Hoekman, 2002; Prowse, 2006). In practice, many of the needs at the country and regional level are services-related. Poor countries have found it difficult to attract investment in service sectors and create contestable markets that provide consumers – firms, farmers, and households – with high-quality services. One reason for the weakness of these sectors is the persistence of explicit or implicit barriers to foreign and private participation, which are of course the main focus of trade negotiations. But the removal of such barriers needs to be complemented by action to address more fundamental weaknesses in poor countries' services sectors, including in regulatory institutions.

While the WTO is not and should not become a development organisation, we argue that the WTO has a major potential role to play in assisting governments to address the domestic reform agenda in low-income countries by helping to identify these needs and using its 'commitment and monitoring technologies' to mobilise both liberalisation *and* assistance. Specifically, we argue that if WTO members were to expand the transparency mandate of the organisation by making the WTO a focal point for multilateral discussions and assessments of the state of members' service sectors, the institution could do much to help address the needs of its poorer members. It would do so by raising the policy profile of the services agenda in poor countries, helping governments identify where development assistance is needed and monitoring the delivery and effectiveness of such assistance.

Technical assistance will not be enough. Even if developing country governments liberalise access to services markets and improve the regulatory framework, poor countries may not see much of an investment response – reputational hurdles, geography, the small size of the market, and sheer poverty may result in a lack of interest and a lack of competition – and thus high prices and/or under-served consumers and regions. Additional aid for trade could make a difference on the ground – by targeting entry by new providers and the delivery of services that otherwise would not be provided by profit-maximising firms. Using aid for trade resources can help ensure universal access for key services, in the process increasing the perceived benefits to poor countries from multilateral engagement.

The plan of this chapter is as follows. The first section discusses the economic fundamentals – why services and services trade and investment matter for development. The second section turns to the WTO market access negotiations and discusses the challenges in harnessing traditional negotiating mechanics to deliver openness in services and presents some specific options that could foster additional liberalisation. This 'traditional' approach is relevant primarily for the larger members of the WTO. The third section focuses on what could be done to make the WTO more relevant for all developing countries, including smaller and poorer members – the majority of the WTO membership. Much of the agenda here revolves around appropriate sequencing of autonomous reforms, provision of development assistance to strengthen and improve regulation, and using multilateral commitments to overcome political constraints and resistance to opening markets to greater (international) competition. A fourth section concludes.

Economic fundamentals

There is no denying that agricultural reform is central to poverty reduction. In low-income countries agriculture often accounts for 20–30 per cent of GDP and over 50 per cent of employment. From a poverty-reduction perspective, the agricultural sector is even more important than these statistics suggest, because within low-income economies poverty is greatest in rural areas that depend on agriculture. Over 70 per cent of the world's poor reside in rural areas (Hertel and Winters, 2006). But even in the poorest countries, services account for 40–50 per cent of GDP and a significant share of employment. Not only would improved performance in services produce significant direct benefits, large indirect benefits would come from domestic farmers, households, and firms obtaining access to better and cheaper services than they have today. Similarly, while the opportunity to export more agricultural and manufactured products is important, actions to improve the efficiency of service sectors are vital to exploiting these opportunities.

An efficient and well-regulated financial sector will improve the transformation of savings to investment by ensuring that resources are deployed where they have the highest returns. Improved efficiency in telecommunications generates economy-wide benefits, as this service is a vital intermediate input and also crucial to the dissemination and diffusion of knowledge. Similarly, transport services contribute to the efficient distribution of goods within a country, and are particularly important in determining the ability of firms to contest international markets. Business services such as accounting and legal services are important in reducing transaction costs associated with the operation of financial markets and the enforcement of contracts. Retail and wholesale services are a vital link between producers and consumers, and the margins that apply in the provision of such services influence competitiveness. Education and health services are determinants of the ability of citizens to benefit from trade opportunities.

Services, growth, and poverty reduction

Even though empirical studies on services have limitations as a result of data weaknesses, recent research suggests that a comprehensive 'behind-the-border' policy reform agenda focusing on enhancing competition in services industries can help boost growth prospects and enhance welfare. Mattoo, Rathindran, and Subramanian (2006) analyse the effects of trade and investment openness for the financial and telecommunications sector on growth in a cross-sectional analysis. Controlling for other determinants of growth, they find that countries that fully liberalised the financial services sector grew, on average, about 1 percentage point faster than countries that did not. Fully liberalising both the telecommunications and the financial services sectors was associated with an average growth rate of 1.5 percentage points above that of other countries. Focusing on a sample of transition economies, Eschenbach and Hoekman (2006) find that services-related policies play an important role in attracting foreign direct investment (FDI). They explore the impact of financial and infrastructure services policy reforms on per-capita income growth using time-series data covering the 1990–2004 period. Controlling for other potential explanatory variables, they find that improvements in services policies – infrastructure and finance – have a large and statistically significant positive impact on per-capita growth.

Increasing international competition on service markets will reduce what Konan and Maskus (2004) call the cartel effect – the mark-up of price over marginal cost that incumbents are able to charge due to restricted entry; and an attenuation of what they call the cost inefficiency effect – the fact that in an environment with limited competition, marginal costs of incumbents are likely to be higher than if entry were allowed. The latter is more important, as inefficiency imposes a cost on all sectors and households that consume the services involved. Simulation studies for Egypt and Tunisia that analyse the likely impact of services liberalisation conclude that removing policies that increase costs can have much greater positive effects on national welfare than the removal of trade barriers – by up to a factor of seven or eight (see, for example, Hoekman and Konan, 2001; Konan and Maskus, 2004). Instead of the 'standard' 0.5 to 1 per cent increase in welfare from goods liberalisation, introducing greater competition on services markets that removes cost inefficiencies raises the gains to 6–8 per cent. These large effects of services liberalisation reflect both the importance of services in the economy and the extent to which they tend to be protected.

The positive association between more efficient service sectors and overall economic performance implies that services policy reforms will help reduce poverty – as sustained economic growth is the most powerful instrument to reduce poverty. Underlying this aggregate, indirect relationship are many channels through which better services can directly improve economic outcomes for poor households, for example by enhanced consumption of health and education. Another channel is by enhancing the benefits of trade reforms. A number of recent country studies that have investigated the likely impacts of trade reforms on the poor conclude that greater trade opportunities can raise incomes but only if poor households produce products for the market. This may require active intervention to help households switch from subsistence to cash crops and improve productivity – through extension services, access to credit and transportation services, and investments in infrastructure.

Some specific examples are helpful to illustrate the importance of domestic policy actions to enhance the benefits of global trade reforms. Nicita (2007) concludes that, overall, multilateral trade liberalisation would have only a small impact on Ethiopian households. This is partly because the likely policy changes would have only small impacts on the world prices of products exported by Ethiopia and partly because exports represent only a small part of Ethiopia's gross domestic product (GDP), so that even a hypothetical doubling of the country's export values would not have much impact on overall poverty. Critically, within Ethiopia, markets are poorly interconnected and households largely engage in subsistence activities, so that the price and quantity effect of trade polices will be much attenuated.

Balat, Brambilla, and Porto (2007) focus on Zambia and also conclude that only small impacts can be expected from global trade reform because it will generate only small changes in prices for Zambian exports and imports and because home-produced goods account for very large shares of both income and expenditure for households. They show that in the case of cotton, agricultural extension services would have much greater impacts in reducing poverty than the expected rise in the price of cotton that would result from an ambitious Doha Round agricultural reform. They also show that from a poverty perspective it is important that households shift out of subsistence and into cotton. Figure 5.1 summarises their findings. It compares

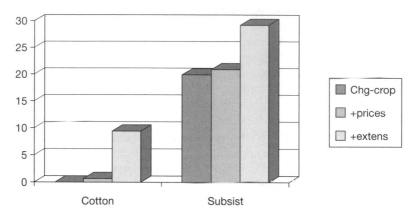

Figure 5.1 Income effects of global trade and complementary reforms for cotton in Zambia

current subsistence farmers with the same characteristics as cotton growers and shows that most of the gains would come from switching to cotton. This would boost incomes by 20 per cent. Extension services that enhance productivity would improve incomes by another 8 per cent. In contrast, higher cotton prices add only 1 per cent to the incomes of existing cotton producers; they would benefit much more from the extension services. Other studies with similar conclusions can be found in Hoekman and Olarreaga (2007) and Hertel and Winters (2006).

Significant gains in poor countries from global trade reforms depend on actions to move households out of subsistence agriculture. Global trade reform by itself will not ensure this. Domestic supply constraints are the main reason for the lack of trade growth and diversification in many of the poorest developing countries. Without action to improve supply capacity, reduce transport costs from remote areas, increase farm productivity, and more generally improve the investment climate, trade opportunities cannot be fully exploited and the potential gains from trade will not be maximised. The needed reforms span numerous areas, but many of them are services-related.

Services export interests

In addition to the 'import dimension' stressed above, developing countries also have an export interest in services. Their exports of services have grown nearly fourfold in the last decade to attain a share of the global marketplace of 18 per cent. In large part this reflects growth in so-called business process outsourcing (BPO) services. This activity arises from the outsourcing (and out-location through FDI) of non-core business processes throughout the value chains of both manufacturing and services industries. Within BPO activities the more advanced developing countries, such as India, are moving from providing only low-end back-office services (such as data entry) to more integrated and higher-end service bundles in fields such as customer care, human resource management, and product development. This move is creating space for other developing countries, from China to Senegal, to step into the more standardised segments of the market.

There is great potential for other services exports as well. Health services are an important example where developing countries have an export interest, either by attracting foreign patients to domestic hospitals and doctors or by temporarily sending their health personnel abroad. A major barrier to this trade is the lack of portability of health insurance in OECD countries. For example, US federal or state government reimbursement of medical expenses is limited to certified facilities in the US or in a specific US state. This constraint is also significant because it deters elderly persons from retiring abroad. Those who do retire abroad are often forced to return home to obtain affordable medical care. The potential impact of permitting portability could be substantial. If only 3 per cent of the 100 million elderly persons living in OECD countries retired to developing countries, they would bring with them possibly $30 to $50 billion annually in personal consumption and $10 to $15 billion in medical expenditures (UNCTAD and WHO, 1998). Mattoo and Rathindran (2005) find that extending health insurance coverage to overseas care for just 15 types of tradable treatments could produce savings for the US of over $1 billion a year even if only one in ten American patients travel abroad. The lower costs of health services abroad offer the opportunity to extend medical benefits to people who currently are not insured.

A major potential source of gain in services is mode 4 of the General Agreement on Trade in Services (GATS) – the liberalisation of temporary movement of service suppliers. Temporary movement offers arguably a partial solution to the dilemma of how international migration is best managed, given the substantial political resistance that exists against it in many high-income countries. It enables the realisation of gains from trade while addressing some of the concerns of opponents to migration in host countries, while also attenuating the brain drain costs for poor source countries that can be associated with permanent migration. Research has shown that if OECD countries were to expand temporary access to foreign service-providers by the equivalent of 3 per cent of their labour force, the global gains would dominate those associated with full liberalisation of merchandise trade (Walmsley and Winters, 2003; Winters, 2004). Both developed and developing countries would share in these gains, and they would be largest if both high-skilled mobility and low-skilled mobility were permitted.

Market access negotiating logic: opportunities and constraints

The economic fundamentals summarised above illustrate that services are a key dimension of multilateral negotiations from a development perspective. The WTO can potentially help to improve services performance by inducing countries to liberalise access to markets, thus increasing competition. The WTO is driven by mercantilism: the desire by members to improve their access to the markets of other members. The role of WTO negotiations is to mobilise export-oriented groups that seek better access to foreign markets to support domestic liberalisation in areas of interest to trading partners. Market access concessions could be exchanged within services or through cross-issue linkages between goods and services. A broad-based multi-issue approach could help define a negotiating set that is large enough for all players to identify potentially Pareto-improving packages of reforms. As noted, a link between services and agriculture will have to be made if protectionist policies in agriculture are to be reduced substantially.

Apart from furthering market access, it is less clear what the WTO can do to improve members' service performance through improved regulation and enhancing the business environment and investment climate. The focus of the WTO process is not on the welfare or growth prospects of members or on the identification of 'good' policy. Nor does the WTO have access to financial resources or to mechanisms to redistribute the gains from global trade and investment reforms across members. This raises the question of what the WTO might do to address many of the issues discussed in the previous section that are important for development. The remainder of this section focuses on the 'bread and butter' of the WTO – market access. The next section turns to the question of what might be done through the WTO to improve the domestic services environment in developing countries.

Identifying goals for the services negotiations

One problem is that negotiators have failed to identify a set of broad goals for the services negotiations that make sense from a development perspective, would provoke engagement from the business community, and satisfy the overall mercantilist constraint of ensuring a 'balance of concessions'. A specific fear created by the GATS is that it will deprive regulators of the freedom they need to achieve social objectives. Because negotiators have failed to provide the necessary reassurance, regulators are reluctant to make new commitments. The implication is that, at this stage of the development of the GATS, a balance needs to be struck between securing improved market access while preserving desirable regulatory freedom. Such a balance could be achieved by limiting commitments to measures that discriminate (pre- and post-entry) against foreign providers of services – as opposed to seeking disciplines that also target measures that do not discriminate in any way: that is, generally applicable sectoral regulation. Making national treatment the primary discipline covering all forms of *de jure* and *de facto* discrimination (pre- and post-establishment) would cover the bulk of the most important prevailing restrictions. A focus on policies that discriminate would not only diminish fears of the intrusiveness of the GATS but also reduce the opacity of current GATS disciplines and the resulting uncertainty regarding the exact implications of making commitments.

Regarding the modes of supply that are distinguished in the GATS, Mattoo (2005) argues that specific objectives should include: (1) locking-in the currently open regimes for cross-border trade in a wide range of services sectors; (2) eliminating barriers to foreign investment in sectors where the regulatory preconditions already exist; (3) committing to phased elimination where these conditions can be met at a foreseeable date; and (4) allowing greater freedom of temporary movement for individual service providers as intra-corporate transferees and to fulfil specific services contracts. The first goal is essentially 'painless' in that openness is the prevailing status quo; however, realisation of the others will involve potential adjustment costs and complementary regulatory reform and institutional strengthening in many developing countries.

Towards de facto *differentiation*

Achieving these objectives will arguably require a change in negotiating approach. WTO members have been proceeding bilaterally, submitting requests to others and responding to requests with (conditional) offers. Requests have tended to be highly ambitious and offers mostly minimalist. This negotiating process has resulted in a low-level equilibrium trap where little is expected and less offered. Assuming agreement to limit negotiations to policies that discriminate, the next question is whether to stick to the bilateral request-and-offer approach or to shift to alternative approaches that are more akin to negotiating formulas. In the sphere of trade in goods, WTO members have sought to use a formula on the basis of which they cut tariffs and/or subsidies. In the Doha Round both agriculture and the non-agricultural market access (NAMA) negotiations revolve in part on formulas-based negotiating modalities. There are a number of reasons to favour formulas/model schedules. In a world of unequal bargaining power, multilaterally agreed formulas that are seen to be equitable and efficient are likely to produce a more favourable outcome for the weaker party than bilateral negotiations. Formulas also help reduce the transactions costs of negotiations – avoiding the need to barter commitments sector by sector, country by country. Thus formulas can help overcome the difficulty in accomplishing an exchange (and balance) of concessions between countries that do not necessarily have a reciprocal interest in each other's markets.

Possible 'formula-type' approaches for services include quantitative targets for the coverage of schedules of commitments and so-called model schedules. In services, quantitative assessments of offers are unlikely to be helpful because even the best available methods of quantifying barriers to trade are hopelessly inadequate. At best it would be possible to measure differences in the sectoral coverage of commitments, possibly weighted by some crude measure of the level of openness. As it is very difficult to determine the restrictiveness of policies, any assessment of the implied level of openness will be inherently subjective. If recourse is made to quantitative indicators, the most straightforward – if not only – possible measure is arguably the number of commitments entailing no restrictions on national treatment by sector and sub-sector (Hoekman, 1996). Any other type of coverage index approach will not be meaningful in so far as there will always be ways for members to schedule sectors while maintaining restrictions – such as economic needs tests or similar requirements. In our view, anything short of full national treatment as the focal point is not meaningful from an economic, systemic, or development perspective. Nor would a less ambitious approach do much in our view to move the broader Doha agenda (agriculture in particular) forward, as anything less will be seen for what it is – an effort to create the impression of progress.

Assuming the national treatment focal point is adopted, the question of sectoral coverage will need to be determined, as will the issue of determining which or how many WTO members need to make commitments. Rather than seek an overall numerical coverage target, a more fruitful collective approach would be for groups of members, akin to the 'friends' groups that already exist, to champion clearly specified goals that are embodied in 'model schedules'. The latter would entail agreement among these countries that the sectors concerned are of economic interest to them and allow clarity as to what types of commitments will be expected in those sectors. This approach could also be used for specific modes – most notably mode 1.[2] The building blocks of model schedules are relatively straightforward, and some have already been proposed for specific modes.[3] The idea is to create a focal point for liberalising commitments, either by agreeing on a certain threshold level of commitments for the model schedule, thus shifting the burden on a member to justify its refusal to concede the threshold level rather than on other members to extract the minimum concessions, or via a 'zero-for-zero' analogue – for example, the number of sectors or sub-sectors without any national treatment exceptions.[4]

These types of approaches allow for *de facto* differentiation between WTO members in terms of participation and depth of services commitments. From the broader perspective of attaining a Doha Round outcome that involves meaningful liberalisation of agricultural policies and merchandise trade, there must be a balance of concessions. In particular, as mentioned, large developing countries – such as the G20 for concreteness – must make liberalisation commitments that are perceived to be of value to OECD countries. But smaller and poor developing countries have little to offer the OECD countries in this type of exchange – their markets are too small. The proposed type of approach discussed above allows for the latter set of countries to be effectively exempted from participation – they would be able to 'free-ride'.

The countries that must be part of the negotiation set cannot be determined ex ante – this is endogenous and will depend on the issue – but past practice suggests that for sectoral liberalisation agreements to be applied on a MFN basis, the 'internalisation' ratio needs to be fairly high – say of the order of 90 per cent of total trade.[5] The pursuit of such a 'k-group' approach (Schelling, 1978) should be more feasible than it is for goods trade because of the way the GATS is structured.[6] It embodies significant scope for flexibility through its use of a positive list approach to define the country coverage of specific commitments. The prospects for pursuit of a k-group approach were enhanced by the Hong Kong Ministerial meeting, which explicitly identified the option of 'plurilateral' talks. These can be pursued on a horizontal or sectoral basis.

What about the poor countries? Many would argue that the proposed 'free riding' will not necessarily be beneficial to them. We share this view, but would argue that the types of beneficial policy reforms that are needed are best pursued through a different mechanism that provides greater assurances that countries will benefit from making commitments. The rationale for the proposed small-group approach to market-access negotiations is not to let poor-country governments 'off the hook' but to recognise that there is little they can do to influence the outcome of market-access negotiations. That is, they have few incentives to play this game and will find it hard therefore to argue domestically that the quid pro quo received justifies potentially painful domestic reforms. A more *à la carte* approach that stresses assistance and co-operation and ex-post clarity of the benefits of making WTO commitments is more appropriate to the needs of the poorest countries. We return to this in the next main section.

Facilitating negotiations through broader co-operation, particularly on mode 4

Facilitating regulatory co-operation could help deal with apprehensions about liberalisation on all modes. For example, in financial services, confidence in co-operation by the home country regulator of suppliers could facilitate greater openness to both commercial presence and cross-border trade by host countries. Similarly, in international transport services, confidence in the enforcement of home-country competition law might increase the willingness to liberalise in importing countries.

The area that is probably of greatest interest to many developing countries – whether large emerging markets or the LDCs – in direct trade terms is to achieve progress on mode 4. To date, mode 4 has been (another) millstone for the services negotiations. To support a positive outcome on mode 4, members need to recognise that simply asserting that mode 4 is about trade in services and *not* about migration cannot dispel the deep-rooted fears raised by the entry of foreign providers in many countries. Whatever one's views of the legitimacy of those fears, to make progress they have to be acknowledged and addressed. One way to take a more co-operative and less antagonistic approach to mode 4 is to draw upon the experience of a few relatively successful bilateral and regional trade agreements.

The inclusion of labour mobility in the framework of a multilateral trade agreement implies that obligations are assumed by host countries to provide market access on an MFN basis regardless of conditions in source countries. Greater progress might be feasible if more were done also to impose obligations on source countries. This is a key element of regional agreements (for example, Asia-Pacific Economic Co-operation – APEC) that have facilitated mobility of skilled workers, and bilateral labour agreements (such as between Spain and Ecuador, Canada and the Caribbean, Germany and Eastern Europe) that have to a limited extent improved access for the unskilled. Source country obligations in these agreements include pre-movement screening and selection, accepting and facilitating return of workers, and commitments to combat illegal migration. Co-operation by the source can help address security concerns, ensure temporariness, and prevent illegal labour flows in a way that the host country is incapable of accomplishing alone. In effect, such co-operation constitutes a service for which the host may be willing to 'pay' by allowing increased access.

How might such elements be incorporated in a multilateral agreement? One possibility is that host countries commit under the GATS to allow access to any source country that fulfils certain pre-specified conditions – along the lines of mutual recognition agreements in other areas. Even if these conditions were unilaterally specified and compliance determined unilaterally, it would still be a huge improvement over the arbitrariness and lack of transparency in existing visa schemes. Although negotiating these conditions multilaterally and establishing a mechanism to certify their fulfilment would be an improvement over the unequal, non-transparent and potentially labour-diverting bilateral context, this is simply not feasible in the short run. Given the large differences in the ability of source countries to satisfy whatever conditions are put in place, there is a clear case for high-income countries also providing assistance to poorer countries to attain them (we discuss the subject of aid for trade in services below).

One other problem needs to be addressed: in the current GATS framework, when a country makes a market access commitment it is obliged to grant a fixed level of access every year in the future regardless of domestic economic conditions. In contrast, bilateral labour agreements allow host countries to vary the level of access depending on the state of the economy. One example is the bilateral agreement between Germany and certain Eastern European countries under which the quota on temporary migrants increased (decreased) by 5 per cent for every 1 percentage point decrease (increase) in the level of unemployment. It may be desirable to consider GATS commitments along these lines which allow necessary flexibility in a transparent, predictable, and objectively verifiable manner. This would be a big improvement over the opaque and discretionary economic needs tests that infest current GATS schedules.[7]

Supporting services reforms in poor countries

Although we have argued that for many developing countries the WTO process cannot deliver – they have very limited ability to negotiate better access and thus do not see much (political) gain to making commitments themselves – their own liberalisation is important for firms and consumers in these countries. The adoption of an explicit k-group strategy should not imply that poor countries are ignored; reforms in these countries are as important as, if not more important than, for the more advanced developing countries. But they may not be able to benefit from liberalisation – and thus GATS commitments – if the preconditions for doing so have not been satisfied. And there is likely to be substantial uncertainty as to what those preconditions are and what the sequence should be in which they are addressed (the same applies for the size and distribution of the associated costs and benefits). Moreover, many of the preconditions have nothing to do with the ambit of the WTO but require domestic efforts or action. We argue that assistance needs to be given to poor countries to remedy domestic inadequacies and that the WTO potentially has a role as a focal point and monitor of not just market access commitments but also trade-related development assistance.

A softer, critical role for the WTO

While market access in services is negotiated within the WTO, policy advice and assistance for regulatory reform and public investments in services infrastructure are provided by international financial institutions and specialised agencies. There is virtually no link between the two processes. This disconnection persists even though it is clear that improved regulation – ranging from prudential regulation in financial services to pro-competitive regulation in a variety of network-based services – will be critical to realising the benefits of services liberalisation in many sectors. Policy intervention will also be necessary to ensure universal service because liberalisation per se will not always deliver adequate access to the poor. There is a need to determine whether there are good reasons to defer liberalisation and/or not to make binding commitments. For example, weaknesses in existing mechanisms for prudential or pro-competitive regulation, the need to alleviate adjustment costs, and the desire to ensure universal access in liberalised markets may be good reasons to hold back on making unconditional liberalisation commitments.

These considerations help explain both the limited use that has been made by poor countries of the GATS and their resistance to making additional specific commitments to guarantee access to their markets. A possible approach to recognising the perceived uncertainty of the magnitude and distribution of the costs and benefits associated with making GATS commitments is to adopt a more flexible and conditional framework. This could involve a 'soft law' form of co-operation that revolves around the creation of a mechanism that focuses explicitly on identification of national objectives for a given sector, collaboration among members in identifying policy instruments that could be used to pursue the objectives, and providing assistance to do so, as well as regular monitoring and assessments of the effects of the policies adopted and assistance provided. Such a process would go beyond the status quo by changing the focus from seeking commitments on the basis of quid pro quo arguments (which are weak to start with and perceived with great suspicion by many governments) to one where the focus is on attaining the objectives of the countries that are currently being asked to make commitments in an efficient manner.

Much of the attention directed at the WTO tends to centre on the process of negotiations and the Dispute Settlement Mechanism (DSM). However, the functions of the WTO extend beyond rulemaking and enforcement. One of its tasks is to increase the transparency of member trade policies through the Trade Policy Review Mechanism (TPRM) (Article III, WTO).[8] Services are included in the ambit of the TPRM. Indeed, the WTO is currently the only multilateral body that has a mandate to review all the services trade-related policies of countries.

Instead of calling for all developing countries to make additional GATS commitments and/or to ignore the majority of these countries because they are of limited commercial interest, an alternative would be to build on the precedent established by the TPRM by adding a process through which national objectives, constraints, and possible policy instruments are identified. Importantly, a goal of the process would be to identify where development assistance could be most effectively used to help attain the national objectives. The TPRM would then be extended to monitor not just national trade-related policies but the services 'performance' of the country concerned and the provision and effectiveness of the aid provided by donor countries. One result would be a reduction in uncertainty regarding the value of making specific commitments to countries over time, as these would be based on the experience obtained by having implemented them already.[9]

In a nutshell, the implications of the suggested approach are that the primary roles of the WTO would be expanded for it to act as (1) a focal point for considering the international dimensions of national services policies on a regular basis; (2) a mechanism for increasing the transparency of policy and outcomes, and monitoring the provision of development assistance; and (3) a lock-in device for policy reforms that have been deemed to be beneficial. Again, the appropriate role of the WTO in this area is not to provide assistance, or to allocate it. What the WTO can best do is to be the focal point for regular policy attention and interaction on services. No other organisation can play that role or has an incentive to do so.

The proposed approach does not imply ceasing to negotiate binding disciplines. Instead, it would put the focus more strongly on a country's identification and pursuit of a national policy agenda and priorities and to link this to aid for trade. Rather than focus predominantly on legally binding commitments, the emphasis would be put on identifying the goals and objectives of governments and how these could be met, with specific commitments under the GATS being one element of the latter.

Mobilising and allocating aid for services trade

Prospects for mobilising the needed assistance have increased with the support that has been expressed for the idea of allocating additional aid to support trade capacity.[10] In Hong Kong a number of specific commitments were made by donors to expand allocations for trade assistance. There is still considerable uncertainty as to how aid for trade is best operationalised. Numerous questions need to be addressed, including how resources should be managed and allocated, which countries will be eligible, and what the role of the WTO and the various development institutions should be.[11]

Whatever is agreed on the allocation mechanisms and modalities, much of the aid for trade agenda at the country level, in our view, revolves around improving the quality and cost of services. The agenda goes far beyond technical assistance to help countries make market access commitments – the focus of the status quo (as illustrated for example by the language on technical assistance for services negotiations in the Hong Kong Ministerial declaration). The agenda spans not just technical assistance for regulatory strengthening but resources to strengthen services-related infrastructure. As discussed previously, to benefit from trade opportunities, many developing countries must bolster the competitiveness of firms and the farm sector through actions to lower the cost of, and increase access to, services such as energy, transport, finance, and communications. This, in turn, requires a mix of policy reforms and investments in infrastructure, training, institutional development, and the like.

The types of intervention that will have the most effect in increasing the gains from liberalisation are unlikely to be uniform across countries. For example, Barth et al. (2006) offer a recent – indeed, the first – comprehensive cross-country assessment of the impact of bank regulation on the operation of banks, and assess the validity of the Basel Committee's influential approach to bank regulation. They conclude that viewing the reform of bank regulation and supervision as a narrow technical issue is risky because the impact of bank regulation reflects host countries' complex economic and political institutions. They find no evidence that any single set of 'best practices' is appropriate for promoting well-functioning banks in every country. Furthermore, their results suggest that the conventional prescriptions of empowering direct official supervision of banks and strengthening capital standards may be ineffectual. Indeed, it may even have perverse results. A key finding is that fortifying official supervisory oversight and disciplinary powers actually impedes the efficient operation of banks, increases corruption in lending, and therefore hurts the effectiveness of capital allocation without any corresponding improvement in bank stability. Their conclusion that societies that emphasise market-based monitoring of banks enjoy superior outcomes may be open to question, but there is no questioning the powerful cautionary message that there are few well-established and standardised prescriptions for bank regulation. There is need, therefore, for a high degree of country specificity in both diagnosis and remedial action.

Supporting regional co-operation on services

For small countries in particular there may be economies of scale that can be realised through regulatory co-operation – harmonisation or mutual recognition of qualifications, technical standards, prudential regulation, and so on. Technical assistance could be used to determine 'what, where, and how much'. For example, should regulations in, say, professional services be harmonised first within a subset of, say, Common Market for Eastern and Southern Africa (COMESA) countries, on a COMESA-wide basis, or directly vis-à-vis the EU (in the context of the future Economic Partnership Agreement), or not at all? To some extent the needs confronting governments with respect to regional co-operation are similar to those that arise in the GATS context: whether to bind (in some or all dimensions) immediate or gradual market opening, or not to bind at all. But much of the agenda at a regional level will span issues that are not relevant to a multilateral context – for example, 'local' cross-border spill-overs or club goods such as roads and shared ports, joint tourism marketing, development of regional infrastructure hubs, and the like.

For smaller countries, regulatory co-operation may allow the substantial fixed costs associated with regulatory bodies to be shared. For example, in basic telecommunications, apart from spectrum monitoring equipment, computers, and programs, there is the cost of professional assistance for activities such as interconnection, cost estimation and spectrum management. An example is the Eastern Caribbean Telecommunications Authority (ECTEL), the first regional telecommunications authority in the world. Although the member countries retain their sovereign power over licensing and regulation, ECTEL provides technical expertise, advice, and support for national regulations. Apart from the economies of scale in establishing a common regulator, there are at least three other advantages. It will promote the development of harmonised and transparent regulation in the region, allow for a greater degree of independence (and hence credibility) in regulatory advice, and enhance bargaining power in negotiations with incumbents and potential entrants.

Improving domestic access to better services

Improving regulation is important but the payoffs to the associated investments are a function of the private sector response. For the poorest countries in particular, this response may be muted and take a long time to materialise. Moreover, structural factors such as economic size or location may imply that some countries or parts of countries will not be attractive enough to induce entry by private firms, whether foreign or domestic. Or the market may be too small to allow vigorous competition.

Such situations could be addressed to some extent by targeting aid for trade on service providers to encourage them to provide services in remote and disadvantaged regions in poor countries and/or to lower the prices of such services below what would be needed to cover costs. In our view this could be an important dimension of an effective 'aid for trade' strategy to complement and support multilateral trade reforms. Here we are not thinking of fiscal investment or entry incentives of the type offered by virtually all developing countries to foreign investors. These are costly and in any event of dubious value in so far as incentives are generally not conditional on performance requirements of the type we are envisaging here. Instead, the idea is to use development aid funds to induce services firms – foreign or nationally owned – to provide specific services to households that otherwise would not be served.

The experience of a number of countries in a number of sectors has improved our understanding of the universal access policies that must complement market-based reforms to ensure improved access for the poor at least in infrastructure services. In network industries such as telecommunications or electricity, private providers could compete for performance-based subsidies related to providing services to the poor.[12] This would ensure that the poor reap some of the benefits of competition, and allow the government to discover the true cost of service provision. For instance, in Chile, government subsidies equivalent to less than 0.5 per cent of total telecommunications revenue, allocated through competitive bidding in 1995, mobilised 20 times as much private investment to extend basic telephone services to rural areas (Wellenius, 2000).

An international arrangement that replicates the key elements of successful national schemes may be one way to use additional aid for trade resources to increase support for pro-competitive reforms. This could involve countries (or regions) that are willing to eliminate barriers to investment both being given assistance to put in place the necessary regulatory reforms *and* being granted access to a 'universal service provision fund' in instances where the investment response from domestic and foreign firms had been inadequate. The fund would provide a subsidy to firms to create infrastructure and/or provide services in the relevant region or country at pre-specified terms. Along the lines of the policies put in place in Chile and several other countries, these terms could be established as the result of an auction or bidding process under which firms would indicate the minimum level of subsidy they would require to fulfil the mandate set out by the government. Note that this form of assistance does not target specific industries or firms, as would industrial policies or trade preferences. Rather, the objective would be to improve the availability and quality of services for all firms, farms, and households.[13]

Conclusions

Numerous recent assessments of the impact of ambitious global trade policy reform (liberalisation) on poverty have concluded that the associated relative price changes will generally benefit the poor disproportionately, including the poor in the poorest countries.[14] Agriculture is very important here – the best available global models clearly reveal that most of the gains in the area of trade reform for goods will be due to agriculture. But the global models neglect what may well be the greatest source of potential gains from trade liberalisation: services.

The Doha negotiations on services are not making much progress. In part this is because liberalisation of trade in goods has been central to much of the discussion to date – there has been less interest in, and thus less attention given to, the services agenda. The neglect matters. Foreign services suppliers can do much to improve competitiveness and consumer welfare in developing countries by providing a greater variety of high-quality services at lower prices. The costs of neglecting services are both direct – less being done through the Doha Round to improve services policies – and indirect – reducing the incentives for the EU and other industrialised countries to do more on agriculture.

There is much that can and should be done through the WTO on services, but this will require a change in approach and emphasis. The focus to date on negotiating market access commitments (liberalisation) on a quid pro quo basis does not do enough to generate the political economy support or incentives needed for countries to take a strong interest in the services talks. This is true especially for small, poor countries that do not offer much in the way of an attractive market to (potential) foreign suppliers and whose private sector does not perceive significant opportunities to contest foreign service markets. But even for larger countries there are legitimate concerns regarding the ability to put in place the regulatory preconditions to benefit from opening up service markets to greater foreign competition.

Moving forward on multilateral services, liberalisation arguably requires a change in negotiating modalities. Shifting from bilateral request–offer methods to a model schedule approach that sets ambitious objectives – full national treatment for the major backbone services – may improve prospects for achieving a more ambitious Doha Round outcome. But a precondition for achieving agreement on an ambitious focal point for the services negotiations is to put in place mechanisms that will bolster pro-competitive regulation and strengthen regulatory authorities in developing countries. It is here that the WTO could play a much more prominent role, both through a shift towards 'model schedules' to define more relevant sectoral commitments and by helping to mobilise the technical and financial assistance that is needed to improve regulatory capacity in poor countries.

Many countries need assistance to put in place the regulatory mechanisms that can help ensure the potential benefits from liberalisation are realised. Such assistance needs to go beyond the public sector in developing countries and be used to attract investment more directly into the poorest countries and generate the incentives for firms to provide services in markets and areas that otherwise would not be served in poor countries. There is great potential for OECD countries to do good – to assist developing countries to benefit from services-related reforms – while also doing well in terms of obtaining better access to developing country markets. The comparative advantage of the WTO in this connection is to act as a focal point, a mechanism to increase transparency and accountability both in developing countries as regards policies and outcomes and in industrialised countries in terms of the assistance that has been granted.

Notes

The authors are grateful to Dominique Njinkeu and Sheila Page for very helpful comments on an early draft. The chapter draws in part on the findings of a research programme supported by the UK Department for International Development (DFID). More detailed analysis and background papers on a number of the issues discussed in this chapter can be found at www.ycsg.yale.edu (Global Trade and Financial Architecture) and http://econ.worldbank. org/programs/trade. The views expressed are personal and should not be attributed to the World Bank.

1   See, for example, Anderson and Martin (2006) and Hertel and Winters (2005).
2   The model schedule approach already has a track record in the GATS, having been used in the Understanding on Financial Services, the Telecommunications Reference Paper, and the Model Schedule for Maritime Transport. In each case the premise was that agreement on standardised commitments would secure a higher level of commitment overall than if members devised their liberalisation offers independently.
3   See, for example, Mattoo and Wüntsch (2004) and Chaudhuri, Mattoo, and Self (2004).
4   From an economic perspective the focus could be on the key 'backbone' sectors – the services that are inputs into all other economic activities: transport, distribution/logistics, telecommunications, financial services, and education as well as on sectors and modes where developing countries have an export interest. We would also argue in favour of a relatively aggregated approach, focusing on 2-digit sectors so as to reduce negotiation and transactions costs and to minimise uncertainty regarding the coverage of new or unclassified services at a more disaggregated level.
5   This was the figure used in the negotiations on the Information Technology Agreement – see Hoekman and Kostecki (2001).
6   In the international relations or game theory literature a k-group is used to describe the minimum number of countries ('K') out of a larger set ('N') that internalise enough of the total potential gains from co-operation to make it feasible (that is, despite the fact that the remaining N–K players will free-ride).
7   We should stress that these types of arrangements constitute managed trade and are certainly not first-best. The suggestions are instead pragmatic ones that in our view

would lead to a Pareto-improving outcome given the political constraints that restrict the feasibility of implementing superior policies.

8 The objective of the TPRM is 'achieving greater transparency in, and understanding of, the trade policies and practices of Members . . . [through] the regular collective appreciation and evaluation of the full range of individual Members' trade policies and practices and their impact on the functioning of the multilateral trading system. It is not, however, intended to serve as a basis for the enforcement of specific obligations under the Agreements or for dispute settlement procedures, or to impose new policy commitments on Members' (Annex 3, WTO). Annex 3 WTO, Section B states further that 'Members recognize the inherent value of domestic transparency of government decision-making on trade policy matters . . . and agree to encourage and promote greater transparency within their own systems, acknowledging that the implementation of domestic transparency must be on a voluntary basis and take account of each Member's legal and political systems'.

9 The type of model we have in mind is discussed in more general terms in Hoekman (2005). As discussed there, the process would need to involve national regulators and economic policymakers – that is, extend beyond the trade officials representing countries at the WTO.

10 An important first step towards mobilising additional resources to address such needs and bolster trade capacity was the commitment by the G8 Heads of Government in 2005 to increase aid to developing countries to build physical, human, and institutional capacity to trade, and to grant additional support for trade capacity-building, to take advantage of the new opportunities to trade that will result from a positive conclusion of the Doha Round. At the September 2005 IMF/World Bank annual meetings, Ministers endorsed the need to expand aid resources to bolster trade capacity in developing countries.

11 See Prowse (2006) for an in-depth discussion of issues and options.

12 But the picture is far less clear in other, especially social, services. We do not know whether this is because these services are inherently different, for example because performance is so much more difficult to measure, or because governments have justifiably been far less adventurous in experimenting with new policies in these areas.

13 In the case of trade preferences, proposals have been made to shift towards financial instruments, on both efficiency and systemic grounds, and as a mechanism to compensate beneficiary countries for the erosion of the value of preferences as MFN barriers are lowered. The services proposals made in this chapter could also be part of an effort to address preferences erosion losses, but they are primarily focused on the set of countries that have not been able to utilise preferences as a result of supply constraints.

14 See, for example, the various papers in Hertel and Winters (2006) and Hoekman and Olarreaga (2007).

References

Anderson, Kym, and Martin, Will (eds) (2006), *Agricultural Trade Reform and the Doha Development Agenda* (Basingstoke: Palgrave Macmillan, and Washington, DC: World Bank).

Balat, Jorge F., Brambilla, Irene, and Porto, Guido G. (2007) 'An Analysis of the WTO Development Round on Poverty in Rural and Urban Zambia', in Bernard Hoekman and Marcelo Olarreaga (eds), *Impacts and Implications of Global Trade Reform on Poverty* (Washington, DC: Brookings Institution, Sciences Politiques, and Yale Center for the Study of Globalization).

Barth, James R., Caprio, Gerard Jr, and Levine, Ross (2006), *Rethinking Bank Regulation: Till Angels Govern* (Cambridge: Cambridge University Press).

Chaudhuri, Sumanta, Mattoo, Aaditya, and Self, Richard (2004), 'Moving People to Deliver Services: How Can the WTO help?', World Bank Policy Research Working Paper 3238 (March).

Eschenbach, Felix, and Hoekman, Bernard (2006), 'Services Policy Reform and Economic Growth in Transition Economies, 1990–2004', *Weltwirtschaftliches Archiv*, 142: 4.

Hertel, Thomas, and Winters, L. Alan (2005), 'Estimating the Poverty Impacts of a Prospective Doha Development Agenda', *World Economy*, 28: 8.

Hertel, Thomas, and Winters, L. Alan (eds) (2006), *Poverty and the WTO: Impacts of the Doha Development Agenda* (London and Washington, DC: Palgrave Macmillan and World Bank).

Hoekman, Bernard (1996), 'Assessing the General Agreement on Trade in Services', in Will Martin and L. Alan Winters (eds), *The Uruguay Round and Developing Economies* (Cambridge: Cambridge University Press).

Hoekman, Bernard (2002), 'Strengthening the Global Trade Architecture for Development: The Post-Doha Agenda', *World Trade Review*, 1: 1 (March).

Hoekman, Bernard (2005), 'Operationalizing the Concept of Policy Space in the WTO: Beyond Special and Differential Treatment', *Journal of International Economic Law*, 8: 2.

Hoekman, Bernard, and Konan, Denise (2001), 'Deep Integration, Nondiscrimination and Euro-Mediterranean Free Trade', in J. von Hagen and M. Widgren (eds), *Regionalism in Europe: Geometries and Strategies* (Dordrecht: Kluwer).

Hoekman, Bernard, and Kostecki, Michel (2001), *The Political Economy of the World Trading System: The WTO and Beyond* (Oxford: Oxford University Press), second edition.

Hoekman, Bernard, and Olarreaga, Marcelo (eds) (2007), *Impacts and Implications of Global Trade Reform on Poverty* (Washington, DC: Brookings Institution, Sciences Politiques, and Yale Center for the Study of Globalization).

Konan, Denise Eby, and Maskus, Keith E. (2004), 'Quantifying the Impact of Services Liberalization in a Developing Country', World Bank Policy Research Working Paper 3193 (January).

Mattoo, Aaditya (2005), 'Services in a Development Round: Three Goals and Three Proposals', *Journal of World Trade*, 39: 6 (December).

Mattoo, Aaditya, and Rathindran, Randeep (2005), 'Does Health Insurance Impede Trade in Health Care Services?', World Bank Policy Research Working Paper 3667 (July).

Mattoo, Aaditya, and Wüntsch, Sasha (2004), 'Pre-empting Protectionism in Services: The WTO and Outsourcing', *Journal of International Economic Law*, 7: 4 (December).

Mattoo, Aaditya, Rathindran, Randeep, and Subramanian, Arvind (2006), 'Measuring Services Trade Liberalization and Its Impact on Economic Growth: An Illustration', *Journal of Economic Integration*, 21: 1 (March).

Nicita, Alessandro (2006), 'Ethiopia', in Bernard Hoekman and Marcelo Olarreaga (eds), *Global Trade Liberalization and Poor Countries: Poverty Impacts and Policy Implications* (Paris: Institut d'Etudes Politiques).

Prowse, Susan (2006), '"Aid for Trade": Increasing Support for Trade Adjustment and Integration – a Proposal', in S. Evenett and B. Hoekman (eds), *Economic Development and Multilateral Cooperation* (Basingstoke: Palgrave Macmillan).

Schelling, Thomas (1978), *Micromotives and Macrobehavior* (New York: W. W. Norton).

United Nations Conference on Trade and Development and World Health Organisation (1998), *International Trade in Health Services: A Development Perspective*. Geneva: UNCTAD/ITVD/TSB/5; WHO/TFHE/98.1.

Walmsley, T. L., and Winters, L. A. (2003), 'Relaxing the Restrictions on the Temporary Movements of Natural Persons: A Simulation Analysis', CEPR Discussion Paper 3719, CEPR, London.

Wellenius, Bjorn (2000), 'Extending Telecommunications beyond the Market: Toward Universal Service in Competitive Environments', Public Policy for the Private Sector, Note 206, The World Bank, Finance, Private Sector, and Infrastructure Network.

Winters, L. Alan (2004), 'GATS Mode 4: The Temporary Movement of Natural Persons'. www.ycsg.yale.edu.

Part III
Principal players

6 How the poor pay for the US trade deficit

And why it matters for the Doha Development Agenda

James Scott

Recent years have seen the US trade deficit rise to unprecedented levels, generating a great deal of concern about the state of the US economy. Much of the response has been based on a profound misunderstanding of the true causes of the trade deficit, namely the disparity between savings and investment rates and the large fiscal deficit. It is not, however, the first time a burgeoning trade deficit has caused political angst. In the 1980s too a large trade deficit emerged, and the period holds interesting parallels to what is happening today. In both cases tackling the underlying causes of the deficit has been effectively politically blocked, leading to a shifting of the blame to other countries. The response of the Reagan administration in the 1980s was twofold: one bilateral, the second multilateral. Bilaterally, the deficit was used to extract concessions from individual countries, particularly Japan, that were claimed to be pursuing 'unfair' trade practices. Multilaterally, it was used to push for the launch of a new Round of trade negotiations in the GATT. This Round, the Uruguay Round, was framed in a certain way by the trade deficit in that other countries were placed in a position of having to deal with the US in the GATT to escape more protectionist policies from a belligerent Congress, tempering what other countries felt they could demand from the US. It also meant that the US had little to give away by way of concessions. The outcome was consequently one-sided, imposing large costs on developing countries, much of which were of direct benefit to industrialised countries, while giving them little in return.

In the present day something strikingly similar is happening. The mounting trade deficit is being used to extract concessions from other countries – although now it is China (rather than Japan) that is the target for particular demonisation. Just as Japan faced in the 1980s, there is pressure from the US on China to revalue its currency, to open its markets to US goods, and to implement more stringent intellectual property protection. These policies are pushed by the US supposedly to reduce the trade deficit, but in reality they would have little, if any, effect on it since they do not address the underlying causes. Concessions by China may partially rebalance the US–China bilateral deficit but any such reduction would be balanced by a concomitant rise in the deficit the US holds with other countries. In the multilateral setting the trade deficit is a key factor in the current negotiations in the WTO, the Doha Development Agenda (DDA). While the DDA was supposed to be skewed towards the interests of developing countries to redress the imbalance of previous Rounds, this outcome is increasingly unlikely while the US trade deficit continues to be the context in which the US delegation participates in the negotiations. The US is politically unable to agree to anything that would exacerbate the trade deficit, or that would be perceived to do so by a belligerent Congress. Consequently, a result of the DDA skewed towards the interests of developing countries is highly unlikely.

The chapter begins with an examination of what the causes of trade deficits are, and where the solution to their reduction lies. This section shows that the deficit is primarily the result of US domestic issues, particularly the low personal savings rate exacerbated by the fiscal deficit. To contextualise US posturing in the DDA the chapter then examines the experience of the 1980s, the bilateral response of the Reagan administration, and the Uruguay Round. The results of the Uruguay Round are examined, paying particular attention to the benefits and costs to developing countries. The chapter then goes on to examine the present day, focusing on the US trade deficit with China. Finally, the chapter turns to the impact of the US trade deficit on the DDA and its bearing on the development content of the Round.

The trade deficit in the 1980s

A plethora of reasons have been put forward to explain the US trade deficits that ballooned in the 1980s and in the 2000s, many of them flatly contradicted by economic theory, as shown below. To understand the reasons underlying the trade deficit, it is best to look at some accounting identities. Accounting identities detail how a country's money is being used and where it is coming from. In any economy, total leakages (that is, money leaving the economy) must equal total injections (that is, money entering the economy). Money enters the economy in three ways – investment, government spending, and export revenue. Likewise, money leaves an economy in three ways – savings, taxation, and to pay for imports. By putting these together and using the fact that leakages must equal injections we get the following equation:

$$\text{Investment} + \text{Government Spending} + \text{Exports} = \text{Savings} + \text{Taxation} + \text{Imports}$$

The trade deficit is the difference between exports and imports, so by making a slight rearrangement to this equation we get:

$$\text{Exports} - \text{Imports} = \text{Savings} - \text{Investment} + \text{Taxation} - \text{Government Spending}$$

From this we can see that if government spending exceeds tax revenues (that is, there is a fiscal deficit) and the investment rate exceeds the savings rate, these imbalances will necessarily be manifest in a trade deficit. Naturally, a fiscal deficit can be counterbalanced by a savings surplus over investment, or a fiscal surplus can offset a savings rate that is lower than the investment rate, leading to a balance of exports and imports, but when the two do not balance each other a trade deficit is inevitable. What is particularly noteworthy about this equation is that it makes no reference to the exchange rate. Fluctuations in the exchange rate will affect the trade balance only to the extent to which they affect the four elements on the right side of the equation above (see Clarida, 1989, for a discussion of this and possible mechanisms through which this effect takes place).

Using this equation, we can understand the huge rise in the US trade deficit that occurred in the 1980s. When Ronald Reagan came to power in 1981 he instigated dramatic cuts in tax rates, with an across-the-board 25 per cent cut in 1981 and further cuts later in his presidency. These were concentrated on the rich, who saw the top rate of federal income tax fall from 70 per cent to 28 per cent. The cuts were combined with an expansion of government spending, notably including a doubling of the defence budget between 1981 and 1989, although this was partly offset by cuts in the federal budget elsewhere, such as in social security spending (Niskanen and Moore, 1996).

Savings rates during the 1980s failed to keep pace with investment rate growth, despite high interest rates, as shown in Figure 6.1. Figure 6.1 shows that the gap between savings and investment rates increased significantly over the 1980s. When combined with the fiscal deficit, the result was a huge trade deficit, which mushroomed from $19.4 billion in 1980 to a peak of $153 billion in 1987 (see Figure 6.2).

A country's trade deficit must be financed somehow (that is, there must be a source of revenue to pay for importing more goods than are being exported. Otherwise, other countries would stop selling to the country with the deficit because

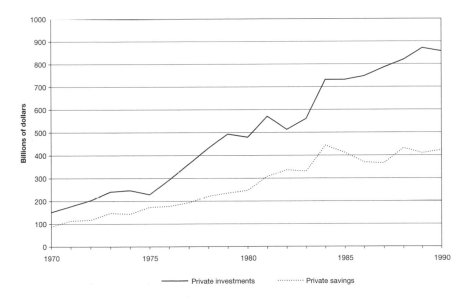

Figure 6.1 US savings and investment rates 1970–90

Source: US Department of Commerce Bureau of Economic Analysis

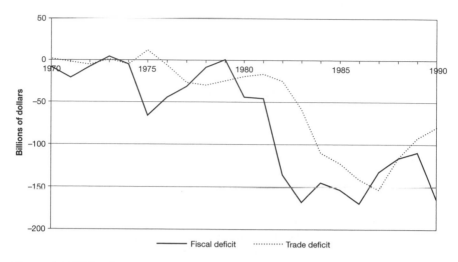

Figure 6.2 US fiscal and trade deficits 1970–90

Source: US Department of Commerce Bureau of Economic Analysis

there would be no money to pay them). To finance a trade deficit, countries must borrow money. In some cases this comes from overseas.[1] The US trade deficit of the 1980s was financed by investment from other countries, particularly Japan, attracted by high US interest rates and good investment opportunities. The removal by the Japanese government of certain controls on foreign investment helped to recycle Japanese savings into the US economy (Baldwin, 1989: 130). Over the four years from 1975 to 1978, foreign direct investment (FDI) in the US totalled $18.5 billion. Between 1981 and 1987 it averaged $22.9 billion *per year* (Panitch and Gindin, 2005: 63).

The US response

Any solution to the problem of the trade deficit would have to come from addressing one or both of the underlying causes – that is, ameliorating the fiscal deficit and/or the deficiency of the savings rate with respect to investment. Interest rates during this period were high as a result of the 'Volcker shock' – the self-imposed structural adjustment programme initiated by the Chair of the Federal Reserve, Paul Volcker, in order to bring the high inflation of the 1970s under control and to break the wage militancy of US labour. Volcker placed limits on the growth of the money supply and allowed interest rates to rise to whatever level was necessary to curb inflation (interest rates rose from 8 per cent in 1978 to over 19 per cent in 1981) (Panitch and Gindin, 2005: 60–64). With interest rates already high, there was no room to stimulate savings. Cutting investment would have dealt a blow to an already ailing economy. The only available method for reducing the trade deficit therefore lay in balancing the fiscal budget, but this was politically difficult. Reagan had pledged in his election campaign not to raise taxes and was ideologically opposed to the idea anyway. He believed (or at least claimed to believe[2]) that cutting federal tax rates would *increase* government tax revenue through what has become known as supply side economics, associated with the work of Arthur Laffer (see Canto et al., 1982), Robert Mundell and Jude Wanniski (1978). This is the counterintuitive idea that taxation removes the incentive for people to work, as they will not receive sufficient remuneration from their efforts. Lowering the tax rate would therefore stimulate people to work more, leading to a large increase in national income. When this extra income is taxed, even at the new lower rate, government revenue is larger than the previous higher taxation of a smaller income (see Krugman, 1994, for an examination of the emergence, and a thorough debunking, of this idea).

Without the option of increasing taxes, the only remaining policy for cutting the fiscal deficit was to cut government spending, which was also politically difficult. Reagan was committed to increasing defence spending, with the result that any fiscal cuts would have to come from the social security budget. This was, however, opposed by Congress members, who feared a backlash among their constituents. All options for tackling the trade deficit were therefore politically blocked; but it could not simply be ignored. As a consequence, both the President and Congress turned to blaming foreigners for maintaining 'unfair' trade practices and for not having sufficiently open markets for US goods (Baldwin, 1989: 130).

The bilateral setting

This turn towards blaming other countries led to the resurrection of Section 301 of the US Trade Act, which became the favoured method of exerting bilateral pressure on countries deemed to be contributing to the trade deficit. Section 301 allowed the President to impose sanctions on countries that were unilaterally determined to be pursuing 'unfair' trade practices. It had originally been passed in 1974 but started to be used only in 1985 (Preeg, 1995: 79). In 1988 it was strengthened with a widening of the definition of unfair practices and the inclusion of 'super' and 'special' 301 provisions. Super 301 allowed the President to push for changes in systemic unfair trade practices of targeted countries, while Special 301 was focused on countries that did not provide 'sufficient' intellectual property protection.

Japan, with which the largest proportion of the trade deficit lay, was the principal target for action under Section 301 between 1985 and 1990, although India, Brazil, South Korea, and others were also targets (see Noland, 1997: 368). In response to pressure from the US, Japan initiated a number of reforms aimed at reducing the bilateral deficit between the two. In 1981 Japan adopted a package of measures to open up its market; and in 1982 it adopted a new package that addressed significant non-tariff barriers to US goods. Between 1984 and 1986 the dollar dropped by 40–50 per cent against the yen in a joint effort between the two countries to manipulate their currencies in order to cut the trade imbalance (Green and Larson, 1987: 22).

Despite these measures, however, the trade deficit between the two continued to climb throughout the 1980s, as did the level of blame levelled at Japan for the US's performance. Illustrative of the blaming of Japan is Green and Larson's (1987) response to the ineffectiveness of these measures. They put this down to Japan failing to go far enough, suggesting that 'Japan will not voluntarily sacrifice its strategic domestic targeting for the sake of the US trade deficit' and that Japan has 'absolutely no incentive to import the most competitive products manufactured by American companies' (Green and Larson, 1987: 22). Their suggested remedy, like that of many Congress members, was to close the US market to Japanese goods. 'If the Japanese do not intend to open their doors to us, we can no longer afford to keep ours wide open to them' (Green and Larson, 1987: 28).

Within Congress, legislation was proposed in 1985 to apply a tariff surcharge on goods from Japan until such time as Japan eliminated barriers to US exports (see Library of Congress, 2006). Claims that the US economy was 'wide open' to Japanese exports were at the very least historically contentious, since there had been a long history of discrimination in the GATT by most (if not all) industrialised countries, including the US, against the exports of Japan, particularly in textiles and clothing but also in virtually every sector in which Japan achieved a significant comparative advantage (for the standard account of early discrimination towards Japan's entry into the GATT see Patterson, 1966: 271–322). None the less, the perception in Congress and elsewhere was that Japan had industrialised through an aggressive export strategy, making use of the open US market while refusing to import US-made products.

The reason why the measures undertaken by Japan failed to address the trade deficit was that they were based on a misconception of what caused it. As examined in the opening section, the origin of the trade deficit lay in the disparity between savings and investment and the excess of government spending over revenue. The only way in which the deficit could be reduced was to address these underlying imbalances. The measures imposed on Japan had only an indirect effect on these imbalances and consequently they failed to have the desired effect.

The multilateral setting

Perhaps more significantly, what these Section 301 actions also led to was a growing acceptance of the US push for a new Round of trade negotiations to be undertaken in the GATT. Other countries preferred to deal with the US within the multilateral setting of the GATT rather than bilaterally since in bilateral negotiations their political and economic weakness vis-à-vis the US was profound (Ostry, 2000: 3). The US began the process of setting the agenda for a new Round in 1981, getting agreement from the GATT Contracting Parties to hold a ministerial meeting the following year (Preeg, 1995: 31). This began five years of political manoeuvring over what topics should be negotiated in the new Round, culminating eventually in the formal decision to launch the Uruguay Round taken in Punte del Este in 1986. The US pushed for a strengthening of the GATT's provisions on agriculture and an extension of the GATT's remit into new areas in which the Americans had a comparative advantage, namely services, intellectual property, and investment. Domestic intellectual property provisions and investment regulations were only dubiously linked to the GATT's remit (which was exclusively trade) so they had 'Trade Related' appended to the front to give Trade-Related Intellectual Property Rights (TRIPs) and Trade-Related Investment Measures (TRIMs) respectively.

Initially, the move to launch a new Round was resisted fiercely by developing countries. Many developing countries opposed the expansion of the GATT's agenda, particularly into services, and wanted any new Round to focus on addressing the historical concerns they had with the institution (such as the exclusion of textiles and clothing from normal GATT coverage, the exclusion of products of export interest to them from tariff cuts in previous Rounds, and restrictions imposed by developed countries on the import of tropical products), and to roll back the increasing protectionism being applied by the industrialised countries (Croome, 1999: 17, 24). The EU was initially unenthusiastic about the prospect of new trade negotiations because it knew that it would face unwelcome pressure to reform the Common Agricultural Policy (CAP). The US set about applying a battery of arm-twisting techniques to grind down resistance to a new Round, including threats of action under Section 301 and threats to move to bilateral agreements if the GATT failed to address US concerns (Wiener, 1995: 97–116). Faced with the prospect of having to negotiate with the US bilaterally and with an increasingly belligerent US Congress seeking to blame others for the growth of the trade deficit, developing countries preferred to negotiate in the multilateral forum offered by the GATT.

The large US deficits also helped indirectly to push developing countries to the negotiating table. The Reagan administration turned the US from the world's largest creditor into the largest debtor, pushing up global interest rates. This was exacerbated by the 'Volcker shock'. Higher interest rates had a terrible effect on highly indebted developing countries. Many developing countries had built up large debts in the 1970s as recycled petro-dollars deposited in Western banks were lent to them to finance development programmes and the increased cost of oil imports. Initially these loans were being made at negative real interest rates as the inflation rate was higher than the interest rate, but as interest rates rose in the early 1980s developing countries found themselves unable to maintain rising interest repayments. Their ensuing balance-of-payments crises led many to undertake IMF-dictated structural adjustment programmes, which included implementing unilateral trade liberalisation. GATT negotiations were built around the notion of reciprocity, by which tariff cuts were used as bargaining chips to be exchanged for trade concessions from other countries. Unilateral liberalisation effectively reduced a country's bargaining strength in subsequent negotiations by reducing its bargaining chips. Those countries that had undertaken such unilateral liberalisation therefore sought recognition of this through retrospective trade concessions from other countries, but these could be delivered only in a new trade round. Turning the US into a sink for global savings in order to finance the US current account deficit therefore inadvertently helped to drive developing countries to the negotiating table largely against their will.

The results of the Uruguay Round showed that developing countries were right to have been sceptical of the process. The 'Grand Bargain', as it was termed by

Sylvia Ostry (2000; also see Chapter 2 above), between developed and developing countries, in which developed countries undertook to phase out the Multi-Fibre Agreement (MFA), bringing textiles and clothing into the GATT regime, and to liberalise their agricultural trade, while developing countries agreed to services, TRIPs, TRIMs, and further market access for non-agricultural goods, was not a balanced agreement. The inequalities in negotiating capacity are well documented, but the context in which the US negotiated the Round must also be borne in mind when explaining the biased outcome. The trade deficit and the protectionist bent it gave Congress served to frame the negotiations in a particular way. As Wiener puts it, the US

> approached the Uruguay Round as a demandeur across the board, from market access to services and from intellectual property to agriculture, yet with a trade deficit of over $150 billion it had little to offer in return. The US could cause the collapse of the GATT system by opting out, but could contribute to its maintenance only by forcing others to renew it.
>
> (Wiener, 1995: 130)

Inevitably the position the US adopted (of demanding concessions in many areas from other countries because of its perception that the world economy was biased against its interests while being unable or unwilling to grant concessions in return) had a marked effect on the balance of the Uruguay outcome. In agriculture the agreement made between the US and EU in a series of closed, bilateral meetings made at Blair House in Washington (see Wiener, 1995: 191–215; Preeg, 1995: 143–147; Coleman et al. 1997: 464) stipulated a reduction in export subsidies of 21 per cent, a reduction in aggregate domestic support provided to farmers of 20 per cent, and full tariffication of agricultural non-tariff barriers, along with a reduction of those tariffs. The details, however, showed a significant derogation from the intentions of the agreement. The base year used in the process of tariffication gave an unusually high level of protection, which was exacerbated by the 'dirty tariffication' used by many countries, by which tariff rates posted were significantly higher than dictated by the agreed conversion process. The consequence was that there was 'markedly little liberalisation for most products in most countries . . . Apart from Japan, the highly protected markets in OECD countries were liberalised little if at all' (Hathaway and Ingco, 1995: 8). Similarly, the base-years used for calculating the level of subsidies (1986–90) were chosen to give an unusually high initial level from which the cuts were to be made, giving both the EU and the US considerable slack between the bound and applied rates of support (Wiener, 1995: 174). As a consequence, industrialised countries' support to their agricultural sectors has subsequently increased from 31 per cent of gross farm receipts in 1997 to 40 per cent in 1999 without violating the Agreement on Agriculture (OECD, 2000). Since then the 2002 US Farm Bill brought into effect an 80 per cent increase in subsidies to its farmers but was still in compliance with the letter, if not the spirit, of the agreement (Watkins, 2002).

The detrimental effect such policies have on developing countries is well documented (see, for instance, Oxfam, 2002a, 2002b). While some constraints have been placed on the behaviour of the largest agricultural supporters, seen through the WTO Dispute Settlement Body (DSB) rulings against EU sugar subsidies (WTO, 2002a, 2002b, 2003) and against US cotton subsidies (WTO, 2004), there was little 'bite' to the Agreement on Agriculture. Furthermore, the provision that negotiations for further liberalisation would begin by 2000 was never going to be anything other than vacuous, given the way the GATT was structured to undertake liberalisation in Rounds.

The Agreement on Textiles and Clothing (ATC) was similarly compromised by the details. The opening of industrialised countries' markets was heavily back-loaded, with 49 per cent of all liberalisation left until the final stage of the ATC phase-in period in 2005. Furthermore, the list of products that had to have quotas removed – included as Annex 1 of the agreement – was packed with products on which there were in fact no restrictions in place. Thus quotas were 'removed' from such items as tyre cords (Canada), ties (the EU) and tents (the US) (Baughman et al., 1997: 408), while almost all politically sensitive items – namely those that would face the greatest competitive pressures from developing country exports and would therefore be of most benefit to developing countries – were left to the final tranche. These spurious items included in Annex 1 which had never been subject to trade restrictions accounted for 47, 34, and 37 per cent of the total 1990 imports for Canada, the EU, and the US respectively (Bagchi, 1994: 36, cited in Baughman et al., 1997: 411).

What developing countries received from the Uruguay Round was therefore severely limited. What they gave away in the Grand Bargain was highly costly. Implementation of the agreements on TRIPs, Sanitary and Phyto-sanitary Standards, and on Customs Valuation was estimated to cost a total of $150 million, representing more than a full year's development budget for many countries, while failing to address the most pressing problems developing countries faced in these areas (Finger and Schuler, 2000: 525). TRIPs alone represented a direct transfer from poor countries to rich of $8.3 billion a year to only six industrialised countries, with the US accounting for $5.8 billion (Srinivasan, 2002: 28, citing Maskus, 2000).

TRIMs meanwhile have prohibited many of the conditions on investment used extensively by industrialised countries during their periods of industrialisation, such as local content requirements, technology-sharing, limitations on local borrowing, export requirements, and so on (see, for instance, Low and Subramanian, 1995: 417). This, it has been argued, is an institutionalised form of List's 'kicking away the ladder' by shrinking the development policies countries have available (Wade, 2003: 632).

The services agreement – the General Agreement on Trade in Services (GATS) – committed signatory countries to ongoing negotiations to progressively liberalise their services markets. This extends the WTO's remit into an area that is critical to the overall performance of the economy, but which is often under-developed in poor countries, making domestic companies unable to compete with foreign competitors. Furthermore, GATS has been used by the US and EU to put pressure on developing countries to liberalise inappropriate sectors of their economy, such as water provision. In many cases this has led to large price increases for water and sanitation provision, putting them beyond the means of poorer sections of the population (World Development Movement, 2003: 22–31).

Economic analyses made after the completion of the Round confirm the inequity of the bargain. The UNDP (1997: 82), for instance, estimated that in the six years following the completion of the Uruguay Round (1995–2001) the 48 least developed countries would be made worse off by approximately $600 million a year and sub-Saharan Africa would be worse off by $1.2 billion a year, despite the Uruguay Round increasing global income by between $212 and $510 billion (see also Stiglitz and Charlton, 2004: 11–12).

We see, then, that the growth of the US trade deficit in the 1980s was blamed on the 'unfair' trade practices of other countries, and was a significant impetus in the drive by the US to get the rest of the world to undertake multilateral trade negotiations in the GATT. The result was the extraction of costly concessions from developing countries in a one-sided bargain that left some of the poorest countries in the world significantly worse off. The present time is showing remarkable parallels.

The present time

The trade deficit, while never returning to a complete balance, began to fall significantly from 1987, reached a trough in 1991 where it almost broke even, before beginning a virtually uninterrupted climb again up to the present. President George W. Bush has overseen a turnaround in Federal spending from a 2 per cent fiscal surplus that he inherited from Clinton to a 4 per cent deficit (see Figure 6.3). However, the real driving force behind the climbing trade deficit this time around has been the comparative decline in private savings rate, while investment has continued to grow at a reasonably constant rate (see Figure 6.4). Figure 6.5 shows that, of this private savings rate, the real fall since 1990 has been in the personal savings rate. Corporate savings have grown over these years but personal savings, which accounted for the largest share of total private savings in 1990, have steadily declined, becoming negative in 2005.[3] The disparity between savings and investment rates, amounting to over $1.5 trillion in 2005, is the principal reason for the current trade deficit. However, it appears that the decline in the savings rate has not occurred across all income brackets but has been driven by a falling savings rate among the richest quintile. A study for the Federal Reserve found that essentially all the decline in the savings rate seen in the 1990s can be attributed to the collapse in savings of the richest 20 per cent of families (Maki and Palumbo, 2001). As Duménil and Lévy (2004: 671) put it: 'The increasing propensity to spend on the part of the richest fraction of households appears as the main, continuous, cause of the decline of US saving rates and of the corresponding external deficits'.

The US is in a unique position with respect to its trade deficit. Any other country running sustained current account deficits would face a declining currency and a

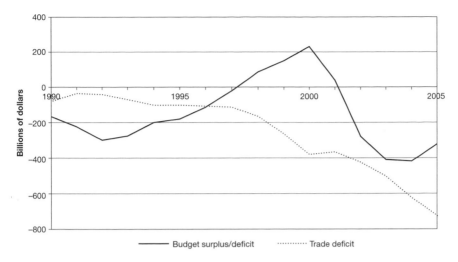

Figure 6.3 US fiscal and trade deficits 1990–2005

Source: US Department of Commerce Bureau of Economic Analysis

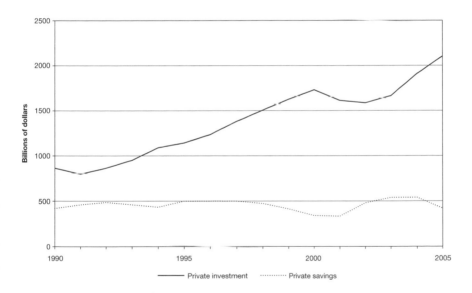

Figure 6.4 US savings and investment rates 1990–2005

Source: US Department of Commerce Bureau of Economic Analysis

decline in its economy, but the centrality of the dollar to the world economy makes the US largely unconstrained by its deficits. The bargain made in 1973 between the US and Saudi Arabia by which the US would tolerate the formation of OPEC if Saudi Arabia guaranteed that all oil transactions must be paid for in

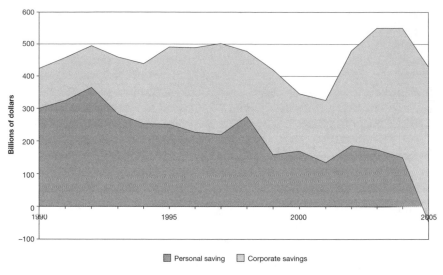

Figure 6.5 US composition of private savings 1990–2005

Source: US Department of Commerce Bureau of Economic Analysis

dollars ensured that the world would have an almost insatiable demand for dollars in order to finance its oil imports. Much of the funding for the US current account deficit has once again come from East Asia, particularly from central banks, which in 2002 accounted for 58 per cent of the world's dollar reserves (Wolf, 2003). China has been central in this. A triangular system has built up whereby China achieves the approximately 8 per cent growth a year it needs (to maintain domestic stability and absorb the migration of workers to urban areas) through exporting manufactured goods to the US; the US consumer is willing to purchase these goods in a consumption boom, even if it means building up more personal debt, financed by a rising housing market; the resulting trade deficit is financed by the Chinese government buying stocks of US bonds. While the flow works at present, and will continue to do so while countries are willing to invest in dollar-denominated debts, in the long term as the burden on the US of mounting debt repayments grows, or as confidence in the dollar diminishes, or even if there is a shift away from using dollars for all oil transactions (as may occur if Iran's plans to create an oil market based in euros take off), something will have to change (see, for instance, Blecker, 1999; Duménil and Lévy, 2004; Rothkopf, 2004).

The bilateral setting

Whereas in the 1980s it was Japan that was blamed primarily for the deficit, now it is China that has become the target of censure from Congress and elsewhere (although there have been many other commentators recognising that simply blaming China is misguided, for instance Stiglitz, 2006; *Washington Post*, 2005c;

Labonte and Makinen, 2004). Official US government figures show a bilateral deficit with China in 2005 of $202 billion (Census Bureau, 2006: 19). However, there is a large disparity between the official figures posted by the US and those posted by China for their mutual bilateral trade deficit, with official Chinese figures putting its surplus with the US at only $114.6 billion (Barboza, 2006). This arises because the US counts Chinese exports to Hong Kong which are then re-exported to the US as imports from China, but it does not count US goods that are first shipped to Hong Kong and then re-exported to China as US exports to China (Zhang, 2000: 312). Such trade through intermediaries is declining but is still a considerable share of total trade. In 2003 approximately 18 per cent of China's total imports from the US came through Hong Kong and approximately 27 per cent of Chinese exports to the US went through Hong Kong (figures calculated using data from Schindler and Beckett, 2005: 47). Furthermore, the US figures attribute the entire value of the products imported from Hong Kong to China, when in fact the Hong Kong intermediary companies accounted in 2003 for approximately 24 per cent of the value of the goods (Schindler and Beckett, 2005: 47; see also Lardy, 1997). Such differences in accounting practices lead to the large discrepancy between the two governments' figures.

It is also unreasonable of critics in the US to place so much attention on the deficit with China because much of the growth of this deficit has come from the relocation of production from Hong Kong, Taiwan, and other Asian countries following the opening of China to FDI. Thus, for example, China's market share of world exports of clothing, toys, sporting goods, and footwear rose from 14 per cent in 1984 to 39 per cent in 1994, but the share of Hong Kong, South Korea, Singapore, and Taiwan combined fell more than China's increase (Lardy, 1997). The single country-of-origin rules do not reflect the true origin of the product either, since the value added in China's production stage is much less than the export value, once inputs have been subtracted (Zhang, 2000: 314–315).

The balance between the two countries is affected also by restrictions placed by the US on exports to China for 'national security' reasons, including a prohibition on nuclear energy technology, high-performance computers, and satellites (Yang et al., 2004: 1048–1051). The export to China of high-performance computer chips (those that operate at or above 2000 million theoretical operations per second) requires a licence. This is not particularly fast – slightly less than two parallel (now outdated) Pentium III processors (Atkinson and Ward, 1999), and nowhere near the performance of the chips found in something like the XBox360 or Playstation 3. The latter is somewhat ironic if Sony follows its previous practice with the Playstations 1 and 2 and has the Playstation 3 assembled in China, giving China access to an abundance of computer chips significantly faster than the threshold requiring a licence for export from the US. These restrictions have meant that a significant amount of Chinese imports has been diverted from US sources to the EU or Japan, exacerbating the US–China trade deficit (Yang et al., 2004).

The bilateral trade deficit between the US and China therefore is not as large as US sources make out, it is exacerbated by self-imposed restrictions on exports to China, and it is not the result of unfair Chinese practices but stems in large measure from the collapse in US personal savings. None the less, the US–China deficit has certainly grown in recent years, and has resulted in heated denunciations of China's policies, focusing on manipulation of the exchange rate, failure to offer sufficient market access for US goods, and failure to offer sufficient intellectual property protection. To take one example, former US Commerce Secretary and US Trade Representative (USTR) Mickey Kantor declared that the US trade deficit is 'the result of unfair practices on the part of China, not only the piracy of US products but also keeping US products out of the Chinese market' (quoted in Yang, 1998: 81). Many articles have appeared in the press on the subject (see, for instance, *New York Times*, 2003, 2006; *The Independent*, 2006; *Washington Post*, 2005b).

A number of actions have been undertaken of a more direct kind. There have been threats to take China to the WTO's DSB for manipulating its currency in order to keep it undervalued against the dollar (despite, as pointed out by Zhang (2000: 319), the fact that following the Asian financial crisis of 1997 China was praised by the US for manipulating its currency to hold the value of the yuan constant while other countries were busy devaluing). On 3 February 2005 two senators, Lindsey Graham and Charles E. Schumer, announced the introduction of a bill which would put tariffs of 27.5 per cent on all Chinese goods in response to the 3 million job losses the two senators claim to have been caused by the trade deficit, and as part of 'a tough-love effort to get the Chinese to stop playing games with their currency in order to level the playing field for American companies trying to compete with goods and services coming from China' (Senate, 2005).

Following discussions with Alan Greenspan and Treasury Secretary John Snow, the two senators decided to postpone the legislation, having had assurances that Beijing would soon allow the value of the yuan to rise (*Washington Post*, 2005a). However, just as the measures undertaken by the Japanese in the 1980s did little to address the bilateral deficit with the US because they did not affect the under-lying causes of the deficit, so any measures that are undertaken by China are likely to have little effect on the current trade deficit it has with the US. A rise in the value of the yuan against the dollar would make Chinese products more expensive to American consumers and US-produced goods cheaper in China, but would have no effect on either the US savings rate or the budget deficit and could in fact stimulate outward investment as US exporters find greater demand in China. Without these underlying imbalances being redressed, the overall US trade deficit would remain at the same level. Although the bilateral deficit with China may be reduced, this would necessarily be compensated by a growth in the US trade deficits with other countries (Stiglitz, 2006).

Pressure on China has nevertheless resulted in a slight loosening of the peg of the yuan to the dollar and a modest revaluation of the yuan along with a number of measures to tackle intellectual property infringement. A number of factories producing pirated CDs have been closed, measures have been taken to improve the border inspections against smuggling of pirated products, restrictions on capital transactions have been partially lifted, and China has opened its market some-what to US software and audio-visual companies (*Financial Times*, 2006a, 2006b; Yang, 1998: 80).

The multilateral setting

As occurred in the 1980s, the trade deficit has had repercussions in the multilateral setting also. A commission was created in 1998 – the US Trade Deficit Review Commission (TDRC) – which produced a report in 2000 detailing the causes and consequences of the trade deficit and providing recommendations for how it should be addressed. In this, one of the recommendations was to launch a new Round of trade negotiations in the WTO, although this policy was supported only by the Republicans on the commission. The Democrats opposed the launching of a new Round unless it included the issues of labour regulation and the environment (TDRC, 2000: 220–221, 208). None the less, the US was not in fact, for the first time in over fifty years of multilateral trade negotiations, the driving force behind the launching of the DDA. It was the EU that provided the greatest impetus towards new negotiations, with the US playing the part of a willing partner (Wilkinson, 2006a: 105–121).

None the less, once again the deficit has had a significant impact on the structure of the negotiations and the likely results. At the time of the launching of the Round, 14 November 2001, the US negotiators did not have fast-track authority,[4] which was passed by the House of Representatives by only one vote on 6 December 2001. Given the increasing deficit and with the extremely close vote in favour of allowing Bush fast-track authority, the US negotiators are once again in a position in which the agreement that they eventually put forward for Congressional approval will have to be of clear, large-scale benefit to the US, just as the Uruguay Round was. At the very least, it must not be seen to exacerbate the alleged 'unfairness' of the system and is likely to be voted down if it makes large concessions in sensitive sectors such as textiles and clothing or steel. The US is once again, to paraphrase Wiener's words quoted above, a demandeur across the board with little to offer in return.

The Doha Round was originally intended to be a 'Development Round', in which the inequities of previous Rounds, particularly the Uruguay Round, were to be (albeit only partially) redressed. It was therefore supposed to be skewed towards the interests of developing countries in the way in which the economic benefits of the Uruguay Round were skewed towards the interests of the industrialised countries, as noted above. Originally it had a target completion date of the end of 2005, but, as with past negotiations, that deadline has proved to be unrealistic. The real deadline is taken to be the expiry of fast-track authority in May 2007 – even though this now looks optimistic (Wilkinson, 2006b: 300–301).

While there is still some way to go with the negotiations, the overall content of the final package is taking shape, particularly after the agreement at the Hong Kong Ministerial Meeting of December 2005. Preliminary indications are that the DDA is not going to live up to the hopes held by developing countries. A number of issues appear to be beneficial to developing countries, but on closer inspection they do not, as yet, appear to offer quite so much (see Stiglitz and Charlton, 2006; Wilkinson, 2006b). Central among these is agriculture, which is for many developing countries the most important issue on the table. Here, the agreement reached in Hong Kong to eliminate export subsidies by 2013 is undoubtedly beneficial, but export subsidies account for only approximately 4 per cent of the overall support given in OECD countries. Much of the remaining 96 per cent of the support given to agricultural producers also has a large effect on the interests of developing countries, by lowering world prices and limiting market access in the industrialised countries (although those developing countries that are net food importers benefit from the lower prices that are the result of these subsidies – see Panagariya, 2005). In fact, the overhang between the bound level of aggregate market support (AMS) and the actual applied level, coupled with the details of how the AMS is calculated, mean that the proposed cuts in support (75 per cent cuts for those countries whose domestic support accounts for 20 per cent or more of production costs, 60 per cent for others, and 40 per cent for developing countries), though they appear to be ambitious, would reduce actual support levels in only six countries: Australia, the EU, Iceland, Norway, Thailand, and the US (Hertel and Winters, 2006: 9).

Cotton has been a particularly important area of the negotiations, with a number of developing countries pushing for a much greater and faster liberalisation in this commodity than in the rest of the agricultural sector. In cotton the US agreed to eliminate export subsidies by 2006. However, this is not a new concession, since it would have had to do just this anyway, following the decision of the Dispute Settlement Panel in the action brought by Brazil against US cotton export subsidies (WTO, 2004). Furthermore, as with agriculture in general, it will do nothing to the domestic subsidies that form 80–90 per cent of total US support. As Stiglitz and Charlton put it, '[i]n short, America, to great fanfare, has made an offer worth essentially zero to the developing countries' (Stiglitz and Charlton, 2006: 3).

A similar conclusion can be raised about the much-trumpeted duty-free and quota-free access for LDCs. This is essentially just a new, extended form of the preference systems that industrialised countries have offered developing countries since 1971. These schemes, though worthy in themselves, have always proved to be of limited benefit, for several reasons. Firstly, they tend to include strict rules of origin which limit the goods to which the scheme applies (see Mattoo et al., 2003; Brenton, 2003: 12–18). These rules of origin usually stipulate that for a product to be eligible for preferential rates, the stage of production undertaken in the exporting country must account for a minimum percentage of the total value of the product. For many goods the stage of production undertaken in LDCs typically accounts for little of the value added to the product, and subsequently many of the exports of LDCs are ineligible for preferential rates. The Doha Round duty-free and quota-free agreement makes no progress on this issue.

Secondly, while LDCs were demanding that the duty-free and quota-free agreement should apply to all tariff lines, this was resisted, particularly by the US and Japan, leading to a compromise in which 3 per cent of product lines would be exempt. While this sounds insignificant, the narrow range of products LDCs manage to export means that this exclusion will allow industrialised countries to leave out the majority of LDC exports (Stiglitz and Charlton, 2006: 4). Past experience, such as that of the ATC mentioned above, suggests that any space for developed countries to implement agreements in such a way as to comply fully with the letter of the agreement, while minimising the impact it has on their economy, tends to be exploited to the full.

Lastly, preference systems have generally been of little benefit because of the difficulties LDCs often face in increasing their supply of a product. This may potentially be addressed in the final part of the Hong Kong agreement, which was included specifically for developing countries – Aid for Trade. This, at least abstractly, could provide the finances to overcome those supply-side constraints, and to provide assistance to groups negatively affected by liberalisation. The details of the Aid for Trade element of the DDA are yet to be drawn up, so it is difficult to assess. A series of problems nevertheless present themselves. Firstly, it is doubtful that the substantial Aid for Trade money pledged by developed countries in Hong Kong is actually available. A Member of the European Parliament (MEP), Caroline Lucas, for instance, argues that

> From a European perspective, the aid for trade is a package of lies . . . the carrot that the Commission wants to provide, it cannot possibly guarantee at a time when member states, especially the British presidency, are talking about slashing European budgets.
>
> (quoted in Focus on the Global South, 2005)

The funds pledged mostly come from existing aid budgets rather than being an increase in development assistance (Oxfam, 2005: 16). Furthermore, Aid for Trade budgets may suffer the problems of other development assistance, such as being used by the donor country as a tool of foreign policy, available only to those countries, for instance, that are 'with us' on the war on terror and tied to the granting of reciprocal concessions. The rhetoric from the EU is increasingly looking towards demanding reciprocity from developing countries (Stiglitz and Charlton, 2006: 6). In return for the inclusion of Aid for Trade in the DDA, developing countries are being expected to give up concessions on market access for industrial goods (South Centre, 2005: 5–6).

The preliminary evidence therefore suggests that whatever comes out of the DDA, it is unlikely that it will be significantly skewed towards the interests of developing countries. A recent large-scale report by the World Bank on the expected benefits of the DDA predicted a mixed effect on poverty, with a rise in some countries (particularly those that are net importers of agricultural products) and a fall in others, although in the long term there is likely to be a greater poverty reduction effect (Hertel and Winters, 2006: 26). The context in which it is being negotiated, with an increasingly belligerent Congress seeking others to blame for the trade deficit, precludes any happy ending for developing countries. Until the US government opts for the (admittedly difficult) path of addressing the causes of the trade deficit, the world's poor will have to wait for a more equitable trading system.

Conclusion

There are, then, striking parallels between what is happening at present and the experience of the 1980s and early 1990s that augur badly for developing countries. In the 1980s the US experienced a massive increase in its trade deficit – the result of low savings and a fiscal deficit. The response, however, was to blame the 'unfair' trade practices of the rest of the world and to extract unilateral concessions from Japan and others bilaterally while pursuing an aggressive market-opening strategy in the GATT to mould the world economy more in their favour.

In the late 1990s and 2000s a similar pattern has emerged. The trade deficit has reached record levels as a result of the very low, or indeed non-existent, personal savings rates, exacerbated by the budget deficit George W. Bush has overseen. The response has once again been to blame other countries, particularly China, for maintaining an undervalued exchange rate and for not giving sufficient protection to intellectual property. However, any revaluation of the yuan will have little if any impact on the US trade deficit since it will not affect the underlying causes.

The Uruguay Round of trade negotiations was undertaken within the context of Congressional disquiet over the US trade imbalance, with the result that US negotiators had little to offer the rest of the world in concessions, adding to (though by no means the most important element in) the imbalance of the outcome. The DDA was supposed to redress this imbalance, but the unprecedented US trade deficit makes such an outcome less likely, if not impossible. If the Round concludes when it is expected to in time to submit the package to Congress by May 2007 before fast-track authority expires (which, with the collapse of the negotiation in July 2006, now looks unlikely), there is every chance that it will do so at a time when the trade deficit is at another record high. It is hard to see Congress approving an agreement that is tilted towards developing countries when much of the US trade deficit is with developing countries, and one of the key beneficiaries of the trade Round is likely to be China since it is in an excellent position to take advantage of any increased market access opportunities. Furthermore, the current Round does nothing to address the two key concerns Democrats were pushing for inclusion in any new agreement, namely labour standards and environmental standards.

The US negotiators therefore know that they have little to give away. The agreement cannot make concessions that are politically difficult, such as providing significantly improved market access in textiles and clothing. Indeed, it must be seen to redress the perceived 'unfair' trade practices of other countries and to be opening up the markets of those developing countries that have much higher tariffs on average than the US. There is little chance of the DDA fulfilling what it was set up to do, namely to redress the imbalances of previous GATT Rounds. The result of the US trade deficit is therefore to structure the negotiations in such a way as to ensure that the results are skewed towards US interests – a course of action that it is in a unique position to take. While China is likely to be able to weather the storm of bilateral pressure, within the WTO the result of the US inability or unwillingness to address the underlying causes of the trade deficit is likely to be the exclusion of the development content from the DDA.

Notes

The author would like to thank Rorden Wilkinson and David Smith for their comments on earlier drafts of this chapter.

1 More formally, a current account deficit (which is the sum of the trade deficit plus profits on overseas investments and interest payments) must be balanced by a capital account surplus (which measures capital flowing into and out of a country for investment, grants and loans).
2 The architect of Reagan's 1981 tax cuts, David Stockman, later admitted that the supply side argument was 'always a Trojan horse to bring down the top [income tax] rate' (Greider, 1981: 47). The administration's advocacy of supply side economics may therefore have been purely to give a rationale for the tax cuts it was determined to make for ideological and political reasons without Reagan or his advisers actually believing the theory.
3 A negative savings rate indicates that people on average spent slightly more than they earned in 2005, financing the rest by spending past savings or running up debts. This has been encouraged by the strong growth in the US housing market.
4 Fast-track authority limits the Congressional vote on trade agreements negotiated by the president to a yes–no decision, without being able to make amendments.

References

Atkinson, R. D., and Ward, J. M. (1999), 'The Emerging Export Control Crisis: Reinventing the Computer Export Control Regime', PPI Backgrounder (1 June). www.dlc.org/print. cfm?contentid=1409.

Bagchi, S. (1994), 'The Integration of the Textile Trade into GATT', *Journal of World Trade*, 28: 6.

Baldwin, R. E. (1989), 'US Trade Policy: Recent Changes and Future US Interests', *The American Economic Review*, 79: 2.

Barboza, D. (2006), 'China's Trade Surplus Tripled in 2005', *New York Times*, 11 January.

Baughman, L., Mirius, R., Morkre, M. E., and Spinanger, D. (1997), 'Of Tyre Cords, Ties and Tents: Window-Dressing in the ATC?', *The World Economy*, 20: 4.

Blecker, R. A. (1999), 'The Ticking Debt Bomb: Why the US International Financial Position Is Not Sustainable', Briefing Paper, Economic Policy Institute. www.epi.org/content.cfm/briefingpapers_debtbomb.

Brenton, P. (2003), 'Integrating the Least Developed Countries into the World Trading System: The Current Impact of EU Preferences under Everything but Arms', World Bank Policy Research Working Paper Number 3018 (Washington, DC: World Bank).

Canto, V. A., Joines, D. H., and Laffer, A. B. (1982), *Foundations of Supply-Side Economics: Theory and Evidence* (New York: Academic Press).

Census Bureau (2006), 'Trade in Goods (Imports, Exports and Trade Balance) with China'. www.census.gov/foreign-trade/balance/c5700.html.

Clarida, R. (1989), 'That Trade Deficit, Protectionism, and Policy Coordination', *The World Economy*, 12.

Coleman, W. D., Atkinson, M. M., and Montpetit, E. (1997), 'Against the Odds: Retrenchment in Agriculture in France and the United States', *World Politics*, 49: 4.

Croome, J. (1999), *Reshaping the World Trading System: A History of the Uruguay Round* (The Hague: Kluwer Law), second edition.

Duménil, G., and Lévy, D. (2004), 'The Economics of US Imperialism at the Turn of the 21st Century', *Review of International Political Economy*, 11: 4.

Financial Times (2006a), 'Beijing in Move to Relax Control over Capital', 15 April.

Financial Times (2006b), 'China Moves to Allay US Anger on Unfair Trade: Concessions Announced', 12 April.

Finger, J. Michael, and Schuler, Philip (2000), 'Implementation of Uruguay Round Commitments: The Development Challenge', *World Economy*, 23: 4 (April).

Focus on the Global South (2005), 'Aid for Trade – Another Empty Promise'. www. focusweb.org.

Green, R. T., and Larson, T. L. (1987), 'Only Retaliation Will Open up Japan', *Harvard Business Review*, 65: 6.

Greider, W. (1981), 'The Education of David Stockman', *The Atlantic*, 248.

Hathaway, D. E., and Ingco, M. D. (1995), 'Agricultural Liberalization and the Uruguay Round', in W. Martin and L. A. Winters (eds), *The Uruguay Round and the Developing Countries* (Washington, DC: World Bank).

Hertel, T. W., and Winters, L. A. (eds) (2006), *Poverty and the WTO: Impacts of the Doha Development Agenda* (Basingstoke and Washington, DC: Palgrave and the World Bank).

Independent, The (2006), 'Congress Heaps Pressure on China as US Trade Deficit Soars', 11 February.

Krugman, P. (1994) *Peddling Prosperity* (New York and London: W. W. Norton).

Labonte, M., and Makinen, G. (2004), *Changing Causes of the US Trade Deficit*, Congressional Research Services Report for Congress. Available from www.senate.gov.

Lardy, N. R. (1997), 'Is China an Effective Foreign Policy Tool? [*sic*]', Background Paper (22 May), The Brookings Institution. www.brookings.edu.

Library of Congress (2006), Bill H.R.1944, sponsored by Rep. Elwood H. Hillis. http://thomas.loc.gov.

Low, P., and Subramanian, A. (1995), 'TRIMs in the Uruguay Round: An Unfinished Business?', in W. Martin and L. A. Winters (eds), *The Uruguay Round and the Developing Countries* (Washington, DC: World Bank).

Maki, D. M., and Palumbo, M. G. (2001), *Disentangling the Wealth Effect: A Cohort Analysis of the Household Saving in the 1990s* (Washington, DC: Federal Reserve).

Maskus, K. (2000), *Intellectual Property Rights in the Global Economy* (Washington, DC: Institute for International Economics).

Mattoo, A., Roy, D., and Subramanian, A. (2003), 'The Africa Growth and Opportunity Act and Its Rules of Origin: Generosity Undermined?', *The World Economy*, 26: 6.

New York Times (2003), 'Report Faults China's Policy since It Joined Trade Group', 20 December.

New York Times (2006), 'Made in USA Isn't a Hot Label on Goods in China', 26 February.

Niskanen, W. A., and Moore, S. (1996), *Supply Tax Cuts and the Truth about the Reagan Economic Record*, Cato Policy analysis document No. 261. www.cato.org.

Noland, M. (1997), 'Chasing Phantoms: The Political Economy of USTR', *International Organization*, 51: 3.

OECD (2000), *Agricultural Policies in OECD Countries: Monitoring and Evaluation 2000* (Paris: OECD).

Ostry, S. (2000), 'The Uruguay Round North–South Grand Bargain: Implications for Future Negotiations', prepared for the Conference on the Political Economy of International Trade Law, University of Minnesota. www.utoronto.ca/cis/Minnesota.pdf.

Oxfam (2002a), *The Great EU Sugar Scam: How Europe's Sugar Regime Is Devastating*

Livelihoods in the Developing World, Oxfam Briefing Paper No. 27. www.oxfam. org.uk.

Oxfam (2002b), *Cultivating Poverty: The Impact of US Cotton Subsidies on Africa*, Oxfam Briefing Paper No. 30. www.oxfam.org.uk.

Oxfam (2005), 'What Happened in Hong Kong? Initial Analysis of the WTO Ministerial, December 2005', Oxfam Briefing Paper No. 85. www.oxfam.org.uk.

Panagariya, A. (2005), 'Agricultural Liberalisation and the Least Developed Countries: Six Fallacies', *World Economy*, 28: 9.

Panitch, L., and Gindin, S. (2005), 'Finance and the American Empire', in *Socialist Register* (London: Merlin Press).

Patterson, G. (1966), *Discrimination in International Trade: The Policy Issues 1945–1965* (Princeton: Princeton University Press).

Preeg, E. H. (1995), *Traders in a Brave New World* (Chicago and London: University of Chicago Press).

Rothkopf, D. J. (2004), 'Anyone Seen Our Economic Policy?', *Washington Post*, 25 July.

Schindler, J. W., and Beckett, D. H. (2005), 'Adjusting Chinese Bilateral Trade Data: How Big Is China's Trade Surplus?', *International Journal of Applied Economics*, 2: 2.

Senate (2005), 'Schumer-Graham Announce Bipartisan Bill to Level Playing Field on China Trade', Press release, 3 February. www.senate.gov/~schumer.

South Centre (2005), *Aid for Trade*, Trade Policy Brief, No. 2. www.southcentre.org.

Srinivasan, T. N. (2002), 'Emerging Issues in the World Trading System', in R. Adhikari and P. Athukorala (eds), *Developing Countries in the World Trading System: The Uruguay Round and Beyond* (Cheltenham: Edward Elgar).

Stiglitz, J. (2006), 'A Tale of Two Deficits', *Global Agenda*, Magazine of the World Economic Forum.

Stiglitz, J., and Charlton, A. (2004), *The Development Round of Trade Negotiations in the Aftermath of Cancún*, Report for the Commonwealth Secretariat with the Initiative for Policy Dialogue (London: Commonwealth Secretariat).

Stiglitz, J., and Charlton, A. (2006), 'The Doha Round after Hong Kong', paper prepared for the conference 'An Assessment of the Doha Round after Hong Kong', 2–3 February, University of Manchester.

TDRC (2000), 'The U.S. Trade Deficit: Causes, Consequences and Recommendations for Actions'. http://govinfo.library.unt.edu/tdrc/reports.

UNDP (1997), *Human Development Report* (Geneva: UNDP).

Wade, R. H. (2003), 'What Strategies Are Viable for Developing Countries Today? The WTO and the Shrinking of "Development Space"', *Review of International Political Economy*, 10: 4.

Wanniski, J. (1978) *The Way the World Works* (New York: Basic Books).

Washington Post (2005a), 'Senators Told China Will Loosen Policy on Currency', 1 July.

Washington Post (2005b), 'Both Parties to Punish China Trade', 15 July.

Washington Post (2005c), 'The Senate's Hypocrisy', 24 April.

Watkins, K. (2002), 'Greed in Action', *The Guardian*, 5 June.

Wiener, J. (1995), *Making Rules in the Uruguay Round of the GATT* (Aldershot: Dartmouth).

Wilkinson, R. (2006a), *The WTO: Crisis and the Governance of Global Trade* (London: Routledge).

Wilkinson, R. (2006b), 'The WTO in Hong Kong: What It Really Means for the Doha Development Agenda', *New Political Economy*, 11: 2 (June).

Wolf, M. (2003), 'Asia Is Footing the Bill for American Guns and Butter', *Financial Times*, 19 February.

World Development Movement (2003), *Whose Development Agenda? An Analysis of the EU's GATS Requests of Developing Countries* (London: WDM).

World Trade Organisation (2002a), *Panel Report on Brazil vs. EC: Export Subsidies on Sugar*, Dispute DS266. www.wto.org.

World Trade Organisation (2002b), *Panel Report on Australia vs. EC: Export Subsidies on Sugar*, Dispute DS265. www.wto.org.

World Trade Organisation (2003), *Panel Report on Thailand vs. EC: Export Subsidies on Sugar*, Dispute DS283. www.wto.org.

World Trade Organisation (2004), *Panel Report on Brazil vs. US: Subsidies on Upland Cotton*, Dispute DS267. www.wto.org.

Yang, J. (1998), 'Some Current Issues in US China Trade Relations', *Issues and Studies*, 34: 7.

Yang, J., Askari, H., Forrer, J., and Teegen, H. (2004), 'US Economic Sanctions against China: Who Gets Hurt?' *The World Economy*, 27: 7.

Zhang, J. (2000), 'Sino-US Trade Issues after the WTO Deal: A Chinese Perspective', *Journal of Contemporary China*, 9: 24.

7 Negotiating with diminished expectations

The EU and the Doha Development Round

Alasdair R. Young

With the 2004 and 2007 enlargements and the completion of the single European market programme, the EU has become the world's largest market. It is also the world's largest exporter of goods and services. In terms of imports and as a home to, and host of, foreign direct investment, it is comparable to the US. Reflecting its economic weight, the EU has emerged as one of the dominant players in multilateral trade negotiations. The EU, however, is not an international actor in the traditional sense; it is also an international organisation that brings together 27 member states.

The need to manage the diverse interests of the 27 member states has been the driving force behind the EU's approach to and strategy in the Doha Round. In particular, the focal issue for the EU has been on managing the internal political costs of reforming the Common Agricultural Policy (CAP). To do so the EU has applied the American football aphorism that 'the best defence is a good offence': seeking to broaden significantly the negotiating agenda, in particular by seeking negotiations on non-agricultural market access. It has also sought to promote a 'deep trade agenda', seeking to agree international disciplines, often procedural, on domestic rules (Young and Peterson, 2006). This includes the 'Singapore issues' of competition policy, investment, government procurement, and trade facilitation, as well as environmental protection and core labour standards. This deep trade agenda is, at least in part, a response to the emergence of the new politics of trade, which has brought new actors into the trade policy process.

The need to keep the member governments on side makes the EU an unwieldy and difficult negotiating partner. None the less, under persistent pressure from its negotiating partners, particularly Brazil and the US, the EU has made a number of non-trivial concessions on agriculture, including the elimination of export subsidies by a specific date and cuts in protection. This despite vocal opposition from a significant number of member states, led by France, and with relatively little to show for them other than the continuation of the Round itself. These concessions have been possible because several member states, including Denmark, the Netherlands, and the UK, favour reform of the CAP.

I will begin by surveying the contours of the EU's trade policy, the point of departure for the Doha negotiations. I then briefly explain how the EU's character as an international organisation affects its participation in multilateral trade negotiations before turning to examine the EU's approach to, and strategy in, the Doha Round. I conclude by evaluating the EU's strategy.

EU's trade regime: liberal with (big) exceptions

How easy it is for foreign products to enter the EU depends on a combination of policies, some that are intended to affect imports and others that affect imports as a side-effect of other policy objectives. As a consequence of multiple rounds of multilateral negotiations, the EU's average most-favoured-nation tariff (MFN) is only 4.2 per cent, and 20 per cent of tariff lines enter duty-free (WTO, 2002). Further, the vast majority of the EU's trading partners enjoy some kind of preferential access to the EU market, although the value of such preferential access has diminished as the EU's tariffs have fallen (Winters, 2001).

The EU's 'nominal' liberalism, however, is tempered by a number of very important exceptions (Winters, 2001: 25). The most prominent concerns agriculture. The CAP functions through a system of price supports, which requires that imports are subject to levies to prevent them undercutting EU prices. The EU's average agricultural tariff is 23 per cent (Mandelson, 2005b), and tariffs are significantly higher on a number of other products such as wheat, sugar, and dairy (Winters, 2001). Further, the price supports encourage overproduction, which is disposed of through a system of export subsidies. In addition, there are particularly high tariffs – 'tariff peaks' – on some manufactured goods, particularly footwear, leather, textiles, and clothing (Winters, 2001). The EU is also an extensive user of anti-dumping measures (WTO, 2005).

As tariffs have fallen and quantitative restrictions have been eliminated, the EU's regulations have emerged as significant barriers to market access for manufactures and a number of agricultural products (WTO, 2002). Although the single-market programme has generally benefited non-EU firms by providing access to the whole EU market without having to comply with different national rules (Commission, 1998; WTO, 1995), in some cases it has resulted in very strict common rules, thereby increasing regulatory barriers to imports. These 'regulatory peaks' tend to result from the political dynamics of overcoming pronounced regulatory differences among the member states rather than from an explicitly protectionist motive (Young, 2004).

As with goods, the development of the single-market programme has given the EU a liberal regime in most service sectors with regard to investment and cross-border trade (Commission, 1998; WTO, 1995). As with goods, however, there are some significant exceptions. Access to the single market in air, inland waterway, and maritime transport is restricted to EU-controlled firms. EU rules on audio-visual services require minimum European content, and so are explicitly discriminatory. There is also strong resistance to liberalising (at the national level) services associated with the welfare state, such as education and health services. In addition, the EU's rules on consumer protection, such as on data protection, although not discriminatory, can impede trade in services. There are also numerous member-state-specific measures regulating services, particularly with regard to 'Mode 4', which involves the politically sensitive issue of people immigrating, at least temporarily, to provide services (Langhammer, 2005).

Table 7.1 The EU's sensitive sectors

Agriculture	Goods	Services
Common Agricultural Policy	Footwear	Transport
	Leather	Audio-visual
	Textiles and clothing	Education
		Healthcare

As with other large economies, the EU's importance as a market for goods and services, whether supplied through trade or investment, means that its policies affect producers in other countries whether intentionally or not. The importance of EU firms as providers of goods and services, whether through trade or investment, means that the EU takes an interest in the policies of other countries. The EU's economic importance thus gives it an interest in the functioning of the global economy and the capacity to influence it.

The politics of the EU's participation in multilateral trade negotiations

Because the EU is an international organisation there is an issue about how it participates in international trade negotiations. This issue is related to, but is also distinct from, the substance of the positions that it adopts in those negotiations. One of the defining features of the EU is that it is a customs union. A customs union requires the ability to pursue a common approach to trade with the rest of the world. For this purpose the 1957 Treaty of Rome established the common commercial policy (CCP). Under the CCP the member states delegate the conduct of trade negotiations to the EU's executive, the European Commission, 'assisted' by a committee of trade policy officials from the member states – the 133 Committee. Significantly, the 2004 enlargement of the EU to 25 member states seems to have enhanced the Commission's leadership role (Woolcock, 2005) – a situation likely to have been reinforced by enlargement to 27.[1] The Council of Ministers, composed of the representatives of the member governments, authorises the Commission to negotiate and ratifies the resulting agreements by a qualified majority vote – a super majority. In practice, however, the member governments proceed on the basis of consensus, albeit one that is reached in the 'shadow of the vote' (Johnson, 1998; Lamy, 2004; Woolcock, 2005).

From the outset there has been a persistent tension between the member states and the Commission about the allocation of authority for all aspects of trade policy. Although the February 2001 Treaty of Nice extended the EU's authority, there are still some important issues, reflecting the sensitivities of particular member states, for which the member states retain authority. Audio-visual services, educational services, and social and human health services fall under the shared authority of the EU and the member states. In addition, FDI in non-service sectors and non-trade-related intellectual property rights were not included under EU authority (Holmes and Rollo, 2001; Meunier and Nicolaïdis, 2001). Despite these legal complexities, the EU's member governments have agreed to participate in the DDA, as they did in the Uruguay Round, 'as if' the EU has exclusive competence (Commission, 1999). Thus only the Commission represents the EU across the full breadth of the agenda.

The EU's institutions for aggregating the member governments' trade policy preferences are extremely important because of the pronounced differences among those preferences. There are some member states that tend to favour liberalisation, most notably the Czech Republic, Denmark, Estonia, the Netherlands, and the UK, while others tend to be more protectionist, particularly on agriculture, most notably France, Italy, Poland, Portugal, and Spain. With respect to the Doha Round there are three main cross-cutting tensions among the member states: agriculture, development, and the deep trade agenda. There is also a general consensus about the desirability of liberalisation in non-agricultural products and services, which can sit uneasily with the other objectives. These tensions are discussed in greater detail below.

The EU's institutions and the diversity of trade policy preferences among the member governments have implications both for the substance of the EU's positions and for how it pursues them. Because any wide-ranging multilateral agreement is likely to address issues of mixed competence, the entire agreement will require the unanimous approval of the member governments. This means that the most protectionist member governments effectively have a veto over the whole agreement. As a consequence, the EU's negotiating position is likely to be quite protectionist, at least on those issues of most concern to the protectionists – that is, agriculture.

Given the diversity of interests among the member governments and their active involvement in trade negotiations, agreeing common positions is extremely difficult. This applies both to the opening position and to any changes. Importantly, although the EU's negotiating positions may be difficult to change, there are usually actors within the EU that are dissatisfied with the initial position and that will seek to exploit opportunities to revisit the issue. None the less, the EU tends to be a very cumbersome negotiator, reacting only slowly to changes in the negotiating environment. Greater flexibility therefore tends to come only from the Commission making concessions that are within its mandate. The precise limits of the mandate are necessarily vague, which can lead to tensions between the Commission and at least some member governments, as has happened repeatedly since Cancún, most notably concerning the Commission's offers on agricultural market access in the run-up to Hong Kong.

To an extent these two issues come together. The Commission repeatedly makes use of the difficulty of reaching internal agreement to extract significant concessions from trading partners for any concession by the EU (Meunier, 1998, 2005). The logic is simple. Under unanimity, protectionist member states have the power to block any deal. In order for their opposition to be overcome, either they need to realise sufficient gains in other areas to offset the losses or other member governments must have a sufficiently large stake in a successful negotiation that they will put enough pressure on the reluctant member governments to go along. This has been the driving motivation behind the EU's approach to the Doha Round.

The EU's initial negotiating agenda[2]

The origins of the EU's approach to the Doha Round lie in the unresolved issues from the Uruguay Round (Young et al., 2000; Kerremans, 2005; Woolcock, 2005). Given the political sensitivity of reform of the CAP, the 'built-in agenda' of negotiations on agriculture (and services) presented a significant problem for the EU. The Commission's response was to seek to broaden the negotiating agenda beyond agriculture and services in order to secure benefits in other areas to offset the anticipated political costs associated with concessions on agriculture (Allen and Smith, 2001; Kerremans, 2005). This informed the Commission's proposals to launch a 'Millennium Round' at the Seattle Ministerial in December 1999 and persisted as the basis of the EU's negotiating mandate for Doha (see Table 7.2 for a summary).

Agriculture

The EU's position on agriculture in Seattle, and subsequently Doha (2001), was based on the limited Agenda 2000 reforms of the CAP. The EU was willing to negotiate on tariffs, although it preferred the Uruguay Round formula that reduced all tariffs by the same proportion, and domestic and export supports, so long as all forms of export support were treated equally. It insisted that the concept of 'Blue' and 'Green' Boxes should continue, and called for the recognition of the 'multifunctional' role of agriculture, which captures the role of agriculture in rural development and environmental protection (Council, 1999). It also wanted improved market access and sought discussions on food safety (including the precautionary principle), food quality, and animal welfare. Thus the EU's opening position on agriculture was very defensive.

Services

The EU's negotiating position on services could not have been more of a contrast. As the EU's market was already relatively open to non-EU firms and as EU firms are major exporters of services, the EU has pressed for more market opening. At the very least it wanted governments to bind all unilateral liberalisation that had taken place since the Uruguay Round was concluded. It also wanted further liberalisation, particularly in professional services, energy-related services, and e-commerce. In addition, it wanted progress on a number of issues left unresolved by the Uruguay Round, such as disciplines on subsidies, government procurement, and safeguard measures. The only sensitive sectors for the EU were audio-visual services, education, and health services.

Table 7.2 The EU's diminished negotiating objectives

Issue	Seattle/Doha	Hong Kong
Agriculture	Agenda 2000 provides basis	2003 reform provides basis
	Retain 'Blue' and 'Green' Boxes	Develop 'Blue Box' disciplines
	'Multifunctionality'	[Secured]
	Uruguay Round formula to tariff reductions	G20 formula to tariff-cutting with a cap, but protection for sensitive sectors
	Reductions in all export support	Eliminate all export support
	Protect geographical indications	Protect geographical indications
Services	Bind unilateral liberalisation	Ambitious mandatory numerical targets
	Further liberalisation	
	Progress on subsidies, government procurement, safeguard measures	Progress on subsidies, government procurement, safeguard measures
Non-agricultural products	Swiss formula	Swiss formula (applied tariffs)
	Comprehensive initiative on non-tariff barriers	
'Singapore issues'	Competition policy	[Dropped]
	Investment	[Dropped]
	Government procurement	[Dropped]
	Trade facilitation	Negotiations
Other new trade issues	Environment	Narrow mandate
	Core labour standards	[Dropped]

Sources: Council (1999); Commission (2005b)

NAMA

The EU also pursued an offensive liberal agenda with respect to non-agricultural products. This reflects that with only a few exceptions most European manufacturing industries are now export-oriented.[3] As the EU has a higher average tariff, but fewer tariff peaks, than the US, it favoured the Swiss formula, which is a mathematical formula that implies steeper cuts in higher tariffs (Council, 1999; Woolcock, 2005). The EU also wanted a 'comprehensive non-tariff initiative' to make sure that non-tariff barriers – including customs valuations, licensing, origin, product safety standards, and certification procedures – were not used to counter the benefits of tariff reductions (Council, 1999: 5).

'Singapore' and other new trade issues

The EU has been the principal proponent for addressing the 'Singapore issues' – competition policy, investment, government procurement, and trade facilitation, as well as two issues sidelined at the WTO's first Ministerial Meeting in Singapore in December 1996 (the environment and core labour standards) in the multilateral trading system (Lamy, 2002). These are diverse issues with diverse origins. There are four different explanations for why the EU has championed them, although some explanations work better for some issues than for others:

1   They are believed to be beneficial to the world trading system – this is the pure 'postmodern' agenda about governing globalisation.
2   They are a cynical ploy intended to disrupt progress in the Round and thus reduce pressure on the CAP.
3   They bring benefits to the EU that will offset the political costs of concessions on the CAP.
4   They represent disguised protectionism (Rollo, 2003; Woolcock, 2005; Young et al., 2000).

Competition policy comes closest to being associated with the deep trade agenda. The Commission, prompted by its own experiences using competition policy to combat residual trade barriers within the EU, wants every country to have a competition law of some basic kind (Woolcock, 2005; Young et al., 2000). Although there was no strong support from European firms (Woolcock, 2005), the Commission got some support from some member governments, such as the British government, which see promoting competition policy as a way of benefiting consumers in developing countries (Holmes, 2005). The EU, therefore, advocated developing a 'basic framework of binding core principles and rules on domestic competition law and policy and its enforcement' (Council, 1999: 5).

The motives for EU's position on foreign direct *investment* were more mixed. Although there was some support for an investment agreement from some medium-sized EU firms, the larger European multinationals did not think it was necessary (Woolcock, 2005). In addition there were some ideological differences among the member governments. While some, such as the British government, supported an agreement that would discipline governments, others, such as the French, wanted to discipline firms (Young et al., 2000). The EU thus called for the negotiation of a framework that would both create a stable and predictable climate for investment and 'take into account' concerns about investors' responsibilities (Council, 1999: 5).

Multilateral rules on *government procurement* and *trade facilitation*, by contrast, clearly promised benefits to European firms (Woolcock, 2005). The EU hoped to improve the chance of EU firms providing goods and services to foreign governments by increasing the transparency of public procurement practices and curbing discriminatory purchasing practices. Trade facilitation addresses the customs and other administrative costs associated with conducting trade. As tariffs are reduced, such costs become more evident and important. Such barriers are particularly painful for small and medium-sized firms and are particularly prevalent in developing countries.

Trade and the environment and *core labour standards* were pushed on to the agenda by the mobilisation of a new trade-policy constituency of environmental non-governmental organisations and by an established constituency of trade unions reframing its agenda (Hocking and Smith, 1997; Lamy, 1999; Woolcock, 2000). These issues are also seen as components of a deep trade agenda which became influential in Brussels and other European capitals, including Berlin, in the late 1990s (Falke, 2005; Lamy, 2001, 2002). In addition to promoting values that appeal to newly mobilised trade-policy actors, such measures may also serve to protect firms and industries from 'unfair' competition.

The environment was propelled up the trade agenda by WTO disputes concerning trade discrimination on environmental grounds, most notably the 1996 Shrimp-Turtle complaint against the US. The desire to protect national environmental rules and the enforcement mechanisms of multilateral environmental agreements from WTO disciplines, rather than explicit attempts to export environmental standards, were the focus of the EU's negotiating position (Council, 1999).

The EU's member governments are divided over the desirability of incorporating core labour standards into the WTO. Some, such as the UK, are disinclined to go beyond the Singapore Ministerial Declaration (Wilkinson, 1999). Others, with strong social democratic traditions, such as Sweden, see the WTO as a way to promote human rights. For yet others, such as France, linking core labour rights to trade provides a means to provide protection (Young et al., 2000). Essentially unable to reconcile these different positions, the EU's position did not represent much of an advance on the status quo (Council, 1999).

The EU thus entered the Seattle Ministerial with an ambitious agenda, which was at best of little interest to developing countries and in a number of instances was anathema to them. The governments of the US and the Cairns Group accused the EU of trying to negotiate about everything but agriculture (Young et al., 2000). When the ministerial failed to launch a comprehensive Round, the EU was among the most obvious losers as the 'built-in agenda' on agriculture (and services) kicked in automatically.

The Doha Ministerial

In the wake of Seattle, the Commission and some member governments proposed revisiting the EU's agenda in order to make it more flexible in approach if not in substance (Lamy, 2000; *European Report*, 22 March 2000). The difficulty of agreeing a new position, however, meant that in March 2000 the Council stuck with the Seattle agenda, as had been agreed in October 1999. The EU, therefore, went to Doha with the most ambitious agenda pushing for wide-ranging negotiations that would encompass non-agricultural market access, the Singapore issues, trade and environment, and trade and labour standards, as well as the 'built-in' talks on agriculture and services.

Consequently, whereas the Uruguay Round began with the US and the developing countries on opposing sides with the EU in the middle, in Doha the EU was in opposition to the developing countries on a number of key issues. Not only did the EU, particularly France, resist the inclusion of the objective of phasing out agricultural export subsidies in the agenda, it was alone in advocating a comprehensive agenda that would have included the 'Singapore issues' that many developing countries, India in particular, disliked so much (Panagariya, 2002; Thompson, 2001).

At the final hour of the ministerial a form of words was found for the agenda that satisfied the EU, and, after a delay, clarifications of the text enabled India also to accept the agenda. On agricultural export subsidies the Ministerial Declaration (WTO, 2001: 3) stated that the agenda did not 'prejudge the outcome of the negotiations' and clarified that the aim was the 'reductions [*sic*] of, with a view to phasing out' export subsidies. The decision to start negotiations on the Singapore issues was postponed to the Cancún Ministerial in September 2003. India sought, and received, explicit clarification that the decision to start negotiations on the 'Singapore issues' could be blocked by any member. Given the evident hostility from developing countries the Commission decided not to push for the inclusion of core labour standards on the agenda (Lamy, 2002).

The EU did score some successes. In exchange for accepting the deferment of the start of negotiations on investment and competition policy, the EU secured a commitment that the negotiations would seek to clarify the relationship between the WTO and multilateral environmental agreements (Thompson, 2001), although it did not secure a commitment to discuss strengthening the protections for national environmental rules or the inclusion of the 'precautionary principle', which holds that policymakers may act to protect the environment or public health before the existence of a risk has been scientifically established, in WTO rules (Lamy, 2002). The EU also got formal recognition that 'non-trade' aspects of agriculture – its 'multifunctionality' – would be taken into account in the negotiations (Commission, 2001). In addition, the ministerial, facing the threat of a veto by the African, Caribbean, and Pacific (ACP) countries, granted a waiver for their preferential trading relationship with the EU (*Financial Times*, 14 November 2001).

The EU was not consistently in opposition to the developing countries. For example, the EU pressed other developed countries to adopt equivalents to its 'Everything But Arms' initiative. This initiative, adopted in February 2001, grants duty-free access to imports of all products except arms and munitions from the least developed countries, although the full liberalisation of certain sensitive products is delayed – bananas (January 2006), sugar (July 2009) and rice (September 2009).

In addition, the EU played an important role in securing an agreement in principle that the TRIPs agreement should be interpreted and implemented in such a way as to permit WTO members to manufacture or import drugs necessary for dealing with public health crises (Panagariya, 2002; Thompson, 2001). This position, at the expense of European pharmaceutical companies, was supported by a number of member governments, including Germany's, and civil society groups concerned about developing countries (Falke, 2005). The Commission may also have hoped, ultimately unsuccessfully, that this would help to blunt developing country demands for reforms to the CAP (Falke, 2005).

The crunch in Cancún

Even before the ministerial meeting in Cancún in September 2003 ended without agreement, the Round had lost momentum. Initially, the US and EU were at the core of the problem. The US was guilty of sins of commission by imposing safeguard measures on steel imports and substantially increasing its agricultural subsidies. The EU was guilty of sins of omission by having trouble agreeing negotiating positions in agriculture and services and struggling with agricultural reforms.

Agriculture was an early sticking point. The US, the Cairns Group, and a number of other developing countries said that unless the EU aggressively reduced import barriers and slashed subsidies, there could be no deal (*Financial Times*, 23 January 2003). Although not alone in resisting agricultural liberalisation – Japan, Norway, South Korea, and Switzerland do as well – the EU received the brunt of the criticism. In part this was because it was the last of the major trade powers to table firm agricultural proposals, which was due to French and Irish insistence that references to the elimination of export subsidies for specific products be removed (*Bridges Trade BioRes*, 7 February 2003).

There was a breakthrough of sorts in June 2003 when the EU agreed reforms to the CAP. To an extent this was a response to internal pressures: the then impending enlargement, which threatened to drive up the cost; the budgetary constraints faced by the members of the euro; and the resistance of some member governments to being significant net contributors to the EU budget (Young et al., 2000). As a consequence the British, Dutch, and Swedish governments wanted reforms. These internal pressures were compounded by external pressures associated with the end of the 'peace clause', which protects agricultural subsidies that comply with the Agreement on Agriculture from being challenged under other WTO agreements; the framing of the CAP as a development issue; and the need to move the Doha Round forward (Dinan and Camhis, 2004; Rieger, 2005; Woolcock, 2005). There was, however, fierce resistance to reform, particularly from the French and Spanish governments (Dinan and Camhis, 2004). Consequently, the reforms focused more on changing the modalities of EU subsidies than their generosity and did not apply to the sensitive sectors of sugar, cotton, olive oil, and tobacco (Commission, 2003a). None the less, they moved further towards decoupling support from production (shifting support from 'Amber' to 'Blue' and 'Green' Boxes), so that by 2006 market price support and export subsidies will fall to about 20 per cent of expenditure (Commission, 2003a).

Although these reforms sent a positive signal, they were far from a panacea. For starters, the EU indicated that it would not bind these cuts in domestic support unless there were comparable cuts from its important trading partners (Allen and Smith, 2004). More importantly, the reform did not directly affect the EU's agricultural tariffs or its export subsidies, although it has implications for both. The tariffs are particularly significant as they are estimated to represent the lion's share of the benefit from the liberalisation of developed country agricultural markets (Anderson and Martin 2005).

The EU's reform, combined with the 2002 US Farm Bill, did, however, clear the way for a joint EU–US proposal on agriculture in the run-up to Cancún (Woolcock, 2005). That proposal focused on reconciling their different approaches to agricultural tariff reductions and limiting less trade-distorting domestic subsidies and export subsidies, but was short on specific reductions and dates (*Financial Times*, 15 August 2003).

A new alliance of developing countries (the G20) – including Brazil, China, India, and South Africa – was highly critical of the EU–US proposal, demanding more extensive liberalisation from developed countries while offering less. Another group of developing countries (the G90), mostly from Africa, were very concerned that agricultural liberalisation would erode the value of their preferential trading relationships with developed countries and expose their small farmers to intense competition (*The Economist*, 20 September 2003).

The ministerial, however, concentrated first on the Singapore issues, for which the EU had been the principal demandeur. These issues were anathema to most of the developing countries, 90 of which had stated their opposition to beginning negotiations on them at the start of the ministerial.[4] It was only on the last day of the talks that the Commission dropped its insistence on talks on investment and competition policy. The G90, however, were deeply dissatisfied with the draft text on agriculture and refused to negotiate on any of the Singapore issues (*The Economist*, 20 September 2003). On the other side of the coin, Japan and South Korea, both of which had been resisting liberalising their agricultural markets, insisted that all four Singapore issues be included in the Round (*Bridges Trade BioRes*, 19 September 2003). Thus although the EU eventually showed some flexibility, the two issues in the Round to which it was central – agriculture and the Singapore issues – were linked in a destructive way by others. The Cancún Ministerial, like the one in Seattle, ended without agreement.

To a negotiating framework and on to Hong Kong

In the wake of the failure at Cancún the Commission undertook an extensive consultation with the member governments, EU business and civic interest groups, and its negotiating partners. On the basis of this consultation it concluded that it was in the EU's best interests to continue to pursue the Doha Round. Further, it concluded that the EU's 'fundamental objectives' that it had taken into Seattle had 'stood the test of time' (Commission, 2003b: 5). It did, however, conclude that it needed to review its strategy for achieving those objectives.

Central to this new strategy was a willingness to be more flexible on the Singapore issues. The Commission proposed dropping the demand that all four issues be treated the same way and considering whether any, some, or all of the issues should be negotiated as plurilateral issues outside the single undertaking (Commission,

2003b). It also proposed shifting the discussions on the relationship between multilateral environmental agreements and the WTO from a legal approach to a focus on political principles and adopting a slightly more flexible approach to the precise arrangements governing geographical indications. The Commission, however, signalled that it would not improve on its commitments on agriculture and stressed that those already tabled would be delivered only if its trading partners 'show real movement' (Commission, 2003b: 2). It also flagged its intention to maintain the EU's ambitious objectives in non-agricultural market access and services. The Commission's proposals received the unanimous support of the member governments, even though some, such as the British government, would have been happy to see competition policy and investment dropped entirely (*Financial Times*, 3 December 2003).

In May 2004, in an effort to revive the negotiations, the Commission went further. In a letter to WTO members, it:

- offered to bind the cuts in domestic support stemming from the 2003 CAP reforms;
- offered to eliminate all agricultural export subsidies, provided others made similar cuts in their export promotion schemes;
- indicated a willingness to drop negotiations on investment and competition and also public procurement if that is what others wanted; and
- proposed that the poorest WTO members not be asked to further open their markets (Commission, 2004a).

The French government, however, strongly criticised the letter for exceeding the Commission's mandate and for being 'tactically very dangerous' (*Financial Times*, 11 May 2004). The Commission, however, had the backing of the British and German governments, the latter of which supported concessions on agricultural export subsidies only after the collapse of talks at Cancún (*Financial Times*, 3 December 2003; Falke, 2005).

The Commission's initiative contributed to the adoption of a framework for the negotiations on 31 July 2004. This framework essentially enshrined the concessions in the Commission's letter, establishing the objective of eliminating agricultural export subsidies by a date to be agreed and dropping competition, investment, and public procurement (Commission, 2004b). Again the French government objected to the concessions on agriculture, but it was the only member government to do so, and the Commission accepted the framework agreement anyway (*Financial Times*, 31 July 2004; 2 August 2004; *Le Monde*, 2 August 2004).

The EU's next concession came at an informal meeting in Dalian, China, in July 2005. The Commission accepted in principle the G20's framework for cutting agricultural tariffs, which was a compromise between the EU's insistence on the Uruguay Round formula (which would have preserved tariff peaks) and the US proposal (which targeted tariff peaks) (*Financial Times*, 18 July 2005). This framework groups tariffs into bands, with the bigger cuts applying to tariffs in the higher bands. Even though the boundaries of the bands and the size of the cuts were not agreed and the Commission insisted on some flexibility in applying the formula to particularly sensitive sectors, this latest concession provoked further criticisms from the French, Irish, and Italian governments for going too far (*Financial Times*, 18 July 2005).

At the informal WTO ministerial meeting in Zurich on 10 October 2005, however, the Commission went further still (Commission, 2005a). Most significantly, for the first time, along with the other major players, the Commission tabled initial proposals on agricultural market access. It also indicated limited scope for reducing the ceiling on 'Blue Box' support below 5 per cent of total agricultural production, subject to clarification of what constitutes 'Blue Box' support.

In response, 13 member states, led by France, wrote to the Commission calling on it to consult with the member states before offering any concessions in agriculture (*GAIN Report*, E35189, 13 October 2005). At a special meeting of the EU's foreign ministers on 18 October France sought to force the Commission to withdraw its negotiating proposal (EurActiv.com, 19 October 2005). Although the French initiative was supported by the Greek, Irish, Polish, Portuguese, and Spanish governments, it did not command a sufficient majority to be adopted. In particular, the British government, holding the EU's rotating presidency, and the German government, along with the governments of Denmark, Finland, the Netherlands, and Sweden, opposed constraining the Commission (EurActiv.com, 19 October 2005; *Financial Times*, 18 October 2005). The Commission, however, undertook to strengthen the mechanisms by which it keeps the Council informed of the negotiations. In addition, the Council confirmed that 'the [2003] CAP reform is Europe's important contribution to the DDA and constitutes the limits for the Commission's negotiating brief in the WTO Round' (Council, 2005a). On 27 October 2005 French President Chirac underlined this position, warning that France reserved its right to veto any agreement if it went beyond the 2003 CAP reform (*Le Monde*, 27 October 2005; *Financial Times*, 28 October 2005).

Despite Chirac's warning, and apparently with the explicit or tacit backing of the other 24 member governments (*Financial Times*, 29 October 2005), the Commission responded to heavy pressure from its major trading partners by improving its offer on agricultural market access on 28 October. The EU offered to cut its highest agricultural products by 60 per cent and its average agricultural tariff by 46 per cent (to 12 per cent) and accept a cap of 100 per cent (Mandelson, 2005b). The EU, however, also indicated that it would want to classify up to 8 per cent of its tariff lines as covering 'sensitive products', which would most likely include beef, poultry, and sugar (Commission, 2005b; *Financial Times*, 29 October 2005).

In making this improved offer the Commission explicitly invoked the need for significant concessions from others in order to sell the Round to the 'increasingly sceptical' member governments (Commission, 2005b: 1). It also stressed that it had gone to the 'outer limit of its mandate' and that the offer on agricultural market access represented the EU's 'bottom line' (Mandelson, 2005b; Fischer Boel, 2005).

Hong Kong and beyond

Given this inauspicious background it was not surprising that the outcome of the Hong Kong Ministerial was disappointing. The last, best (though never very great) hope that the EU would make a significantly improved offer on agriculture in Hong Kong was scuppered when the European Council Summit in December 2005 did not agree any further reforms to the CAP as part of setting the parameters for the EU's budget for 2007–13. The agreement did include a review of the EU's spending, including the CAP, but not until 2008/9 (Council, 2005b). Thus the Commission was not given any additional room for manoeuvre in Hong Kong.

The Commission thus stuck to its guns: the only concession it made, and that grudgingly, was to accept 2013 as the date by which to eliminate export subsidies. By then the 2003 CAP reform will have largely eliminated the need for export subsidies anyway. Further, the EU will continue to press for the elimination of export subsidies to be expressed in value terms and the Commission has assured the member states that the phasing out of the export subsidies will be 'fully in line with' agreed reforms of the CAP (Council, 2005c: 7). The EU did not gain a lot either. Its preferred 'Swiss formula' was accepted for the non-agricultural market access talks, but the crucial decisions on the coefficients by which tariffs are to be reduced were deferred and there was almost no progress on services. Consequently, the Council was less than satisfied with the outcome of the talks, noting 'certain deficiencies and a lack of ambitious progress on various issues' (Council, 2005c: 7).

There is next to no chance that the EU will adopt any significant reform to the CAP prior to the review of finances in 2008/9, particularly given the French presidential election due in the spring of 2007. This is critical, as it would appear that the Commission has already approached the outer limits of what it can offer on the basis of the reforms already agreed.[5] The only area of agriculture where further 'concessions' might be made is on the non-trivial issue of sugar, as the EU's sugar regime is reformed in the wake of successful WTO complaints. Thus it is likely to take significant concession on non-agricultural market access and services by the other key players even to open the possibility of further EU concessions on agriculture for several years to come. Given the importance that several of the other key participants in the Round, most notably Brazil and the US, have attached to EU concessions on agriculture, this has significant negative implications for the Round as a whole. It raises the prospect of failure and suggests that even success is likely to be modest.

Conclusions

The EU entered the Doha Round with a very ambitious agenda as part of a grand strategy to offset the anticipated political costs of agricultural reform and as an attempt to improve the governance of globalisation. In the wake of Hong Kong the EU's strategy seems to have failed. The negotiating agenda, while broader than the built-in agenda carried over from the Uruguay Round, is much narrower than the EU had hoped (see Table 7.2). Moreover, the negotiations have remained focused on agriculture, with very little progress on non-agricultural market access and services. In the meantime the EU has adopted a significant reform of the CAP, albeit largely for internal reasons, accepted a date for the abolition of all export subsidies, and accepted a more liberalising approach to agricultural market access than it had wished.

This account would appear to belie the EU's vaunted negotiating strength. Although the resolute negotiating of the US, the G20, and, to a lesser extent, the G90 has been important, these concessions are largely due to the internal pressures for, and advocates of, agricultural reform. In addition, the Commission, supported by a number of member governments, including the British and German governments, wants the Round to succeed to benefit EU firms and developing countries. Consequently, the Commission has led the member states, repeatedly making concessions beyond what the more protectionist governments have been happy with. Their patience having been severely tested, the Commission's further room for manoeuvre now seems severely limited.

The Commission is now seeking to leverage the evident reluctance of a significant number of member governments to extract concessions from its negotiating partners (Mandelson, 2006), even threatening to scupper an agreement. This is credible because each member state will effectively have a veto over the ratification of any agreement. To forestall any member government exercising its veto the Commission needs significant concessions from the other WTO members on non-agricultural products and services in particular. Hence Trade Commissioner Mandelson's rather mournful observation that 'this aircraft will not fly long on one engine alone'.

Notes

1 Interview with a German trade official, Brussels, 16 March 2005.
2 This section draws heavily on Young et al. (2000).
3 Interview, trade association representative, Brussels, 26 March 2004; former Commission trade official, London, 10 March 2005.
4 See Rollo et al. (2003) for a summary of the opposition.
5 I am grateful to Jim Rollo and Wyn Grant for sharing their assessments with me.

References

Allen, D., and Smith, M. (2001), 'External Policy Developments', *Journal of Common Market Studies*, 39, Annual Review.

Allen, D., and Smith, M. (2002), 'External Policy Developments', *Journal of Common Market Studies*, 40, Annual Review.

Allen, D., and Smith, M. (2004), 'External Policy Developments', *Journal of Common Market Studies*, 42, Annual Review.

Anderson, K., and Martin, W. (2005), 'Agricultural Market Access: The Key to Doha Success', *World Bank Trade Note* 23 (27 June).

Commission (1998), *External Access to European Markets*, The Single Market Review,

Subseries IV, Volume 4 (Luxembourg: Office for Official Publications of the European Communities).

Commission (1999), 'The EU Approach to the Millennium Round', 8 July.

Commission (2001), '4th WTO Ministerial Conference, 9–14 November, Doha, Qatar – Assessment of Results for the EU'. http://trade-info.cec.eu.int/europa/2001newround/compas.htm.

Commission (2003a), 'EU Agriculture and the WTO: Doha Development Agenda: Cancún – September 2003', September.

Commission (2003b), 'Reviving the DDA Negotiations – the EU Perspective', 26 November.

Commission (2004a), 'WTO-DDA: EU Ready to Go the Extra Mile in Three Key Areas of the Talks', 10 May.

Commission (2004b), 'WTO Doha Development Agenda: WTO Mid-point Agreement Paves the Way for Future Conclusion of Trade Round A Stronger Multilateral Trading System', 31 July.

Commission (2005a), 'Statement of EU Conditional Negotiating Proposals – With Explanatory Annotations', 10 October.

Commission (2005b), 'Making Hong Kong a Success: Europe's Contribution', 28 October.

Council (1999), 'Preparation for the Third WTO Ministerial Conference – Draft Council Conclusions', Document 12092/99 WTO 131 (22 October).

Council (2005a), 'Extraordinary Meeting of the General Affairs and External Relations Council', Luxembourg, 18 October, 13378/05 (Presse 267).

Council (2005b), 'Financial Perspectives 2007–2013', DQPG 15915/05, CADREFIN 268, Brussels (19 December).

Council (2005c), 'Special Council Meeting General Affairs and External Relations, Hong-Kong, 13–18 Dec. 2005', 15945/05 (Presse 366).

Dinan, D., and Camhis, M. (2004), 'The Common Agricultural Policy and Cohesion', in M. G. Cowles and D. Dinan (eds), *Developments in the European Union 2* (Basingstoke: Palgrave).

Falke, A. (2005), 'Waking-up from Trade Policy Hibernation? Germany's Role in the Doha Development Round', in M. Overhaus, H. W. Maull, and S. Harnisch (eds), *European Trade Policy and the Doha Development Agenda: German Foreign Policy Dialogue* (15 February) (www.deutsche-aussenpolitik.de).

Fischer Boel, M. (2005), 'Statement to the Press on the EU's New Offer on Agricultural Market Access', 28 October.

Hocking, B., and Smith, M. (1997), *Beyond Foreign Economic Policy: The United States, the Single European Market and the Changing World Economy* (London: Pinter).

Holmes, P. (2005), 'British Trade Policy and the Doha Development Round', in M. Overhaus, H. W. Maull, and S. Harnisch (eds), *European Trade Policy and the Doha Development Agenda: German Foreign Policy Dialogue* (15 February) (www.deutsche-aussenpolitik.de), 7–12.

Holmes, P., and Rollo, J. (2001), 'EU Commercial Policy after Nice', *Euroscope*, 19, Spring Term (Falmer: Sussex European Institute).

Johnson, M. (1998), *European Community Trade Policy and the Article 113 Committee* (London: Royal Institute of International Affairs).

Johnson, M., with Rollo, J. (2001), 'Enlargement and the Making of Commercial Policy', SEI Working Paper 43 (Falmer: Sussex European Institute).

Kerremans, B. (2005), 'Managing the Agenda: The EU's Rationale for a New Round of Trade Negotiations', in M. Overhaus, H. W. Maull, and S. Harnisch (eds), *European*

Trade Policy and the Doha Development Agenda: German Foreign Policy Dialogue (15 February) (www.deutsche-aussenpolitik.de).

Lamy, P. (1999), 'World Trade Organisation Ministerial Conference in Seattle: Appraisal and Prospects', Speech to the European Parliament (13 December).

Lamy, P. (2000), 'What Are the Options after Seattle?', Speech to the European Parliament (25 January).

Lamy, P. (2001), 'The WTO New Round: Perspectives for Hamburg and Europe', Speech to the Handelskammer Hamburg (3 September).

Lamy, P. (2002), *L'Europe en première ligne* (Paris: Editions du Seuil).

Lamy, P. (2004), 'Europe and the Future of Economic Governance', *Journal of Common Market Studies*, 42: 1.

Langhammer, R. J. (2005), 'The EU Offer of Service Trade Liberalisation in the Doha Round: Evidence of a Not-Yet-Perfect Customs Union', *Journal of Common Market Studies*, 43: 2.

Lehmann, J.-P. (2005), 'France and the Doha Debacle', in M. Overhaus, H. W. Maull, and S. Harnisch (eds), *European Trade Policy and the Doha Development Agenda: German Foreign Policy Dialogue* (15 February) (www.deutsche-aussenpolitik.de).

Mandelson, P. (2005a), 'Statement by Commissioner Peter Mandelson to the WTO on the State of DDA Talks', Geneva (28 July).

Mandelson, P. (2005b), 'New EU offer in Doha Talks: Statement by Peter Mandelson', 28 October.

Mandelson, P. (2006), 'EU Trade Policy after Hong Kong', Speech to the Haus der Deutschen Wirtschaft (23 January).

Meunier, S. (1998), 'Divided but United: European Trade Policy Integration and EU–US Agricultural Negotiations in the Uruguay Round', in C. Rhodes (ed.), *The European Union in the World Community* (Boulder: Lynne Rienner).

Meunier, S. (2005), *Trading Voices: The European Union in International Commercial Negotiations* (Princeton: Princeton University Press).

Meunier, S., and Nicolaïdis, K. (2001), 'Trade Competence in the Nice Treaty', *ECSA Review*, Spring.

Panagariya, A. (2002), 'Developing Countries at Doha: A Political Economy Analysis', *World Economy*, 25: 9.

Rieger, E. (2005), 'Agricultural Policy: Constrained Reforms', in H. Wallace, W. Wallace, and M. A. Pollack (eds), *Policy-Making in the European Union* (Oxford: Oxford University Press), fifth edition.

Rollo, J. (2003), 'An Earlier Sign of EU Flexibility Might Have Managed to Head Off the Cancún Breakdown', *Financial Times*, 24 September.

Rollo, J. et al. (2003), 'Expanding WTO Rules? Should There Be WTO Rules on Competition, Investment, Trade Facilitation and Transparency in Government Procurement?', The Federal Trust.

Thompson, R. (2001), 'Doha Diary'. www.freetradewritersgroup.org.

Wilkinson, R. (1999), 'Labour and Trade-Related Regulation: Beyond the Trade–Labour Standards Debate?', *British Journal of Politics and International Relations*, 1: 2.

Winters, L. A. (2001), 'European Union Trade Policy: Actually or Just Nominally Liberal?', in H. Wallace (ed.), *Interlocking Dimensions of European Integration* (London: Palgrave).

Woolcock, S. (2000), 'European Trade Policy: Global Pressures and Domestic Constraints', in H. Wallace and W. Wallace (eds), *Policy-Making in the European Union* (Oxford: Oxford University Press), fourth edition.

Woolcock, S. (2005), 'Trade Policy: From Uruguay to Doha and Beyond', in H. Wallace, W. Wallace, and M. A. Pollack (eds), *Policy-Making in the European Union* (Oxford: Oxford University Press), fifth edition.

WTO (1995), *Trade Policy Review: European Union 1995* (Geneva: World Trade Organisation).

WTO (2001), 'Ministerial Conference, Fourth Session, Doha, 9–14 November 2001: Ministerial Declaration', WT/MIN(01)/DEC/W/1. www.wto.org.

WTO (2002), *Trade Policy Review: European Union*, WT/TPR/S/102 (26 June) (Geneva: World Trade Organisation).

WTO (2005), 'Report (2005) of the Committee on Anti-Dumping Practices', G/L/758 (2 November).

Young, A. R. (2004), 'The Incidental Fortress: The Single European Market and World Trade', *Journal of Common Market Studies*, 42: 4.

Young, A. R., and Peterson, J. (2006), 'The EU and the New Trade Politics', *Journal of European Public Policy*, 13: 6.

Young, A. R., Holmes, P., and Rollo, J. (2000), 'The EU's Multilateral Trade Agenda after Seattle', in I. Falautano and P. Guerrieri (eds), *Beyond Seattle: A New Strategic Approach in the WTO 2000*, IAI Quaderni No. 11, Istituto Affari Internazionali (October).

8 The cotton club

The Africa Group in the Doha Development Agenda

Donna Lee

Introduction

One of the most heralded characteristics of the Doha Development Agenda (DDA) is the increased level of participation and influence of developing countries. Much is made of the increased presence of developing countries at all levels of WTO trade negotiations, from their membership of mini-ministerials and various negotiating committees to participation in the so-called exclusive 'Green Room' meetings. Indeed, depending on which version of the Cancún Ministerial meeting (September 2003) one finds most convincing, developing countries played a major role in the collapse of the trade talks. During the December 2005 Hong Kong Ministerial meeting, developing country participation was, once again, key to the completion of the negotiations. In particular, the Africa Group's involvement in the agricultural negotiations – and specifically the talks on cotton, where there was a minimal agreement – was vital to the overall outcome.

This chapter explores the role and influence of the Africa Group in the DDA through a case study of the cotton negotiations. A key theme explored here is the emergence of the African countries as major protagonists in the DDA. After a brief discussion of Africa's economic and political interests in multilateral trade negotiations, I discuss the theme of the increased participation of developing countries – including the Africa Group – in trade negotiations. I then go on to discuss the political economy of cotton production and the cotton trade in order to highlight the fundamental importance of the commodity to African development and, in turn, the fundamental importance of building a strong pan-African coalition within the WTO in order to secure a satisfactory agreement on cotton. I also consider the political economy of cotton subsidies in the United States (US) and European Union (EU) as a way of demonstrating the importance of state-level analysis in understanding outcomes in international economic diplomacy. The final section of the chapter returns to the theme of the increased participation of the Africa Group through a detailed examination of the cotton negotiations in the DDA from April 2003 to the Hong Kong Ministerial.

Although the Africa Group is one of the largest blocs in the WTO, dwarfed only by the G90, it is probably the weakest vis-à-vis the dominant powers. The members of the group – with the exception of South Africa – suffer from high levels of vulnerability in relation to the major trading nations because they are particularly exposed to bilateral pressure from the Americans and Europeans due to existing preferential trade agreements, as well as aid and finance programmes such as the Africa Growth and Opportunity Act (AGOA) and the Cotonou Agreement. The Africa Group's diplomatic weight is also diminished by internal divisions that prevent the degree of co-ordination of strategy necessary for effective influence in the DDA. Apart from the cotton issue, where the Group sustains a consensus position, there are also fundamental policy splits within the Group on all other issues in the DDA, including serious fault lines on agriculture, TRIPs, and the Singapore issues. Uganda, Kenya, Senegal, and Nigeria, for example, argue against substantive negotiations in agriculture because they want to retain subsidies as they rely on imports of subsidised food and because they already enjoy access to EU markets through existing preferential trade agreements. South Africa and Tanzania, however, seek greater access to agricultural markets and therefore support negotiations on the removal of subsidies, anti-dumping, and increased market access. The differences on agricultural subsidies, according to one African newspaper, left the 'continent polarised into two camps' (*The East African*, 23 June 2003). And while most African countries are opposed to the inclusion of the Singapore issues in the DDA, South Africa is prepared to trade-off the inclusion of these in the hope of achieving movement by the US and EU on implementation issues.[1]

On the cotton issue the Africa Group has achieved a remarkable degree of unity in the deliberations and synchronised its diplomatic strategies in the DDA through regular meetings of the Africa WTO Group (weekly meetings of Geneva-based African trade representatives) as well as the United Nations Economic Commission for Africa (UNECA), which hosts workshops for African trade negotiators to prepare for ministerial meetings, and the African Union (AU) Conference of Ministers of Trade. These in-house efforts to increase their deliberative capacities are vital to African countries because trade negotiations have become the key instrument of development now that other policy tools have been removed by the Uruguay agreements. The importance of the international trade regime to African development cannot be emphasised enough.

Africa and the importance of the international trade regime

The recovery of the global economy from mid-2003 onwards has produced increased demand for African commodities. The 5 per cent growth in world trade in 2003 – up from 1.7 per cent in 2002 – was largely driven by increased demand from fast-growing developing countries such as China, Brazil, and India, and many African countries (especially the new oil producers such as Chad, Equatorial Guinea, and Angola) have benefited from this demand. The rise in Chinese imports of raw materials from Africa such as oil, nickel, copper, and aluminium, for example, is a key growth area for African exports; African trade with China has risen by over 50 per cent (UNECA, 2004).

China's accession to the WTO is just one factor heightening the importance of the Doha negotiations for African countries. The persistence of protectionist attitudes in the US and the expanded EU in the agricultural sector is another. As a result, African countries can ill afford to remain politically isolated within the WTO. Moreover, Africa needs to impose its development agenda on to the WTO negotiations so that developed countries move from a position of intent to open up market access, increase export competition and reduce domestic subsidies, to a position of firm action on these issues.

Despite some export growth in trade with the emerging economies, Africa has become increasingly marginalised in international trade during the last 25 years. African economies have endured sharp decreases in their share of world exports from 4.1 per cent in 1980 to 1.6 per cent in 2000, as well as a fall in their share of total world imports from 3.2 per cent to 1.3 per cent in that same twenty-year period (UNECA, 2004: 55). These figures, combined with the trends of persistent protectionism in the US and EU, and the growing influence of fast-developing countries such as China, Brazil, and India in the WTO negotiations during the DDA, underline the importance for the Africa Group of increasing its influence in multilateral trade negotiations.

The course of trade liberalisation over the last twenty years has not favoured African countries. Africa's opening up to exports from developed countries through the implementation of the Uruguay Agreements and in response to the demands of structural adjustment programmes has not brought economic development. While trade has grown as a result of the lowering of tariff and non-tariff barriers to exports and the devaluation of currencies in Africa, the reduction in world prices of key commodities such as cotton has meant that the value of African exports has actually fallen. Furthermore, most of Africa has little, if any, manufacturing production capacity and as a result its share in world manufacturing trade has been stuck at less than 1 per cent for the last twenty years.[2]

The WTO is important to the *strategic* as well as economic interests of Africa. To begin with, the WTO is one of many multilateral forums in which African countries can project their ideas regarding development. Additionally, active participation in trade negotiations enhances Africa's international standing, assisting its slow transition from an *object of trade negotiations* (a passive victim or receiver of the decisions of economic diplomacy) towards a *subject of international trade negotiations* (enjoying participant status in the deliberations), albeit in a limited way. In this way the characteristics of international economic diplomacy in the WTO (as well as the United Nations Conference on Trade And Development – UNCTAD) contrast sharply with the characteristics of international economic summitry in the G8, G20, and World Economic Forum (WEF), where African countries continue to play little, if any, part in the negotiations – though of course development has been the major item on the agenda.[3] In the WTO – as opposed to the G8, G20, and WEF – Africa has at least the opportunity to influence decisions affecting the continent's development – or continued underdevelopment, as is the case.

It is in this rather positive context of WTO multilateralism that I explore Africa's role and influence in the DDA multilateral negotiations, focusing in particular on the cotton negotiations. It is highly unlikely, however, that the Africa Group will achieve much of what it sets out to achieve in the DDA. This is because of the institutional structural constraints (the relative material power of the Quad – both the old and the new Quad[4] – compared to the Africa Group), ideational constraints within the WTO (the dominance of market-led approaches to development) that work against Africa's effective influence, and the political economy of cotton in America and, to a lesser extent, Europe.

As is now commonly known, the creation of the WTO led to an extension of the rules and regulations of international trade that leaves national trade policymaking severely restricted, adding to the importance of Africa's meaningful participation in the trade negotiations. Restricting the use of national trade policy leaves little room for developing countries to pursue development strategies outside the trade liberalisation norms that dominate the WTO (and other international economic institutions). In other words, developing country members of the WTO have no alternative to the trade liberalisation route to development; there is no other option than to seek to influence outcomes in WTO negotiations.

But just how much influence does the Africa Group have in WTO negotiations? One of the more interesting developments in the WTO during the DDA has been the increased activism of developing countries. In a recent study of developing country participation in the WTO, Kapoor points out that these members wrote 'almost half of the submissions' for the Ministerial Declarations at both Seattle and Doha (Kapoor, 2004: 530). This increased participation reflects two important changes during the DDA: (1) a greater willingness on the part of the major powers to pull key developing countries like Brazil, India, Uganda, Kenya, and South Africa into the negotiations process; and (2) significant developments within the South that have increased their negotiating capacities.

Two developments in the South are particularly noteworthy. First, developing countries have increased their deliberative capacity by enhancing the skills of their delegations through increased personnel, training, and better preparation.[5] Indeed, Walker, for example, notes the effectiveness of the Egyptian, Algerian, and South African delegations in multilateral conferences (Walker, 2004: 239). More noticeable, however, has been the establishment of developing country coalitions such as the G20,[6] the Africa Group,[7] and, to a lesser extent, the G90,[8] which have all at one stage actively opposed the majors on key issues in the DDA such as agriculture, cotton, implementation, and the Singapore issues.

Recent studies provide details of the involvement of developing countries in WTO deliberations (Akyüz, 2003; Jawara and Kwa, 2004; Kapoor, 2004; Martin and Winters, 1996; Krueger, 1999; Kufour, 2004; Narlikar, 2003, 2004; Narlikar and Odell, 2004). They show that developing country activism is for the most part restricted to the upper-income-level countries and the middle powers such as Brazil, China, and India. Few of the active developing countries are African. Most African countries, and especially the LDCs in Southern Africa, are rarely involved in key decisions and they are seldom consulted during the deliberative process. Moreover, even the African countries that do participate – including South Africa, Uganda, and Kenya – seem to have little impact on the drafts and final texts of

Ministerial Declarations despite putting forward proposals such as the highly significant April 2003 Cotton Initiative. However, procedurally, African countries can have a decisive impact on whether final agreement is reached at ministerials – as the collapse of the Cancún talks illustrates. On substantive issues, however, increased participation by developing countries in general, and the Africa Group in particular, has not resulted in meaningful transformation of rules and regulations governing trade during the DDA. This chapter seeks to explain why, using a case study of the cotton negotiations.

The political economy of cotton

Cotton production and exports play a vital strategic role in the development – or, to be more accurate, the continued underdevelopment – of the 33 net cotton-exporting African countries. Exports from a majority of Central and West African countries are dominated by cotton. For example, cotton accounts for some 60 per cent of agricultural exports in countries such as Benin, Burkina Faso, Chad, Mali, and Togo (WTO, 2003a). These countries are essentially single-commodity producers, dependent on market access for their goods and stability in (as well as relatively good) world prices. Cotton production and export in Central and West Africa are not, therefore, simply about export earnings, as they are in the developed world. Cotton is an issue of development, of food security, and of poverty in peasant communities.

Despite remarkable successes in increased production and efficiencies in costs that make African countries the most competitive cotton producers in the international economy (peasant farmers in Togo produce a ton of cotton at half the cost that American farmers produce it) – African country earnings from cotton continue to fall, causing rising levels of poverty in Central and Western Africa. Thus while production of cotton in these regions in the period 1999 to 2002 increased by 14 per cent, at the same time export earnings fell by 31 per cent (WTO, 2003a).

The current international political economy of global cotton production ensures the continued underdevelopment of its most competitive producers. If liberal trade practices prevailed and cotton production and export were left to market forces, many African countries would enjoy economic growth greater than the Millennium Development Goal of 7 per cent and the 10 million Africans working in cotton production would be lifted out of abject poverty. But liberal trade practices do not prevail in cotton; quite the opposite. A handful of the most powerful developed countries within the WTO – particularly the US, which accounts for 30 per cent of all cotton trade and is the most important player in world cotton markets – subsidise cotton production to a level that costs African countries an estimated over $1 billion in export revenue. The EU has only a marginal influence on market prices since it accounts for only 2 per cent of world trade, yet, in terms of volume, EU cotton production in Greece, Portugal, and Spain represents 70 per cent of West and Central African exports (Commission of the European Communities, 2004). First and foremost, however, African cotton farmers' concerns are with US domestic subsidies because they are the single most important factor depressing cotton prices on the world market and depressing African producers export income. Here are some details of the subsidies:

- The US spends $3.7 billion a year in 'Amber Box'[9] domestic subsidies to its cotton farmers in Alabama, Arizona, Arkansas, California, Georgia, Louisiana, Mississippi, Missouri, New Mexico, South Carolina, Tennessee, and Texas.
- The US also spends some $700–800 million each year on export credit guarantees and a further $110–350 million on other cotton export subsidy programmes (ICTSD, 18 December 2005).
- The EU provides 'Amber Box' domestic subsidies to Spanish and Greek cotton farmers totalling $700 million per year (United States Department of Agriculture Foreign Agriculture Service, 2002). The EU does not subsidise cotton exports.

US policies on domestic subsidies keep the global market price of cotton artificially low. Indeed, the price of cotton has continued to fall (with the exception of a small rise in 2003) throughout the period of the DDA negotiations by approximately 0.9 per cent per year (Commission of the European Communities, 2004). In essence the US and the EU subsidise a few thousand farmers working on large-scale production units, putting the livelihood of 10 million small-scale peasant farmers in Africa at risk.

In Washington and Brussels domestic support for farmers is a political rather than an economic necessity; it is strategically important in the politics of the American and European state since agricultural interests are powerful political actors. The US houses the three largest and most powerful cotton-trading organisations in the world. American-based organisations such as the Plains Cotton Cooperative Association (PCCA) and the International Cotton Advisory Committee (ICAC) enjoy observer status at WTO negotiations as well as huge political influence within the North American Free Trade Agreement (NAFTA) and the US polity. This influence is reflected in the passage of the 1996 and 2002 Farm Acts, which secured huge domestic subsidies for cotton-trading organisations in the South West and Delta regions and in the almost continuous passage of 'supplemental payments' to cotton-trading organisations to compensate for market loss. Agricultural subsidies are deeply entrenched in the political economies of the US (and the EU) despite the fact that there are few convincing economic arguments for supporting cotton subsidies in developed countries. Cotton exports in Texas, Arizona, Georgia, Mississippi, and Tennessee topped the list of most important agricultural exports in those states. President Bush's own state of Texas relies heavily on cotton exports, which in 2003 were worth $803 million (United States Department of Agriculture Foreign Agriculture Service, 2003a), and in California cotton exports totalled $335 million in 2003 (United States Department of Agriculture Foreign Agriculture Service, 2003b). No US Congressman from the South West and Delta states can vote against cotton interests in their state; it would be political suicide. It is no wonder the US trade negotiators defend US cotton subsidies in trade negotiations. In the EU, cotton production has risen by some

227 per cent in the last 20 years. In Greece cotton has become the major crop for export income, making the country one of the world's largest cotton exporters. One consequence of this increase in production has been to depress world cotton prices significantly (MacDonald, 2000). This, in turn, has had a detrimental impact on rural livelihoods in cotton-producing areas of Africa.

In African countries, however, cotton holds strategic importance as a means of development and an escape from poverty for its peasant communities. The cotton industry in most African countries offers the only prospect of economic growth, especially for the land-locked countries in Central Africa. The DDA cotton deliberations are, as a result, essentially about African development; and the lack of progress therein means that the situation for cotton growers in Africa has continued to decline throughout the Doha talks. It is this development dimension that informs and acts as a source of solidarity for the Africa Group's proposals in the DDA cotton negotiations.

The cotton negotiations

To date there has been little progress on the cotton negotiations despite high levels of activism on the issue by the Africa Group. What emerged from the Hong Kong negotiations was an agreement to eliminate export subsidies in 2006 – an agreement that was largely forced by the 2005 WTO Appellate Body ruling against the US on Uplands Cotton rather than the influence of the African group in the DDA talks (Zunckel, 2005). In September 2002 Brazil requested that the Dispute Settlement Body (DSB) create a panel to review its complaint against US cotton subsidies. In April 2004 that Panel found in favour of Brazil and ordered Washington to eliminate export subsidies. Although the US appealed against the decision, the subsequent Appellate Body Report of March 2005 supported the ruling of the Panel Report (WTO, 2005a). In April 2005 the Bush government began complying with the Report and set out measures for reducing domestic subsidies in cotton.[10]

There is as yet no significant agreement on cotton to eliminate domestic subsidies. Rather, there is only a promise to discuss these over the coming months. The Hong Kong Ministerial Text sets out as a priority objective the reduction of domestic subsidies through further negotiations (WTO, 2005b). US domestic subsidies, however, are the crucial issue for the African cotton producers because these subsidies cause the market price of cotton to fall year after year. Put starkly, two years of negotiations on cotton have produced meagre results, and without the landmark Appellate Body ruling on cotton – which brought much-needed judicial pressure to bear on the negotiations – the outcome of the negotiations to date would have been even more derisory. While the Africa Group has put forward firm proposals on cotton throughout the DDA, pressured the US and the EU to set specific dates for the elimination of their domestic subsidies, and called for compensation in cash to African cotton-producing countries while US and EU domestic subsidies continue, the Americans (supported by Japan and Canada) continue to stall and postpone discussion of these proposals. In July 2005, two years after the Africa

Group submitted its 'Initiative on Cotton' calling for an end to developed country subsidies, the delegate from Benin complained that 'we have not made any progress. There has been no advance' (WTO News, 2005a). The tone of paragraph 21 of Annex A of the Hong Kong Draft Ministerial Declaration reveals yet further African frustration and disappointment when it states that on cotton 'Members remain at this point short of concrete and specific achievement' (WTO, 2005c).

The lack of any progress in the DDA negotiations prior to the March 2005 Appellate Body ruling at first reveals the back-burner status of the cotton negotiations in the DDA, which in turn demonstrates a lack of meaningful political influence by the Africa Group in the negotiations, despite its very proactive diplomacy. The Africa Group – one of the largest coalitions within the WTO – cannot translate its numerical advantage into raw negotiating power. Assertive African agency at the negotiating table has produced very little movement by the major powers. Only judicial power through the Dispute Settlement Mechanism (DSM) forces their hand in the WTO. Even though the Africa Group occupies the moral high ground on agricultural issues in general and cotton in particular (it is difficult for all but the most hard-nosed American delegate to argue that developed country subsidies have anything other than a very negative impact on cotton farmers in Africa and should be eliminated in a Trade Round that claims to prioritise development), it has little negotiating strength in the WTO relative to other coalitions. The dynamics of the agricultural trade negotiations work against African influence even where there are high levels of Africa Group participation in negotiations. These dynamics include the tendency for the negotiations to be dominated by the US and EU; the American use of bilaterals with developing countries to undermine solidarity in developing country coalitions like the Africa Group; the existence of a range of preferential trade agreements between African countries and the US and the EU (such as the AGOA and Cotonou Conventions) which provide potential retaliation measures should African countries not co-operate with their patrons; the presence of several coalitions (the G20, the Cairns Group, the Africa Group, G90, and MERCUSOR) all vying for influence; as well as the dynamics within the Africa Group – having members that are net importers of agricultural products and thus benefit from subsidised food, as well as members that seek market access and thus lose out because of developed country subsidies – which undermines African solidarity in the wider agriculture negotiations. The Africa Group is far from homogeneous, and it has found it extremely difficult to sustain collective action in the DDA on all issues other than cotton.

This next section of the chapter analyses some of the details of the cotton negotiations. I begin by discussing the key proposals in the April 2003 Cotton Initiative tabled by members of the Africa Group and then go on to highlight reactions to the Initiative at the Cancún Ministerial in September 2003, the discussions on cotton in the July Package deliberations, the discussions of the Cotton Sub-Committee in the lead-up to the Hong Kong meeting in December 2005, and finally the Hong Kong Ministerial itself.

The April 2003 Cotton Initiative

In April 2003 four African countries – Benin, Burkina Faso, Chad, and Mali – submitted a four-page document titled 'Poverty Reduction: Sectoral Initiative in Favour of Cotton' to the WTO Director-General in the hope that it would kick-start meaningful discussions in the DDA on cotton. This initiative was also presented to the WTO Trade Negotiations Committee on 10 June 2003 and discussed at two Special Sessions of the Committee on Agriculture in July 2003. It was then submitted to the ministerial meeting at Cancún in September 2003 (WTO, 2003c, 2003d).

Arguing that the key objective of the DDA is the development of a liberal trade system in which distortions in world agricultural markets were to be reformed – since African countries suffer most from developed country agricultural subsidies – the Cotton Initiative made firm and wide-sweeping proposals on cotton. The Initiative called for:

•   the total elimination of domestic subsidies on cotton in the period 2004–6, taking the form of a one-third reduction each year of all cotton-supporting measures. By December 2006 a free market in cotton should be in place;
•   transitional arrangements in the form of cash compensation for cotton-producing countries to offset their loss of revenue until domestic subsidies in developed countries were eliminated.

The Cancún Ministerial meeting

Despite vigorous efforts by the Africa Group, these cotton proposals were not included in the Draft Ministerial Text for the Cancún meeting. However, the Initiative was presented to the Cancún Ministerial meeting by the Africa Group on the first day of deliberations. On the second day the WTO Director-General, Supachai Panitchpakdi – who had taken responsibility for chairing the cotton discussions – consulted all WTO members on the Initiative. The consultations and subsequent discussions on the third day of the Cancún meeting were characterised by American and European resistance to the substantive and procedural aspects of the proposal. Substantively the Americans and Europeans argued that the discussions should avoid what they saw as a narrow focus on domestic subsidies and should consider the long-term state-level obstacles to the development of the cotton industry in Central and Western Africa and the need to reform the cotton production to create more demand for garment rather than fibre (leading one commentator to quip that the US was suggesting to African countries that they should create a bigger market for T-shirts – Aziz, 2003). On the issue of transition funding the Americans and Europeans stalled the discussions on procedural grounds, stating no more than an intention to consider compensation measures, but only after the trade-related issues of cotton had been resolved. The Americans also raised a procedural obstacle to progressive deliberations on cotton by arguing for the linkage of cotton to the overall agricultural talks. In effect they agreed that a cotton agreement had to be part of a single undertaking in agriculture, thereby ensuring that cotton would remain on the back burner in the agriculture negotiations.

Vocal African disquiet at what Africans perceived to be an attempt to bury the cotton issue in the broader, and hugely contentious, agricultural negotiations at least forced specific proposals on cotton to be included in the September Derbez Text,[11] although the wording of the Text on cotton again signalled no more than an intention to reduce subsidies rather than any specific action on subsidies or compensation.

The July Package

Throughout 2004 the Africa Group continued to push for progress on its cotton proposals but with only limited success on procedural matters. In March 2004 the WTO hosted a workshop on cotton in Benin and these discussions led to specific proposals on cotton finding their way into the 2004 July Package. A more assertive African consensus emerged at the July Package negotiations in summer 2004 where the Africa Group threatened to block the negotiations if its demands on subsidy reductions were not achieved by 2005. This more aggressive strategy produced some results in that the July Package instructed the WTO Agriculture Committee to give cotton 'appropriate priority' and ensure cotton is discussed independently, going on to stipulate that cotton will be dealt with 'ambitiously, expeditiously and specifically' on the issues of market access, domestic support, and export competition (the so-called three pillars of the agriculture negotiations). In the July Package we see the first official recognition of the complementarity between development and the establishment of a free trade regime in cotton (WTO News, 2004a). But while the Africa Group optimistically viewed the July Package as a meaningful first step towards reductions in US and EU domestic subsidies, it was also aware that the text contained no commitments on dates or percentages and that much would depend upon the goodwill of the Americans and Europeans; 'we hope that this agreement will be applied in good faith', pleaded a member of the Burkina Faso delegation (News24.com, 2004). Yet a key obstacle to goodwill would be the looming 2004 US Presidential and Congressional elections where cotton is king in key electoral battlegrounds in the so-called blue states of Alabama, Arizona, Arkansas, Georgia, Louisiana, Mississippi, Missouri, New Mexico, South Carolina, and Tennessee. As already mentioned, these states enjoy huge domestic cotton subsidies and, tellingly, tend to punch above their weight in the Senate and the House of Representatives (in the Senate, for example, a voter in New Mexico has 19 times the representation of a voter in California as a result of the US electoral system). Clearly cotton subsidies translate into votes for George W. Bush and the Republicans in the cotton belt.

During this period there is evidence that African agency in the WTO was having some influence in so far as the cotton issue remained high on the Agricultural Committee agenda. In November 2004 Africa Group persistence on the point that cotton should be given priority in the agricultural negotiations and discussed independently led to the creation of the WTO sub-committee on cotton. This, however, was an easy compromise for the US and EU to accept since it involved no firm commitments on domestic subsidy reduction. The Africa Group had gone to Geneva demanding reductions by the 'beginning of the 2005 harvest' and it came away with a sub-committee. This was active participation – but not meaningful influence.

WTO sub-committee on cotton: towards the Hong Kong Ministerial

Throughout 2005 the Africa Group used the sub-committee on cotton as a vehicle for putting continuous pressure on the Americans and the Europeans to begin elimination of domestic subsidies and compensation. With the April 2005 Appellate Body ruling upholding Brazil's complaint against US cotton subsidies setting the pace for the negotiations, the Africa Group tabled a document at the cotton sub-committee meeting in April 2005 setting out modalities on cotton that included a call for the elimination of domestic subsidies by 21 September 2005 and the elimination of all export subsidies by 1 July 2005. The proposal also called for the immediate creation of an emergency support fund for African cotton producers. There were also additional demands that the Africa Group signalled it would be making in the agricultural deliberations at the Hong Kong meeting. These included the development of disciplines to prevent box-shifting (the re-categorising of supports without reducing their distorting effect) of domestic subsidies within the agricultural negotiations – a favoured tactic of the US and the EU – as well as cotton-specific criteria for measures authorised under Green and Blue Boxes. Also, the Africa Group would be demanding agreement on the creation of a 'safety net programme' for all African cotton-producing and net exporting countries to 'contain the serious socio-economic consequences for the farming communities of loss of revenue' (WTO, 2005d).

The Africa Group proposals were supported by Cuba, Paraguay, Brazil, Argentina, and China, but opposed by major developing countries, including the US, EU, Canada, and Japan. The EU response to the proposal was to argue against the phasing out of domestic subsidies in cotton and issue an intention to implement reductions in trade barriers and subsidies agreed in the context of the agricultural negotiations. Similarly, the US and Canada argued against fast-tracking cotton, rehearsing yet again the position that the outcome of the cotton negotiations should be part of the 'single undertaking' of the DDA and part of the 'comprehensive agriculture package'. As US Texas Congressman Randy Neugebauer remarked:

> Singling out one commodity, and one nation's policies on that commodity, is not the path to take for fair trade. When all of the 148 WTO countries put their tariffs, export subsidies and unfair trade barriers on the table, then and only then can we have a full discussion of agriculture support.
>
> (Southwest Farm Press, 29 April 2004)

The American position is that a separate decision on cotton would undermine the 'cross-cutting approach' of the agriculture negotiations. With respect to the proposal to create an emergency fund, the US and the Japanese repeated their opposition, arguing that such a fund would be anti-competitive and that a better response to the economic crisis in peasant farming communities would be to extend bilateral aid programmes (WTO News, 2005b).

In the meantime, in September 2004, 'The Upland Cotton Ruling' (Chad's and Benin's participation as third parties to the dispute was the first time an African country has been a party in a WTO dispute either as plaintiff or defendant) found in favour of Brazil's complaint about American cotton and, following the Appellate Body's March 2005 decision to uphold the Panel's ruling, forced the Bush Administration to begin reducing its export subsidies in April 2005.[12] This will bring some relief to African as well as Brazilian cotton farmers. It will, however, lead only to the elimination of US export subsidies, not the more important (in terms of the effect of depressing world prices) domestic subsidies. The Uplands Cotton ruling was a judicial shot in the arm of the DDA cotton negotiations. Had Brazil not won this case it is unlikely that there would have been any progress towards African goals in the cotton negotiations.

Using the impetus provided by the ruling on cotton in November 2005, the Africa Group – making one more push in advance of the Hong Kong meeting – called for the elimination of export subsidies for cotton by the end of 2005 and called for the phasing out of domestic subsidies by January 2009 (80 per cent by the end of 2006). It repeated the call for an emergency fund for African cotton producers and free access for African cotton exports. Within days of this announcement the EU stated that it would eliminate all tariff barriers to African cotton exports upon completion of the Round and also that it would be willing to eliminate most domestic subsidies autonomously from 2006. This left the US somewhat isolated – a position it is well accustomed to in trade negotiations. The US went into the Hong Kong meeting holding firm to its position that agreement on cotton could only be part of an overall agricultural package and that domestic subsidies on cotton could not be negotiated separately from domestic subsidies in agriculture generally (International Centre for Trade and Sustainable Development, 2005b). Clearly, if there were going to be any agreement, it would require a huge shift on substantive as well as procedural issues by the Americans on domestic subsidies.

The Hong Kong Ministerial

In the lead-up to Hong Kong the Benin delegate stated that the Africa Group 'disagreed with the view that progress in cotton has to wait for progress in the agriculture negotiations as a whole' and other African delegates warned that the Africa Group would not allow cotton to be sidelined at the Hong Kong Ministerial meeting (WTO News, 2005a). At the plenary session on the first day of the meeting the Minister for Chad highlighted how Africa's specific demands on cotton had been ignored to date and appealed for progress in the negotiations.

In advance of the meeting the EU also offered to eliminate what export subsidies it had in place (these were really quite minor). It seemed there was some impetus for movement towards African demands. The Americans, however, held fast to their position on domestic subsidies and as a result the meeting ended without specific progress beyond what had already been forced by the 2005 Appellate Body US Uplands Cotton ruling. Paragraph 11 of the Hong Kong Ministerial text sets out the results of the cotton negotiations. These were the elimination of developed export subsidies by 2006, quota-free and duty-free access for LDC cotton exports to developed country markets, and a commitment to prioritise discussions on reducing domestic subsidies more ambitiously and more expeditiously than reductions on agricultural domestic subsidies. Paragraph 12 of the text also outlines provision for development assistance for cotton producers (WTO, 2005b).

In sum, the negotiations produced an agreement to eliminate export subsidies on cotton which had already been deemed illegal by the WTO. The agreement to provide free access for African cotton exports to the US and other developed countries was also meaningless since these are not key markets for African producers. What African producers need are real market prices for their cotton so that they have equal access to all markets. Yet market prices are depressed by US domestic subsidies. On this principal issue the Africa Group came away with only US assurances that the Americans would continue to negotiate to reduce domestic subsidies more quickly than under the general framework of agricultural subsidy reductions. Thus cotton subsidies continue to be linked to agricultural subsidies in general and the US was able to duck this most foremost issue for the Africa Group in the DDA.

Conclusions

While it is easy to identify Africa's increased participation in the DDA, it is much more difficult to pinpoint substantive impact in key areas of negotiation such as cotton. It is only on procedural issues – such as the creation of the cotton subcommittee – that the Africa Group has exercised any kind of influence. Attempts to force substantive changes in US domestic cotton subsidies – the single most important factor depressing market prices for African cotton – have failed. As the analysis of these negotiations in this chapter has shown, explanations for the lack of substantive influence on the cotton issue by an assertive and active Africa Group must take account not only of the relative structural weaknesses of the coalition in the DDA negotiations but also of protectionist pressures within the US and Europe which lobby for, and continue to receive, huge levels of domestic agricultural subsidy.

The tragedy of the lack of substantive influence for the Africa Group in the DDA is that it is locked into the WTO process. The political economy of the international trade regime dictates that the Group has no alternative to participating in the DDA and working towards its completion in the hope that it can secure better market access and fairer prices for its products. And so, despite the lack of progress on the Cotton Initiative and the passing of deadlines it set out for reductions in US and EU domestic subsidies and compensation measures, the Africa Group maintains support for the WTO process, a process that continues to be undemocratic and 'tilted towards richer countries' (Jawara and Kwa, 2004: 65). A very small number of African countries such as South Africa, Uganda, Ghana, and Kenya are sometimes involved in the early 'consultation' process in the 'Green Room' meetings and the mini-ministerials organised and chaired by the WTO Director-General. But 'Green Room' meetings and negotiating committee meetings lack transparency; minutes are not produced. Instead the Chair submits a briefing to the WTO of their 'sense' and 'understanding' of the meeting. These briefings are then reflected in WTO Drafts such as Ministerial Texts. Ministerial Texts act as agendas for Ministerial Conferences, forming the basis for the negotiations. African countries feel marginalised in this process and are, not surprisingly, often very critical of this procedure since African positions get lost in the system and are often absent from the Ministerial Texts. And all this despite record levels of African participation in the WTO.

As a Japanese commentator recently pointed out, a developing country appointment as 'Friends of the Chair' was 'meant to give the impression that the third world is participating in trade discussions as an equal partner, but that is not the case' (*The Monitor*, 15 September 2003). Developing countries are only participating at the behest of the Secretariat and they cannot hope to negotiate on an equal footing with the major powers in the WTO. African members are constrained by their dependence upon the majors and the inequalities within the international political economy.

This chapter has shown that the Africa Group has been an active participant in the DDA, driving the cotton negotiations forward for the last two years. It has also shown the limitations of this activism such that, despite participation in influential meetings and membership of key committees, the Group can claim very little influence over the key substantive matters in cotton. Since its key goals were to secure the reduction of American and European domestic subsidies in cotton, the continued failure to get agreement on these means that the DDA is yet to yield anything meaningful in trade for the Africa Group.

In the world of trade negotiations, the Africa Group has insufficient material and ideational capacity to challenge the power of the major developed countries whatever diplomatic strategies it pursues. While the Africa Group can rightly claim to have increased its participation in the trade negotiations, it can claim to have had only procedural influence. Lacking the capacities to challenge the protectionist forces dominating the political economy of cotton in America, the Africa Group will struggle to carve out for itself an influential role in the substantive negotiations on cotton in the DDA post-Hong Kong. It is only where the rule of law governs international trade in the Dispute Settlement Mechanism (DSM) that African countries have been successful in challenging domestic protectionist forces in the US – albeit as third parties to disputes – as the Uplands Cotton Ruling demonstrates. In sum, African countries have more influence on the rules governing cotton where the rule of law prevails in the DSM than they can in WTO trade negotiations conducted under conditions of anarchy. In this sense, assertive Pan-Africanism is better placed in the WTO's DSM than it is in the DDA.

Notes

Thanks to Craig Murphy, Rorden Wilkinson, Jeff Ladewig, and Julie Gilson for comments on an earlier draft of this chapter. I am also indebted to the Department of Political Science and International Studies, University of Birmingham, for funds in support of the research for this chapter.

1 For detailed analysis of the splits within the Africa Group at Cancún see Lee (2006).
2 This compares with a rise share in the share of manufactured trade in Asia from 7.1 per cent in 1980 to 21.5 per cent in 2000 (United Nations Economic Commission for Africa, 2004: 64).
3 South Africa has, however, has been invited by the majors to attend recent G8 summits and is also a member of the G20 of Finance Ministers. Given its high level of economic development, the high level of FDI within Africa, and its hegemonic trade relationship with its South African neighbours, Pretoria can hardly claim to represent adequately the 'voice of Africa' in these negotiations. Indeed, other African nations are somewhat wary and resentful of South Africa's promotion to this self-appointed – or, perhaps more accurately, appointed by the North – position. For a discussion of the problems South Africa faces in its African diplomacy see Hamill (2006).
4 The old Quad consisted of the US, EU, Japan, and Canada. The so-called new Quad consists of the US, the EU, Brazil, and India.
5 The WTO has provided funds and technical assistance to help developing countries improve their negotiating skills. The United Nations ECA has also provided much-needed expert advice and analysis of WTO negotiations, policies, and procedures to the Africa Group.
6 The G20 group includes Argentina, Bolivia, Brazil, Chile, China, Colombia, Costa Rica, Cuba, Ecuador, Egypt, Guatemala, India, Indonesia, Mexico, Pakistan, Paraguay, Peru, the Philippines, Nicaragua, South Africa, Thailand, and Venezuela. El Salvador was originally a member but it withdrew at the Cancún Conference.
7 The Africa Group consists of 44 members from the African Union.
8 The G90 comprises all the developing and less developed country members of the WTO.
9 Amber Box subsidies are those to be reduced. Green Box subsidies are those permitted and Red are those forbidden.
10 For details of the ruling on US Uplands Cotton see WTO documents on Dispute Case DS267 at http://www.wto.org/english/tratop_e/dispu_e/cases_e/ds267_e.htm.
11 The so-called Derbez Text was the Second Revision of the Draft Cancún Ministerial Text distributed on 13 September 2003.
12 For a detailed discussion of the ruling see Zunckel (2005).

References

Akyüz, Yilmaz (2003), *Developing Countries and World Trade: Performance and Prospects* (London: Zed Books/UNCTAD/Third World Network).

Aziz, Naeesa (2003), 'Eye on Africa/Africa's WTO loss', *The Hill Top – Nation & World.* http://www.thehilltoponline.com.

Commission of the European Communities (2004), Communication from the Commission to the Council and the European Parliament, *Proposal for an EU–Africa Partnership in Support of Cotton Sector Development* (Brussels: Commission of the European Communities).

Drahos, Peter (2003), 'When the Weak Bargain with the Strong: Negotiations in the World Trade Organization', *International Negotiation*, 8: 1.

Hamill, James (2006) 'South Africa in Africa: The Dilemmas of Multilateralism', in Donna Lee, Ian Taylor, and Paul Williams (eds), *The New Multilateralism in South African Diplomacy* (Basingstoke: Palgrave).

Hampson, Fen O. (2004), 'Lilliputians to the Rescue: Small and Middle Power Mediation in International Multilateral Negotiations', Paper presented at the annual general meeting of the International Studies Association, Montreal.

Hoekman, Bernard M., and Kostecki, Michel M. (2001), *The Political Economy of the World Trading System* (Oxford: Oxford University Press), second edition,

Hoogvelt, Ankie (1997), *Globalization and the Postcolonial World: The New Political Economy of Development* (Basingstoke: Macmillan).

International Centre for Trade and Sustainable Development (2005a), *Bridges Daily Update*, Issue 10 (December), www.ictsd.org.

International Centre for Trade and Sustainable Development (2005b), *Bridges Daily Update*, Issue 6 (December), www.ictsd.org.

Jawara, Fatoumata, and Kwa, Aileen (2004), *Behind the Scenes at the WTO: The Real World of International Trade Negotiations* (London: Zed Books), updated edition.

Kahler, Miles, and Odell, John (1989), 'Developing Country Coalition-Building and International Trade Negotiations', in John Walley (ed.), *Trade Policy and the Developing World* (Ann Arbor: University of Michigan Press).

Kapoor, Ilan (2004), 'Deliberative Democracy and the WTO', *Review of International Political Economy*, 11: 3 (August).

Krueger, Anne (1999), 'The Developing Countries and the Next Round of Multilateral Trade Negotiations', *World Economy*, 22: 7.

Kufour, Kofi Oteng (2004), *World Trade Governance and Developing Countries: The GATT/WTO Committee System* (London and Oxford: The Royal Institute of International Affairs/Blackwell).

Lee, Donna (2004), 'Understanding the WTO Dispute Settlement System', in Brian Hocking and Steven McGuire (eds), *Trade Politics* (London: Routledge, 2004), second edition.

Lee, Donna (2006), 'South Africa in the WTO', in Donna Lee, Ian Taylor, and Paul Williams (eds), *The New Multilateralism in South African Diplomacy* (Basingstoke: Palgrave).

MacDonald, Stephen (2000), 'The New Agricultural Trade Negotiations: Background and Issues for U.S. Cotton Sector', *Cotton and Wool Situation Outlook/CWS-2000/November 2000*, Economic Research Service, US Department of Agriculture.

Martin, Will, and Winters, Alan (eds) (1996), *The Uruguay Round and the Developing Countries* (Cambridge: Cambridge University Press).

Narlikar, Amrita (2003), *International Trade and Developing Countries: Bargaining Coalitions in the GATT and WTO* (London: Routledge).

Narlikar, Amrita (2004), 'Developing Countries in the WTO', in Brian Hocking and Steven McGuire (eds), *Trade Politics* (London: Routledge), second edition.

Narlikar, Amrita, and Odell, John S. (2004), 'Explaining Negotiation Strategies and Bargaining Outcomes: The Like-Minded Group and the 2001 Doha Agreements', Paper presented at the annual general meeting of the International Studies Association, Montreal.

News24.com (2004) 'WTO: More Promises for Africa', 01/08/2004. http://www.news24.com/news24/Africa/News/0,,2-11-1447_1566443,00.html.

Odell, John S. (2000), *Negotiating the World Economy* (Ithaca: Cornell University Press).

Payne, Anthony (ed.) (2004), *The New Regional Politics of Development* (Basingstoke: Palgrave).

Peet, Richard (2003), *Unholy Trinity: The IMF, World Bank and WTO* (London: Zed Books).

Putnum, Robert (1988), 'Diplomacy and Domestic Politics: The Logic of Two-Level Games', *International Organization*, 42: 3.

Soko, Mills (2005), 'The Political Economy of African Trade in the Twenty-first Century', in Dominic Kelly and Wyn Grant (eds), *The Politics of International Trade in the Twenty-first Century: Actors, Issues and Regional Dynamics* (Basingstoke: Palgrave).

Southwest Farm Press (29 April 2004) http://southwestfarmpress.com.

Steinberg, Richard, H. (2002), 'In the Shadow of Law or Power? Consensus-Based Bargaining and Outcomes in the GATT/WTO', *International Organization*, 56: 2.

Tussie, Diane, and Glover, David (eds) (1995), *The Developing Countries in World Trade: Policies and Bargaining Strategies* (Boulder: Lynne Rienner).

United Nations Economic Commission for Africa (2004), 'Economic Report on Africa 2004: Unlocking Africa's Potential'. http://www.uneca.org/era2004.

United States Department of Agriculture Foreign Agriculture Service (2002) 'What's at Stake for Cotton', July. http://www.fas.usda.gov.

United States Department of Agriculture Foreign Agriculture Service (2003b), 'Trade and Agriculture: What's at Stake for California'. http://www.fas.usda.gov/info/factsheets/wto/states/ca.html.

United States Department of Agriculture Foreign Agriculture Service (2003a) 'Trade and Agriculture: What's at Stake for Texas'. http://www.fas.usda.gov/info/factsheets/wto/states/tx.html.

Walker, Ronald A. (2004), *Multilateral Conferences: Purposeful International Negotiation* (Basingstoke: Palgrave).

Wolfe, Robert (2004), 'Crossing the River by Feeling the Stones: Where the WTO Is Going after Seattle, Doha and Cancún', *Review of International Studies*, 11: 4.

Woolcock, Stephen (2003), 'The ITO, the GATT and the WTO', in Nicholas Bayne and Stephen Woolcock (eds), *The New Economic Diplomacy* (Aldershot: Ashgate).

WTO (2003a), 'Poverty Reduction: Sectoral Initiative in Favour of Cotton', Joint proposal by Benin, Burkina Faso, Chad, and Mali, WTO TN/AG/GEN/4 (16 May).

WTO (2003b), WT/MIN (03)/W (17 September).

WTO (2003c), WT/MIN (03)/W/2 (15 August).

WTO (2003d), WT/MIN(03)/W/2/Add.1 (15 August).

WTO (2005a), WT/DS267/20 (24 March).

WTO (2005b), 'Doha Work Programme: Draft Ministerial Text (Revision)', WT/MIN (05)/W/3/Rev.2 (18 December).

WTO (2005c) 'Doha Work Programme Draft Ministerial Declaration (revision)', WT/MIN (05)/W?3/Rev.2 (18 December).

WTO (2005d) 'Proposed Elements of Modalities in Connection with the Sectoral Initiative in Favour of Cotton: Communication from the Africa Group', TN/AG/SCC/GEN/2 (22 April).

WTO News (2004a), 'Text of the "July Package" – the General Council Decision', 1 August, http://www.wto.org/english/tratop_e/dda_e/draft_text_gc_dg_31july04_e.htm.

WTO News (2004b), 'Sub-committee Set Up on Cotton', 19 November. http://www.wto.org/english/news_e/news04_e/sub_committee_19nov04_e.htm.

WTO News (2005a), 'Africans Keep Up Pressure for Progress by end of July'. http://www.wto.org/english/news_e/news05_e/cotton_18july05_e.htm.

WTO News (2005b), 'Africa Group Proposes Cotton Distortions Scrapped by September', 29 April. http://www.wto.org/english/news_e/news05_e/cotton_19april05_e.htm.

Zartman, William I., and Berman, Maureen R. (1982), *The Practical Negotiator* (New Haven: Yale University Press).

Zunckel, Hilton (2005), 'The African Awakening in United States-Upland Cotton', *Journal of World Trade*, 39: 6.

9 The periphery strikes back?
The G20 at the WTO

Ian Taylor

Bargaining coalitions at the World Trade Organisation (WTO) are of increasing interest and importance in advancing negotiating positions in the emerging global trade regime (Narlikar, 2003). This chapter seeks to discuss and analyse the implications for this regime of the emergence of an important network of coalitions from the developing world as exemplified by the G20. The chapter argues that the activism demonstrated by the G20 reflects an inherent frustration with the results of WTO negotiations for key exporting states from the Global South. Thus the G20 can be seen as an experimental attempt to push forward an agenda in resistance to the stalling and compromises that stake out the WTO thus far on important matters vis-à-vis trade, market access, and dismantling non-tariff barriers. In particular the G20 has concentrated on insisting on removing the delays to reciprocal liberalisation in the developed world, above all with regard to agriculture. However, in doing so, the G20 is actually demanding that the North implements its own rhetoric regarding the supposed benefits of 'free trade'. It is an interesting sign of the times – as well as the hegemonic status of liberal norms regarding economics – that the elites from key developing countries are demanding greater liberalisation, not less. This was most graphically illustrated at the WTO meeting in Hong Kong.

Origins and membership of the G20

The G20 is an informal body in which developing economies have come together in order to construct a united front of sorts in pushing for greater liberalisation on agricultural trade and, in particular, the reduction of the massive subsidies on agriculture in the Group of 7 (G7) economies. The G20 was initially composed of Argentina, Bolivia, Brazil, Chile, China, Colombia, Costa Rica, Cuba, Ecuador, El Salvador, Guatemala, India, Mexico, Pakistan, Paraguay, Peru, the Philippines, South Africa, Thailand, and Venezuela. Its current membership is 21 and is made up of five countries from Africa (Egypt, Nigeria, South Africa, Tanzania, and Zimbabwe); six from Asia (China, India, Indonesia, Pakistan, the Philippines, and Thailand); and ten from Latin America (Argentina, Bolivia, Brazil, Chile, Cuba, Guatemala, Mexico, Paraguay, Uruguay, and Venezuela).

The impetus for its founding was in the lead-up to the WTO Ministerial meeting in Cancún in 2003 following the spectacular breakdown in Seattle. The immediate motivation for the formation of the G20 was the fact that certain deadlines relating to the construction of a framework for the reduction of agricultural subsidies, agreed to at the 2001 Doha Ministerial meeting, were missed before the Cancún meeting. According to the G20, '[t]he Group was born to try . . . to avoid a predetermined result at Cancún and to open up a space for negotiations in agriculture . . . the Group's main objective was to defend an outcome in the agricultural negotiations which would reflect the level of ambition of the Doha mandate and the interests of the developing countries' (G20 'History', www.g-20.mre.gov.br/history.asp). Indeed, the motive for the G20's formation was summed up by the Brazilian Permanent Representative of Brazil to the WTO, Luiz Felipe de Seixas Corrêa, when he asserted that

> [w]hat prompted the creation of this group in the WTO was a recurrent phenomenon that we think has to be changed in order to cope with the new realities of multilateral negotiations. There is the belief or understanding that everything can be solved when the two majors get together and carve out a deal that represents their convergence of interests. And that the rest of the world, being so disunited or being so fragmented or having so many different perspectives, ends up one by one being co-opted into an agreement – for lack of an organizational framework.
>
> (South Centre, 2003)

Apart from a wish to prevent a 'stitch-up' by the developed world at the WTO – perceived to be inimical to the interests of the developing world – was the desire to put on the table the issue of trade subsidies by the North. South Africa's chief director of trade negotiations, Xavier Carim, noted that an additional reason for the G20 coming together was in response to 'a particular problem' (for instance, the US$300-billion agricultural subsidies paid to farmers in the US and European Union (EU) member states). 'The G20 was not mobilised around a political banner of developing versus developed countries, but around trying to address a fundamental problem in the global economy', said Carim (quoted in *Sunday Times* (Johannesburg), 28 September 2003). Corrêa has also been keen to assert that the G20 harbours no political ambitions: 'the G20 was formed around agriculture, it has no other object than to influence the course of the agricultural negotiations' (South Centre, 2003).

At the time of the formation of the G20, a common position was adopted that was distributed as an official document of the WTO, both prior to and during the Cancún summit. This document remains the core platform of the G20 (see WTO, 2003). The platform was a restatement of the Doha Round, supporting 'the objective to establish a fair and market-oriented trading system'. Importantly, special and differential treatment for developing countries was seen to be an integral part of the negotiations, as was that 'non-trade concerns should be taken into account'. The platform urged the intensification of work 'to translate the Doha objective into reform modalities, including by adopting . . . approaches for reduction/ elimination commitments and related disciplines on key outstanding issues on market access, domestic support and all forms of export subsidies'. Thus the G20 demanded that all 'developed countries shall achieve substantial reduction in trade distorting support with Members having the higher trade distorting subsidies making greater efforts', as well as 'substantial improvement in market access for all products, in an effective and measurable way'. Tariff cuts were central to this, whilst there was a demand that 'all developed countries shall provide duty-free access to all tropical products' (WTO, 2003). The G20 also called for the elimination of export subsidies 'for the products of particular interest to developing countries'. Finally, the Group strongly underlined the need that '[t]he particular concerns of recently acceded members and Least Developed Countries shall be effectively addressed' (WTO, 2003).

The G20 position sprang from a realisation that subsidies in the developed world will not simply disappear through goodwill but require strong lobbying, political pressure, and organisation from those interested countries. Implicit in the creation of the G20 is an understanding that negotiations have not worked so far and have perhaps served to prolong the existing situation. In other words, the G20 has emerged as a result of a fundamental distrust held by the developing, agriculturally inclined nations, vis-à-vis the industrialised stance towards free trade in agricultural products. The G20 is thus using the hegemony of neo-liberalism within the WTO to delegitimise the position of the North. According to Brazil, this is a result of the G7's inflexibility and hypocrisy:

> Some people say we have introduced the North–South dichotomy into the WTO and we are blamed for that . . . We did not introduce it. It was the North that introduced the North–South dichotomy in these negotiations. The United States and the European Union got together and drafted a proposal from which they said they cannot move. So, if it was anyone who introduced the North–South dichotomy in the WTO, it was the North, not the South. Let us make this point very clear.
>
> (Corrêa, quoted in South Centre, 2003)

In essence, the G20 countries were incensed by the moves made by the US and EU prior to Cancún, which, rather than maintaining the Doha Declaration, wanted to safeguard subsidy regimes in return for negligible reforms and also pushed for the 'Singapore issues' to be discussed. These were those issues that the industrialised countries wished to negotiate, namely global rules governing investment, competition policies, transparency in government procurement processes, and the co-ordination of customs procedures (known as trade facilitation). Prior to Cancún, Brazil, Argentina, and India thus set up an alliance to push for negotiations in line with the commitments made at Doha, with South Africa, Nigeria, Egypt, China, Mexico, and most of Latin America also joining up. It can be inferred from such a move that work within the structures of the WTO had not resolved matters to the satisfaction of key elites in the developing world. What this also meant was that this grouping accounted for over 20 per cent of the globe's agricultural GDP, 26 per cent of total agricultural exports, 51 per cent of the world's population, and

63 per cent of all farmers – a not insignificant grouping, in other words. This formation can be perhaps seen as a watershed in global trade politics as developing countries were taking the lead in promoting free and fair trade within a liberalised framework. As Brazil's President, Luiz Inácio Lula da Silva, remarked, '[a]t Cancún, no one believed the G21 (developing nations) [i.e. G20] could create such an impact. But we did, which makes us believe 20 countries representing more than half the world's population, can change rules of the world trade' (quoted in *Star* (Johannesburg), 29 January 2004). In fact it seems that what happened at Cancún was that there was a clash of styles between the attitude adopted by the EU and US, which assumed their usual brinkmanship-style negotiation strategy, and the line of attacks favoured by many of the developing countries which were simply not prepared to go along with this game any more, and were ready to walk out if they were not happy with the process. Furthermore, there was growing anger at the '[a]symmetries in power [which] are exploited by the US, EU, Canada, and Japan'. This exasperation at the developed world's intransigence was specifically aimed at '[t]he WTO's richest members [who] jealously guard the "flexibility" and "informality" of its decision-making processes. Meetings are conducted in secret without record, and pressures and inducements are deployed, such as threats to withdraw aid or report non-compliant delegates to their superiors back home. If trouble stirs, more brutal methods against Third World delegates are used' (Eagleton-Pierce, 2003).

Though the Cancún meeting clearly failed, the close consultation process established at the summit invigorated the formation of the G20 as a central player in the construction of some form of meeting point between the developed and developing world over the issue of agricultural trade and other matters, as well as an alliance of supposed like-minded states in its own right:

> The group of 21 developing countries (G-21), led by Brazil, India and China, represented a critical grouping which empowered the developing world into being able to reject unfair conditions and pressures. From this point of view, Cancún has strengthened the international community. It has raised self-confidence among delegates from the South and encouraged more South–South cooperation. The challenge now remains to move from a common opposition against the unfair to the achievement of fairer agreements.
>
> (*Daily Mail* (Islamabad), 10 April 2004)

However, during and after Cancún the US and the EU became determined to target the G20 countries and lost little time in seeking to undermine this nascent grouping. At a briefing on 10 September 2003 an American official referred to the G20 as the 'Group of the Paralyzed' (quoted in Bello, 2003), whilst the proposals to put right the global agricultural trading system were characterised as 'welfare measures' and illegitimate intrusions into the 'serious' side of the negotiations. Consequently, an intensive operation to divide the G20 was conducted by Washington and the EU, with states perceived to be vulnerable to persuasion being the main targets. Offering special deals to smaller members was the immediate strategy, with co-ordinated efforts by private capital:

Alongside the US government trade team, the US corporate lobby also went to work to split the G-21. Consumer Alert, a business group masking as a consumer's organisation, said that 'while ostensibly representing the views of developing countries', the G-21 programme 'better represents the positions of several powerful exporting countries, who want greater market access without opening up their own countries' markets to importers'. But despite the intense pressures, the US was [initially] able to detach only one country from the group: El Salvador.

(Bello, 2003)

In fact '[t]he EU is reported to have warned former colonies in Africa and the Caribbean that their joining the G20 could endanger their "privileged access" to the European market [whilst] the US reportedly told Costa Rica, El Salvador and Guatemala that if they left the G20 they would get a "sweetheart deal" giving them "increased access" to the U.S. economy' (*TML Daily*, 2003). When the Cancún negotiations ended, the US rushed to blame the G20 as the prime culprit, with the US trade representative at the Cancún talks, Robert Zoellick, asserting that 'Whether developed or developing, there were "can do" and "won't do" countries here. The rhetoric of "won't do" overwhelmed the concerted efforts of the "can do"' (quoted in *BBC News Online*, 15 September 2003). The G20 grouping was cast as very much the 'won't do' group. And to emphasise Washington's contempt for the G20, it was made clear that the US would now pursue bilateral and/or regional trade deals in the absence of any agreement at Cancún. Thus President Alvaro Uribe of Colombia was warned that 'remaining in that group [the G20] will not lead to good relations between Colombia and the United States' (quoted by *Our World Is Not for Sale*, 2003). Colombia, along with Peru, also a country under powerful pressure, subsequently left the G20. 'Republican Senator Charles Grassley, the Chairman of the US Senate Finance Committee, was quoted as saying he would use his position as head of the committee with jurisdiction over international trade policy "to carefully scrutinize the positions taken by many WTO members during this ministerial"' (Berthelsen, 2003). The actions of the US moved a British parliamentary committee to state that the G20 'are a serious grouping . . . and should be treated with respect rather than contempt' (House of Commons, 2003: 17).

In addition, negotiations related to the planned Central American Free Trade Area (CAFTA) were utilised as ways of trying to undermine the G20. For instance, after Cancún, Zoellick asserted that 'the emergence of the G20 might pose a big problem to this agreement since our Congress resents the fact that members of CAFTA are also in the G20' (quoted in *Our World Is Not for Sale*, 2003). Furthermore, Zoellick attempted to raise the spectre of Brazilian hegemony as a reason why countries like Costa Rica and Guatemala should not be in the G20 as Brazil, and their own interests diverge, seeing that Brazil 'is a big country that can defend its interests by itself' (quoted in *Our World Is Not for Sale*, 2003). When Colombia, Peru, and Costa Rica left the Group the *Washington Times* (13 October 2003) commented approvingly that 'The splintering of the Group of 21 could moderate the positions taken by poor countries – which could be helpful for talks'. At the same time, it became clear that Washington was raising the very real spectre that the world trade system would fragment into regional and bilateral agreements, which would hit the developing nations hardest. These and other problems informed the G20's position at the next major WTO meeting, in Hong Kong in December 2005.

The G20 and Hong Kong

The sixth WTO Ministerial meeting took place in Hong Kong in December 2005. Four key items set out the agenda for Hong Kong, namely services, agriculture, non-agricultural market access (NAMA), and the development package (that is, the demand for 'special and differential treatment' for developing countries). From the start the EU and the US offered relatively minor reductions in agricultural subsidies in exchange for developing countries opening up their markets further in both services and industrial goods. As the negotiations proceeded, it became apparent that developing countries were backed into a corner. In return for the ending of export subsidies by 2013 the developing nations agreed to liberalise services and industrial products. But this agreement was not formally tied down and was dependent on further progress vis-à-vis the agriculture talks on subsidies and access. The end result of this was that export subsidies would remain an important bargaining chip for the developed world in advancing further liberalisation. Thus the so-called 'core modalities', involving the formulas for cutting tariffs and subsidies, were left unclear. In short, the deal arrived at in Hong Kong was based on considerable concessions by the developing countries whilst little was given in return by the developed economies.

One of the interesting dynamics at Hong Kong was the extent to which the G20 allied itself with the G33, ACP countries, LDCs, the Africa Group, and the Small Economies, in seeking to advance developing countries' interests. This led to the formation of the Group of 110 (G110) on 16 December 2005, and was in response to the developed countries' insistence on pushing the services agenda. Kamal Nath, the Indian Trade Minister, was quoted as saying that 'Our bonds [in forming the G110] are perpetuated by the desire not to put up anymore with the inequities of global trade. We need to move forward not in the direction of a handful of countries, but in the direction of 120 countries that represents four-fifths of humanity – this developed countries must recognise.' Nath went on assert that 'We have been seeing an amazing development in the discussions in Hong Kong whereby the developed countries talk in the plenary halls of a "Round for Free" for developing countries. Then they move to the green room and continue to ask for a "Round for Free", this time for themselves' (quoted by Trade Justice Movement, 2005). Expressing even greater anger, the Brazilian Foreign Minister, Celsio Amorim, reportedly asked the EU, 'which part of NO don't you understand?' (quoted by Trade Justice Movement, 2005). Hong Kong was the first time that either the G20 or the G90 had convened a meeting at an actual WTO ministerial conference.

However, the strength of the G110 was compromised by later developments as 'in the end, the developing country governments caved in, many of them motivated solely by the fear of getting saddled with the blame for the collapse of the Organisation. Even Cuba and Venezuela confined themselves to registering only "reservations" with the services text during the closing session of the ministerial in the evening of December 18' (Bello, 2005). The role of the G20 founders, Brazil and India, in this climbdown was key. Brazil's main aspiration at the Hong Kong meeting was obtaining a date for the phase-out of export subsidies on agricultural products by the developed world. Both countries accepted a Swiss formula on NAMA and the plurilateral approach in services (India took Brazil's lead on agriculture). According to Bello, 'the main gain for Brazil and India lay not in the impact of the agreement on their economies but in the affirmation of their new role as power brokers within the WTO' (Bello, 2005).

This occurrence had been developing before Hong Kong and demonstrated the growth of key developing countries within the WTO in pushing for further liberalisation, whilst ostensibly being in conflict with the developed world. With the materialisation of the G20 at Cancún, the developed countries realised that their apparent overbearing dominance of the WTO process was delegitimising the organisation. New blood needed to be brought in (or, arguably, co-opted) in order to give the organisation a semblance of legitimacy and equality. Consequently India and Brazil were invited (alongside Australia) to join the 'Five Interested Parties' (FIPs) with the EU and the United States. It was within the FIPs that the Framework Agreement at the General Council meeting in July 2004 was arrived at, paving the way for Hong Kong. And before the ministerial meeting the 'New Quad' was formed, consisting of the EU, US, Brazil, and India. This informal grouping set out the agenda and the course of the Hong Kong negotiations and fulfilled the expressed view of the G20 that the WTO was necessary for the developing world. But as Bello puts it:

> [T]he role of Brazil and India was to extract the assent of the developing countries to an unbalanced agreement that would make this possible in the face of the reluctance of the EU and US to make substantive concessions in agriculture. Delivering this consent was to be the proof that Brazil and India were 'responsible' global actors. It was the price that they had to pay for full membership in [the] new, enlarged power structure.
>
> (Bello, 2005)

In essence both Brazil and India played a quite central middlepowermanship role: 'the notion of "middle power" orient[ates] the . . . state to a role supportive of the hegemonic global order . . . [and] by fulfilling an important role of facilitator and mediator, [the middle power] help[s] defuse potential conflicts which, if not addressed, might . . . undermine . . . the stability of the global order' (Neufeld, 1995: 16–17). In short, the middlepowermanship role of Brazil and India acted as a facilitating agent to advance neoliberalism at the WTO, albeit in ostensibly defending the developing world. This continued the broad trajectory of the G20 overall since the Cancún summit.

The G20 in its global context

Central to the G20's existence is the importance of a predictable, rule-based, and transparent multilateral trading system as a means through which developing countries can maximise their development via trade and their competitive advantage. As Corrêa has asserted, the WTO 'is an irreplaceable organisation. We need it. We need it badly. We need a strong WTO and from the perspective of developing countries, this is really an irreplaceable forum – with all its shortcomings, with all its problems – this is where [the G20] can make a difference. We can get some predictability. We can get some rules and we can get some enforceable rules in an area where in the past we had none' (South Centre, 2003). Thus as Kirsty Nowlan, World Vision's delegate at Cancún, noted: 'the emergence of the G20 as a strong force on the negotiating scene represents a sea change in the way developing countries approach the WTO. It is the first time they have used their potential power as a negotiating block to balance out negotiations' (World Vision, 2003). This same ethos informed the G20's position at Hong Kong.

Aside from this broader context, other states are increasingly developing ties with the less developed world, creating axes that bypass and perhaps in the long run may threaten American dominance. Thus China is clearly more and more keen to establish special relationships with regional powers in the developing world and, in particular, in Africa (Taylor, 2004). This, in particular, has the potential that such overlapping developments may come together and create a nascent bloc of the developing world to forge greater participation in the global trading system – particularly its regulation – as well as providing alternatives to simple north–south directions in trade. Indeed, the G20 might be seen as nascent attempts to create a 'new trade geography' which does not ignore the primary importance of trade with the Group of 8 (G8) but does at the same time seek both to restructure global trade along liberal lines *and* to create new and exciting options. Certainly the growth of trade ties among developing countries has the possibility of democratising global trade relations and may help rein in the current domination of the US – something which clearly worries Washington, as its aggressive reaction to the G20 demonstrates. The India–Brazil–South Africa Dialogue Forum (IBSA) is another potential grouping of note (see Alden and Vieira, 2005).

Increased trading ties within the IBSA bloc demonstrate this potential: South Africa's trade with India and Brazil has grown 1334 per cent and 268 per cent respectively during the past decade; and between Brazil and India trade has grown 450 per cent over the same period (*Star* (Johannesburg), 2 February 2004). Indeed, initiatives such as the IBSA have very interesting implications for global politics. It could, *if* it holds together, create a market of 1.2 billion people and amount to a $1.2 trillion domestic market and foreign trade of $300 billion. IBSA's trade figures at present correspond to 15 per cent of that of the EU and USA, but by 2015 its trade is forecast to be equal to 25 per cent of EU trade and 20 per cent of the US's. In terms of GDP in purchasing power parity, IBSA accounts for 10 per cent of the globe's GDP, and by 2015 its share is forecast to increase to 12 per cent. This should be compared to 18 per cent and 20 per cent for the EU and US respectively.

Furthermore, the IBSA countries have major economic presences in their respective regions and in fact can be seen as growth poles within the developing world. And the future looks relatively bright for the IBSA states, given that by 2015 the IBSA countries will have 208 million college-educated people below the age of 40 as against only 127 million in the G7. Comparatively cheaper skilled human resources have the potential of making the IBSA nations globally competitive in niche industries (India's call centres being a prime contemporary example), and technological innovation may well grant the IBSA states the ability to leapfrog, making them more and more important in the global production process. Furthermore, the IBSA is also based on the notion that its members could quickly expand their exports if they could gain better access to foreign markets. The prediction is for Brazil to increase its trade by 200–300 per cent (Schott, 2001) whilst India could well attain huge growth numbers in the next decade or so if New Delhi is able to accomplish its reform programme and integrate into the global economy – a process that would be facilitated by easier access to developed markets (Srinivasan and Tendulkar, 2003). These facts make the G8's current domination of the global agenda seem more and more incongruous and perhaps opens up strategic spaces for groupings such as the G20.

Problems facing the G20

In a splintered global trading milieu, bilateralism and agreements with the developed world seem paramount and trump so-called South–South co-operation strategies, despite the rhetoric of multilateralism. For instance, talks between the US and the five-nation Southern African Customs Union (of which Pretoria is the dominant member) appear to be currently far more pressing than building up the G20. Besides, the G20 countries are actually competitors for export shares to the G7 markets rather than obvious partners for co-operation, certainly on the economic front. Are G20 states really ready to forgo advantages in trade between themselves for the greater good of the 'developing world', whatever that might be? Indeed, India currently is reluctant to open its own agricultural markets, whilst Brazil and South Africa are ready to do so. How will the G20 overcome this contradiction and how will such divergences play out in WTO negotiations? In addition, whilst the G20 'sees itself as leader of the developing world as a whole, [this] is often contested by the G33 and the G90'[1] ('Blue, Amber, Green', 2005).

Furthermore, the current dialogue carries within it the dangers of emasculating any interrogatory position regarding the inequities of the global system: '[s]ince the prevailing consensus is the free-market liberalisation model that is promoted by the Bretton Woods institutions and the WTO, [such a position] seems to be seeking a role to be relevant to this model and to be accepted, for instance, by the WTO and the International Chamber of Commerce, rather than to challenge or provide alternatives to the model' (Hormeku, 1998: 1). In fact the G20's position is built upon the premise that liberalisation *has not gone far enough* and the G7 needs to accept the logic of its own rhetoric regarding free trade. This was made clear at the Hong Kong meeting.

However, this position has engendered opposition within G20 states by those critical of an accommodating position towards the WTO. The international peasant federation Via Campesina, for example, regards the G20's stance as a thinly veiled attempt to advance the material interests of agro-exporters and agri-business. From this position the effect this would have on peasant producers is not on the agenda and indeed will be damaged by the G20's strategy (see www.viacampesina.org). As a result, Via Campesina chose not to support a statement by trade-related NGOs denouncing American attempts to split the G20.

However, the G20 takes the stance that a world without the WTO or other multilateral institutions would only strengthen the G7's ability to extract concessions from the weaker states in the developing world. It is the latent collective bargaining power, shown in Seattle and Cancún, where they pulled the plug on the US and the EU, that has seemingly inspired the G20's formation. In this regard it would be true to say that the interests of peasant farmers are not high on the agenda.

Indeed, realising the latent power of key developing world exporters and attempting to harness it by forming a coalition of like-minded reformist partners in the developing world *in defence* of the WTO's ostensible agenda is the cornerstone of the G20. This turns the tables on the dominant powers in the global economy and highlights their hypocrisy vis-à-vis 'free trade' and 'liberalisation'. Such a stance is expressed in the rhetoric of the rules-based system that the WTO puts forward. Indeed, the former Director-General of South Africa's Department of Foreign Affairs suggested back in 1999 that the promotion of such a global regime is a major plank to South Africa's foreign policy and is integral to the government's pro-growth policies:

> [T]he creation of a rules-based international system of interaction between states contributes to our domestic agenda. The setting of international standards and rules, the creation of transparent trading and other systems and ensuring that no single country or group of countries can dominate world affairs . . . creates an environment within which growth and development can take place.
>
> (Selebi, 1999)

Within such an international system there are 'obligations' that member states must abide by. At the same time there are 'rights' which a member state can expect and it is this flip-side of the rules that the G20 advances and which Pretoria attempts to push in its engagement with the organisation and also within its broader economic diplomacy. This is based on the understanding that the WTO manages a rules-based trade regime in which even relatively weak states are in principle entitled to confront and challenge the dominant developed powers. The G20's position is, then, an endorsement of the liberal themes that underpin the body – whilst pressing for full adherence to the idea of a rules-based regime and a reform of the global system.

Concluding remarks

It is increasingly apparent that a number of leading countries from the South have emerged as advocates of reform on issues related to global trade. Importantly, they are proactive and not simply spoilers in the WTO process (Narlikar and Tussie, 2004). 'These initiatives are not to be seen as a revival of the third-world movement of the 1960s and 1970s. None of their declarations openly question the principles of liberal economic globalisation. But the agreements do start a new phase in a process that has continued since 1945: the South's gradual self-assertion on the world stage' (Ruiz-Diaz, 2005).

However, whilst the reformist positions of the G20 might well be the policies of pragmatism in the present international context, this means in the final analysis advocating the intensification of international competition for markets in which states have relatively limited control over their own economies. Related to this is the conundrum facing the G20, namely what strategy exists within the common-sense approach adopted by the group vis-à-vis global trade to both promote greater exports and market access for agri-business *and* protect the peasantry and small farmers of many of the G20's members? Apparent from G20 statements is the absence of positions on protecting markets or steadying primary commodity prices. So, whether or not the group can both liberalise and safeguard domestic interests outside of the agro-exporting fractions remains an unanswered and, indeed, unexplored question. Why this is so is probably answered by the dominant position within key G20 states (certainly the most active ones) of large-scale agricultural capitalists. Thus in Brazil 50 per cent of agricultural land is controlled by just 4 per cent of landowners whilst 50 per cent of Brazil's GDP and jobs depend on the export sector. This explains Brasilia's concentration on agri-business within the G20 and Brazil's assertiveness regarding opening up new markets. Consequently, 'the challenge remains of determining precisely which agenda motivates [the G20]. The trade agendas of many developing countries have been heavily dominated by the interests of farm export groups, with a disproportional emphasis on access to markets' (Soares, 2005). And this explains the behaviour of both Brazil and India at Hong Kong.

Such contradictions imply that keeping together a broad-based coalition, such as the G20, may prove to be very difficult. Moving forward necessitates that the G20 chooses which subjects at the WTO it should negotiate on and also implies, given resource constraints and the lack of capacity, that key states from the developing world take a lead. But this is much easier said than done and serves to flag caution. Consolidating incompatible interests within any such developing world grouping such as the G20 is highly problematic and, whilst Pretoria or Brasilia may argue (or even think) that what is good for South Africa or Brazil is good for the rest of their respective continents, others may not think so and may even be highly suspicious of intentions. This became especially evident at the Hong Kong meeting.

It is true that '[w]hat we are looking at is a shift in paradigm, an inverting of roles with developing nations now heading the fight for trade liberalisation in the face of resistance from rich countries' (Osava, 2003). But any critical positioning of the G20 is offset by a broader acceptance of the orthodoxy of neoliberalism and the G20's limited scope, which is largely focused on agricultural trade liberalisation, and the implicit reluctance to expand the group's concerns regarding globalisation's effects beyond the push for further trade liberalisation, restricts the transformative potentiality of developments so far. Whilst there are clear limitations to the G20 developing into a nascent opportunity through which an alternative power bloc might be developed, strategic space that has opened up in the last five years or so will remain underutilised as long as the initiatives remain so constricted in scope.

It can be argued that the emergence of the G20 demonstrates that the retreat of the developing world may be in abeyance as neoliberal globalisation is being seen to be more and more one-sided. But this pregnant agenda needs broadening beyond its current narrow confines. It does of course have to be noted that only a small number of the WTO's members actually have the capacity and indeed bargaining power to push forward complex trade negotiations, particularly on the key issue of market access (the majority of African countries, for instance, are actually quite woeful on this score). Cancún seemed to show that an effective counterbalance to the G7 could be found in a group of the large and dynamic developing countries coming together; an emerging bloc of powers within the global trading regime may be nascent. However, we should be aware that 'unlike the third-world movements of the 1960s and 1970s, the G20 does not explicitly challenge the international economic system, nor propose an alternative social model. It is still too early to envisage any fundamental changes to the power relationships that structure international society' (Ruiz-Diaz, 2005). And the actions of Brazil and India at Hong Kong militate against any over-enthusiasm for the G20 as it is currently constructed. After all, 'it is paradoxical that the G20, whose formation captured the imagination of the developing world during the Cancún ministerial, has ended up being the launching pad for India and Brazil's integration into the WTO power structure' (Bello, 2005).

Whether the G20 and the blossoming call for a reformed global trading order can move forward and beyond the current global impasse, and in effect try to tip the global scales back into balance, will be of extreme interest in the future. In doing so, at least two big hurdles will have to be overcome. Firstly, as Hong Kong showed, putting together a coherent position that can be advanced as a 'developing world' position is problematic. And secondly, there will be a need to confront the almost inevitable US tactic of pursuing bilateral negotiations with individual favoured nations, which can both fracture the global trading system and quickly undermine any nascent G20 unity.

Whilst we may not be witnessing a rebirth of the New International Economic Order (NIEO), interesting times seem to await us with regard to the management of the international system. It is true that at Cancún 'the talks ended before any substantial negotiations on the draft agriculture text, so the balance of forces was not tested' (Bello, 2005). However, interactions involving the G20 in the WTO will probably continue to be sites of an important ongoing debate and, it could be argued, the testing – if not reformulating – of important global balances. As one commentator notes, 'As long as the WTO exists as a Western-driven unreformed regulator of global discipline it will face resistance for its institutional and moral failures. The message from Cancún is clear: a strong Southern framework can give poorer nations more time and space to defend themselves and the hope of negotiating a more equitable deal for their peoples' (Eagleton-Pierce, 2003). Though this was somewhat undermined at Hong Kong, the emerging coalitions of developing countries within the ambit of the WTO are developments that will be of profound interest in future trade Rounds.

Notes

1 The G33 has 42 members, of which ten are also in the G20 and 28 in the G90. Its priority is to defend developing countries' right to maintain high tariff barriers on imports. The G90 is made up of 79 countries from the African, Caribbean, and Pacific group of states, linked to the EU by the Cotonou convention. It includes the world's 49 least developed countries and the African Union nations. It shares the G33's objective of maintaining high tariff barriers for its own members, and also fears that if developed countries drop their tariffs – as the G20 wants them to do – then it will lose the tariff preferences, from which it benefits greatly, and not just for bananas and sugar ('Blue, Amber, Green', 2005).

References

Alden, C., and Vieira, M. (2005), 'The New Diplomacy of the South: South Africa, Brazil, India and Trilateralism', *Third World Quarterly*, 26: 7.

Bello, W. (2003) 'Washington's Vendetta'. www.geocities.com/ericsquire/articles/ftaa/frontlin031025.htm.

Bello, W. (2005), 'The Real Meaning of Hong Kong: Brazil and India Join Big Boys' Club', *Focus on the Global South*, 22 December.

Bergsten, F. (2004), 'The G20 and the World Economy', Speech to the Deputies of the G20 Leipzig, Germany, 4 March. www.iie.com/publications/papers/bergsten0304-2.htm.

Berthelsen, J. (2003), 'Cancún: A Good Idea at the Time', *Asia Times*, 12 November.

'Blue, Amber, Green: The Three Boxes' (2005), *Le Monde Diplomatique*, December.

Eagleton-Pierce, M. (2003), 'Doing the Canc?', *Oxford Student*, 2 October.

Embassy of Brazil, London (2003), *Meeting of Foreign Secretaries of Brazil, South Africa and India Brasilia Declaration*, 6 June.

Hormeku, T. (1998) 'NGOs Critical of UNCTAD's Investment and Pro-Business Approach', *Third World Economics*, 187/188, 16 June to 15 July.

House of Commons (2003), International Development Committee, *Trade and Development at the WTO: Learning the Lessons of Cancún to Revive a Genuine Development Round*, First Report of Session 2003–04, vol. I (London: The Stationery Office).

India-Brazil-South Africa (IBSA) (2004) Dialogue Forum: Plan of Action. www.dfa.gov.za/docs/2004/ibsa0305a.htm.

Narlikar, A. (2003), *International Trade and Developing Countries: Bargaining Coalitions in the GATT and WTO* (London: Routledge).

Narlikar, A., and Tussie, D. (2004), 'The G20 at the Cancún Ministerial: Developing Countries and Their Evolving Coalitions in the WTO', *World Economy*, 27: 7.

Neufeld, M. (1995), 'Hegemony and Foreign Policy Analysis: The Case of Canada as a Middle Power', *Studies in Political Economy*, 48 (Autumn).

Osava, M. (2003), 'G20+ Might Just Add Up for the WTO', *Inter Press Service*, 11 October.

Our World Is Not for Sale (2003), 'We Demand a Halt to US and EU Bullying and Intimidation of the G 21'. www.ourworldisnotforsale.org/statements/wto/20.html.

Ruiz-Diaz, H. (2005), 'G20: The South Fights for the South', *Le Monde Diplomatique* (English edition), September.

Schott, J. (2001), *Prospects for Free Trade in the Americas* (Washington, DC: Institute for International Economics).

Selebi, J. (1999), 'Address by Mr J. S. Selebi, Director-General of the Department of Foreign Affairs, to the South African Institute of International Affairs', issued by Media Section, Department of Foreign Affairs, Johannesburg, 18 May.

Soares, A. (2005) 'G20, G90 and G33: Challenges for Building a New Politics', *Global Policy Forum*, 23 (January).

South Centre (2003), 'G20: A Powerful Tool for Convergence in Negotiations', *South Bulletin* 68 (Geneva).

Srinivasan, T., and Tendulkar, S. (2003), *Reintegrating India with the World Economy* (Washington, DC: Institute for International Economics).

Taylor, I. (2004) 'The "All-weather Friend"? Sino-African Interaction in the Twenty-first Century', in I. Taylor and P. Williams (eds), *Africa in International Politics: External Involvement on the Continent* (London: Routledge).

TML Daily (2003), 'WTO Ministerial Meeting Collapses without Agreement', 15 September.

Trade Justice Movement (2005), 'Developing Countries Hold Firm with New Alliance'. www.tjm.org.uk/wto/hongkong/day4.shtml.

World Trade Organisation (2003), *Agriculture: Framework Proposal*, WT/MIN(03)/W/61 (4 September).

World Vision (2003) 'Cancún Collapse: Developing Countries Stand Firm, but Future Uncertain', 16 September.

10 The shift from duopoly to oligopoly in agricultural trade

Wyn Grant

Ever since it was effectively brought back within the scope of international trade negotiations in the Uruguay Round, agricultural trade has been one of the major obstacles to securing a fair and effective international trade agreement. As Peter Mandelson, the EU trade commissioner, has commented, agriculture has proved to be the 'most complex, challenging and most politically charged' part of the Doha Round discussions (*Agra Europe*, 23 September 2005: EP/6). The fundamental reason is that agricultural trade is highly politicised because of the high levels of domestic support still provided for agriculture in most countries.[1] This, in turn, means that rent-seeking coalitions cluster around agricultural politics with a strong attachment to preserving the status quo or at least disturbing it as little as possible. It seems that the first thought of any farmer when a new product opportunity comes along (for example, biofuels) is: can I get a tax break or a subsidy? However, agricultural privileges are gradually being eroded, and the most important factor in bringing about change is the liberalisation of farm trade.

The farmers themselves, particularly the large-scale farmers who enjoy economic muscle and political clout, are highly prominent in these rent-seeking coalitions. The farm vote has not completely disappeared in significance, as Wilson has shown in relation to close Senate races in the United States (Wilson, 2005: 75). However, it is important not to overlook the other beneficiaries of systems of farming support. In terms of farm outputs, the food processing industry can benefit substantially from some aspects of the provision of agricultural subsidies. Even more important are the various input industries, generally dominated by multinational companies, which provide inputs to farmers: fertilisers and pesticides; machinery and equipment; veterinary medicine; and, often overlooked, finance.

These factors are relatively constant over time, but what is changing is a shift in the balance of power in international trade negotiations away from the formerly prevalent duopoly of the EU and US towards the emerging economic powers such as Brazil. This can be characterised more generally as a shift from a stable duopoly to a less stable oligopoly with more players between whom agreement has to be reached. Hence the first section of this chapter sets out the key coalitions and groupings that have emerged in the Doha Round. The next section then sets out the main developments in the agricultural negotiations since Cancún. This discussion provides a way of introducing the main themes in the negotiations, which are centred on the three pillars of import protection, domestic support, and export subsidies. The specific issues are then discussed in more depth, with a particular emphasis on the question of market access, which has proved particularly difficult to resolve. The chapter then concludes with an assessment of prospects for a fair and effective settlement in the agricultural trade talks in the Doha Round. Although the approach adopted in this chapter is necessarily a sectoral one, it is important that agriculture is considered within the wider context of the Doha Round negotiations.

Coalition formation

Given the size of the WTO, it is not possible to have a genuinely multilateral agreement in which every member is a more or less equal participant; but nor can there be a unilateral imposition of the will of one member country. Hence agreement is reached by countries coming together in more or less formal and more or less enduring alliances. Narlikar has drawn attention to the 'spaghetti bowl of coalition activity' that occurs in trade rounds (Narlikar, 2003: 177). Many of these informal arrangements undergo a series of bewildering metamorphoses. For example, the Jamarillo process in the Uruguay Round subsequently became the G20, the *Café au Lait* and then the G48 (Narlikar, 2003: 96). Although Narlikar argues (2003: 178) that 'coalitions . . . have begun to change from the secret societies of GATT days to more publicly prominent ones', it is not easy to trace all the informal groupings that occur, but it is hoped that the principal ones are identified here.

The stylised facts about the agricultural trade agreement in the Uruguay Round are that it was largely a mutual adjustment of their respective interests by the US and the EU with some side payments to other countries (for example, Japan and Korea on rice) and some token concessions to developing countries. This was exemplified in the Blair House agreement between the EU and the US. It would be very easy to come to the conclusion that the EU–US decision-making duopoly no longer matters, but such a judgement would be hasty and premature. It may be more constrained than it was before, and there will certainly be nothing as blatant as a Blair House deal in the Doha Round. The EU–US joint position on agriculture arrived at in August 2003 failed, according to then US Trade Representative (USTR) Robert Zoellick, in part because other countries 'thought it was Blair House all over again' (*Agra Europe*, 5 March 2004: EP/5). However, the fact that there is more suspicion of EU–US joint initiatives does not mean that this axis of protection no longer matters.

The biggest change in the negotiating map in the Doha Round has been the emergence of the G20, led by countries such as Brazil, China, India, and South Africa.[2] In part this reflects the increasing displacement of emerging countries in the global economy. This particular grouping may be placed within Narlikar's framework in terms of what she describes as a 'type 1' coalition. 'These newer coalitions are confined to smaller groups of developing countries. Rather than attempt to restrict themselves to a single issue . . . these blocs evolve common positions in different issue areas' (Narlikar, 2003: 201). Such groups benefit from log-rolling that is not indiscriminate, given that membership is restricted to a subset of countries sharing common problems or interests. 'When the large diversified developing countries are involved . . . the bloc in turn enjoys considerable bargaining power and is able to trade concessions across issue areas that can help in facilitating agreement' (Narlikar, 2003: 538). Although such blocs may be initially prone to inflexibility, Narlikar suggests that a learning curve may lead this tendency to be overcome by a greater attention to strategy choice and the process of negotiation.

There are significant tensions within the G20, in particular between its export-oriented members such as Brazil and Argentina and those more concerned with protection such as India. Countries such as India and China have to think about how agricultural liberalisation would impact on their millions of peasant farmers, while Brazil is eager to exploit its comparative advantage in agricultural exports. It is also important not to fall into the trap of thinking that the G20 can necessarily speak on behalf of developing countries more generally, especially least developed countries (see Ian Taylor, Chapter 9 above). Although the group does include a few relatively impoverished countries, its leadership comes from countries like Brazil that would benefit from a substantial liberalisation of agricultural trade. For example, Brazil would be a very successful exporter of sugar in a regime that maximised free market access. Such a regime would harm poor sugar exporters such as Jamaica and Mauritius, which benefit considerably from their protected access to the EU market.

The emergence of the G20 also raises questions about the role of the Australian-led Cairns Group of agricultural exporting countries.[3] The eight developing country members of the Cairns Group are also members of the G20. The Cairns Group did not play its cards particularly well during the Uruguay Round negotiations, eventually being marginalised because of its hard-line position. Since the emergence of the G20, the Cairns Group has been somewhat undermined and the two groups met in February 2004 to collaborate more closely and come up with a new negotiating position. The real tension between the groups is over the difficult question of market access. Developed countries such as Australia want substantially increased market openings in both developed and developing country markets. Countries such as India, Pakistan, and South Africa also want substantial improvements in market access in developed countries, but are not prepared to offer substantial improvements in access to their own domestic markets. The communiqué from the February 2004 meeting got around these difficulties by evading the more difficult question of access *to* developing countries.

The G10 bloc of protectionist countries, led by Japan and Switzerland, was somewhat overlooked in the aftermath of Cancún, but it has been important, given the centrality of market-access issues in the negotiations. The G10 is often seen as an ally of the EU, with some of its members in the European Economic Area and also supportive of EU efforts to set up a 'multifunctionality club' to build support for wider public goods argument for agricultural subsidies. However, on market access the G10 has tended to take an even harder line than the EU and has been portrayed as an obstacle to the successful completion of negotiations. The tariff plans presented in October 2005 were considered to be too extreme by the G10 group, with Switzerland's economy minister, Joseph Deiss, claiming that the cuts called for by the US would 'wipe agriculture out of our landscapes' (*Agra Europe*, 14 October 2005: EP/4). The G10 also takes the hardest line of any grouping on tariffs for so-called 'sensitive products' (discussed later).

Although the G10 primarily comprises OECD countries, Mauritius is also a member.[4] It was Mauritius that in 2004 hosted a meeting of the G90 group of developing countries, which includes in its membership the African, Caribbean, and Pacific countries (ACP) and the 50 least developed countries. There is a clear difference of interest between developing countries that export farm products and poorer, food-importing countries and it is possible for developed countries to exploit these differences so as to pursue a 'divide and rule' strategy.

With all these groupings, some mechanism has had to be found in order to broker agreement, and that has emerged in the form of the New Quad, the Group of Five (or 'five interested parties' – FIPs) and the 'Quint'. Of these the FIPs are arguably the key group. It will be recalled that the old 'Quad' (US, EU, Canada, and Japan) played an important mediating role in the Uruguay Round. The 'New Quad' is made up of the EU, the US, Brazil (representing emerging countries that are agricultural exporters), and India (representing developing countries anxious to protect their subsistence farmers from competition from cheap imports). The 'five interested parties' are the New Quad plus Australia, although in 2006 a version of this grouping emerged which also included Japan. The Quint, which last met in Australia in August 2005, is the old Quad plus Australia and thus includes Japan, which has become less important since China displaced Japan as the world's third largest trader.[5] Because of the divergence in the positions of the G20 and the EU and US it has not been possible to develop enough common ground to facilitate agreement, but it could be an important negotiating forum in the final stages of the negotiations.

The development of the negotiations

The EU–US trade pact

The negotiations saw an attempt to revive the EU–US deal that was successfully utilised in the Uruguay Round, but the changing balance of economic power meant that this was no longer effective. The attempt to conclude an EU–US deal did not have the desired impact on the negotiations in Cancún, but it is a useful guide to those issues that divide the EU and US and those where they can find agreement. The EU and US agreed to put to one side for the time being the most difficult issues between them, including the question of the peace clause (technically, the Due Restraint provisions of the Uruguay Round Agreement on Agriculture), which protected subsidies from legal challenge at the WTO. This was designed to limit the number of disputes in the area of agricultural trade by exempting key EU and US programmes from challenges such as compensation payments in Europe and deficiency payments in the US. It subsequently lapsed in any case. The EU and US also agreed not to pursue at that stage of the negotiations the implementation period of any deal and Geographical Indications (GIs). The basis of the compromise between the EU and US was that the EU, having reformed the CAP, could give ground on trade-distorting domestic support, while the Americans would give ground on market access. The proposals on market access were particularly vague and this EU–US paper was seen as a failed attempt to impose a settlement on the Cancún talks.

The Derbez text

The Cancún negotiations failed largely because of a conflict over so-called 'new' issues in the Doha Round: investment, competition policy, government procurement, and trade facilitation. The compromise text on agriculture produced by the Mexican Foreign Minister, Luis Ernesto Derbez, has no formal status, as it was never adopted, but it was influential as a survey of the issues and possible means of resolving them, although it says little on the subject of cotton, which was a high-profile issue at Cancún. On domestic support the text calls for substantial reductions to be made, with members having the higher support making greater efforts.

What was particularly alarming for the EU, and is likely to be a significant issue in the future, was the suggestion that Green Box criteria should 'be reviewed with a view to ensuring that Green Box measures have no, or at most minimal, trade-distorting effects on production' (*Agra Europe*, 19 September 2003: EP/4). How the word 'minimal' is used in relation to the Green Box has never been properly explained (see Rude, 2001: 1015). The problem here is that, as the OECD has argued, almost all agricultural subsidies have some effect on agricultural production (an exception might be a subsidy that required farmers to keep the land 'in good heart' for environmental reasons but not to cultivate it or graze livestock).

Oxfam has spelt out why all subsidies have such effects more clearly than the somewhat cautious language of the OECD (Oxfam, 2005). It identifies four main ways in which decoupled subsidies might maintain production at what would otherwise be uneconomic levels:

- There is a 'wealth effect' whereby the stream of direct income guaranteed by the subsidy payment increases producers' willingness to produce.
- The payments give farmers a sense of security, which encourages the taking of greater productive risks than in the absence of the subsidy.
- The way in which subsidy schemes are administered encourages farmers to maintain land in production.
- There is an accumulation effect whereby decoupled payments are linked with production-linked payments.

The emergence of a draft text

Following the disappointments of Cancún, it took some time for progress to be made in resuming negotiations. They were revived by an offer by the EU in May 2004 to abolish all of its agricultural export refunds, subject to parallel concessions on export credits, food aid, and state trading enterprises.[6] This offer involved political costs for the EU, provoking a split within the Farm Council and also carrying long-term policy risks for the Union. Without export subsidies it will be difficult to offload surplus EU production, itself the result of domestic subsidy regimes, on the world market. In any event the EU's concession on export subsidies was sufficient to kick-start the negotiations and allow the WTO to come close to meeting its self-imposed end of July deadline for a draft framework agreement on reducing agricultural subsidies.

The final draft agreement was concluded in the early hours of 1 August 2004, just missing the 31 July deadline. It was known as the Oshima text as it was formally submitted by the Chair of the WTO's General Council, Shotaro Oshima. In fact, however, the text was effectively agreed in a meeting of the five key players in the Doha Round agricultural trade negotiations: the EU, US, Brazil, Australia, and India (the FIPs). Perhaps its most innovative feature was a so-called 'down payment' that required all members to cut the overall level of trade-distorting domestic support by at least 20 per cent of the base level in the first year of the agreement's implementation. Officials were quick to point out that this was equivalent to the entire six-year reduction of domestic subsidies in the Uruguay Round, although, as far as the CAP is concerned, the reforms already agreed mean that the EU will have no difficulty in meeting this target.

The question of *de minimis* payments was left in the air with reductions to be negotiated (see Table 10.1). This is not an entirely straightforward issue, as developing countries (represented on this issue by Barbados) have argued that for such countries the level should be kept at 10 per cent (as against the current 5 per cent for developed countries). The EU and US have countered that the framework agreement requires reductions in *de minimis* payments for everyone, except payments mainly for subsistence farmers. Blue Box payments would be capped at 5 per cent of a member's average total value of agricultural production during an unspecified historical period. The definition of the Blue Box would be changed to

Table 10.1 The coloured boxes and *de minimis* explained

Red Box: A category of banned domestic subsidies that was dropped from discussion in the Uruguay Round in 1990.

Amber Box: Objectionable domestic subsidies that should be reduced over time, the amount and speed being a matter for negotiation.

Green Box: Policies that are claimed to have no, or only minimal, trade-distortion effects or effects on production.

Blue Box: Introduced in the Uruguay Round to cover programmes that were notionally production-limiting such as area aids in the EU and deficiency payments in the US.

De minimis: *De minimis* support is that which does not exceed 5 per cent of the total value of production either of individual products (for product-specific support) or of the total value of agricultural production (for non-product-specific support)

---

allow the counter-cyclical payments introduced in the 2002 Farm Bill to qualify, a useful concession won by the US.

In the face of strong opposition from France, which had terms inserted in the original Doha Round declaration that it thought would protect export subsidies, the EU agreed to phase out all export subsidies by a date that was set in Hong Kong at 2013. In return, more binding language was inserted in the text to ensure that export subsidy elements within the US's export credit and food aid programmes, and within 'single-desk' export selling bodies such as the Canadian Wheat Board (CWB), are also subject to WTO disciplines. These draft agreements on export subsidies represented a substantial step forward given the size of the subsidies (almost €4 billion for the EU in 2004) and their damaging impact on farmers in the Global South.

Import tariffs would be reduced in accordance with a 'tiered' formula, with higher tariffs being subject to bigger cuts. The crucial issues of the number of bands, the thresholds for defining the bands and the type of tariff reduction in each band were left for further negotiation and these discussions have, not surprisingly, proved to be very difficult. However, the role of a 'tariff cap' (a maximum tariff for each product) was left on the table for further evaluation; that is, an attempt was made to kick it into the long grass, although it was subsequently revived by the G20, to the chagrin of Japan (which is concerned to maintain its very high tariffs on rice).

A significant and potentially difficult innovation was the idea that countries would be able to nominate certain products as 'sensitive'. These products would be subject to less exacting tariff reductions, although there would have to be some improvement in market access through a combination of tariff cuts and tariff quota increases. The actual language on 'sensitive' products says that countries may 'designate an appropriate number, to be negotiated, of tariff lines to be treated as sensitive'. What the appropriate number should be is itself a highly controversial issue, given that what sensitive really means is 'politically sensitive'. Given the admission of the Trojan horse of sensitive tariffs to the negotiations, this seems to be more like a hopeful aspiration than an achievable objective. 'This clause has the potential – probably more than any of the others – to derail the whole trade liberalising thrust of the trade negotiations, should the definition of a "sensitive product" be drawn too broadly' (*Agra Europe*, 13 August 2004: A/2).

The October 2005 talks

The negotiations were given a new boost when substantial new offers were tabled by the EU and the US at meetings in Geneva on 11 October 2005 and Zurich on 13 October 2005, followed by a third paper tabled at the Zurich meeting by G20 which was seen as an attempt at compromise between the EU and US positions. Both the American and the EU offers were more ambitious and detailed than what had been put on the table previously. The US offered to cut trade-distorting Amber Box support by 60 per cent over a five-year period. The EU's offer to cut its Amber Box support by 70 per cent looked even more generous, but reforms already undertaken had more or less brought spending down to that level. The US called on the EU to cut its domestic support by 83 per cent, with the G20 calling for an 80 per cent cut from all developed countries. The US and Australia were critical of the EU's offer on import tariffs as lacking ambition, although disputes about its calculation confused the debate about how good the offer was. The US offer on domestic subsidies was launched with something of a fanfare and did seem, at least temporarily, to put the EU on the back foot and under increased pressure to make an improved offer on market access. As *Agra Europe* remarked (14 October 2005: A/1), these developments remarked the end of the 'shadow-boxing' phase of the agricultural trade talks.

Although these largely secret talks were reported to have been encouraging, some difficult issues were left unresolved. Both the main players also faced increased internal opposition. An attempt by France[7] to restrict the EU Trade Commissioner Peter Mandelson's room for manoeuvre and to water down EU concessions failed after an emergency meeting of the EU Council of Foreign Ministers, but France nevertheless indicated that it could derail the talks if further concessions were not offered. In the US, Senator Saxby Chambliss, chair of the agriculture committee, warned the US administration not to agree to reduce overall farm spending as a result of a WTO agreement, although that is exactly what the Bush administration would like (and has unsuccessfully tried) to do in order to reduce the budget deficit. France mounted a major diplomatic and media offensive in defence of the CAP, which it saw as threatened with being dismantled by the American proposals and the acquiescence of the Commission. At the EU Hampton Court economic summit on 27 October 2005 President Chirac warned that he would block a Doha Round deal rather than make deep cuts to the EU's farm subsidy regime (*Financial Times*, 28 October 2005).

On 28 October 2005 the EU made a fresh offer on market access with a higher average cut in tariffs across all bands. The Commission claimed that this would mean an average cut of 46 per cent, whereas the US said that it actually amounted to 39 per cent, reflecting the difficulty of agreeing how one calculates the mean for such reductions. The EU tried to counterattack the US – which makes extensive use of *de minimis* provisions to shield politically expedient subsidies – by calling for a bigger reduction in the *de minimis* threshold. The EU also made an explicit link with other areas of the negotiations, stating that the proposals were conditional on movement on services and industrial tariffs. The US gave the new proposals at best a lukewarm reception and was in particular critical of the EU's insistence on maintaining steeper tariffs on 8 per cent of its 'sensitive' imports, identified as beef, poultry, sugar, and some fruit and vegetables. However, these loopholes were politically necessary if there was to be any chance of retaining French agreement. The EU's view was that its new proposal was 'a final offer which stretches to the very limits of its negotiating mandate' (*Agra Europe*, 28 October 2005: EP/2).[8] Subsequently, however, the EU has shown willingness to expand tariff-rate quotas for sensitive products which would enlarge access to the European market.

The issues

The issues dealt with here in some detail are export subsidies; domestic support; market access; geographical indications; and state trading enterprises.

Export subsidies

Export subsidies have always been an issue of particular concern for both developed and developing countries because of their disruptive effect. In developing countries they can drive local producers out of business (for example, dairy farmers cannot compete with skimmed milk powder). They can also intensify price competition in third-country grain markets (for example, between the EU and the US in Egypt and North Africa). For the EU, however, they have been an important way of getting rid of surplus product in intervention stores, a very real issue as grain intervention stocks grew rapidly in 2005.

At the Hong Kong Ministerial it was agreed to eliminate agricultural export subsidies by 2013. Importantly, there is to be a substantial degree of 'front-loading', with the majority of export subsidies to be phased out by 2010. This will put real pressure on the EU, although the Farm Commissioner, Mariann Fischer Boel, insisted that 'substantial' would be defined in such a way that did not make new CAP reforms necessary. In return the EU demanded precise language on alternative forms of export subsidisation, known in the jargon as 'parallelism'. The concept of a 'safe box' was introduced which will enable food aid to be provided when there are real humanitarian emergencies but will hopefully ensure that food aid programmes do not serve as a means of providing back-door export subsidies. The elimination of these subsidies, if finally put into effect, would be a very real gain from the Doha Round.

Domestic support

According to Canadian figures, the EU's bound levels of domestic support represent 41 per cent of the global total of domestic support, followed by Japan with 19 per cent and the US with 18 per cent (*Agra Europe*, 11 February 2005: EP/1). There is a huge volume of 'water' between the EU's Amber Box ceiling and its actual level of spending (at least €25 billion) and therefore it is easy for the EU to make concessions on domestic support, provided that the Single Farm Payments (SFPs) which are at the heart of the reformed CAP are deemed eligible for placement in the Green Box. Questions have been raised about that issue by a decision by the WTO's Dispute Settlement Panel against the Green Box status of the US's cotton subsidy programme because recipients of the aid may not produce fruit and vegetables. There is also a question about how the EU's scheme meets the Uruguay Round Paragraph 6 criteria about decoupled support, in particular criterion (*d*) that the 'amount of such payments in any given year shall not be related, or based on, the factors of production employed in any year after the base period'. As

Swinbank and Tranter point out, '[n]o doubt the EU would dispute our claim, but the insistence that SPS payments are tied to land that is "maintained in good agricultural and environmental condition" . . . weakens the EU's case. An SPS payment in any year depends upon the amount of land "farmed" that year' (Swinbank and Tranter, 2005: 54).

There is at least the basis of an argument to challenge the Green Box compatibility of the SFPs, but whether such a challenge would be mounted is a political decision that would be influenced by the state of negotiations in the Doha Round. As Swinbank and Tranter point out (2005: 58): '[i]f the round can quickly be brought to an amicable solution, we suspect the chances [of a challenge] are slight . . . If, however, negotiations become protracted and bitter, we would not discount the possibility of a WTO challenge to the green-boxing of the EU's new subsidy mechanism.' It is quite likely that any agreement will include a provision for a future review of Green Box definitions, which could leave a time bomb ticking away under the EU's reformed subsidy regime.

Although the discussion here has focused on the EU, it should be noted that there has been criticism of the US for failing to make clear how far it is prepared to go in terms of cuts in domestic support. There is also an outstanding issue about so-called 'indirect' subsidies in developing countries which operate via the maintenance of high internal prices rather than direct payments. The European Commission takes the view that if developing countries such as India and Brazil were assessed in this way, their total level of trade-distorting support would look much higher than it does at present.

In October 2005 the US offered to cut 'Amber Box' subsidies, the most distorting type, by 60 per cent and to halve the agreed cap on the less trade-distorting 'Blue Box' subsidies. This would allow the US to retain its controversial counter-cyclical payments (introduced in the 2002 Farm Act) that compensate farmers for low prices. However, they would be limited to $5 billion a year rather than the current $7.6 billion a year. The actual cuts in subsidies would be less than the US offer implies even though they would require a changed Farm Bill. The EU's view was that the offer could not be assessed without commitments to reform and discipline payments such as the counter-cyclical subsidies. In March 2006 Commissioner Mandelson launched a major attack on the US offer, arguing that it had offered only 'paper reductions' in subsidies. He argued: '[t]he United States has supported rice and wheat production massively' (*Agra Europe*, 3 March 2006: EP/6). The problem for the US in terms of domestic politics is that these interests are very politically influential and are major political donors. Moreover, the US global ceiling for Amber Box aid at around $19 billion is less than a third of the $60 billion that the EU is providing in farm subsidies, albeit most of it classified as Green Box. The bottom line is that 'Brussels does not really care what the US does with its internal subsidies – since it still has plenty of its own' (*Agra Europe*, 17 March 2006: A/1).

The EU has continued to be concerned about the issue of single-desk exporters such as the Australian and Canadian Wheat Boards, maintaining that the question of whether they are privately owned (as in the Australian case) is irrelevant, as they still have monopoly control of exports of a given commodity. The Hong Kong text did not demand the elimination of monopoly powers for national agricultural export bodies, but specified that such powers could not be used to circumvent disciplines on export subsidies. The question remains how enforceable such a provision is. The seriousness with which the EU takes this issue was demonstrated by a visit by Commissioner Fischer Boel to Australia and New Zealand in March 2006. She argued that Australia's wheat monopoly would be an impediment to further progress in the Doha Round talks. She also reiterated her criticisms of New Zealand's dairy co-operative, Fonterra, arguing that it should end its monopoly over access to export quotas.

Market access

Market access is undoubtedly the most intractable issue in the negotiations and it is important to understand why this is the case. 'Market access opportunities for developing countries, and especially for poor producers in those countries, are to be found much more in agriculture than in other sectors' (Anderson and Martin, 2006: 5). For the agricultural exporting countries this is the key issue in the negotiations so that they can boost markets for their price-competitive products, whereas for the EU how tariff reductions are implemented 'could make the difference between survival or extinction for many of the EU's less competitive producers' (*Agra Europe*, 14 January 2005: A/2). These uncompetitive producers are often situated in politically sensitive areas (such as dairy farmers in Bavaria or Brittany). In the UK, dairy farmers, who have been squeezed by falling nominal prices for their produce, have been at the forefront of a wave of militant action, blockading milk processing factories or retailer distribution depots. What appear to be (and are) highly technical issues become very charged politically and this mixture of real technical complexity and political passion is very difficult for even the most skilled negotiator to handle.

Agricultural tariffs average 60 per cent across the OECD area, with most OECD countries having peak tariffs of at least 200 per cent and Japan having a 500 per cent tariff for rice. 'More than 7% of the fixed-rate tariffs currently applied by the EU to protect European agricultural markets against imports are set at an equivalent level of 100% or more' (*Agra Europe*, 22 July 2005: EP/1). Although the highest *ad valorem* equivalent (AVE) is 407 per cent for chilled skirt of beef, many of the very high tariffs are in the dairy sector. This is not surprising given that, despite the introduction of dairy quotas, the EU has a structural surplus of milk and many dairy farmers are both economically marginal and politically vocal. Even so, it is surprising to find that in a number of tariffs the applied tariff is higher than the gap between domestic and world prices. 'No fewer than 38 of the 158 [EU] individual tariff lines for dairy products . . . have returned three-figure values when converted into [AVEs]' (*Dairy Markets*, 21 July 2005: 1). The highest AVE in the dairy sector is for buttermilk of more than 27 per cent fat (tariff code 04039039), which has an estimated AVE of 264 per cent.

There were three main formulas for tariff reduction on the table:

- The Uruguay Round approach, a simple average rate of tariff reduction with a minimum percentage cut for any one product. This did not have any advocates, but was an important historical reference point and was used in the 'blended' formula.
- The Swiss formula approach under which the largest tariffs are reduced most rapidly in order to achieve tariff convergence at some point in the future. This formula was supported by the Cairns Group because it would impose bigger cuts on the highest tariffs, thus reducing the gap between low- and high-tariff products.
- The 'blended' formula advanced by the United States and EU, which combines the Uruguay Round formula, the Swiss formula, and tariff elimination. This approach meets the US need for substantial cuts in tariffs as well as the EU need for flexibility to shield sensitive sectors. It was included in the Derbez Text. However, it was opposed by the G20, most members of the Cairns Groups, and the G10 because it was not thought to do enough to achieve cuts in high-end tariffs in developed country markets and did not take sufficient account of the needs of fragile farming sectors in poor countries. The only agreement reached at Hong Kong was to create four bands for tariff cuts. These will undoubtedly use a blended formula, but the real controversy is about sensitive products.

The agenda on establishing tiers for tariff reductions was initially moved forward by a proposal to group tariffs into five tiers put forward by the G20 with tariffs reduced at the same rate for all products in each group (as distinct from an Australian proposal which envisaged three tiers but progressively bigger cuts within them). The EU and the US signalled that they were comfortable with the broad outlines of this proposal, although the Commission was subsequently criticised in the Article 133 committee for making too many concessions on market access. The G20 proposal also envisaged a maximum tariff level for any product of 100 per cent, which was not welcomed by Japan. The upshot was that the G10 blocked any agreement at the end of July 2005 (Canada also argued for a progressive formula for each band).

However, some further progress was made at the Paris discussions between the FIPs in September 2005.[9] Considerable secrecy surrounded the talks, in itself a sign that real negotiations were taking place rather than posturing for the benefit of domestic audiences. In particular the EU and US put concrete tariff reduction figures on the table on the basis of a tiered approach and also indicated that they would keep the number of sensitive products to a minimum.

The three offers (EU, US, G20) tabled in October 2005 all embraced a four-tier approach. The US proposed cuts in import tariffs of between 55 per cent and 90 per cent, depending on the size of the tariff. With the G20 taking an intermediate position that involved maximum 75 per cent reductions, the EU proposed a reduction of 50 per cent for very high tariffs. The percentage of sensitive products would be cut from 10 per cent to 8 per cent of tariff lines compared with a US proposal of 1 per cent. This would still leave 180 EU products treated as 'sensitive'. According to US calculations, this would result in an average cut in EU farm tariffs of 24.5 per cent, less than the 36 per cent average agreed in the Uruguay Round. The US made it clear that it thought the EU offer was inadequate. However, implementing the US offer would require, for example, a 25 per cut in the intervention price for butter (*Agra Europe*, 14 October 2005: A/1), which would be a severe blow to a European dairy industry troubled by rising fuel and packaging prices.

Geographical Indications (GIs)

This is a very important issue for the EU. The EU has seen animal welfare and multifunctionality disappear from the agenda (although the latter is less important if Single Farm Payments (SFPs) can be placed within the Green Box). 'But strengthening protection of GIs has remained as a potential "victory" for the EU to soften the blow of ending export subsidies, cutting tariffs and reducing trade-distorting payments for farmers' (Josling, 2005: 13–14). This is not just a question of chalking up a win to appease domestic political audiences. GIs are integral to the whole CAP reform strategy of the EU, displacing quantity by quality. In particular they are seen as offering a means of bolstering the position of marginal farmers, helping them to move into high-quality, value-added products for niche markets. Indeed, the EU has already 'negotiated bilateral treaties with Australia, Chile and South Africa that mutually protect a number of GIs' (Josling, 2005: 8).

GIs were covered by the Uruguay Round TRIPs agreement, which defines them in Article 22.1 as follows:

> Geographical Indications . . . identify a good as originating in the territory of a Member, or a region or locality in that territory, where a given quality, reputation or other characteristic of the good is essentially attributable to its geographical origin.

Article 22.2 requires member states to provide legal means to prevent 'the designation or presentation of a good that indicates or suggests that the good in question originates in a geographical area other than the true place of origin in a manner that misleads the public as to the geographical origin of the good' as well as any use 'which constitutes an act of unfair competition'. An example would be Parma-type ham that did not come from the Parma region of Italy. Article 23.4 provides for special protection for wines and spirits, but no agreement has been reached in the negotiations on a multilateral registry. In short, the dispute is between a voluntary system advocated by the US and allies in the Cairns Group plus Japan and a compulsory system advocated by the EU and other European countries such as Switzerland (plus Sri Lanka).

One of the difficulties in this area arises from transatlantic differences in the way in which protection is offered. As one would expect in a 'company state', the US bases its protection on trademarks granted to individual firms, although it has also used trade agreements to protect GIs such as Tennessee Whiskey and Bourbon (Josling, 2005: 8–9). However, trademarks are a subtly different means from GI protection of creating a monopoly over the use of certain terms:

> The difference is that the value of trademarked terms must be created through marketing. GI protection takes a term that already has market recognition and value and limits its use to a small subsection of existing producers, appropriating a value that is currently spread among producers worldwide.
>
> (Henning, 2005: A/2)

The temperature of the dispute over GIs was raised by a WTO dispute panel finding that the EU had given insufficient protection to US trademarks, making registration difficult by demanding rights for EU goods in third-country markets. The US chose to interpret this as a finding that the EU's system of GIs is illegal. This was a rather broad interpretation of the findings, quite apart from the breach of confidentiality involved. When the final report came out in March 2005 both the EU and US again claimed victory.

The GI issue does raise difficult questions of principle, policy, and procedure which can all too easily lead to entrenched positions being adopted. The question of principle is clearly stated by Josling: '[t]o some, it is a form of protection for producers in a particular region against competition from new entrants . . . To others the question is one of giving consumers accurate information on which to make choices' (Josling, 2005: 2).

It also raises fundamental questions about the nature of globalisation and in particular whether cultural globalisation is to be welcomed or resisted. In particular, 'the choice of foods that individuals and communities make, the combinations of foods that they prepare for meals, and the ways in which these foods are prepared are integral parts of culture' (Coleman, Grant, and Josling, 2004: 17). One view is 'that . . . there is little to be gained by impeding the natural spread of food cultures and habits that accompany movement of people' (Josling, 2005: 13). An alternative perspective is that the globalisation of foods and food preparation could 'lead to fewer differences between cultures around the world and thus a decline in cultural diversity' (Coleman, Grant, and Josling, 2004: 17).

The EU wants the GI protection offered to wines and spirits to be extended to food on a multilateral basis, although it has indicated that there might be negotiating room on whether any register would be legally enforceable. The food-exporting countries see this as another protectionist device dreamt up by the EU. As far as the framework agreement was concerned, the GI question is simply described as an issue of interest not yet agreed. The US, Australia, South Africa, and New Zealand among others claim that the GI issue has no place in the framework of the agricultural negotiations and should be dealt with within the TRIPs Council. On the other side, some countries, notably Switzerland and Bulgaria, are threatening to derail the entire agricultural negotiation process unless progress is made on the GI issue within the Doha Round. Perhaps it is the potentially damaging character of this dispute that has led the EU and the US to privately discuss how it might be resolved. The only reference to the issue in the Hong Kong text was a note that the consultative process on the issue had to be 'intensified'.

State trading enterprises (STEs)

Three key issues have arisen in the negotiations in relation to STEs:

*   Export subsidies to STEs should be subject to the same limits as ordinary export subsidies.
*   There should be an end to government financing or refinancing for STEs.
*   There should be an end to underwriting of losses.

Even more sensitive is the core issue of whether the monopoly export powers of STEs (such as the CWB) should be abolished. The EU and the US complain that the lack of transparency, notably on price transmission, was one of the key problems with such enterprises. Cairns Group states, where the three most controversial single-desk exporters are located, counter that there is no evidence to suggest that such enterprises do not operate on a commercial basis and that more information was already available from the STEs than from private trading companies.

In some respects this is one of those issues that can be used as a counter to extract concessions elsewhere or as part of a divide and rule strategy. 'EU officials privately admit that the Union has few problems with the notion of STEs, but the Commission has been only too pleased to offer support to Washington's campaign against STEs as a highly convenient way of driving a wedge between the US and Cairns Group' (*Agra Europe*, 14 May 2004: A/1).

Conclusions: from duopoly to oligopoly

The old EU–US power duopoly has been replaced by an oligopoly represented by the FIPs. However, the EU and the US are still the most powerful entities within the grouping and indeed there is still an expectation that they will exercise leadership in the negotiations. The EU and the US still engage in a dialogue with each other designed to reach a mutually satisfactory reconciliation of divergent interests and positions. They are still able to extract key concessions on issues such as the treatment of the Amber and Blue Boxes. The G20 has become an important actor, far more so than the Cairns Group in the Uruguay Round. For example, it played a key, and broadly accepted, agenda-setting role in relation to the issue of tiers in the market-access discussions. So far potential tensions within this grouping have not come to the surface. Brazil is the cheapest producer of many agricultural commodities in the world and can easily expand its cultivated area. India and China have large peasant populations they wish to protect, but China has not been prominent in the leadership of the group. South Africa has a number of areas of niche, high-value production such as wine. There is, thus, always the potential for competition *within* G20 as well as *between* G20 and other groupings or states. Oligopolistic competition is inherently more unstable than duopolistic competition (which can be very intense), given that more parties are involved, but the risk of instability is intensified if one of the participants is, in effect, a joint venture between partners with potentially conflicting interests. It will be interesting to see if G20 is more successful as a mediator between the US and EU than the Cairns Group, which tended to adhere too closely to the US position.

The EU has effectively been conducting a strategic managed retreat on key issues such as export subsidies. However, the Commission is ultimately constrained by member states, as was evident during the Uruguay Round negotiations, and there has been increasing restiveness that it has given away too much, too quickly. Peter Mandelson has asked rhetorically, '[c]ould you name a stage in any trade round when France did not express concerns?' (*Financial Times*, 29 October 2005). Nevertheless, French concerns are more than superficial posturing and could still derail the whole Round. The stance of the US is less clear, in part for structural reasons arising from the checks and balances within the US government and the debate about the next Farm Bill. The commitment of agri-business interests to trade liberalisation is less unambiguous than it was in the 1990s, and other domestic and international issues have a greater priority. This enhances the opportunities for the G20 to exercise leadership, and Brazil in particular has shown sophistication and flexibility, marking its arrival as a great agricultural power. What is sometimes overlooked is the influence exerted by the G10 group led by Switzerland, which is well resourced, influential, and sometimes intransigent.

Little progress was made in early months of 2006 in dealing with the issues left unresolved by the Hong Kong Ministerial and in particular on establishing the 'modalities' or broad parameters for agreement, which were supposed to be resolved by April 2006. It was observed that 'the negotiation is essentially a zero-sum game – no-one can gain without someone else losing. The politically painful reality is that gains and losses are not just between nations but particularly between different groups within individual nations' (*Agra Europe*, 17 March 2006: A/1). It will not be as easy to make an agreement between five or six participants, one of them made up of 20 countries, as it was to conclude a bilateral agreement to resolve agricultural issues in the Uruguay Round. Ultimately, much will depend, particularly for the developed nations, on trade-offs with other areas of the negotiations.

Notes

1 The main exceptions are Australia and New Zealand, although Australia provides quite a lot of aid to farmers in the form of drought relief. 'Drought' is a socially constructed phenomenon – there is no generally accepted definition of what constitutes a drought.
2 The full list of members is Argentina, Bolivia, Brazil, Chile, China, Colombia, Costa Rica, Cuba, Ecuador, Egypt, El Salvador, Guatemala, India, Mexico, Nigeria, Pakistan, Paraguay, Peru, the Philippines, South Africa, Thailand, and Venezuela. Originally it was G22, but Indonesia and El Salvador subsequently left.
3 The full list of members is Argentina, Australia, Bolivia, Brazil, Canada, Chile, Colombia, Costa Rica, Guatemala, Indonesia, Malaysia, New Zealand, Paraguay, the Philippines, South Africa, Thailand, and Uruguay. Hungary was a member before it joined the EU.
4 The other members include Iceland, Mauritius, Norway, South Korea, and Taiwan.
5 There was a three-year gap since the last full meeting in Japan in 2002, although

discussions on agriculture were held by the five in the margins of the UNCTAD summit in São Paulo in June 2004.
6 Indeed, the EU was particularly insistent subsequently on food aid, arguing that of a total of US$3 billion of food aid offered by the US government, US$2 billion actually stays in the US.
7 France was initially backed by Austria, Belgium, Cyprus, Finland, France, Greece, Hungary, Ireland, Italy, Lithuania, Luxembourg, Poland, and Spain.
8 It should be emphasised that the mandate is not some tablet of stone but rather a series of statements from the Council between 1999 and 2004 specifying how far the Commission should go in negotiations.
9 There is some ambiguity about the presence of Australia. *Agra Europe* listed the participants as the EU, US, Brazil, and India; the *Financial Times* (22 September 2005) says that Australia joined later.

References

Anderson, K., and Martin, W. (2006), 'Agriculture, Trade Reform and the Doha Agenda', in K. Anderson and W. Martin (eds), *Agricultural Trade Reform and the Doha Development Agenda* (Washington, DC, and Basingstoke: The World Bank and Palgrave Macmillan).

Coleman, W., Grant, W., and Josling T. (2004), *Agriculture in the New Global Economy* (Cheltenham: Edward Elgar).

Grant, W. (2004), 'Is a More Multilateral Trade Policy Possible?', *Review of International Studies*, 30: 4.

Henning, S. (2005), 'Geographical Indications (GIs): Squaring the Doha Round Circle', *Agra Europe*, No. 2180 (28 October).

Josling, T. (2005), 'Geographical Indications: Protection for Producers or Consumer Information?', Paper presented to the Annual Conference of the Australian Agricultural and Resource Economics Society, Coffs Harbour, 7–11 February.

Narlikar, A. (2003), *International Trade and Developing Countries: Bargaining Coalitions in the GATT and WTO* (London: Routledge).

Oxfam (2005), 'A Round for Free: How Rich Countries Are Getting a Free Ride on Agricultural Subsidies at the WTO'. http://www.oxfam.org/eng/pdfs/bn050615_dumping_roundforfree.

Rude, J. (2001), 'Under the Green Box: The WTO and Farm Subsidies', *Journal of World Trade*, 35: 5.

Swinbank, A., and Tranter, R. (eds) (2004), *A Bond Scheme for Common Agricultural Policy Reform* (Wallingford: CABI Publishing).

Swinbank, A., and Tranter, R. (2005), 'Decoupling EU Farm Support: Does the New Single Payment Scheme Fit within the Green Box?', *Estey Centre Journal of International Trade and Policy*, 6: 1.

Wilson, G. (2005), 'Farmers, Interests and the American State', in D. Halpin (ed.), *Surviving Global Change: Agricultural Interest Groups in Comparative Perspective* (Aldershot: Ashgate).

Part IV
Fairness and legitimacy

11 All's fair in love and trade?

Emerging powers in the Doha Development Agenda negotiations

Amrita Narlikar

Balvānashcha yathā dharmam lokē pashyati purushah
Sa dharmo dharmavelāyām bhavatyabhihatah parah
The Mahabharata, II – 69.15

Conceptions of justice are almost inextricably linked with notions of power. What the weak see as just can differ radically from the interpretations of the strong. The ancient Sanskrit verse quoted above advances precisely this idea, and further suggests which notion of fairness or justice (literally 'Dharma') wins out in the real world:

> In this world, the mighty decide whatever is just, which is accepted by people as justice. It always overrides what the weak interpret as just.

Such a conceptualisation reduces the notion of fairness to little more than a function of power and interests. By extension, discourses of fairness appear little more than window-dressing for the harder interests that motivate the actions of individuals and states. According to this argument, interests would provide the central causal explanation for outcomes; fairness would appear only in the realm of rhetoric – an intervening variable between interests and outcomes with very little weight, playing but a minor role in any explanatory accounts for outcomes. And yet, even in the context of the hard bargaining that is associated with multilateral trade negotiations in the WTO, we find ample occurrence of references to fairness, justice, and legitimacy in academic scholarship (see, for instance, Suranovic, 2000; Albin, 2001; Kapstein, 2005; Steffek, 2006) as well as diplomatic practice.

The fairness discourse appears in the diplomatic-speak of both developed and developing countries, albeit the substance and frequency of the discourse varies with the actors involved, particular issue-area, and the forum within which the negotiation occurs. In this chapter I examine the concepts of fairness that certain developing countries have appealed to in trade negotiations, how and why these notions have changed over time, and the impact that they have exercised on nego- tiated outcomes. I conduct this analysis with specific attention to the role of interests and power. In certain instances developing countries advance notions of fairness that conform perfectly to their immediate material interests; in such instances

I argue that it is impossible to argue that fairness 'matters' in any real or falsifiable way. However, I also point to instances when developing countries have endorsed notions of fairness that go against their material interests and actually generate some costs. Here I argue that something more than a power-based explanation is at work, and suggest ways in which ideas about fairness can make a difference.

Before I launch into the chapter, two points of clarification may be useful. First, while much of the literature on trade-related concepts of fairness has focused on developing countries as a group, I will be paying considerably more attention to the role played by Brazil and India in this discourse. This is partly because the collective vision of fairness has borne a strong imprint of the vision espoused by the bigger developing countries, which were influential in the GATT and continue to be so in the WTO. For instance, both countries were frequent invitees to the Green Room in the days of the GATT, and continue to be involved in small-group meetings in the WTO. Perhaps even more importantly, though, their large size, regional and international presence, and economic weight mean that, unlike least developed countries (LDCs), they have no obvious reasons to resort to discourses of fair-ness rather than rely on discourses of power. That they continue to do so, however, provides us with stronger reasons for why fairness might matter in trade negotiations in ways that go beyond a simple window-dressing of interests. The role of these countries is also interesting because of the tutelage they have provided to weaker developing countries in voicing their demands in the GATT and the WTO. Particularly as the LDCs emerge as increasingly accomplished players in the WTO system and the interests of developing countries diverge further, we may expect some differences to emerge between the notions of fairness they support versus those supported by the middle powers. If, in spite of these differences, the various subgroups end up supporting each other's interpretations of fairness, we may have a case for a particularly strong notion of fairness in operation. Second, notions of fairness have a close interplay with the institution within which they are advanced. This, however, is not the focus of the present chapter (see Narlikar, 2006a). Rather, this chapter traces the evolving notions of fairness, particularly as espoused by Brazil and India, and further suggests conditions under which fairness may be thought of as mattering more than under others in the context of the current Round of negotiations.

The chapter proceeds in four parts. Following this introduction, the second section presents the theoretical framework. The third section discusses changes in the notions of fairness over time through a brief account of competing ideas in the days of the GATT, but devotes greater attention to the role that demands for fairer trade have played in the DDA negotiations. The fourth section presents the conclusions.

Theoretical framework

Rational choice approaches provide us with a simple explanation of the formation and survival of international organisations: states create international organisations and abide by their rules to overcome classic problems of collective action and thereby avail themselves of the gains of efficiency that derive from inter-state co-operation. As recent public demonstrations against international economic organisations have shown, however, efficiency is not enough; decisions arrived at in international forums must also be seen to be fair by their stakeholders. It is this imperative that leads the staff and members of international organisations to engage in the fairness discourse.

Definitions of fairness remain contested, and the substance of a fair agreement depends considerably on who the affected parties are. In this chapter I use Thomas Franck's definition of fairness as

> a composite of two independent variables: legitimacy and distributive justice. Fairness discourse is the process by which the law, and those who make law, seek to integrate those variables, recognizing the tension between the community's desire for both order (legitimacy) and change (justice), as well as the tensions between different notions of what constitutes *good* order and *good* change in concrete instances.
>
> (Franck, 1995: 26–27)

Franck further associates concerns about legitimacy as fairness with procedural matters, and concerns about distributive justice as fairness with substance and equity of outcome.

The simplest translation of the two types of fairness into trade politics suggests a North–South divide. We might expect the weak to endorse fairness thought of as distributive justice and change, whereas the powerful would support fairness conceived as process-driven legitimacy and order. In the GATT and the WTO this would translate into process-related demands for rules of reciprocity and equal obligations by developed countries, and demands for more equitable outcomes through mechanisms such as differential obligations by developing countries. At least at a very high level of generalisation we could argue that this has been the case. Jens Steffek (2006), for instance, makes an interesting argument about the postwar conflict between the American vision of global governance based on embedded liberalism versus the developing countries' vision that was based on a different notion of justice that Steffek terms 'redistributive multilateralism'. He attributes the difference in these visions to the fact that embedded liberalism presupposes that countries have enough resources to finance domestic policies to mitigate the disruptive effects of market liberalisation. He writes: 'embedded liberalism only works for industrialised countries. Not surprisingly then, a major line of contestation runs between the US as the most passionate promoter of embedded liberalism and developing countries.' There are, however, two problems with such an approach.

The first problem is theoretical: despite the appeal to fairness, the account given above is primarily interest-based. In an analysis where the weak demand distributive justice and the strong demand order and legitimacy, the fairness variable has but a marginal place. Weaker and poorer countries would naturally demand redistribution of wealth, whilst the stronger and richer countries would naturally demand preservation of the existing order. Even if we completely eliminated fairness as a causal variable, we would still see the same expected behaviour patterns of the strong versus weak states, more or less. Fairness at its best plays a secondary role in serving some kind of a legitimacy function; more often it seems just a polite – but perfectly substitutable – term for interests.

Second, an empirical analysis of trade politics in the GATT and the WTO reveals a much more complex picture than that suggested by a pure interest-based account. States may have started out with a North–South division of fairness-related demands, but developing countries have gradually incorporated ideas of process and legitimacy into their notions of fairness, whilst developed countries too have incorporated at least minimal notions of distributive justice. These evolving visions of fairness are explored in the next section. I focus mainly on developing countries, using learning and adaptation as the central causal explanation for these changes.

Given the positive correlation that we see between the interests that states have and the type of fairness they endorse, how can we show in any rigorous way that fairness can have an impact on trade negotiations? In instances when developing countries support notions of fairness even when they impose costs on them, it would be possible to argue that something more than a short-term interest-based explanation is necessary. Two forms of explanation are plausible, with only the first and minimal one being falsifiable. The first explanation takes cognisance of the costs. But according to this explanation, costly commitment to a notion of fairness might involve some longer-term, non-material gains. For instance, even though they may incur the costs of free-riding by endorsing special and differential treatment (SDT) provisions for LDCs, the larger developing countries might accumulate significant gains in the form of their acceptance as leaders of the developing world. This status, in turn, would allow them a bigger voice in trade negotiations, and possibly greater influence across regimes. The commitment to fairness in these instances is 'real', given its costs, but it is strategic. The second explanation relies on a stronger commitment to the notion of fairness: the countries do not use the fairness discourse simply to meet strategic ends but because they actually buy into the particular vision. Here the commitment is not strategic but ideological. There is no reason to assume that apparently strategic uses of fairness do not also entail some ideological commitment, so the two explanations are not mutually exclusive. However, the second explanation is more difficult to prove. The only way of showing that countries actually believe in a particular notion of fairness or justice would be to examine the visions that these countries end up endorsing after achieving Great Power status. If the countries continue to endorse ideas of distributive justice even after achieving dominance in the international system, then it would be possible to argue that the driving force for their behaviour was indeed an ideological commitment to the fairness idea. However, if the countries end up abandoning these notions on achieving Great Power status, and resorting to a notion of fairness that is process- and order-based, then only the first and minimal explanation would hold true: fairness was a strategic tool to achieving greater power. As neither Brazil nor India has fully achieved this Great Power status, the second explanation is difficult to test. However, the following section will examine current trends of the fairness debate, and will offer some conjectures on how deep the commitment of the middle powers to their fairness principles is.

Brazil and India in the GATT and WTO

Both Brazil and India were founding members of the GATT. However, for various reasons, including the misadventure with the aborted International Trade Organisation (ITO) and subsequent decision-making processes, the GATT ended up espousing process-related fairness (as we would expect developed countries to do) rather than equity-based, outcome-related fairness (which developing countries had favoured) (Narlikar, 2006a). How developing countries, led by Brazil and India, managed to voice their own version of fairness in the institution, and with what degrees of success, can be traced in three phases. I give a brief account of the first two phases, and present a more detailed account of phase III.

Phase I: late 1940s to early 1980s

In the first phase of their dealings with the GATT, developing countries tried hard to incorporate their own concerns with equity and distributive justice. The position of developing countries was typified in the statement of the Indian representative: 'Equality of treatment is equitable only among equals. A weakling cannot carry the burden of a giant' (quoted in Kock, 1969: 289).

Developing countries were convinced at the time that institution of the GATT was weighted against them owing to its commitment to liberalisation, lack of balancing development provisions or special treatment for primary commodities, the shenanigans of Green Room diplomacy, and negotiating formulas like the Principal Supplier Principle that made their participation even more difficult. To counterbalance these problems, developing countries called for preferential treatment in the GATT through special market access and exemptions from certain obligations.

These demands, though framed in terms of fairness understood as equity, are difficult to separate from the interests of developing countries. For Brazil and India, following protectionist models of growth driven by import-substituted industrialisation, engagement with the GATT on a reciprocal basis potentially had real costs. In contrast, by standing on the margins of the GATT, they could continue to enjoy a free ride on concessions that developed countries engaged, and gain additional concessions to suit their economic priorities via special preferences. As such, it appears that the fairness discourse to which developing countries appealed may have served a strategic function. Given strong sentiments of Third Worldism and anti-colonialism that were prevalent at the time, it is of course also possible that appeal to fairness thought of as equity in outcomes had deeper sources. But given the perfect conformity of these demands with the politico-economic interests of developing countries, claims to such deeper motivations would have to be speculative.

The demands for a system that was conducive to fairer outcomes generated some success, for instance the inclusion of Article XVIII*b* in 1954–55, the Haberler report in 1958, and the addition of Part IV on Trade and Development in 1965. In 1971, following developments in the UNCTAD, the GATT provided a waiver to the most-favoured-nation (MFN) principle, thereby allowing the Generalised System of Preferences (GSP) for the next ten years. The GSP was given a permanent and legal basis in 1979 through the 'Enabling Clause'. A closer inspection, however, suggests that these provisions did not amount to a reworking of legitimacy and process-related fairness in the GATT into a notion of fairness associated with outcomes and equity. The Enabling Clause, negotiated in the Tokyo Round, was accompanied by the 'Graduation Principle'. Effectively this meant that the Enabling Clause was a stopgap measure allowed until developing countries resumed their 'normal' responsibilities of reciprocal trade liberalisation. The foundational principles of the GATT continued to be MFN and reciprocity rules, and what the GATT treated as fair continued to be a matter of process and legitimacy rather than outcomes and equity.

Not only were the successes of developing countries in inducing norm change in the GATT limited, but their gains from SDT were also few. Authors such as Martin Wolf have argued that GSP was used as a bait to divide the South (Wolf, 1984); for late entrants the costs of GSP were especially high, as markets were distorted by other developing countries already enjoying preferences. Even for beneficiaries the system of preferences had decreasing marginal utility with increasing overall trade liberalisation. And by accepting such schemes that represented a violation of the MFN principle, developing countries could no longer legitimately demand the end to exceptions that developed countries had granted themselves in areas like agriculture, and textiles and clothing. Unsurprisingly, as interests changed, the fairness discourse too evolved in phases II and III.

Phase II: mid-1980s to late 1990s

By the time of the launch of the Uruguay Round, notions of fairness that developing countries espoused appeared to be changing. No longer content with standing on the sidelines, developing countries gradually began to engage with developed countries on an equal and reciprocal basis to create what later came to be known as the 'Grand Bargain' of the Uruguay Round (see Sylvia Ostry, Chapter 2 above). They agreed to an inclusion of the so-called 'new issues' of services, TRIPs, and TRIMs. In return they obtained the inclusion of agriculture and textiles and clothing – areas which had been governed through exceptions and waivers to meet the interests of developed countries – within the multilateralised reciprocity of GATT rules. The Grand Bargain also facilitated institutional innovations in the GATT, the most important of which were the creation of the Single Undertaking and the establishment of the WTO.

This improved willingness by developing countries to participate in the GATT on reciprocal terms – at the cost of the fairness-as-equity agenda – was a product of several factors. In some countries at least, new constituencies for liberalisation emerged as the failures of central planning became evident, the debt crisis reinforced these limitations, while the successes of the East Asian economies through export-oriented growth models provided a powerful new alternative (Hoekman and Kostecki, 2001). For many developing countries, however, this conversion to economic liberalisation was not a choice that they had exercised voluntarily. The economic downturn of the 1980s, and their weak BATNA (best alternative to negotiated agreement), inevitably drove developing countries to the negotiating table.

While economic imperatives and power politics together rendered rhetorical appeals to equity of outcomes an indulgence that few countries could afford, institutional learning specific to the GATT had also shed doubt on their old strategies. The hard-won SDT provisions generated only minimal gains, and developing countries began to realise that the multilateralism of the GATT provided them with one of the few defences against the 'aggressive unilateralism' that they faced from the developed world. Further, the utility of old-style Third Worldist coalitions (like the Informal Group of Developing Countries and the G10) that had relied on ideas of distributive justice was on the decline. In contrast, new issue-based coalitions had emerged (like the G48 in services and the Cairns Group in agriculture), which combined developed countries with developing countries, and signalled commitment to the reciprocity principle by recognising the possibility of trade-offs (see Narlikar, 2003, 2006a).

Irrespective of whether one sees these changes as voluntarily arrived at or as a result of outside pressures and institutional learning, however, it would seem that the preferences of developing countries had changed. In keeping with this realist account, one could argue that as the willingness of developing countries to engage with the world economy increased, their notions of fairness and justice also evolved. As a result, their call for SDT became considerably muted. They bargained through coalitions on a reciprocal basis, in a genuine good-faith effort to participate in the GATT and the WTO according to the rules of the institution. Again, in this explanation, fairness is driven by interests and hence plays only a secondary role. However, the cases of Brazil and India suggest that something more than interests may have been at work.

Even as most developing countries were converting to the new issue-based coalitions, Brazil and especially India showed great reluctance to surrender their old ideologies and loyalties. In the run-up to the launch of the Uruguay Round, Brazil and India had led the G10 into resisting an inclusion of trade in services within the GATT. After the launch of the Round at Punta del Este in 1986, when most members of the G10 coalition had defected, Brazil and India continued to try to resist the inclusion of TRIPs. In the late 1980s a newly democratised Brazil facing some serious domestic economic problems was brought into line by the US with an additional set of threats, including Super 301. India, isolated, continued to try to limit TRIPs, still appealing to old ideas of fairness in terms of outcomes, and finally had to cave in.

In the Brazilian case it could be argued that preferences and priorities had changed with democratisation, the emergence of new elites, and a more conducive political economy for liberalisation, albeit later than in most other developing countries. Further, the promised prize of engaging in give-and-take in the GATT was too big for Brazil – as a leading agricultural exporter – to ignore. Unsurprisingly it became an active member of the Cairns Group, which typified the new diplomacy based on new notions of fairness.

In the Indian case, however, even after the launch of the liberalisation programme in 1991, negotiators continued to use a distributive strategy that still relied on the old rhetoric. This could be partly explained by interests. The relative imperviousness of Indian negotiators to pro-liberalisation pressures at home was partly just a result of the diplomatic establishment: Geneva diplomacy until the late 1990s remained relatively distant from pressures from New Delhi, and the technical nature of the Uruguay Round negotiations meant that Geneva-based negotiators were often better informed than their counterparts in the capital. Additionally, India's liberalisation programme was a slow and controlled one, while popular suspicion of international institutions like the GATT and traditions of anti-colonialism and Third Worldism remained strong.[1] But the strategy of resisting the Uruguay Round, especially as the lone dissident, was a risky one. Countries that had defected early from the G10 had benefited from some side-deals from developed countries; India in contrast attracted considerable flak for its obstructionist behaviour. The fact that India held to a course that all its allies had abandoned suggests that trade negotiators (supported by the anti-imperialist rhetoric of their populations) may have borne these costs because of their commitment to a particular vision of fairness. But even this commitment may have been strategic, though evidence suggests that there were certain quixotic elements in this strategy.

Besides a supportive domestic political culture that resisted liberalisation, some mileage was to be gained by India for its relentless nay-saying to the developed world. For long India had been seen as a leader of the developing world; in the Uruguay Round, by trying to resist pressures for liberalisation, it could have seen itself as standing for all the other developing countries. Whether it was actually seen as a leader of the developing world in the late 1980s to early 1990s is an empirical question that needs more analysis. On the basis of research conducted by this author so far, it appears that most other developing countries had taken on issue-based coalitions with gusto and good faith. India's continued adherence to bloc-type, Third Worldist coalitions demanding distributive justice may have appeared somewhat anachronistic at the time. However, as the inadequacies of the Uruguay Round began to emerge soon after the formation of the WTO (see Ostry, 2001; Finger and Schuler, 2002; and Narlikar, 2006a), India's hard-line diplomacy and suspicion of reciprocal bargains were vindicated.

Phase III: late 1990s to 2005

Even after having participated in the GATT in accordance with its dominant norm of liberalisation, and on terms of fairness based on process-related legitimacy and reciprocity rather than outcomes and distributive justice, developing countries found themselves effectively in a disadvantaged position in the WTO. While their old call for distributive justice had not generated significant success, neither had their conversion in the 1980s to notions of fairness conceived as equal participation and reciprocity. Revised concepts and strategies had become necessary. Interestingly, while changes from Phase I to Phase II were prompted partly by changes in epistemic consensus (for example, dependency theory in Phase I to standard theories of free trade in Phase II), the revision in the late 1990s was driven by some pragmatic learning and adaptation by developing countries within the WTO rather than any radical epistemic reformulations. Under these new conceptions and strategies, developing countries framed the fairness discourse in terms of both equity in process and equity in outcomes. For many developing countries the return to a Third Worldist discourse was a reversal of strategy in comparison to the 1980s; for India, however, it was a logical continuation.

A unique feature of the GATT (in comparison to the Bretton Woods institutions) – and one that developed countries had frequently referred to whilst demanding concessions from developing countries – was its one-member-one-vote system. Particularly from the Seattle Ministerial onwards in 1999 to the Cancún Ministerial in 2003, developing countries began to point to inequalities in the seemingly egalitarian decision-making procedures of the WTO and thereby began to challenge the fairness of the system in terms of legitimacy and process. They bitterly criticised the WTO for its invitation-only Green Room meetings and its various *de facto* and informal processes that were used to arrive at consensus that led to the marginalisation of its smaller members. At the Seattle Ministerial conference African trade ministers issued the following statement:

> There is no transparency in the proceedings and African countries are being marginalized and generally excluded on issues of vital importance for our peoples and their future . . . We reject the approach being employed, and we must point out that under the present circumstances, we will not be able to join the consensus required to meet the objectives of the Ministerial Conference.[2]

In the aftermath of Seattle and leading up to the negotiations at Cancún, developing countries advanced detailed formal and informal proposals for institutional reform within the WTO. These proposals were a far cry from the aloofness of developing countries from the 'Rich Man's Club' in Phase I. Recall further that in Phase I, developing countries had questioned the notion that equitable processes sufficed to produce equitable outcomes; now they transformed their challenge into questioning the assumption that the much-vaunted decision-making processes of the WTO were equitable in the first place. Interestingly, India was at the forefront of demands for improving transparency for developing countries – an agenda that offered little direct benefit to it as it had, along with Brazil, always had individual access to Green Room meetings since GATT days.

On substance too, developing countries were forced to question whether they had been hasty in their readiness to take on reciprocal obligations in the 1980s to early 1990s. Problems of implementing the reciprocally negotiated Uruguay Round were many and expensive, the promises of the Grand Bargain had remained unfulfilled, and LDCs found themselves especially disadvantaged in the negotiation process as well as implementation of the agreements. Faced with these problems, the Like Minded Group (LMG) – led by India – became one of the first coalitions to bring back equity back on to the agenda (Narlikar and Odell, 2006). It focused on the so-called 'implementation issues', and argued that there was no question of launching a new Round until the imbalances of the Uruguay Round were corrected. It brought back the demand for expanded SDT arrangements that were of special relevance for its LDC members and it was accompanied in this call by the LDC grouping.[3]

Brazil was not a member of the LMG, but it echoed the demands of the LMG on key areas. The Brazilian Foreign Minister, Celso Lafer, stated at the Doha Ministerial Conference of 2001:

> Developing countries have always attached great weight to the principle of special and differential treatment. Yet, after more than five decades, there is not much to show for it. On the contrary, if we look at the sectors that were left behind in the process of liberalisation, or even at many specific rules in the WTO Agreements, it is easy to perceive that there is a large measure of special and differential treatment in favour of the developed countries. Such is the case, for instance, of the Agreement on Subsidies and Countervailing Duties which grants a special exemption to members of the OECD Consensus with regard to rules on export subsidies that other Members of the WTO must comply with.[4]

The Indian Commerce Minister, Murasoli Maran, was vitriolic in his indictment of the draft ministerial text; note in particular his appeal to notions of fairness:

> [T]he draft Ministerial Declaration is neither fair nor just to the view points of many developing countries including my own on certain key issues. It is a negation of all that was said by a significant number of developing countries and least-developing countries . . . The only conclusion that could be drawn is that the developing countries have little say in the agenda setting of the WTO. It appears that the whole process was a mere formality and we are being coerced against our will.[5]

Many of these claims have continued even after the launch of the DDA. Coalitions such as the G20 on agriculture included some strong language on SDT issues at the Cancún Ministerial Conference in 2003. These demands were included even though the leaders of the coalition – including Brazil and India – would not be direct beneficiaries of any SDT provisions that might be negotiated in the future.

At the Hong Kong Ministerial (2005), development and outcome-oriented demands by developing countries persisted. The Indian Commerce Minister, Kamal Nath, continued to stress the importance of achieving fairer substantive outcomes:

We are mandated to correct the *'development deficit'* bequeathed to us by the Uruguay Round. Our negotiations here will have failed if they do not contribute towards creating a rules-based world order, which not only makes trade free, but also makes trade fair . . . Trade commitments which throw hundreds of millions of people already on the edge of subsistence into a chasm of poverty and unemployment simply cannot be supported. The ambitions of developed countries cannot and must not trample on the aspirations of four-fifths of humanity.[6]

While all the instances above suggest that Brazil and India have acted as leaders of the developing world in the DDA negotiations, consulting and carrying the interests of the majority of developing countries, at least some observers have argued that these countries speak and negotiate only for themselves at the expense of the collective (Bello and Kwa, 2004). It is certainly true that as and when deadlocks over agriculture and non-agricultural market access (NAMA) are overcome, and attention turns to SDT, rifts between the larger developing countries, LDCs, and small island economies may emerge. However, this author has found little evidence to support this charge so far. Even as members of the Five Interested Parties (FIPs – Australia, EU, US, Brazil, and India) that negotiated the July Package in 2004, Brazil and India were careful to hold close consultations with G20 members as well as parallel groupings; they have continued with such consultations in the run-up to Hong Kong and thereafter. At the ministerial itself, Minister Kamal Nath stated:

We need to finalise the proposal for duty-free quota-free access for exports of LDCs to developed country markets, without hedging. Developing countries too are ready to play their part, according to their abilities. India shall not be founding wanting in this respect.[7]

That this support is not merely rhetorical is suggested by several further actions that India has taken. Some developing countries had protested against certain SDT provisions for the LDCs; Indian negotiators pointed out in private interviews that, irrespective of costs to country, India's long-standing position as a leader of the developing world would make it impossible for them to present any opposition to such proposals. Further, Indian officials have also talked about giving across-the-board high-preference margins for exports from LDCs to Indian markets, suggesting a willingness to allow at least some free riding by the poorer developing countries.[8] Co-operation between the emerging powers and their less developed counterparts takes several forms. Besides co-ordinating positions across coalitions around ministerial conferences, India has provided technical assistance to LDCs in the run-up to the Hong Kong Ministerial and thereafter; that the four West African cotton producers joined Brazil (which, along with India, is one of the most active litigants in the Dispute Settlement Mechanism (DSM)) in its official complaint against the US on cotton subsidies provides another instance of this co-operation.

This third phase of Brazilian and Indian participation in the WTO presents us with a particularly interesting case. At least within the politics of the multilateral regimes, the two countries seem to have made it. They are invited to many small-group meetings and mini-ministerials, the group of FIPs seems to have replaced the Quad in decision-making, their threats to block negotiations have acquired unprecedented credibility since Cancún, they were closely involved in small-group consultations at Hong Kong. In the past, one of the sources of India's influence at the negotiating table was its claim that it represented the Third World rather than large market shares; progressive trade liberalisation and a growth in GDP figures, however, have provided it with a more concrete source of power. In fact both Brazilian and Indian influence has increased radically since these countries' integration into the global economy, in contrast to Phases I and II. Their need for allies from the developing world is far less than before. Were a discourse of fairness simply a function of interest, we might have expected a swing by these countries towards alliances with developed countries, or at least more of a go-it-alone attitude in contrast to their previous Third Worldism. The fact that fairness questions resonate in their speeches as well as actions, conceived in terms not only of procedure-related questions but also of outcome-related questions, suggests that their commitment to a certain type of fairness may run deeper than an immediate, material-interests-based account would indicate.

It is of course possible that the commitment of these emerging powers is still strategic. Larger developing countries may have become regular invitees to Green Room meetings in the WTO, but it is to their advantage to have more of their allies present in the meetings than fewer, so we could argue that it is not surprising that they have lobbied for greater inclusiveness and transparency in decision-making.

That said, several counter-arguments could be made in response. Once within the club of the powerful, especially if prospects of expanding the club are few, Brazil and India could equally well have calculated that it would be more beneficial for them to act as power-brokers and mediators for other developing countries, rather than lobby for greater inclusiveness. Similarly, they could have preferred to cave in to bilateral deals that they were offered (at Doha and at Cancún) rather than work in coalitions that involve costly log-rolling and free riding by weaker allies. At Hong Kong they could have chosen alternative strategies, for instance pushed solely for the demands of the G20 (which includes many of the larger, middle-income developing countries) but decreased their expression of solidarity with the LDCs. They could also have shown their willingness to make trade-offs by opposing the more radical SDT stance that has been advanced in various forms through coalitions of the LDCs, the ACP group, the Small and Vulnerable Economies group, the Africa Group, and the G33. Interestingly, however, as mentioned earlier, Brazil and India have willingly allowed at least some free riding by their weaker counterparts, both by giving them technical assistance and also by log-rolling their agenda on to their coalitions as well as individual proposals. Further, at Hong Kong, negotiators began to talk of the G110, which comprises the G90 (LDC, ACP, and Africa groups), overlaps with the G33, and includes the G20 – admittedly a very diverse group of countries, but one that is attempting to put development first and preserve some co-ordination of the positions of the weak and the strong within the developing world.[9] Given their growing power in the trade context, the fact that Brazil and India have none the less adhered to a fairness discourse aimed at genuine procedural equality and distributive justice suggests that the logic may extend beyond strategy into the world of ethics.

Conclusion

In this chapter I have relied on the distinction made by Franck between the two notions of fairness as legitimacy and equity. A narrow interest-based account would suggest that while developed countries would push for the first notion of fairness, developing countries would support the second. While we do initially see such a division of fairness-related demands, the success of developing countries in bringing equity-based fairness into the mainstream trade discourse was very limited. The failures of Phase 1 prompted an extreme swing by developing countries to Phase II, when traditional Third Worldist politics took a back seat, and developing countries seemed to have converted wholesale to assumptions of reciprocal trade concession. In the wake of the disappointments of the Uruguay Round, a more nuanced position is evident in Phase III. Issues of equity have returned to the fore, but are premised this time upon at least a qualified commitment to economic liberalisation rather than an epistemic alternative. Developing countries have been careful to frame their demands for equity of process and substance in the WTO within the norms and rules of the organisation.

It is interesting to note the implications that these changing notions of fairness have had for trade negotiations. In Phase I, despite the deeply divided notions of fairness between North and South, deadlocks were few. In contrast, even though Phase III involves developing countries advancing notions of fairness that combine notions of legitimacy and equity that fit within the dominant norms of the organisation, two of the past four ministerials (Seattle and Cancún) ended in deadlock; Doha and Hong Kong did not collapse, but it would be hard to treat them as clear successes. In part the difference lies in the marginalisation of developing countries in Phase I in the GATT, versus their active engagement in Phase III. But another explanation lies in the fact that even though current notions of fairness are less antagonistic to developed country notions, they provide an important basis for the cohesiveness of coalitions of developing countries. The outcomes-based notion of fairness in Phase I placed much of the onus of overcoming inequalities on developed countries; the Phase III version, which relies on both process-related legitimacy and outcome-related equity, is accompanied by a recognition that the larger developing countries would have to bear at least some costs of providing greater equity of outcomes. As a result, coalitions of developing countries, even while retaining their diversity, have also proved to be more cohesive and long-lasting so far. Developed countries are still learning to deal with such coalitions (Narlikar, 2006b).

As this learning progresses, it seems realistic to hope that these notions of fairness would facilitate rather than deter agreement. It is also worth bearing in mind that, while this chapter has focused on the evolving notions of fairness in the developing world, developed country conceptualisations of fairness have not been static. For instance, even a minimalist DDA would have been impossible to foresee in the early 1990s; the same might also be said of the Millennium Development Goals (MDGs) for that matter. Developed countries have responded to pressures (strategic and normative) from developing countries, but have also learnt that they cannot ignore their domestic constituencies on multilateral trade matters. Pro-development NGOs form a part of this domestic constituency.

Finally, to return to a question that was raised in the introduction, how far could the evolving fairness discourse be explained in terms of narrow national interest? The previous sections demonstrated that despite their growing influence in trade matters, Brazil and India have so far willingly borne the costs that their adherence to the current fairness discourse entails. These costs suggest that something more than immediate self-interest underlies the continued support of these countries for fairness norms thought of in terms of process-based legitimacy and also outcome-based equity. Two interpretations are plausible. The first is still a strategic one: even though Brazil and India have gained increasing importance in a WTO context, grand strategy requires their continued allegiance to Third Worldist coalitions in trade, which provide them with leadership status and influence in other issue areas. This argument would be especially convincing if we saw similar behaviour patterns by these countries across regimes. In practice, however, the picture is much more mixed. India, which has proudly accepted the status of being the 'voice of the voiceless' in the WTO, has also simultaneously pursued closer bilateral relations with the US on nuclear co-operation. President Lula's presence in the World Social Forum (WSF) may have been a signal of Brazilian commitment to the Global South, but his attendance at the WSF was followed immediately by his participation in the World Economic Forum (WEF). The picture is much more complex than any Grand Strategy logic might indicate.

The alternative explanation would be that the commitment to fairness – at least in trade matters – by these two countries transcends strategic imperatives: at least certain elites within the countries – and their constituencies – are genuinely committed to foreign policies that they see as fair. Sources of this commitment could be historical (memories of colonialism), political (institutions and bureaucracies), politico-economic (interest groups), or cultural (domestic political culture).[10] One way of evaluating this hypothesis would be to see whether these countries continue with a similar discourse after their rise to power, when their need for Third World allies is considerably diminished. Interviews with Indian officials indicate that, at least at this point, there seems to be a commitment to an Indian world-view; India as a Great Power would behave quite differently from the Western Great Powers.[11] Admittedly this argument cannot be tested just yet as these countries are still emerging powers rather than established Great Powers (neither, for instance, is a permanent member of the Security Council). Purely in trade matters, however, their influence today is unprecedented. That they continue to bear the costs of a discourse that stresses legitimacy of process and equity of outcomes suggests that fairness matters in trade negotiations.

Notes

The author thanks the Nuffield Foundation for financial support that enabled her to conduct research on this subject. She is grateful to Pieter van Houten, Shogo Suzuki, Rorden Wilkinson, Duncan Bell, and especially Andrew Hurrell and Sheila Page for stimulating discussions and helpful comments. These friends should not be held responsible for the use that the author made of their advice or any errors that might remain in the chapter. A significant part of the argument presented in this chapter has been discussed at length in Amrita Narlikar (2006), 'Fairness in International Trade Negotiations: Developing Countries in the GATT and WTO', *The World Economy*, 29: 8.

1 None the less, it seems surprising at first glance that a liberalising Indian government did not use the GATT for domestic political economy ends as much as it could have done. For instance, like other developing countries, it could have gained concessions by engaging in issue-based reciprocity and also pushed for economic reform at home under the pretext that the GATT had tied its hands.
2 Statement available at http://www.africaaction.org/docs99/wto9912.htm; a group of Caribbean and Latin American delegations issued a similar statement, http://www.twnside.org.sg/title/grulac-cn.htm, accessed on 7 May 2006.
3 WT/GC/W/442, Proposal for a Framework Agreement on Special and Differential Treatment, 19 September 2001.
4 Statement by Mr Celso Lafer, Brazil, WT/MIN(01)/ST/12, 10 November 2001, www.wto.org.
5 Statement by HE Mr Murasoli Maran, India, WT/MIN(01)/ST/10, 10 November 2001, www.wto.org.
6 Statement by HE Mr Kamal Nath, India, WT/MIN(05)/ST/17, 14 December 2005, www.wto.org.
7 Statement by HE Mr Kamal Nath, India, WT/MIN(05)/ST/17, 14 December 2005, www.wto.org.
8 Private interviews, New Delhi, December 2005, April 2006.
9 http://www.actionaid.org/index.asp?page_id=743; accessed on 7 June 2006.
10 Work in progress, Narlikar and Hurrell, Nuffield Foundation Project.
11 Interviews with current and former officials in the Ministry of Commerce and Ministry of External Affairs, New Delhi, January and April 2006.

References

Albin, Cecilia (2001), *Justice and Fairness in International Negotiation* (Cambridge: Cambridge University Press).
Bello, Walden, and Kwa, Aileen (2004), 'G20 Leaders Succumb to Divide and Rule Tactics: The Story of Washington's Triumph in Geneva', 10 August. http://www.focusweb.org/main/html/Article408.html; accessed on 15 May 2006.
Finger, Michael, and Schuler, Philip (2002), 'Implementation of WTO Commitments: The Development Challenge', in Philip English, Bernard Hoekman, and Aaditya Mattoo (eds), *Development, Trade and the WTO: A Handbook* (Washington, DC: World Bank).
Franck, Thomas (1995), *Fairness in International Law and Institutions* (Oxford: Clarendon Press).
Hoekman, Bernard, and Kostecki, Michel (2001), *The Political Economy of the World Trading System: From GATT to WTO* (Oxford: Oxford University Press).
Kapstein, Ethan (2005), 'Power, Fairness, and the Global Economy', in Michael Barnett and Raymond Duvall (eds), *Power in Global Governance* (Cambridge: Cambridge University Press).

Kock, Karin (1969), *International Trade Policy and the GATT, 1947–67* (Stockholm: Almqvist and Wiksell).

Narlikar, Amrita (2003), *International Trade and Developing Countries: Bargaining Coalitions in the GATT and WTO* (London: Routledge).

Narlikar, Amrita (2006a), 'Fairness in International Trade Negotiations: Developing Countries in the GATT and WTO', *The World Economy*, 29: 8.

Narlikar, Amrita (2006b), 'Breaking the Deadlock: A Model Involving a Signalling Mechanism in North–South Negotiations', Paper presented at the Annual Conference of the International Studies Association, San Diego, March.

Narlikar, Amrita, and Odell, John (2006), 'The Strict Distributive Strategy for a Bargaining Coalition: The Like Minded Group in the World Trade Organization', in John Odell (ed.), *Negotiating Trade: Developing Countries in the WTO and NAFTA* (Cambridge: Cambridge University Press).

Ostry, Sylvia (2001), 'Why Has "Globalization" Become a Bad Word?' http://www.utoronto.ca/cis/ostry.html.

Steffek, Jens (2006), *Embedded Liberalism and Its Critics: Justifying Global Governance in the American Century* (London: Palgrave).

Suranovic, Steven (2000), 'A Positive Analysis of Fairness with Applications to International Trade', *The World Economy*, 23: 3.

Wolf, Martin (1984), 'Two-edged Sword: Demands of Developing Countries and the Trading System', in Jagdish Bhagwati and John Ruggie (eds), *Power, Passions and Purpose* (Cambridge, Mass.: MIT Press).

12 Democracy, development, and the WTO's legitimacy challenge

Assessing the Doha Development Round

Elizabeth Smythe

Introduction

Over five years have passed since the launching of a new Round of trade negotiations when WTO members met in Doha in 2001. The agreement was hailed by
its supporters as putting the WTO back on track after the collapse of the ministerial
meeting in Seattle in 1999 amid mutual recriminations and clouds of tear gas in
the street. The Round was to be a development one which would reflect the interests
of the majority of WTO members and go some way to addressing the growing
debate over the very legitimacy of the WTO itself and the multilateral process of
trade rule-making.

Questions had been growing in the 1990s as the agenda of trade negotiations
penetrated ever more deeply into areas of traditional national regulation and the
WTO confronted the problem of being both too remote from and too intrusive in
the lives of citizens (Woods and Narlikar, 2001). Since Seattle, critics and even
supporters of the WTO recognise that it faces a legitimacy challenge that risks
undermining support and ultimately the basis of authority for the organisation
(Baldwin, 2004; Ostry, 2004; Esty, 2002). While the imperatives of strengthening
the WTO's underlying basis of legitimacy and improving its transparency and
openness, both externally to new voices and internally to its state members, has
been recognised, the response to date has gone only part of the way in addressing
the legitimacy challenge. This chapter examines the debate about legitimacy and
the WTO, focusing on the period since the launch of the Doha Development Agenda
(DDA). It argues that while the WTO has made some strides in external transparency
– an important element in enhancing legitimacy – it has failed to date to address
fully issues regarding internal processes and inequitable outcomes. The meagre
development outcomes of the DDA thus far, as evidenced in Hong Kong as well
as in the collapse of the negotiations shortly thereafter, I argue will not go far in
addressing legitimacy questions. The pressing questions of power asymmetries
among WTO members, reflected in the lack of internal transparency, informal
decision-making processes which marginalise WTO members, and the resulting
inequitable outcomes, are likely to continue to undermine legitimacy.

This chapter begins with a discussion of the concept of legitimacy and its links to norms of democracy and transparency and then examines the WTO's legitimacy challenge. The second section examines the progress to date at the WTO in responding to critics and their increasing demands for openness – a response which has focused on a limited range of measures to increase external transparency. The third section examines criticisms of decision-making processes and demands for greater internal transparency which have emerged since the Seattle Ministerial meeting and assesses progress during the Doha Round in addressing these concerns. The fourth section discusses the question of output legitimacy in light of the claim that the Doha Round has had development 'at its heart'. In particular the participation of the least developed countries (LDCs), the achievement of development outcomes and the preservation of policy space for development in the negotiation process are examined. The final section examines the contribution of the Hong Kong Ministerial to input and output legitimacy and argues that the WTO has not yet fully met the legitimacy challenge.

Legitimacy and the WTO

Legitimacy is generally defined as a degree of acceptance or consensus around rules or norms in a society. Krajewski defines it as follows:

> A norm can be called legitimate in any political or societal system if it is based on fundamental principles or values adhered to by the subjects of that system. These principles can either define certain procedural conditions of the law-making process (input legitimacy) or material conditions measuring the results of the norm (output legitimacy).
>
> (Krajewski, 2001: 169)

In democratic political systems input legitimacy is normally tied to the procedures by which laws are made and the ability of citizens to hold governments accountable for the decisions made on their behalf and with their consent. Citizens hold governments accountable, first, by the formality and clarity of the decision-making process and, second, via the public's right to information about that decision and how it has been made (that is, transparency). Output legitimacy, however, deals with the likelihood of public acceptance of the decision based on its results, especially its effectiveness in advancing or attaining community values.

Beyond the borders of the nation state and defined political communities the issue of legitimacy becomes more complex. In the case of intergovernmental organisations legitimacy is derived from sovereign member states which make the decisions. National political executives direct officials who negotiate or, as state representatives, make decisions in the key bodies of organisations such as the WTO. In turn the national political executive is accountable to its own citizens either directly, via election, or indirectly, via a body of elected representatives (normally a national legislature) which ratifies treaties or expresses confidence in the decisions of the executive (McGillvray, 2000).

Traditionally the General Agreement on Tariffs and Trade (GATT) and the WTO (which succeeded it in 1995) have operated outside public scrutiny. Confidentiality was justified as necessary to facilitate inter-state bargaining and negotiating (the key activity of the GATT). States had a firm grip on this 'member-driven institution' and thus they, not the secretariat, were accountable for decisions made. The WTO's opaque negotiating process was justified as the only way in which conflicting narrow (and often protectionist) domestic interests could be traded off against each other, outside the scrutiny of domestic publics. Resulting agreements would liberalise trade, open markets, and enhance national and, ultimately, global prosperity. Florini outlines this argument as follows:

> Pushing reform through the political system, therefore, requires that government officials be insulated from parochial, selfish interests. Bypassing citizens groups takes politics out of the process and leads to deeper and more comprehensive reform.
>
> (Florini, 2003: 114)

This process, it was claimed, accounted for the successful lowering of trade barriers and expansion of trade in the postwar period. In recent years, however, the persuasive power of both the input and the output legitimacy narratives in the case of the WTO has been eroding.

With the removal of many barriers to cross-border movements of goods has come a widening scope of trade rules and agendas that now reach deeply into domestic regulatory practices (Zürn, 2004; Ostry, 2004). This has been accompanied by more effective and binding dispute-resolution processes at the WTO, even more at arm's length from state members. Multilateral negotiations have become protracted, increasingly complex affairs with huge agendas, as the history of the GATT Uruguay Round (1986–94) illustrates. National legislatures have become marginal to this process. In many cases elected representatives have limited capacity to scrutinise large, complicated agreements presented to them as *faits accomplis*. These agreements, often a result of informal deals among a few powerful WTO members and negotiated as a single undertaking, have left little capacity for citizens to hold their governments accountable (Scharpf, 2000: 115). Thus the procedural basis of input legitimacy, based on what Keohane and Nye have called the 'Club Model' of multilateral organisations, has been called into question as these chains of accountability linking citizens to WTO rule-making lengthened and weakened (Keohane and Nye, 2001: 264–294).

The output basis of WTO legitimacy has also been eroding. While it may have been possible in the early days of the GATT to claim benefits to citizens or the global economy from greater trade liberalisation, more recent agreements and the distribution of benefits and costs of adjustment among members have raised questions. Critics, for example, see the negotiation of the Trade-Related Aspects of Intellectual Property (TRIPs) as reflecting a WTO that operates only in the interests of a few powerful actors and their corporate allies in the North, marginalising the least developed countries despite a formal decision-making process based on equality and consensus (Birdsall et al., 2005: 136–152). Even the World Bank notes the troubling questions of both process and inequitable outcomes that the WTO faces:

> Within the World Trade Organization (WTO), for example, each country has a vote and each can block proceedings. Even so, WTO processes are at times perceived as unfair because of the underlying power imbalance between strong commercial interests and the public interest, in both developed and developing countries. These imbalances manifest themselves, for instance, in the number of staff employed in Geneva by different WTO members. More effective representation of poor countries in global institutions would help improve processes and may lead to more equitable outcomes.
>
> (World Bank, 2005: 17)

Concerns with both process (input legitimacy) and outcomes (output legitimacy) have been forcefully articulated by networks of citizens and non-governmental organisations (NGOs) which have organised in opposition to, and criticism of, the WTO (Scholte et al., 1999). Their efforts, and the deeper penetration of trade rules into national and local policy areas, have resulted in increased media attention to, and public awareness of, WTO activities. In turn, a number of WTO members have faced growing pressures to open up their trade policy process to a broader range of interests.

Democratic norms, as Keohane and Nye note, are widely held internationally (Keohane and Nye, 2001). Despite declining trust in governments and representative institutions in many countries, evidence shows that citizens remain firmly committed to democratic norms (Inglehart, 1999: 236–256). These embedded norms, coupled with increased access to information technologies, mean that citizens are demanding more transparency as a key aspect of the accountability of governments and, therefore, legitimacy. The OECD shows a huge increase in the passage of access to information laws in member countries in the 1980s and 1990s (OECD, 2001). Transparency has also expanded to mean more than a public legislative process and citizens' access to a few government documents. In the age of globalisation, transparency is seen as a key element of good governance. Transparent state regulation is necessary to ensure clear, predictable, and non-discriminatory treatment of traded goods and foreign investors, particularly in developing countries. Transparency is a virtue preached by every international economic organisation from the International Monetary Fund (IMF) to the WTO and by business NGOs such as Transparency International.

The final factor influencing the debate over legitimacy and the WTO has been the trend in other international governmental organisations, beginning with United Nations agencies followed by the World Bank, to accord much more access, and in many cases formal status, to NGOs than is the case at the WTO (ICTSD, 1999; Florini, 2003: 95–119).

In addition to these pressures the WTO has been affected also by transnational advocacy campaigns that have been highly critical of trade agreements and the processes by which they have been negotiated. These campaigns have been accompanied by a growing capacity of NGOs to scrutinise the operation of the WTO and insert themselves into trade policy debates. Organisations like the International Centre for Trade and Sustainable Development (ICTSD), Third World Network, the Institute for Agriculture and Trade Policy (IATP) and Focus on the Global South have regular reports on WTO activities provided by their own representatives in Geneva which are circulated widely via electronic media. Increased scrutiny, NGOs' demands for greater access and accountability, along with protests, and the growing demands of developing-country WTO members for changes in the decision-making processes, have increased the pressures on the WTO and member states to address legitimacy questions. The WTO response to date has been limited largely to enhancing external transparency – much of which was undertaken prior to the launching of the Doha Round.

External transparency

The legal basis for the WTO to engage with NGOs is found in Article 5.2 of the 1995 Marrakesh Agreement, which states:

> The General Council may make appropriate arrangements for consultation and cooperation with non-governmental organisations concerned with matters related to those of the WTO.
>
> (Marceau and Pedersen, 1999: 5–49)

This mandate was clarified somewhat in 1996 and has come to involve several aspects, including more public access to documents, a well-developed website, the accreditation of NGOs at ministerial meetings, and symposia and briefings that allow for delegate, NGO, and secretariat interaction (Wilkinson, 2002).

In the case of documents, rules have been adopted to de-restrict documents. Given that many member countries do not restrict access to their submissions to the WTO, officials estimate that about 96 per cent of documents are now available to the public. The WTO website, established in 1995, has been frequently enhanced, with an NGO page added in 1998. It has become the information gateway, and by the end of 2003 the number of 'hits' had reached 270 million. The website is a widely accessed source of information prior to ministerial meetings. In September 2003 (just prior to the Cancún ministerial meeting) there were 868,950 visitors to the site from 179 countries.

Technology has also allowed the External Relations Office to communicate with a large number of NGOs via an NGO Bulletin and listservs which provide information to groups. Since the Seattle Ministerial meeting, one listserv has gone from 400 contacts to over 1400. About 35,000 individuals now get daily information on WTO activities, and visitor sessions on the website have topped 650,000 a month in 2003, compared to an average of just under 400,000 in 2001.

The presence of NGOs at ministerial meetings dates from the Singapore Ministerial and is based on the 1996 guidelines. The process, however, has remained ad hoc, largely because the General Council has been reluctant to provide more specific criteria or a permanent process. While NGOs are not at the negotiating table, the real benefit of their accreditation at the ministerials is that they have access to the meeting venue itself and thus to delegates and international media. Accreditation thus affords a real opportunity to lobby delegates, to network with other NGOs and influence media coverage. In addition the WTO provides meeting space and access to technology, which permits NGOs to transmit their version of events to their audience quickly and cheaply. It also affords many groups the capacity to co-ordinate an inside/outside strategy of linking their efforts inside the meeting venue with protests and other activities in the streets. Although the location in Doha, Qatar, depressed the number of NGOs present, overall the number has continued to increase from the 108 in Singapore to almost 800 groups in Cancún in 2003. By the 2005 ministerial meeting in Hong Kong the number of NGOs attending was 812, with 1596 accredited representatives, accompanied, of course, by thousands demonstrating in the streets and on the water. The WTO's External Relations Office has also provided daily briefings and meeting spaces for a large number of NGO-organised events. The large NGO presence, along with protests, has resulted in intense media scrutiny, changing the atmosphere and, some say, increasing the pressure and problems at ministerial meetings. There is a recognition, however, that this will not change and the WTO must accommodate this reality if it is to continue the bi-annual high-profile ministerial meetings. Most recently the acceptance of that reality was reflected in Director-General Lamy's meeting with civil society groups in October 2005 in Hong Kong in anticipation of the December ministerial.

The WTO also provides space to host a large annual public symposium held in Geneva. By 2004 attendance had reached over a thousand participants and provided for interaction among NGOs, academics, and delegates. In addition, myriad smaller briefings and ad hoc meetings are held in Geneva.

The WTO's progress in the dissemination of information was recognised by the British-based One World Trust in its *Global Accountability Report* in 2003. In its study of five IGOs, including the World Bank, the United Nations High Commissioner for Refugees (UNHCR), the OECD, and the Bank for International Settlements, the WTO came second in ranking in online access to information. On the dimension of member control of the organisation, however, the WTO ranked lower, primarily because of problems of internal transparency and the domination of large members in its informal decision-making processes – a serious problem which I address below.

Still, more needs to be done, it can be argued, partly because the WTO suffers from a fallacy also common to trade officials. Officials often believe that if they share information and consult with the NGOs critical of trade policy, the NGOs will come to understand and accept the official position. Consultations and information-sharing are often seen by trade officials and governments as a one-way process, useful to inform and persuade the public. NGOs call it a 'Tell and Sell' strategy and find it unacceptable (Smythe and Smith, 2006). The Doha Declaration's very weak commitment on external transparency reflects this 'Tell and Sell' attitude.

While emphasizing the intergovernmental character of the organization, we are committed to making the WTO's operations more transparent, including through more effective and prompt dissemination of information, and to improve dialogue with the public. We shall, therefore, at the national and multi-lateral levels continue to promote a better public understanding of the WTO and to communicate the benefits of a liberal, rules-based multilateral trading system.

(WTO, 2001a: paragraph 10)

Of perhaps even greater concern is the way in which broader questions of internal transparency and full participation of WTO members in decisions and negotiations have been addressed. Here the Doha Declaration is equally limited:

Recognizing the challenges posed by an expanding WTO membership, we confirm our collective responsibility to ensure internal transparency and the effective participation of all members.

(WTO, 2001a: paragraph 10)

the negotiations shall be conducted in a transparent manner among participants in order to facilitate the effective participation of all.

(WTO, 2001a: paragraph 49)

Yet the declaration is full of more frequent and stronger demands for transparency of member states' domestic regulations and policies, such as government procurement, especially in developing countries.

Input legitimacy and internal transparency: a way to go

Achieving real internal transparency and input legitimacy is vital if the WTO's rules and agreements are to be seen as authoritative. It is clear that the WTO still has a long way to go. After the Doha Ministerial the chair of the General Council reiterated at the meeting of the Trade Negotiations Committee on 1 February 2002 a commitment to conduct negotiations according to the best WTO practices and 'in a transparent, inclusive and accountable manner' (WTO, 2003: 77). Many critics of the WTO's internal processes might have been bemused by this commitment and the similar one expressed in the Doha Declaration, given that the Doha negotiations, like those in Seattle, were characterised by processes seen by many to be less than transparent and inclusive (Jawara and Kwa, 2003: 90–111). In fact the Doha Round as a whole has been characterised by a lack of action on these procedural issues.

Coming after the failure in Seattle and the events of 11 September 2001 it should not be surprising that there was enormous pressure to have a successful ministerial launching negotiations. But the November 2001 Doha Ministerial has been seen by many critics and a number of developing country delegates as epitomising non-transparent and undemocratic procedures. Whilst it advanced the agenda of the most powerful members, others argued that it marginalised the concerns of many developing countries, undermined legitimacy, and eroded trust (South Centre, 2001). Critics cited a number of problems, including:

- a draft declaration based on a chair's text that did not reflect the disagreements (that is, had no square brackets)
- a process of informal, invitation-only, high-pressure meetings of key actors (Green Room meetings) which, in some cases, went on for twelve hours at a time
- the appointment by the Conference chair (a minister from the host country) of facilitators to undertake consultations and forge consensus positions on key issue areas, many of whom were seen to be sympathetic to the positions of the US and EU
- sudden, last-minute extensions of the schedule of negotiations after some delegates had already departed for home
- pressure tactics targeted at developing countries which some NGO critics have characterised as a 'misuse of economic and political power by developed countries', in particular the EU ('NGOs' Perspective on Doha', 2001)
- a Secretariat and Director-General who were biased in favour of, and worked openly for, the launching of negotiations on a number of issues.[1]

The experience of Doha led 15 developing countries (the Like Minded Group, as they were called) to put forward a set of modest proposals designed to address some of these problems. These were presented to the General Council of the WTO in May 2002. They included:

- adopting the meeting's agenda at the first formal plenary and not at the opening ceremony
- using a 'committee of the whole' as the main forum for all major decisions
- choosing facilitators by consensus after consultation with members
- open-ended consultation meetings which are transparent and inclusive and open to any interested members to attend
- all drafts and texts to be presented only at open meetings
- no late-night marathon meetings
- clear and unambiguous language in declarations (a problem reflected in the question of new issues in the Doha Round discussed below)
- adherence to a previously agreed timetable for the ministerial meeting and any decision to extend negotiations to be made only by consensus
- a Chair, Director-General and Secretariat that remained neutral and impartial during the process
- holding lower-key regular ministerial meetings in Geneva to lower costs and burdens on smaller developing country delegations (WTO, 2001b).

However, despite discussion at a General Council meeting in July 2002 no consensus emerged. Most interesting was the way in which a number of developed-country members argued in favour of the need to preserve 'flexibility' in procedures and rejecting the notion 'that one size fits all' when it came to process. Many of these same members had argued in the past that concepts such as flexibility were unacceptable when it came to developing countries seeking policy space for development and flexibility in implementation. Sensing a lack of political will on the part of the most powerful members, the Canadian chair of the General Council, Sergio Marchi, did not pursue the matter further.

In the wake of Doha, progress in many areas of negotiations was limited. Missed deadlines, little progress in agriculture, and ominous signs of US protectionism added to the difficulties of forming a consensus. Progress on the development part of the DDA was less than might have been expected, with deep concerns remaining about implementation issues still outstanding from the Uruguay Round.

NGOs continued to draw attention to the lack of progress on internal transparency and democracy and mounted a 'democracy challenge' to the WTO prior to Cancún in June 2003 which focused exclusively on this continued lack of internal transparency (The Cancún Democracy Challenge, 2003). Their open letter to WTO members drew attention to the limited participation of developing countries in decision-making processes and outlined a series of modest changes similar to those that had been demanded by the Like Minded Group in 2002.

The continued problems of opaque and questionable procedures at the WTO in this post-Doha period can be illustrated by looking at the way in which the issue of launching negotiations on the so-called 'Singapore issues' (investment, competition policy, government procurement, and trade facilitation), despite the clear opposition of a bloc of developing countries, was dealt with. Negotiations on these issues – a priority for only a minority of WTO members – had been pushed relentlessly at the Doha Ministerial, where the EU successfully isolated India and managed, after a marathon all-night session, to get wording on negotiations into the draft declaration. Given the opposition of a number of members and a clear absence of any consensus to launch such negotiations, the wording generated much confusion. When a small group of developing countries, led by India, the next morning requested a change to the text to ensure that consensus would be required to launch negotiations on the Singapore issues at the DDA's intended mid-term review (the September 2003 Cancún Ministerial), and not merely to establish the modalities of negotiations, total confusion followed and the chair had to intervene to clarify the meaning of the text. Proponents and opponents of negotiations continued to dispute its meaning and significance for the next two years, right up until the Cancún Ministerial.

The growing divisiveness of the Singapore issues was reflected in a communication to the General Council's July 2003 meeting from 12 frustrated developing countries that directly refuted the continued insistence of the EU that the Doha declaration in fact had authorised the start of negotiations after Cancún as part of a single undertaking. It reminded delegates, once again, of the explicit consensus provision of the Doha Declaration (Comments on the EC Communication, 8 July 2003).

Despite the clear and growing opposition to negotiation of the Singapore issues, the draft ministerial declaration discussed by the General Council in August 2003 reflected more sleight of hand. The draft seemed, at first glance, to fully capture divisions on these issues. However, the second part of the annexe appeared to presuppose that negotiations would begin post-Cancún and clearly laid out the modalities for negotiations (WTO, 24 August 2003) as they had been outlined in the position papers of the EU and Japan, but which had not been agreed to in the working groups dealing with these issues. Similar concerns about other issues in the draft text were brought forward at the General Council meeting of 26–27 August 2003. The chair at the time, Carlos Pérez del Castillo, refused to alter the text, but was forced by protests of members to prepare a cover letter to accompany the text that reflected the extent of members' disagreement over the draft. The atmosphere of mistrust which such procedures had instilled clearly did not bode well for the ministerial two weeks later. As a South Centre analysis of the Cancún meeting indicated, 'an opaque and restricted participation process had been adopted to prepare for the conference' (South Centre, 2004: 14).

Upon arrival in Cancún the Singapore issues were given an additional boost by the Mexican chair when Canada's trade minister, Pierre Pettigrew, was chosen as facilitator for the Singapore issues. For the many and ever-increasing number of developing country members that opposed negotiations on these issues, this choice must have rankled since Canada had been one of the most active proponents of negotiations, especially of new investment rules (one of the most controversial of the four issues). On 12 September 2003 a group of about 30 countries plus Bangladesh (representing the least developed countries) sent a letter to Pettigrew expressing their opposition to negotiations on any of the four Singapore issues and raising concerns about their capacity both to negotiate new issues and to implement resulting commitments (Aziz and Jaitley, 2003). Nevertheless, the option to negotiate on these four issues pushed by the EU and others remained in the final version of the draft declaration and on the table until the bitter end, contributing to the failure of the meeting.

What had changed by the time of the Cancún meeting, however, was the increased capacity of developing country members, especially large countries like Brazil and India, with the addition of China, to use the more informal processes and meetings to forge stronger coalitions. It has been the emergence of these coalitions that has changed the dynamics of the Doha Round despite the lack of progress on procedural issues.

Another opportunity to engage the debate on internal reform came in 2005 with the release of a report titled *The Future of the WTO*. In June 2003 the then WTO Director-General, Supachai Panitchpakdi, appointed a group of eight eminent persons, led by the former GATT Director-General Peter Sutherland, to 'examine the functioning of the WTO and consider how well equipped it is to carry out future responsibilities and demands' (WTO, 2004: 2). While this was not specifically connected to the Doha Round, optimists might have expected that, given the failure to get real reform of the internal processes of the WTO, this report might spur a debate and possible reform. The report raised the issue, but a question remains as to whether it has encouraged changes that would enhance democratic decision-making and internal transparency. While the report does acknowledge the legitimacy challenge the WTO faces, and deals with external transparency and internal decision processes, it is largely focused on defending the case for trade liberalisation. The emphasis tends to be on what is 'efficient' process rather than democratic. In terms of more transparent procedures the report's attitude is summed up in the statement, 'we do not believe a set of inflexible rules for the conduct and preparation of ministerial conferences is the answer'. As the South Centre pointed out in 2001:

> It does not bode well for the future of the organization if three quarters of the membership feels alienated and marginalized. Efficiency can never replace democracy. Inclusiveness and transparency may mean less scope for the mighty to have their way, but this will mean that the organization is stable and can claim true legitimacy.
>
> (South Centre, 2001)

For the Sutherland group, however, efficiency trumped legitimacy, as reflected in its recommendations for a 30-member consultative board with permanent and rotating members to act as a sort of executive committee, a stronger role for the Director-General and the Secretariat and annual ministerial meetings. Most recommendations have not been embraced by members. Given that the report was not authorised by the General Council and does not specifically address Doha Round negotiations, many developing country delegates have seen no need to comment. Others, already concerned about what they see as the bias of the Secretariat and the marginalisation of many developing country members, have not been supportive of the recommendations as reflected in the presentation of the report to an informal heads of delegation meeting on 25 January 2005 (ICTSD, 2005; South Centre, 2005).

With the failure in Cancún and deadlines slipping further, it looked as if the Doha Round was doomed. However, after two weeks of intensive negotiations in July 2004 in the face of looming autumn elections in the US and the imminent departure of two key negotiators, the EU Trade Commissioner, Pascal Lamy, and the US Trade Representative (USTR), Robert Zoellick, a high-level meeting involving many ministers in Geneva resulted in the General Council adopting a framework of instructions for a work programme, restarting the faltering negotiations. The result of many informal meetings and negotiations on agriculture among a small group known as the Five Interested Parties (FIP – the US, the EU, India, Brazil, and Australia), the framework provides more detail on agriculture. It also officially dropped three of the four Singapore issues, indicating that for investment, competition policy, and government procurement, 'no work [would] take place in the Doha Round' and added the issue of cotton to the agriculture negotiations (WTO, July 2004). On so-called development issues the July Declaration merely reiterated the earlier vague commitments of the Doha Declaration on special and differential treatment, implementation, and technical assistance for the least developed countries. Problems of process and transparency remained, as a number of developing countries (notably the G33) and Switzerland complained of being marginalised.

Output legitimacy: stylised logos or real development?

If the internal procedures and decision-making processes of the WTO have fallen short of the highest standards of democracy and transparency, WTO supporters claim it still has legitimacy based on the decisions made and the agreements it has produced. These achievements or outputs, they claim, should be the criteria by which the legitimacy of the WTO should be measured. It is useful to remember that output legitimacy rests on the notion that outcomes have a positive impact in advancing or attaining the goals or values of a community. This raises two questions for the WTO. First, what are the community's key values? Supporters claim that the GATT and the WTO have liberalised international trade and thus contributed to global economic growth to the general benefit of its member countries and their citizens. However, critics claim that the fairness of the distribution of both the benefits of agreements and the costs of adjustments among member countries is also an important value that the WTO has been less successful in attaining.

The second question is one of the nature of the community that needs to be satisfied with the output. Is it simply to be the 149 member states of the WTO or some broader global community? Given the discussion in the first section of this chapter, a case can be made for the latter. As the WTO's rules have reached deeply into domestic matters, economic integration has increased, and the capacity of citizens to hold governments directly accountable has weakened, public attention has shifted to the WTO itself. This has occurred alongside the emergence of a global discourse that addresses questions of the distribution of the costs and benefits of globalisation. Within the WTO itself the composition of its membership (the community) has altered drastically in the past decade. The increased developing country membership and its demand for more influence, along with the growing public attention that WTO meetings and agreements have attracted, were clearly manifested at the Seattle Ministerial meeting. Since then, WTO officials and developed country members have become more cognisant of the need to portray any new rounds of trade negotiations in a more development-friendly way.

Shortly after the conclusion of the Doha Ministerial meeting in November 2001 the Secretariat, and the Director-General in particular, began calling the Round that had just been launched 'the Doha Development Agenda'. This renaming and the stylised logo produced were based on the claim, as the text of the Declaration indicated, that since the 'majority of WTO members are developing countries . . . [w]e seek to place their needs and interests at the heart of the Work Programme adopted in the Declaration' (WTO, 2001a: paragraph 2.2). The declaration further promised to

> make positive efforts designed to ensure that developing countries, especially the least-developed among them, secure a share in the growth of world trade commensurate with the needs of economic development. In this context enhanced market access, balanced rules, and well targeted, sustainably financed technical assistance and capacity-building programmes have an important role to play.
>
> (WTO, 2001a: paragraph 2)

The Declaration went on to acknowledge the particular problems of the least developed countries and committed the membership to addressing their marginalisation. Thus the Declaration had two development-friendly aspects. The first was substantive in terms of the issues, the priorities in the negotiating agenda, and outcomes which would advance development. The second was in reducing the marginalisation of the smallest and least developed countries, which, it had to be acknowledged, bore heavy costs of adjustment to obligations for limited gains. The efforts to be more inclusive in the negotiating process centred on an enhanced programme of technical assistance and capacity-building targeted at the LDCs. But the purpose of this assistance is made clear in the Doha Declaration:

> The delivery of WTO technical assistance shall be designed to assist developing and least-developed countries and low-income countries in transition to adjust to WTO rules and disciplines, implement obligations and exercise the rights of membership, including drawing on the benefits of an open, rules-based multilateral trading system.
>
> (WTO, 2001a: paragraph 38)

A careful reading of the Doha Declaration, however, also indicates that many of the references to technical assistance and capacity-building were tied to new issues (such as the Singapore issues), on which many developing countries were reluctant to negotiate, as outlined above. For example, in the run-up to the Cancún Ministerial over 40 events were held dealing with investment, either in Geneva or in various locations in developing countries, to provide intensive training on an issue that the vast majority of developing countries did not want to see as part of the negotiation round (Smythe, 2005).

Funded by voluntary donations from the developed country members, this extraordinary increase in training events has not necessarily added to negotiating capacity. Some of the initial evaluations of programmes found that they did not contribute to long-term capacity-building, were too short, or were not sufficiently tailored to the country's needs. Some improvements have been made but critics still claim that what is needed is a capacity in the least developed countries to empower them to fully pursue or realise their interests during negotiations. WTO staff admit that in many instances what would have been more helpful and useful was policy-relevant advice on the particular country's interests and options which might help in setting their priorities and deciding what to do on the issue (Smythe, 2005). WTO staff, however, do not see this as part of their mandate.

In terms of developing-country priorities and development-enhancing outcomes, what the Doha Round has offered to date appears to be limited. Aside from the ongoing issues, such as agriculture and services, two issues in the Doha Declaration were seen by many developing countries as key elements of the development aspect of the Round because they reflect their priorities and issues. The two – implementation and special and differential treatment – are part of the unfinished business of what has been called the 'North–South Grand Bargain' (Ostry, 2004: 94–114) of the Uruguay Round of the GATT. Under that final trade agreement developing countries agreed to a set of obligations in new areas, such as services, TRIPs, and Trade-Related Investment Measures (TRIMs) which were of interest primarily to the US and its corporate sector. In return they were supposed to have enhanced market access for agricultural goods, textiles, and other products of interest to developing countries, along with some flexibility in conforming to these new obligations. As Ostry points out, in this Grand Bargain, or 'Bum Deal', developing countries got less than expected, and benefits in trade expansion predicted at the time by various analysts never materialised, nor did the extent of flexibility promised (Ostry, 2004: 94–114).

By the Seattle Ministerial a number of developing countries had made clear that an array of measures and issues had to be addressed if the commitments of the Uruguay Round and fairer distribution of its costs and benefits for developing countries was to be achieved, and before any new issues were to be added to the negotiating agenda (ICTSD, 2004). Despite the commitments to address implementation and the issue of special and differential treatment, little progress has been made. As ICTSD notes, in the various relevant committees and bodies:

> little progress has been seen, either at the Cancún Ministerial or since. In the wake of the Cancún conference, many of the so-called 'development issues' – including special and differential treatment, implementation-related issues and concerns, technical assistance and capacity building and the unique challenges faced by least developed countries (LDCs) and small economies – have been put on the back burner. The lack of movement on these issues, which are crucial to many developing countries, calls into question the description of the current round of negotiations as a 'development round'.
>
> (ICTSD, 2004b)

If the development aspect of the current Round turns out to be nothing more than a cynical rebranding exercise it will only further erode the legitimacy of the WTO in the eyes of many of its members and the broader international community.

While the unfairness and inequity of the current system of global trading rules has been a persistent theme of many critics of the WTO, it could be argued that norms of fairness, equality, and poverty reduction have been embraced even more broadly at the global level in recent years (Stiglitz and Charlton, 2004). The UN Millennium Declaration in September 2000 and the Monterrey Consensus are reflective of states adopting, at least at the rhetorical level, commitments to these goals. Fair trade campaigns such as Oxfam's 'Make Trade Fair' and the current Make Poverty History campaign are also – whatever the shallowness of the commitment – popularising and embedding a discourse of social justice at the global level. The linking of the outcome of the Doha Round to development puts the WTO in front and at the centre in contributing to the achievement of these goals. Many doubt, however, that as 'a mercantilist institution that works on a principle of self-interested bargaining' (Stiglitz and Charlton, 2004: 496) the WTO is currently on the road to achieving development goals.

The Hong Kong Ministerial: a tale of fig leaves and band-aids

The Hong Kong Ministerial, it could be argued, provided an opportunity to demonstrate that the Doha Round does have development at its heart. As the ministerial meeting came to a 'successful' conclusion and the final Declaration was adopted, the Director-General, Pascal Lamy, wearily proclaimed that the Round was back on track. Moreover: '[t]here has been a rebalancing in favour of developing countries, whose interests have now been placed at the heart of our negotiations as we provided for in 2001 when we launched this round' (WTO, 2005a). While a few commentators, such as economist Jagdish Bhagwati, concurred, the most common assessment among media and NGO critics was that what *The Economist* called an 'expensive experiment in sleep deprivation' had at best a limited or at worst a negative impact in terms of development outcomes. Given that efforts had been under way prior to the meeting to lower or 're-calibrate' expectations, this was indeed faint praise. As the newsletter *Bridges* aptly summed it up, 'Low Ambitions Met' (ICTSD, 2005). The Hong Kong Ministerial and the Doha Round to date have made a very marginal contribution, if any at all, to addressing the legitimacy challenges of the WTO in terms of either input or output legitimacy.

Outputs

The Chair of the Ministerial, John Tsang, is quoted as saying negotiations were so tough 'that it looked as though we might not emerge with any document at all or one so lean and mean it would have been seen as little more than a flimsy fig leaf' (Shih, 2006). An examination of the outputs of the meeting suggests that while they may have gone beyond a 'flimsy' fig leaf, it has not been by much. One could argue that the fig leaf, at best, has been supplemented by a few band-aids.

Among the achievements of the Declaration was the agreement in paragraph 6 to 'elimination of all forms of export subsidies and disciplines', to be completed by the end of 2013, reflecting the concession made on the Saturday evening by the EU. Developing countries had pushed for 2010 throughout the meeting, though the EU had refused to set a date. As a number of observers pointed out, however, this 'concession' was already part of the planned reforms to the EU's Common Agricultural Policy (CAP) and had been reflected in the budget. It is, however, the issue of cotton – considered the litmus test of the WTO's development heart – which deserves the fig-leaf label. As *The Economist* summarised it, 'The Americans offered just enough on cotton and duty-free access to avoid being painted as enemies of the poor' (2005). As development NGOs and other analysts point out, while the declaration states that all forms of developed-country export subsidies for cotton will be eliminated (meaning the US), its export subsidy and credit programmes had already been ruled WTO-inconsistent in April 2005. Duty- and quota-free access for LDC cotton exports will not have much impact on the four small African countries devastated by US domestic cotton subsidies since they do not export to the US. Moreover, domestic US subsidies will remain in place with only vague commitments to address them in the future. In the meantime, LDCs still face stiff competition with subsidised US cotton in other markets (Oxfam, 2005).

Paragraph 7 and Annex F of the Hong Kong declaration also outlined developed-country obligations to provide duty- and quota-free access for LDC exports as of 2008. However, again the devil is in the detail, which required developed countries to cover only 97 per cent of tariff lines, which is sufficient, many experts conclude, to keep LDC (especially Bangladesh textile) exports out of key developed country markets. LDCs had wanted 100 per cent coverage. On the issue of special and differential treatment, negotiations remained deadlocked. While the goal was to make these measures 'precise and effective', of the 88 proposals made by developing countries only 5 are reflected in the declaration, with a new deadline of December 2006. While some observers hope the new deadline will create some impetus, the reality is that most developed countries have shown little interest or willingness to negotiate on these issues. Implementation issues face a similar stalemate. Because these issues are scattered across WTO bodies and developed countries appear largely uninterested since they were raised in Singapore, little has been done and they seem to have fallen off the agenda.

Aid for Trade

Since the launching of the Doha Round in 2001 there has been a growing consensus among developing country members and trade policy analysts that trade liberalisation may have limited benefits for some developing countries and involve increased costs of adjustment for them in the short term. Some developing countries lack the trading capacity to benefit from increased access to export markets and face immediate negative consequences of trade reforms such as the loss of preferential market access or subsidies. Acknowledging this reality, the G8 leaders requested the development of a programme of technical and financial assistance to compensate developing countries for costs and enhance their future capacity to realise benefits from trade agreements. These proposals, outlined in an IMF/World Bank paper (IMF, 2005), have become known as 'Aid for Trade'. Paragraph 57 of the Hong Kong Declaration, which has been hailed by Lamy and others as showing real commitment to development in the DDA, embraces this approach. Based on earlier discussions at the World Bank and the IMF, the Hong Kong Declaration welcomes discussions and calls upon the Director-General to establish a task force to operationalise the concept, which is intended to

> help developing countries, particularly LDCs, to build the supply-side capacity and trade-related infrastructure they need to assist them to implement and benefit from WTO agreements and more broadly expand their trade.
>
> (WTO, 2005b)

The composition of the task force was announced on 8 February 2006 and represents a range of members, including many developing and developed countries and representatives of the African and LDC groups. However, there is little clarification on details, especially regarding the moneys involved and whether or not they are merely recycled or rebranded assistance funds. The role of the IMF and the World Bank and US public statements already suggest that funds would be tied to further developing country market liberalisation.

Process

During the Hong Kong Ministerial, 450 meetings were organised, and six major gatherings and over 200 consultations by facilitators were held. Reflecting on the meeting, the WTO Director-General, Pascal Lamy, claimed that a successful and inclusive process based on bottom-up consultations had taken place (WTO, 2005b). Others have also claimed that despite the lack of formal decision-making procedures for ministerials some progress has been made since Seattle in improving informal practices so they are more inclusive and consultative (Pedersen, 2006; Odell, 2005). However, problems have arisen around the processes of transferring discussions in Geneva into text for ministerial Declarations. Particularly troublesome, as outlined above, have been chair's or single negotiating texts which do not include the traditional bracketing, fail to properly reflect the lack of consensus, and appear to marginalise or ignore issue positions of certain members.

Just as the Singapore issues raised questions regarding transparency in development of the Cancún draft text, so services did in the case of the Hong Kong Ministerial. Developing countries and NGOs sounded alarms over the 26 October 2005 draft services text. Controversial elements had first appeared in a note prepared by the Mexican chair of the negotiating group on 13 October 2005 which referred to sectoral and modal objectives, plurilateral and multilateral approaches, and numerical targets and indicators – all of which had been opposed by the majority of developing countries. Despite much opposition and the existence of alternative proposals for the text from developing countries, the wording remained. Sixty civil society organisations were so concerned that they sent an open letter to Lamy regarding the process used to 'manufacture' the services text. The text reflected the interests, in particular of the EU and the European Services Forum, which had been pushing hard to open service sectors in developing countries and, according to Action Aid, had vigorously lobbied EU negotiators. A number of developing countries called for the removal of Annex C of the services text from the 7 December draft of the ministerial text, fearing that its mandatory language would require members to enter negotiations in the event of a plurilateral (that is, collective) request made to them, a context in which they could be vulnerable to pressures. As such, the text appeared to undermine the development protections and 'flexibility' supposedly built into the framework of services negotiations. The G90's opposition was strong and despite some softening of the language of the text in the final declaration was not overcome until the early hours of the final Sunday morning when India played a key role in persuading the group to accept the modified text. As the South Centre has pointed out, however, 'the primary focus of Annex C is to increase the levels of liberalisation without any consideration of the development impacts or gains' (South Centre, 2005).

Conclusion

The WTO has been under increased pressure in recent years as its rules and agreements have expanded and penetrated further into domestic matters. With the launching of the Doha Round as one centred on development, the WTO faces further challenges in delivering outcomes that not only conform to values of democracy, fairness, and equity but also advance the goals of development. The response of the WTO to this challenge, to date, has been limited. While there has been some increase in external transparency, it has meant that the WTO is under closer scrutiny. Problems with internal transparency, especially in the drafting of negotiating texts, remain, although the stronger coalitions of developing countries have ensured that the developed countries must now be more attentive to including them or their representatives in the informal meetings and processes. Further gains on external transparency are unlikely without attention to the internal factors and the asymmetries of negotiating capacities among members.

NGOs, especially aid organisations, are working in co-operation with smaller developing countries to get their issues heard and on to the WTO agenda, as was the case with cotton in West Africa. This co-operation, along with the emergence of stronger developing country coalitions within the WTO and the growing impact of international norms of democracy and equity, has increased the pressure on the WTO. Recognising this, the WTO claimed in forging the Doha agreement and launching the Round that it was development-centred in order to enhance its legitimacy. Development has not, however, been at the heart to date, as this chapter shows. As the Jamaican ambassador noted in Hong Kong, the paradox of Doha is that (as the World Bank has acknowledged) the projected gains for many developing countries will be much diminished from the claims made in 2001; and the demands being made on developing countries by the developed in this Round have only increased (Knight, 2006: 604). Failure to deliver on the development commitments so far, the impasse in Cancún, and the meagre results of Hong Kong appear only to increase the legitimacy challenge. Ultimately the Doha Round will have to deliver more than rhetoric otherwise critics will continue to ask 'what, exactly, is the point of the WTO' (*New York Times*, 2005). Perhaps, as Oxfam suggests, the time has come for the rich-country negotiators to 'examine their consciences' and 'turn this into a development round for the world's poor' (Oxfam, 2005: 2).

Notes

1 One example was the Director-General Mike Moore's open advocacy in a *Financial Times* of London article of launching new negotiations on the Singapore issues, championed by the EU and Japan, but opposed by the many developing countries and ultimately a majority of the WTO membership.

References

Aziz, Seri Rafidah (Malasyia) and Jaitley, Arun (India) (2003), *Letter to Hon. Pierre Pettigrew*, 12 September.

Baldwin, Robert (2004), 'Key Challenges Facing the WTO', in Mike Moore (ed.), *Doha and Beyond: The Future of the Multilateral Trading System* (Cambridge: Cambridge University Press).

Bhagwati, Jagdish (2005), 'A Blend of Strong Measures Put the Trade Talks Back Together', *Financial Times*, 20 December.

Birdsall, Nancy, Rodrik, Dani, and Subramanian, Arvind (2005), 'How to Help Poor Countries', *Foreign Affairs*, 84: 4 (July/August).

The Cancún Democracy Challenge (2003), 'Civil Society Call to WTO Members for the 5th Ministerial in Cancún', July. www.globalpolicyforum.org.

Comments on the EC Communication (2003) Communication from Bangladesh, Cuba, Egypt, India, Indonesia, Kenya, Malaysia, Nigeria, Pakistan, Venezuela, Zambia and Zimbabwe commenting on the EC communication on the modalities for the Singapore issues (WT/GC/W/491, 8 July).

CUTS (Consumer Unity and Trust Society) (2001), 'Capacity Building for WTO Participation: African Perspectives', African Resource Centre, Policy Brief No. 8.

Economist, The (2005), 'Hard Truths, World Trade', 24 December.

Esty, Daniel (2002), 'The World Trade Organization's Legitimacy Crisis', *World Trade Review*, 1 (March).

Florini, Ann (2003), 'From Protest to Participation: The Role of Civil Society in Global Governance', in Host Siebert (ed.), *Global Governance: An Architecture for the World Economy* (Heidelberg: Springer-Verlag, 2003).

Gerhart, Peter M. (2004), 'The World Trade Organization and Participatory Democracy: The Historical Evidence', *Vanderbilt Journal of Transnational Law*, 37 (October).

Halle, Mark (1999), 'Legitimacy: The New Frontier' *Bridges*, 3: 2 (March).

Hart, Michael, and Dymond, Bill (2006), 'The WTO Plays Hong Kong: So Little Accomplished by So Many', *Policy Options*, February.

International Centre for Trade and Sustainable Development (ICTSD) (1999), 'Accreditation Schemes and Other Arrangements for Public Participation in International Fora: A Contribution to the Debate on WTO and Transparency', November (Geneva: ICTSD).

ICTSD (2004a), *Implementation Related Issues and Concerns 3*, Doha Round Briefing Series: Developments since the Cancún Ministerial Conference (December). www.ictsd.org.

ICTSD (2004b), *Special and Differential Treatment 13*, Doha Round Briefing Series: Developments since the Cancún Ministerial Conference (December). www.ictsd.org.

ICTSD (2005) 'Low Ambitions Met: Members Adopt Declaration', *Bridges*, 7 (19 December). www.ictsd.org.

Inglehart, Ronald (1999), 'Postmodernization Erodes Respect for Authority but Increases Support for Democracy', in Pippa Norris (ed.), *Critical Citizens: Global Support for Democratic Governance* (Oxford: Oxford University Press).

International Monetary Fund (2005), *The Doha Development Agenda and Aid for Trade*, 9 September (Washington: IMF).

Jawara, Fatoumata, and Kwa, Aileen (2003), *Behind the Scenes at the WTO* (London: Zed Books and Focus on the Global South).

Keohane, Robert, and Nye, Joseph S. (2001), 'The Club Model of Multilateral Cooperation and Problems of Democratic Legitimacy', in R. Porter, P. Sauve, A. Subramanian, and A. Zampetti (eds), *Efficiency, Equity and Legitimacy: The Multilateral Trading System at the Millennium* (Washington, DC: Brookings Institution).

Knight, Keith (2006), 'Doha Paradox: Decreasing Returns, Increasing Demands', *South Bulletin*, 116 (30 January).

Krajewski, Markus (2001), 'Democratic Legitimacy and Constitutional Perspectives on WTO Law', *Journal of World Trade Law*, 35: 1.

Lerner, Josh (2004), 'Beyond Civil Society: Public Engagement Alternatives for Canadian Trade Policy' (Toronto: Canadian Institute for Environmental Law and Policy, 2003). www.cielap.org.

McGillvray, Fiona (2000), 'Democratizing the WTO', Essays in Public Policy 105 (Stanford: Hoover Institution).

Marceau, Gabrielle, and Pedersen, Peter (1999) 'Is the WTO Open and Transparent?', *Journal of World Trade Law*, 33: 1 (February).

New York Times (2005), 'Hong Kong Holding Pattern', 20 December.

'NGOs' Perspective on Doha: A Development Disaster' (2001), *South Letter*, 3: 4.

Nordstrom, Hakan (2005), 'The World Trade Organization Secretariat in a Changing World', *Journal of World Trade*, 39: 5 (October).

Odell, John (2005), 'Chairing a WTO Negotiation', in Ernst-Ulrich Petersmann (ed.), *Reforming the World Trading System: Legitimacy, Efficiency and Democratic Governance* (Oxford: Oxford University Press).

One World Trust, *Global Accountability Report* (London: 2003).

Organisation for Economic Co-operation and Development (OECD) (2001), *Citizens as Partners: Information, Consultation and Public Participation in Policy Making* (Paris: OECD).

Ostry, Sylvia (2004) 'External Transparency: The Policy Process at the National Level of the Two-Level Game', in Mike Moore (ed.), *Doha and Beyond: The Future of the Multilateral Trading System* (Cambridge: Cambridge University Press).

Oxfam (2005), 'What Happened in Hong Kong: Initial Analysis of the WTO Ministerial', Briefing paper, December.

Pedersen, Peter Norgaard (2006), 'The WTO Decision-Making Process and Internal Transparency', *World Trade Review*, 5: 1 (January).

Scharpf, Fritz W. (2000), 'Interdependence and Democratic Legitimation', in Susan J. Pharr and Robert D. Putnam (eds), *Disaffected Democracy: What's Troubling the Trilateral Countries* (Princeton: Princeton University Press).

Scholte, Jan Aart, with O'Brien, Robert, and Williams, Marc (1999), 'The World Trade Organisation and Civil Society', in Brian Hocking and Stephen McGuire (eds), *Trade Politics: International Domestic and Regional Perspectives* (London: Routledge).

Shih, Toh Han (2006), 'WTO Talks a Close Shave', *South China Morning Post*, 7 January.

Smythe, Elizabeth (2005), 'What Do You Know? Knowledge, Capacity-Building and Trade Negotiations: The Case of Investment Rules and the World Trade Organization', Paper presented at the Annual Meeting of the International Studies Association, Honolulu, Hawaii (3 March).

Smythe, Elizabeth, and Smith, Peter J. (2006), 'Legitimacy, Transparency and Information Technology: The World Trade Organization (WTO) in an Era of Contentious Trade Politics', *Global Governance* 12: 1 (January).

South Centre (2001), 'From Punta del Este to Doha and Beyond', *South Letter*, 3: 4.

South Centre (2004), *From Cancún to Hong Kong: Lessons from the 5th Ministerial Conference of the WTO*, South Centre T.R.A.D.E. Working Papers.

South Centre (2005), 'The Sutherland Report: Further Marginalizing the South', *South Bulletin*, 96 (30 January).

South Centre (2006), *South Centre Analysis of the Hong Kong Ministerial Meeting*, South Centre T.R.A.D.E. Working Papers.

Stiglitz, Joseph, and Charlton, Andrew (2004), 'Common Values for the Development Round', *World Trade Review*, 3: 3.

Sutherland, Peter et al. (2004), *The Future of the WTO: Addressing Institutional Challenges in the New Millennium* (Geneva: WTO).

Third World Network (1999), 'Transparency, Participation and Legitimacy of the WTO', Statement of the Third World Network at the WTO Symposia on Trade and Environment and Trade and Development, Geneva (15–18 March).

Wilkinson, Rorden (2002), 'The Contours of Courtship: The WTO and Civil Society', in Rorden Wilkinson and Steve Hughes (eds), *Global Governance: Critical Perspectives* (London: Routledge).

Wolfe, Robert (2005), 'Decision-Making and Transparency in the Medieval WTO: Does the Sutherland Report Have the Right Prescription?', *Journal of International Economic Law*, 8: 3.

Woods, Ngaire, and Narlikar, Amrita (2001), 'Governance and the Limits of Accountability: The WTO, the IMF and the World Bank', *International Social Science Journal*, 53 (December).

World Bank (2005), *Equity and Development: World Development Report 2006* (New York: World Bank and Oxford University Press, October).

World Trade Organization (WTO) (2001a), *Doha Declarations* (Geneva: WTO).

WTO (2001b), 'Preparatory Process in Geneva and Negotiating Procedure at the Ministerial Conferences: Communication from Cuba, Dominican Republic, Egypt, Honduras, India, Indonesia, Jamaica, Kenya, Malaysia, Mauritius, Pakistan, Sri Lanka, Tanzania, Uganda and Zimbabwe', WT/GC/W/471 (24 April).

WTO (2003), Preparations for the Fifth Session of the Ministerial Conference Draft Cancún Ministerial Text Revision (24 August).

WTO (2004), Second draft of post-Cancún decision for the General Council (30 July).

WTO (2005a), Summary of 18 December 2005, Day 6: Ministers agree on declaration that 'puts Round back on track'. www.wto.org.

WTO (2005b), Doha Work Programme, Ministerial Declaration, 18 December, Ministerial Conference, Sixth session, Hong Kong (WT/MIN (05)DEC).

Zürn, Michael (2004), 'Global Governance and Legitimacy Problems', *Government and Opposition*, 39: 2 (April).

Part V
Concluding the Round

13 The Doha Round and its impact on the WTO

Gilbert R. Winham

The Doha Round began with the WTO Doha Ministerial Declaration of 14 November 2001 (WTO, 2001). This negotiation was launched with the intention of ensuring that developing countries, and especially the least developed, received 'a share in the growth of world trade commensurate with the needs of their economic development' (WTO, 2001). The Declaration established a work programme of approximately 21 subjects, a number of which were to be negotiated formally on the basis of a single undertaking. These subjects mainly included agriculture, services, non-agricultural market access (NAMA), WTO rules, regional trade agreements and environment, as well as certain aspects of the implementation of Uruguay Round Agreements and the TRIPs Agreement. The Doha Declaration also included four subjects – investment, competition policy, government procurement, and trade facilitation (the so-called Singapore issues) – for later inclusion on the basis of the single undertaking, but the first three later failed to receive consensus and were dropped from the negotiation (WTO, 2006a).

The Doha Round, which is the ninth multilateral negotiation held under the GATT/WTO regime, was originally scheduled to conclude not later than 1 January 2005. This deadline was rendered impossible by the impasse that occurred between developed and developing countries at the Cancún WTO Ministerial meeting in September 2003. Following this setback, delegations managed to put the negotiation back on the rails with a new approach to the Doha Work Programme adopted in the 'July Package' by the WTO General Council on 1 August 2004 (WTO General Council, 2004a). The Work Programme extended the Doha Round deadline beyond January 2005, and established December 2005 as the date for the next ministerial meeting in Hong Kong. Most importantly, it singled out the subjects of agriculture, NAMA, and to a lesser degree services for priority attention in the negotiation (Cho, 2005: 1). Additionally, the July Package of 2004 reaffirmed the importance of a sectoral negotiation on cotton, and agreed to pursue the matter in the negotiations on agriculture.

The negotiation slowed in early 2005, with developing countries pressing developed countries mainly in agriculture, while the latter insisted they could not take unilateral action in agriculture without receiving reciprocal concessions on industrial tariffs and services from developing countries. A meeting in July 2005 of some 30 trade ministers in Dalian, China, attempted to bridge this impasse, but it achieved little. Further attempts to set specific negotiating targets were made in the run-up to the Hong Kong Ministerial meeting set for December 2005. In the ministerial meeting itself, gruelling negotiations managed to keep the negotiations alive, but they failed to produce specific numbers or formulas for moving to the next level of tariff and subsidy bargaining (ICTSD, 2005: 1). The ministerial produced an agreement to eliminate agricultural export subsidies by 2013, but it also adopted some changes to reinvigorate the negotiations on services, which had been largely stalled. The major accomplishment of the ministerial was to set a deadline of 30 April 2006 for the tabling of full modalities in the agricultural and NAMA negotiations, and a deadline shortly thereafter of 31 July for draft schedules of commitments in both sectors. In the hopeful words of the WTO Director-General, Pascal Lamy, this result put the Doha Round 'back on track' (ICTSD, 2005: 1), though it was short-lived. The collapse of the negotiations in July 2006 yet again revealed the extent of discord over the direction and content of the negotiations.

Progress of the Doha Round after the Hong Kong Ministerial meeting

By the end of December 2005 two general observations could be made about the negotiation process of the Doha Round. First, depending on how one counted, there were at the outset about a dozen issues placed on the negotiating agenda by developing and developed countries, but three of concern to developed countries had been dropped outright, and the legitimacy of a fourth (services) was subject to challenge by developing countries. The negotiation very much devolved into an exchange over agriculture and NAMA, with the remaining issues dependent on movement and progress on the former subjects. Second, in the period from July 2005 onward, negotiations were more clearly focused on process than substance, or alternatively, on setting dates for action rather than taking action. At some point any negotiation requires the parties to agree on the workable boundaries of an acceptable settlement. When the negotiation entered the year 2006 this had not been done.

Following Hong Kong, the timetable of the Doha Round appeared obvious. Legislation authorising US officials to negotiate on a 'fast-track' basis expired in July 2007, thereby effectively setting a deadline of February/March 2007 for the negotiation (Interview with WTO official). Moving backward, delegations obliged themselves, as spelled out in the Hong Kong Ministerial Declaration, 'to submit comprehensive draft Schedules based on . . . modalities' in agriculture and NAMA no later than 31 July 2006 (WTO, 2005: 4, 6). Modalities in turn were mandated to be established no later than 30 April 2006 (WTO, 2005). It goes without saying that substantial and detailed negotiations are required on the draft schedules once they are derived, which were planned for the autumn of 2006. This work was to be conducted alongside text-based negotiations on issues such as rules and environment that have been relatively neglected thus far in the process.

To meet the above schedule a number of actions were taken in the first months of 2006. On 30 January a series of timelines were drawn up based on informal discussions in Davos, Switzerland; this agenda produced no substantive progress, but simply clarified timelines already agreed at the Hong Kong Ministerial (WTO, 2006b). On 1–2 March senior agricultural officials of the G6 countries (Australia, Brazil, India, EU, Japan, and the US) met in Paris to negotiate modalities in agriculture. On 7–8 March senior trade officials of the G10 countries met in Geneva to negotiate modalities in agriculture and NAMA. On 10–11 March, in preparation for the Hong Kong-mandated deadline of 30 April, trade ministers of the G6 met in London to negotiate modalities in agriculture and NAMA. Again on 3 April the US Trade Representative (USTR), Robert Portman, met in Rio with his ministerial counterparts Peter Mandelson from the EU and Celso Amorim from Brazil to achieve a breakthrough on the issue of modalities. These meetings were all unsuccessful. Finally, shortly before 30 April and acting on advice, the Director-General, Pascal Lamy, made it clear that the meeting of trade ministers in Geneva, which was to establish full modalities in agriculture and NAMA for all Doha Round participants, would not take place.

What was the argument over modalities all about? The answer relates to what has been accomplished and not accomplished in the Doha Round up to May 2006. Building on the existing WTO Agreement on Agriculture, Doha negotiators established in the July 2004 Package a three-part Framework for the agricultural negotiation, which was further elaborated in the Hong Kong Ministerial. First, in *export competition*, ministers at Hong Kong established the date of 2013 for the elimination of export subsidies, and they spelled out more clearly various forms of export competition, such as export credit programmes, activities of state trading enterprises, and food aid programmes. Second, on *domestic support*, ministers agreed to measure government aid to domestic agriculture in three tiers or bands, with countries that provide higher levels of trade-distorting domestic assistance making greater overall reductions. Third, on *market access*, the Hong Kong agreement took a tiered approach that structured tariffs into four bands ranging from low to high, in which tariff reductions would later be determined. Additional provisions allowed developing countries to designate certain products for lesser cuts depending on their importance for food security or rural development, as well as to apply special safeguards on certain imports on the basis of quantity and price.

On NAMA the July 2004 Package established a formula-based Framework for the reduction of tariffs. As well, the package provided an important flexibility to developing countries to apply less than formula cuts up to 10 per cent of tariff lines, and it settled a number of details that arise in tariff negotiations, such as base years, product coverage, use of bound versus applied rates, credit for autonomous liberalisation, and so forth. At Hong Kong ministers advanced the Framework by agreeing to apply the Swiss formula for cutting tariffs, noting especially that it should be applied so as to provide less than full reciprocity for developing countries. The Swiss formula is a harmonising mechanism designed to reduce the differences between varying tariff levels, and is expressed as follows:

$Z = AX/(A + X)$, where X = initial tariff rate, A = coefficient, and Z = resulting lower tariff rate

Simply put, the lower the coefficient that is introduced, the greater the tariff reduction and the lower the final tariff.

Modalities are expressed in relation to the frameworks and formulas that have thus far been established in negotiating texts; they are the numbers that must be inserted into the texts. On NAMA they would be coefficients entered into the Swiss formula, and they could be differentiated by country or by groups of countries (for example, one coefficient for developed countries, another for developing countries). In the negotiations over agriculture, modalities would define the limits of bands in a tiered approach to tariff cutting, and also would express the expected tariff cut within each band.

The negotiations over modalities have been exceptionally difficult. For example, in the area of agricultural market access, a US proposal (updated to 12 January 2006) called for the highest tariffs to be cut by 90 per cent, with other tariffs cut in a range of 55–90 per cent; and sensitive products (that is, exceptions) would be limited to 1 per cent of tariff lines (Hanrahan and Schnepf, 2006: 6). An EU proposal, updated to 27 October 2005, called for the highest tariffs to be cut by 60 per cent, with other tariffs cut in a range of 35–60 per cent, and with sensitive products reduced to 8 per cent of tariff lines (Hanrahan and Schnepf, 2006: 7). A proposal from the group called G20 (developing countries, including India and Brazil) called for developed country tariffs to be cut by 45–75 per cent, developing country tariffs cut by 25–40 per cent, and with sensitive products to be limited (Hanrahan and Schnepf, 2006: 9). Yet another proposal was forthcoming from the G10 (developed country agricultural importers).

In order to conclude the modalities stage of the negotiation in agricultural market access, it would be necessary for all countries to agree on the range of tariff cuts and the limits to sensitive products, as well as various other conditions and exceptions. On the basis of these modalities, negotiators would then attach numbers to specific sectors and products as they prepared the draft schedules. But first they have to establish the modalities. It has been estimated by Director-General Lamy that some 27–29 numbers would be required to be inserted in the negotiating texts on agriculture, and some 12–15 numbers needed for the NAMA texts (Stewart-Brown, 2006: 17).

In a speech in November 2005 honouring his predecessor, Arthur Dunkel, Lamy said of the Doha Round that 'we now need to talk quantities, numbers and coefficients' (Lamy, 2005: 4). This is a task that occurs in many negotiations, and it is always one of the most difficult tasks negotiators can face. Numbers create clarity, whereas the natural instinct of negotiators is to fudge or equivocate those positions that are unacceptable. Numbers easily convey who has lost or won a point, and they turn a situation that might have been approached with a modicum of co-operation into a situation where conflict is the norm. Numbers are often the source of zero-sum bargaining. As the Belgian diplomat Francis Walder has expressed it precisely: 'Rien n'est délicat à fixer comme un ordre de grandeur et rien ne répugne davantage à l'esprit diplomatique' (quoted in Lamy, 2005: 4). It is unfortunate that the Doha Round became so unavoidably fixed on a conversation over numbers.

Analysis and commentary on the Doha Round

By mid-2006 it was no understatement to say that the Doha Round was stuck, possibly terminally stuck, on the issue of modalities. This difficulty would not surprise any observer of tariff negotiations, for there is an inherent tendency in negotiating tariffs for the parties to withhold concessions until the last minute in order to extract concessions from the other side. Consistent with this observation was the belief by some participants that the real deadline for the tabling of modalities and schedules was sometime in late 2006 or early 2007 (*Inside US Trade*, 2006a: 15) and that the pressure to settle some issues earlier was an attempt to build leeway into the process. On the other hand, the magnitude of the work remaining to be done in the time allotted suggests that efforts to conclude were neither artificial nor unnecessary. The judgement of Director-General Lamy that missing the end-April deadline would be a 'huge collective mistake' seemed to be the right call (*Bridges*, 2006).

There was a suggestion that in lieu of waiting for WTO members to act, chairs of the negotiating groups might be called on to table texts in agriculture and NAMA that presumably would contain the needed modalities (*Inside US Trade*, 2006b: 3). Such an initiative would be similar to the action taken by the GATT Director-General Arthur Dunkel during the Uruguay Round, when in 1991 he tabled a compromise text (the 'Dunkel Text') that became the basis for the Uruguay Round agreements concluded two years later. Dunkel's action was lauded for being courageous, and it is often cited as an example of a successful initiative by a mediator in international affairs. However, this tactic might be difficult to apply to the Doha negotiation. The Dunkel Text largely compiled rules-based texts that contained malleable verbal constructions rather than precise quantitative limits or obligations. For the same reason that countries have been unable to agree on the numbers that express, for example, the limits of permissible tariff cuts, it also seems unlikely they would accept a third party's determination on what those numbers should be.

Multilateral trade negotiations have never been easy to conclude in the GATT/WTO system. However, the Doha Round seems particularly immune to the negotiating techniques that have had some measure of success in the past. The reasons go to the interplay of *parties*, *issues*, and *negotiating environment* in the current Round.

First, parties. The objectives of the Round established by the Doha Declaration appear, in the conduct of the Round, to be inconsistent. In the first paragraph the Declaration states that the members strongly affirm the principles and objectives of the WTO and 'pledge to reject the use of protectionism'. In the second paragraph the members recognise that international trade can play a major role in economic development and the alleviation of poverty and they agree to place the needs and interests of developing countries 'at the heart of the Work Programme in this Declaration'. The methodology for carrying out these objectives is (as always) negotiation, and, while there is no contradiction between these objectives in principle, there is some uncertainty whether they could be achieved in practice, and, more specifically, in the context of the current WTO negotiation.

The 149 WTO Members at the Doha Round have organised themselves into a plethora of informal negotiating groups (Wolfe, 2006; Odell, 2006). However, in terms of negotiating behaviour there were essentially three *parties* that carried major responsibility for the success or failure of the Round: the US, the EU, and a group of developing countries, led by India and Brazil. This negotiating structure made its first appearance in the Tokyo Round, it was solidified in the Uruguay Round, and it reached fulfilment in the Doha Round. The developing countries are now formally differentiated by the designation of least developed countries (LDCs), and informally by the term 'industrial and emerging countries' that is applied by some analysts to members such as China, India, Brazil, Mexico, Korea, Singapore, and Hong Kong (China) (see, for example, Weintraub, 2006: 1), but in terms of bargaining behaviour in GATT/WTO Rounds the developing countries have usually been remarkably cohesive. They are also powerful, and in terms of trade flows, which are an important indicator in the WTO, five of the developing country members are included in the world's top ten exporters and five are included in the top ten importers.

The trade policies of developing countries have changed over the years. In the Tokyo Round, motivated by domestic economic policies of import substitution industrialisation (ISI), developing countries largely stood aside from the tariff and non-tariff liberalisation produced by that Round. In the Uruguay Round, developing countries strongly supported the WTO and became full adherents to the Uruguay Round Agreements, but in the tariff negotiation their main contribution was to bind tariff lines, usually above applied rates. Therefore, whereas developed countries bound tariffs at the applied rate and reduced average tariff levels by roughly one-third in each of three negotiations since the 1960s, most developing countries have done nothing comparable. For example, Jagdish Bhagwati notes that – despite a popular misconception – poor countries have greater tariff protection on manufactures than do rich countries. He states: 'It is a simple consequence of the fact that the poor countries have conventionally been exempted from making tariff concessions to get tariff concessions' (Bhagwati, 2005: 26). Thus it is that the tariff, more than any other part of the trade regime, reflects the long residue of the ISI policy.

Second, issues. As the Doha Round moved toward its July 2006 deadline, the three major *issues* on the table were agricultural subsidies, agricultural market access (mainly tariffs), and non-agricultural market access – NAMA (again, mainly tariffs). In trade volume terms the latter category simply dwarfs the former two. The US is (deservedly) under particular pressure from developing countries on agricultural subsidies, the EU is similarly (deservedly) pressed on agricultural market access, and both the US and EU countries are facing demands in NAMA to reduce tariff peaks on products of interest to developing countries. There is no question that such peaks exist and should be reduced, although one reason for these peaks is that developing countries have been unprepared to offer reciprocal tariff concessions in the past.

This combination of issues and parties is not fortuitous for a trade negotiation. Developing countries and LDCs participate in the Doha Round under the mandate that their special needs and interests will be taken into account, including 'less than full reciprocity in reduction commitments' (WTO, 2001: paragraph 16). This principle has been accepted by developed countries. However, developed countries recognise that the international economy is changing rapidly and that economic pressure from countries like China, Brazil, and India is a reality (Friedman 2005). Furthermore, *faute de mieux*, all countries recognise that the process of tariff liberalisation in GATT/WTO negotiations is through mercantile bargaining, and developed countries recognise that if they do not achieve some liberalisation from developing countries in this Round they may not have the bargaining chips to do it in the future. Taking India as just one example, the prospect of relieving a rapidly industrialising country with an average bound tariff of around 50 per cent that is applied at 32 per cent from liberalising its tariff structure does not seem consistent with a 'pledge to reject the use of protectionism' (WTO, 2001: 1).

From the perspective of reaching agreement, it is regrettable that the Doha Round has had a contracting agenda (unlike the Tokyo and Uruguay Rounds, which had expanding agendas) which has come down as much as it has to tariffs. Tariffs are a tax, and money changes hands more evidently when tariffs are lowered than when other forms of restrictions are removed. They are hard to negotiate at any time. But it did not have to be this way. There were other issues on the table in this Round, but given the pressure from developing countries, these issues – investment, competition policy, and government procurement – were dropped from the agenda. Ironically, this has forced the flow of negotiation into areas like the tariff where developing countries must face real liberalisation and make painful choices. The reason is that there are no other significant areas, except perhaps services, where developed countries could seek some balancing for the concessions expected in agriculture.

The loss of the three issues may have more significance than appears at first glance. Both investment and competition policy would effectively be new issues to the WTO. Experience shows (for example, with the General Agreement on Trade in Services – GATS) that new issues of this sort are taken up in stages, with the first stage taken up in negotiating the text, and real liberalisation being left to future negotiations. The negotiation of texts in investment and competition policy might have been a way for developing countries to broaden the negotiation and to deflect some of the pressure they are facing on industrial tariffs.

Yet another irony is being faced in the dropping of the Singapore issues. The Doha Round has come down to a negotiation where tariffs are a central concern, and one would have to go back to the Kennedy Round of the 1960s for a comparable experience in GATT history. The Kennedy Round took four years; it negotiated mainly tariffs (and one anti-dumping code); and its conclusion was a difficult and near-run event. The Kennedy negotiations were also between like-minded developed countries, whereas the Doha Round is between very dissimilar parties.

A second observation is that the Doha Round is billed as a development round. There is little doubt that if the developed countries (especially the US and EU) acceded to the demands of developing countries on agriculture, it would promote economic development among agricultural exporters in the developing world. But the focus on the tariff has brought out another aspect of a 'development round' that is less emphasised by developing countries and non-governmental organisations, namely the developmental benefits derived from the increased competition produced by the reduction of tariffs. Any economist will say that, despite the games played in mercantile bargaining, the real beneficiaries of tariff reductions are the countries doing the reducing. This academic wisdom is demonstrated in the real world when countries negotiate regional free-trade agreements like the NAFTA without any concern for who 'gained' or 'lost' from tariff reductions: it is simply the larger, restriction-free market that is the attraction for the parties. However this plays itself out, in the Doha Round the developing as well as the developed countries are facing a head-to-head contest over trade liberalisation that is undiluted by the structural and text-based issues that preoccupied negotiators in the Uruguay Round. Many observers have commented that there is not much on the agenda in the Doha Round, but what is there is especially difficult to settle.

If there is one major discouragement of the Doha Round, it is that the major parties have all said at different times that their current offers are fixed, but that they might be improved were there to be change on the other side. This is an indication of negotiation failure, not where the parties may lack sufficient negotiating authority from their governments to reach a deal, but rather where they appear to have sufficient negotiating instructions to produce a contract zone but are still unable to reach an agreement because of the interaction at the negotiating table. Much of this goes to the *negotiating environment* of the Round, which has not been conducive to settlement.

Third, negotiating environments. The environment of a negotiation is established by its objectives, which in GATT/WTO negotiations are usually set out in the ministerial declaration creating the negotiation. In the Doha Declaration the objectives specified by all signatories clearly identified the main concern to be the betterment of developing and least developed countries. Based on a rough analysis, the Doha Declaration (paragraphs 1–3, 10) contained four statements of *belief*, namely: (1) that the trading system had contributed significantly to development in the past 50 years; (2) that least developed countries are particularly vulnerable in the world economy; (3) that all peoples need to benefit from the increased opportunities generated by the trade system; and, perhaps most importantly, (4) that trade can play a major role in economic development and the alleviation of poverty.

As for what should be done in the Doha Round, the Declaration contained some six statements of *action*, namely: (1) to maintain the process of reform and liberalisation of trade policies; (2) to reject the use of protectionism; (3) to continue efforts to ensure that developing and especially least developed countries share growth in trade commensurate with needs of their economic development; (4) to address the marginalisation of least developed countries in international trade; (5) to ensure internal transparency and effective participation of all members, despite an expanding WTO membership; and, perhaps most importantly, (6) to place the needs of developing countries at the heart of the Doha Work Programme.

The significance of the objectives in the Doha Declaration can be more fully appreciated by comparing them to those of the Uruguay Declaration of 1986 that initiated the Uruguay Round. In the Uruguay Declaration signatories focused on the prosaic tasks of a multilateral trade negotiation and thus agreed: (1) to bring about further liberalisation and expansion of world trade; (2) to improve the multilateral trade system based on GATT principles and rules; (3) to increase the responsiveness of the GATT system to the evolving international economy; and (4) to increase the interrelationship between trade policies and economic policies affecting growth and development. As for developing countries, signatories stated (1) that developed countries did not expect developing countries to make contributions during trade negotiations that were inconsistent with their individual development; and (2) (in sharp contrast to the language of the Doha Declaration) that developing countries expected that their capacity to make contributions or negotiated concessions would improve with the progressive development of their economies.

In sum, a comparison between the two Declarations reveals a change in two directions: first, the greater breadth of the undertaking in the Doha Round; and, second, the lesser responsibilities in the Doha Declaration of developing countries for their own development. What was similar, of course, about the two Declarations was the action to be taken: that is, they both initiated a multilateral trade negotiation. Negotiation is central to the trade regime, and it has been the means through which the trade-liberalising law of the GATT/WTO system has been created. But is it not going a bit far to expect the mechanism of trade negotiation to play a major role in the promotion of economic development of less developed countries or, even more, in the alleviation of poverty? In regard to the responsibilities of parties, negotiation is an interaction in which all sides are expected to defend their countries' interests, and where diplomats seek an accommodation with other parties on the basis of a quid pro quo that can be defended to their political masters. Is it not going a bit far to assume that an interaction between parties that is based on the placement of one side's needs and interests at the heart of the endeavour can still be called a negotiation? This is not to say that the promotion of economic development or the alleviation of poverty are not goals that should be pursued by developed countries. It is only to say that the objectives of the Doha Round have become broader than the mechanism (that is, a trade negotiation) could be expected to fulfil.

Of course language initiating great endeavours is meant to be inspirational. But the language of the Doha Declaration has helped to create an assumption that development-friendly proposals are those that represent the offensive interests of developing countries, while the offensive interests of developed countries are seen as illegitimate. One example of this was the proposal for plurilateral negotiations in Annex C on Services in the Hong Kong Ministerial Declaration, which, as Hong Kong negotiator Thomas Chan has observed, attracted 'vehement criticism by many about how development-unfriendly the text is' (Chan, 2006: 3). Chan goes on to say that 'the line is clearly divided between developed and developing countries in terms of offensive and defensive interests in services' (Chan, 2006: 4). Chan argues that this negotiating behaviour makes little sense since services have a great potential for promoting economic growth in developing countries.

A second example comes from the NAMA negotiation. In a document tabled on 20 March 2006, members of the NAMA 11 group (including Argentina, Brazil,

Egypt, Indonesia, the Philippines, and South Africa) demanded that development should be at the centre of the negotiations (NAMA 11, 2006). By this the document meant that tariff peaks and tariff escalation in developed countries must be eliminated, while developing countries should take lesser percentage reductions than developed countries. The document notes: 'In a Development Round there can be no expectation that developing countries should be making greater cuts than developed countries' (NAMA 11, 2006: 4). This statement raises several issues. First, it comes very close to extending support for tariffs across the board as an engine of economic development and seems more consistent with ISI policies of the past than with the contemporary WTO approach to trade protectionism. Second, it makes no distinction for levels of development, which is inconsistent with reality. Third, it applies a 'one size fits all' approach to the trade policies and development circumstances of developing countries, an approach incidentally that has been bitterly (and correctly) criticised when applied by the IMF and World Bank in development policy. In sum, the paper from the NAMA 11 group is a plausible extension of the objectives of the Doha Declaration, but what is less clear is whether it will serve as a sound basis for negotiations between developed and developing countries.

The language of the development agenda and the Doha Round has gradually shifted toward the rhetoric of fairness and justice (for example, Stiglitz and Charlton, 2005). There are indeed issues of fairness and justice at stake in underdevelopment and poverty, but, since causality is so difficult to establish unambiguously, invoking these issues in a negotiation risks having the interaction descend into charge and counter-charge. Then too, so few parties come to the table with clean hands. For example, the tariff escalation on higher-value goods that is described as unacceptable by non-governmental organisations (NGOs) when applied by developed countries on imports from developing countries is the same tariff escalation applied by India on imports of uncombed cotton, yarn, fabrics and apparel. These tariffs will impact particularly harshly on exports from Bangladesh. The upshot is that the language and the rhetoric of a 'development round' can very quickly be projected into behaviour that is inimical to the search for mutual benefit that usually motivates successful trade negotiations. Negotiators should note the advice of Ben Franklin, who counselled that in negotiations one should speak of interests and not of justice. Presumably all parties in the WTO have an interest in a successful development Round, and if it is to succeed it will be necessary for the negotiation process to bring these interests to the forefront.

Impact of the Doha Round on the WTO

The outlook does not look bright for the Doha Round, hence the more likely impact of the Round on the WTO will be to manage failure than to celebrate success. What kind of failure might be in store, and how it is handled, have become important questions. Failure in negotiation usually comes in the form of forsaken expectations, after which offers are withdrawn from the table. How much of the offers are taken away becomes the important issue. For example, both Congressional and Executive leaders have stated that the US should not sign an agreement unless it provided real enhanced market access for US exporters, which is unlikely to occur if developing countries stay with their offers to make tariff reductions only to bound rates without touching currently applied rates (*Inside US Trade*, 2006c: 6). Were the US to take this action, it would leave on the table other issues where the negotiation has made progress, such as trade facilitation, subsidies, and even services. The problem is that to settle any issues in the wake of a breakdown in agriculture or NAMA would require consensus of all parties, since the Doha Round is being conducted on the basis of a single undertaking. To achieve consensus on a less than complete package might be difficult in the Doha Round, considering the rhetoric and high expectations that have accompanied the Round.

Given the possible loss of the Round, what would the loss mean to developing countries and to the WTO itself, and how would each recover from the failure? As for the first question, Robert Wade in a letter to the *Financial Times* has questioned whether the loss of the Doha Round would be a 'catastrophe' for developing countries (Wade, 2005). Wade's argument is that developed countries have benefited disproportionately from the international economy in the 1990s, and that to complete the Round on the present basis would simply add to this disparity. Developing countries should insist on scope to use the same policy protectionist tools (such as domestic content requirements) that developed countries used in their own development. Developing countries, writes Wade, 'should be prepared to see the Doha Round fail, and then to put their weight behind another Round on terms fairer to them' (Wade, 2005).

Wade's argument, and similar arguments made by some NGOs, resonate in the developing world because it is probably true – as he claims – that 60 per cent of the increase in world consumption over the 1990s accrued to the upper half of inhabitants of developed countries, roughly 10 per cent of the world's population. However, it is wrong to assume that trade is a main cause of this unhappy circumstance, or, even worse, that it is an easy solution. International underdevelopment is simply more complex than international trade or trade policy.

It is true, as Wade argues, that developed countries used protectionist trade policies to promote economic development, but his own book on the remarkable development of Taiwan and Korea showed that the successful use of these policies (for example, infant industry protection) was discriminating, disciplined, and ultimately consistent with the market (Wade, 1990). This is not the kind of protection that is currently employed in many developing countries, nor that seems to be at issue in developing country proposals in the Doha Round.

If trade is to encourage economic development, the weight of economic theory and experience is that it will do so through the operation of comparative advantage, which essentially points to trade liberalism and not protectionism. History shows that trade liberalism is a relative concept, and in its present form took well over half a century to achieve among a few affluent countries. The struggle for trade liberalism took place over many encounters and there were many occasions in which backsliding was the norm. The Doha Round is only one encounter among many, and it will not be a disaster if it fails. But its failure would represent a lost opportunity for developing countries to achieve some incremental liberalisation in their industrial tariffs, which they will most likely have to do unilaterally in any case, only in a negotiation they can get some liberalisation in return from trade partners. Furthermore, the Round's failure would mean a missed opportunity to move forward, even incrementally, the overall agenda of trade liberalisation, especially agricultural liberalisation in developed countries.

Like it or not, developing countries today are more dependent on the modern trade system for their future economic growth than were the developing countries of the nineteenth century. This presents more advantages than it does disadvantages. What is surprising is how completely the rhetoric of developing countries and their supporters has been accepted: namely, that protectionism is what made the developed countries developed, and therefore that protection should be maintained in developing countries until they can compete on an even basis with developed countries. This view is not correct about developed countries, especially small developed countries that, like developing countries, will be price takers in the international market (for example, Katzenstein, 1985). What these countries have found is that protectionism insulates their economies from the international market, promotes inefficiency, and thereby condemns their producers to forgo international trade and to sell mainly on the domestic market. In GATT/WTO history developing countries have never engaged in serious market access negotiations, and by the Uruguay Round they had only bound approximately 70 per cent of their tariff lines. Today the simple average bound tariff of all developing countries is over 35 per cent and the simple average applied tariff is about 12 per cent (Fernández de Córdoba and Vanzetti, 2005). Tariffs this high are unlikely to enable developing countries to progress toward competing on an even basis with developed countries, nor are they likely to make use of international trade as an engine of economic development.

As for the second question, namely what would the loss of the Doha Round mean for the WTO itself, there is little doubt that the organisation would be damaged by a failure to reach a substantial agreement. As a blue-ribbon Consultative Board stated in its report to the WTO Director-General in 2004, 'The World Trade Organization is in large measure a negotiating machine' (WTO, 2004b: 61). Since the 1960s the predecessor to the WTO, the GATT, successfully completed the three multilateral trade negotiations that were initiated during this period. Anything less in the Doha Round would elicit questions about whether multilateral negotiations on trade had come to the end of the line.

The main concern of those who question the WTO's performance as a 'negotiating machine' is that the number of issues and parties has now grown too large for them to be manageable in any single forum. To this inherent complexity has been added the GATT/WTO negotiating principles of consensus and single undertaking: the former ensures that trade-offs will be made between parties, while the latter ensures that trade-offs will be made between issues (Winham, 2006: 11–14). The result is that in the Doha Round (as in the Uruguay Round) any country can withhold consensus by formally objecting to a decision on any issue included under the single undertaking. The positive benefit of this negotiating mechanism is that it obliges the participants to mobilise a strong support behind any negotiating proposals they might initiate or join, to the point where the doubters will be deterred by a widespread agreement. The downside of course is that mobilising such support is very difficult.

The above problems are not likely to be the cause of the paralysis of the Doha Round. Indeed, for some time the WTO (and the GATT before it) has been exceptionally creative in managing the problem of negotiation in the context of an expanding agenda and an expanding membership. Consider for example the analysis of Ambassador Tim Groser, former Chair of the Agriculture Group in the Doha Round, as he responds to a request 'to provide some structure for the negotiations' (Groser, 2005: 4). Groser states:

> The first level [of the negotiations] . . . is . . . the informal Special Session . . . a mechanism for having what we call a first reading of the issues that emerge from a plain reading of the Framework. Secondly . . . is the open-ended informal process . . . intended to be the centrepiece of the informal negotiations. It allows all delegates, even those delegations that may not be equipped to take part in all the technical discussions, to at least hear what the technical matters are and make their own independent judgment about the implications for their country. The third level . . . deal(s) with the most complex issues . . . I will need to gather together a group of colleagues, *on a representative basis* [italics added], to try and develop issues that have been clearly discussed at the first two levels.
>
> (Groser, 2005: 4)

Groser goes on to explain that the negotiations flow back and forth between the three levels, much as barges move back and forth on canals, with the chairman of the negotiating group serving as chief engineer responsible for the flow of water between the locks. In the case of negotiation, the goals that are served by this system are those of transparency and efficiency.

Ambassador Groser's analysis suggests that those who deal with the complexity produced by numerous issues and parties in WTO negotiations are not without tools to manage their situation. One of these tools is the representation of parties by parties, a concept that is unusual in negotiation but that is customarily accepted in political life. Representation is inherent in the republican form of government, and to some extent is practised in almost all domestic governments in existence. The republican principle, as expressed in the Federalist Papers by James Madison, is that 'however small the republic may be, the representatives must be raised to a certain number, in order to guard against the cabals of a few; and that, however large it may be, they must be limited to a certain number, in order to guard against the confusion of a multitude' (*Daily Advertiser*, 1787). This principle of representation is put into practice with the formation of small-group managerial 'Green Rooms' in WTO negotiations, and it is this principle that is invoked in Ambassador Grosser's aforementioned third level of negotiation. In making use of this and other tools of domestic government in international negotiation, WTO negotiators have proved themselves no less capable than domestic leaders in managing a complex decision-making environment.

If the Doha Round has had problems, it is less a matter of how the negotiation is being conducted than of what is being negotiated. The problems of the Round have been *modalities* and *development*. The first is ostensibly a technical issue, the second is profoundly political.

The obligation to establish modalities was contained in the Doha Ministerial Declaration of November 2001. Regarding agriculture, the Declaration stated that modalities were to be established by 31 March 2003 (subsequently extended), after which comprehensive draft Schedules based on the modalities would be submitted. A similar procedure governed NAMA. The decision to establish modalities was more or less consistent with the approach to tariff negotiations in past GATT Rounds. In the Kennedy Round, countries agreed to table offers of 50 per cent linear cuts, with exceptions, which is a form of formula approach. In the Tokyo Round a Swiss formula was loosely followed for tabling offers. No formula was followed in the Uruguay Round. Instead, countries used a mixture of approaches, such as request or offer for individual sectors and products, or a 'zero-for-zero' approach (that is, free trade) for designated sectors. Concerning these three Rounds two generalisations could be made. First, the approach used in the various Rounds was mainly to get something on the table, after which the real (usually bilateral) bargaining began, based on the economic and trade interests of the various countries. Of course, any concessions would be multilateralised through the operation of GATT Article I (most-favoured-nation – MFN – requirement). There was enough imprecision in this process to allow negotiators to avoid tipping their hand on important issues until late in the negotiation. Second, the Rounds were mainly conducted between developed countries that more or less agreed on the principle and practice of reducing tariffs to promote trade. Furthermore, most tariff lines in these countries were bound at the applied rate, meaning that a reduction in a tariff by an importing country produced real enhanced market access for countries with a capacity to export to that market.

The Doha Round began with a commitment to modalities in agriculture and NAMA that was considerably more exacting than what was previously attempted in formula approaches in GATT Rounds. The advantage of the Doha approach was that, once modalities were agreed, it was assumed that roughly 80 per cent of the work of the negotiation would be completed. This approach also produced an up-front transparency that allowed countries and negotiating groups to assess where they stood, particularly the developing countries. On the other hand, the Doha approach had some significant disadvantages for the negotiation process. All negotiators face a problem in dealing with their internal constituents and they generally try to defer the especially sensitive issues until late in the negotiation. This practice can be a matter of unwillingness to face unpleasant realities, but it also serves the function of creating uncertainty and delaying powerful constituents from mobilising an opposition at home to a prospective agreement. In the Doha Round's handling of modalities, country delegations effectively are expected to telegraph major concessions well in advance of the conclusion of the negotiation. This will allow opposition to form, and it is almost a textbook example in how not to create a domestic consensus to support an external negotiation. As a result of the focus on modalities, countries might be expected to place only cautious or minimal offers on the table, which is essentially what has occurred in the Doha Round.

If the main interaction at the Doha Round remains fixed on modalities in agriculture and NAMA, it will be difficult to advance the negotiation. Unfortunately, however, it will not be easy to drop the focus on modalities and move to a less formal process such as traditional bilateral request and offer. Request and offer is a decentralised negotiating process that usually gives the bargaining advantage to countries with larger economies. The reason is that these countries have more imports on which to offer concessions (for example, tariff reductions), in order to reciprocate for similar concessions received from other countries. Above all, any move to a decentralised request and offer negotiation would put more emphasis on the national economic interest of individual countries, which is what traditional GATT tariff negotiations have always been about, and would put less emphasis on the collective efforts of developing countries to wrest trade benefits from the developed countries. A request and offer negotiation would weaken the focus on development as it has been defined in the Doha Round. The upshot is that on the matter of modalities, the Doha Round is damned if it does and damned if it does not. This is a dilemma of the first order that may take more than one WTO negotiating round to solve.

Behind the issue of modalities lies the broader problem of development and the political expectations of the Round. It has earlier been observed that the mandate of the WTO is trade and not development per se. However, the WTO is concerned with trade not for its own sake but rather because governments accept that trade promotes economic growth and rising levels of living standards. This means that development is inherently connected to trade, and, well before the start of the Doha Round, WTO members were on record calling for 'positive efforts designed to ensure that developing countries . . . secure a share in the growth in international trade commensurate with the needs of their economic development' (GATT, 1994). The problem with the Doha Round is not that it has tackled the issue of development but rather in the way that it has gone about it.

First, the Doha Round was initiated as a continuation of past WTO/GATT trade negotiations without sufficient attention being paid to the unique concerns of a development round. For example, in part because of the long-standing impact of the theory of ISI in developing country economic policies, these countries essentially have not participated in the liberalisation of applied tariffs in any previous multilateral trade negotiations. Instead, developing countries have relied substantially on exceptions and special and differential treatment, the purpose of which has been to retain a measure of protectionism when other countries were moving towards liberalisation. This negotiation history is not the best backdrop for a new development round. Not only does it raise the question about whether trade liberalisation or protectionism is really good for development but it also creates a cynical view that liberalising commitments are something that developed countries undertake, while developing countries exercise creativity in avoiding those commitments.

A further issue is the apparent inattention to domestic policy planning that should precede or accompany trade negotiation. For example, many developing countries are reliant on tariffs for a large portion of their government revenues. This unquestionably is a deterrent to trade liberalisation, and in the modern age it is a questionable tax policy as well, but it cannot be rectified overnight. The conclusion is that both on policy issues like tariff revenues and on more profound issues like the role of liberalism and protectionism in development, a development round in the WTO needs a great deal of preliminary planning before members start debating details like modalities. A WTO development round is not simply a matter of new wine in old bottles.

Second, the trade regime has seen the formation of a negotiating group of developing countries which has been surprisingly cohesive throughout GATT negotiations since the 1960s. Even when disparate interests prevented the group from acting together, the concept of and the concerns of the 'developing countries' were never outside the parameters of successive negotiations. This history was largely imported without change into the Doha Round. It informed the politics of the Round and was also built into the legal objectives of the Round. It may be time now to question whether the concept and construct of 'developing countries' is the best way to promote development within the WTO system.

GATT/WTO negotiations, especially on market access, are motivated by economic interest. In the past it has been possible to assume that the interests of developing countries were different from those of developed countries, hence it made sense for developing countries to join together in demanding advantages from developed countries. Today the economic interests of developing countries are becoming more divergent. To assume that developing countries together are a useful bargaining construct may be to infuse interest with ideology, with the result being that developing countries act more like a political party than an economic interest group whose concerns can be addressed through traditional negotiation practices of concession, reciprocity, and convergence. Not only does this make agreement more difficult between developed and developing countries, it also impedes developing countries from reaching agreements between themselves. Even though the situation is improving, one of the regrettable aspects of the contemporary trade system is the difficulty developing countries have in trading over the protectionist barriers of other developing countries.

Developing countries in the WTO are an economically diverse group, which has occasionally been reflected in negotiating behaviour in the Doha Round. The most destabilising dimension of this diversity is, in fact, economic development. In the Doha Round WTO members have succeeded in making a distinction between developing and least developed countries, and the latter have received a 'no-tariff no-quota' treatment on their exports to developed countries and some developing countries (WTO, 2005: Annex F). However, there is no agreement on how to treat developing countries at the more affluent end of the economic spectrum. This raises the sensitive issue of 'graduation' from developing country status and the loss of trading benefits that this self-determined status confers. This issue has not been discussed at the Doha Round even though, apart from the negotiation, officials in the United States have threatened to rescind trade preferences from leading developing countries like Brazil and India (*Inside US Trade*, 2006d). In any future WTO negotiations over development one might expect that economic realism would dictate that the question of graduation be worked out as a precursor to any discussion of future preferential policies for developing countries.

Conclusion

It is important to view the Doha Round as a stage in the maturation of the WTO. However it comes out, the Round appears to have lost the possibility to accomplish the ambitious goals it was intended to achieve. Its impact on the WTO will probably not be positive, but neither is it likely to detract from the large built-in agenda the WTO acquired from the Uruguay Round. The WTO is a rules-based system with both legislative and judicial functions. When the prospect of establishing new rules and trade liberalisation through negotiation is thwarted, one can expect members to turn to the judicial process to interpret and implement the rules that are already in existence. One can therefore expect the future to bring some growth in dispute settlement at the WTO as countries attempt to achieve their concerns through judicial action in lieu of negotiation.

Despite the worrisome growth of regional free-trade agreements, the WTO still offers trading countries the broadest base of trade rules available and is well backed up by the strongest arrangement for adjudicating disputes. For this reason it will maintain its attractiveness for both developed and developing countries. Development remains the most important issue on the agenda, and it will be negotiated again, although most likely not in the manner in which it was taken up in the Doha Round. It is possible the Doha Round will be recalled in much the same way as the Tokyo Round, which produced a methodological breakthrough in the negotiation of non-tariff barriers that led to the successes of the Uruguay Round, even though the Round did not itself result in very much substantial trade liberalisation. In the same manner the Doha Round will have laid the groundwork for future accommodations in the politically difficult area of economic development.

Afterword

This chapter was written in May 2006 and edited in February 2007. In July 2006 the negotiation was formally suspended, but following promising meetings between various Ministers it was restarted by WTO Director-General Pascal Lamy in February 2007. At this point there was widespread consensus that insufficient time remained to complete the Round prior to the expiry on July 1, 2007 of Trade Promotion Authority (TPA) legislation in the United States. The immediate hope for the Round was that the U.S. Administration could succeed in winning an extension to TPA legislation in a manner that would permit the negotiation to continue and conclude successfully. Failing this, a possible outcome would be a suspension of the negotiation until such time as the United States could return to the negotiation with sufficient legislative authority to complete a multilateral agreement.

References

Bhagwati, Jagdish (2005), 'Reshaping the WTO', *Far Eastern Economic Review* (January/February).

Bridges (2006), 'Lamy to TNC: Missing End-April Deadline Would Be "Huge Collective Mistake"', 10: 11 (29 March).

Chan, Thomas (2006), 'Will the Real Demandeurs in Services Negotiations Stand Up, Please?', *Bridges*, 10: 2 (March–April).

Cho, Sungjoon (2005), 'The Troubled Status of the Doha Round Negotiations', *ASIL Insight*, 25 August.

Daily Advertiser (1787), 'The Federalist No. 10, The Utility of the Union as a Safeguard against Domestic Faction and Insurrection (continued)', 22 November.

Fernández de Córdoba, Santiago, and Vanzetti, David (2005), *Coping with Trade Reforms: Implications of the WTO Industrial Tariff Negotiations for Developing Countries* (UNCTAD: Trade Analysis Branch).

Friedman, Thomas L. (2005), *The World Is Flat: A Brief History of the Twenty-first Century* (New York: Farrar, Straus, and Giroux).

GATT (1994), Marrakesh Agreement Establishing the World Trade Organisation, 15 April.

Groser, Tim (2005), Statement by Ambassador Tim Groser, Summary Report on the Twenty-seventh Meeting of the Committee on Agriculture Special Session Held on 19 November 2004, WTO doc. TN/AG/R/16 (4 February).

Hanrahan, Charles, and Schnepf, Randy (2006), 'The Doha Round: The Agricultural Negotiations', *CRS Report for Congress*, 12 January.

ICTSD (2005), 'Low Ambitions Met: Members Adopt Declaration', *Bridges Daily Update on the Sixth WTO Ministerial Conference*, 19 December.

Inside US Trade (2006a), 'Portman Departure Seen as Lessening Trade Priority for Administration', 24: 16 (21 April).

Inside US Trade (2006b), 'WTO Members Turn to Chairs for Possible AG, NAMA Texts in June', 24: 17 (28 April).

Inside US Trade (2006c), 'Portman Says Doha Will Fail without Ambitious Market Access', 24: 18 (5 May).

Inside US Trade (2006d), 'Grassley Warns Brazil, India on GSP; Stops Short of Predicting Graduation', 24: 20 (19 May).

Katzenstein, Peter (1985), *Small States in World Markets: Industrial Policy in Europe* (Ithaca: Cornell University Press).

Lamy, Pascal (2005), 'A Life Dedicated to a More Open and Fair World Trading System'. www.wto.org.

NAMA 11 (2006), 'Submission by NAMA 11 Group of Developing Countries to the WTO Negotiating Group on Non-Agricultural Market Access', 20 March.

Odell, John S. (ed.) (2006) *Negotiating Trade: Developing Countries in the WTO and NAFTA* (Cambridge: Cambridge University Press, 2006).

Stewart-Brown, Ronald (2006), 'Doha Round in the Balance after Hong Kong', *The European Journal*, February.

Stiglitz, Joseph E., and Charlton, Andrew (2005), *Fair Trade for All: How Trade Can Promote Development* (Oxford: Oxford University Press).

Wade, Robert Hunter (1990), *Governing the Market: Economic Theory and the Role of Government in East Asian Industrialization* (Princeton: Princeton University Press).

Wade, Robert Hunter (2005), 'Doha Failure Would Not Amount to Disaster', *Financial Times*, 4 November.

Weintraub, Sidney (2006), 'The WTO's Uncertain Future', *Issues in International Political Economy No. 73* (Washington, DC: Center for Strategic and International Studies, January).

Winham, Gilbert R. (2006), 'An Institutional Theory of WTO Decision-Making: Why Negotiation in the WTO Resembles Law-Making in the U.S. Congress' (Toronto: Munk Centre for International Studies).

Wolfe, Robert (2006), 'New Groups in the WTO Agricultural Trade Negotiations: Power, Learning and Institutional Design', Paper prepared for the Annual Meeting of the International Studies Association, San Diego, 22 March.

WTO (2001), Doha Ministerial Declaration, WT/MIN(01)/DEC/1 (20 November).

WTO (2004a), General Council Decision Adopted on 1 August, WT/L/579 (2 August).

WTO (2004b), *Future of the WTO: Addressing Institutional Challenges in the New Millennium, Report by the Consultative Board to the Director-General Supachai Panitchpadki* (Geneva: World Trade Organisation).

WTO (2005), Hong Kong WTO Ministerial Declaration, WT/MIN(05)/DEC (22 December).

WTO (2006a), Doha Declaration Explained. www.wto.org/English/tratop_e/dda_e/dohaexplained_e.htm.

WTO (2006b), 'Timelines for 2006', JOB(06)/13 (30 January).

14 Building asymmetry

Concluding the Doha Development Agenda

Rorden Wilkinson

Each of the trade Rounds conducted since (and including) the Allies first negotiated the General Agreement on Tariffs and Trade (GATT) in 1947 has, at one point or another, been threatened with collapse, causing commentators to worry about the impact of a breakdown in the negotiations on the multilateral trading system (see Gardner, 1956; Kock, 1969; Evans, 1971; Winham, 1986). The Doha Development Agenda (DDA) is no exception. The run-up to the launch of the Round was couched in terms of the damage to the global economy that might happen if the trade bicycle was allowed to stall; the commentary that followed the collapse of the Cancún ministerial meeting worried about the consequences of a breakdown in the nego-tiations and the resurgence of interest in bilateralism that could result thereafter (see Zoellick, 2003; Lamy, 2003); poor progress in the run-up to the Hong Kong ministerial led one seasoned commentator to argue that '[t]he Doha Round may . . . become the first major multilateral trade negotiation to fail . . . [and that] [s]uch an outcome could mark a historic reversal in the irregular but steady progress toward liberalising world trade over the past sixty years' (Bergsten, 2005: 15–16); despite the modest agreement to move the DDA forward in Hong Kong, lacklustre pro-gress in the wake of the meeting spawned familiar worries about the consequences to the health of the global economy should the DDA be allowed to falter (see Blair, 2006); and the collapse of the negotiations in July 2006 led *The Economist* to warn that 'this week's debacle [the breakdown of the talks] constitutes the biggest threat yet to the post-war trading system . . . If the wreck is terminal – and after a five-year stalemate, that seems likely – everyone will be poorer, perhaps gravely so' (*The Economist*, 2006).

Yet for all the talk of crisis and despair there is good reason to believe that the DDA will be concluded. Not only is the irreconcilable breakdown of a Round without historical precedent, there is too much at stake for the negotiations not to be concluded. For the advanced industrial countries the Round promises greater market access in those areas in which they have significant economic interests (largely services and non-agricultural market access – NAMA) while at the same time forestalling wholesale liberalisation of their most protected sectors (notably agriculture). For the leading rank of developing countries – India, China, Brazil, and South Africa – the Round promises greater access to the profitable markets of the industrial states as well as early market entry into the emerging markets of their less developed counterparts. And for the least developed the Round carries the promise (though probably not the reality) of lifting the most vulnerable out of abject poverty.

The alternatives should the Round not be concluded offer little that is attractive. As successive commentators have noted, for the leading industrial states bilateral and regional approaches, though an important part of a country's commercial portfolio, are too costly (in terms of time and effort) and promise too few gains compared to multilateral negotiations to make them a viable long-term commercial strategy (see, among others, Feis, 1948: 19, 41; Odell and Eichengreen, 1998: 188, 191–192; Wilkinson, 2004: 149–155; de Jonquières, 2006) – despite much worry to the contrary. Moreover, few developing countries (particularly the smallest of their number) relish the prospects of facing large industrial states in bilateral negotiations, preferring instead the relative protection of multilateral fora (see Ruggie, 1998: 128). As such, determining the consequences of the conclusion of the DDA for the long-run development of multilateral trade regulation presents itself as a compelling task. It is this task with which the chapter is concerned.

Before we begin, three points of clarification are in order. First, the WTO, and the GATT before it, has always been, and remains, a political institution that co-ordinates the negotiation of market-opening opportunities among member states. It is not in itself an engine for free trade. As such, it is susceptible to (and indeed deals struck therein reflect) power political bargaining; its design and attendant practices and procedures reflect the preferences of its principal architects; and its functioning and modes of operation have changed through time in accordance with changes in prevailing power configurations. As a result, while the bargains reached may have eased the flow of goods and services in some sectors (and protected and frustrated others), they have done so in a fashion that reflects differences in the power capabilities among the members and the manner in which the institution structures negotiations. This is entirely different from the blanket liberalisation of trade.

Second, the significance of a conclusion to the DDA can be understood only by standing back and observing the development of multilateral trade regulation through time: that is, from its beginnings under the GATT to the present day. It is impossible to assess the likely conclusion of the DDA in isolation as the bargain that will result will be laid on top of an existing legal framework and a corresponding set of economic opportunities. Moreover, any bargain reached will inevitably be affected by what has gone before.

Finally, it is also important to note that as the history of multilateral trade regulation is a history of political bargains, and because these bargains have been negotiated among states of differing power capabilities (both political and economic) and have been affected by the manner in which the institution has developed, each bargain struck has put into place a new layer of regulation that has presented some of the contracting parties (now members) – largely the industrial states – with economic opportunities to be realised while either excluding others or offering them very little – primarily the developing countries. It is also instructive to note that as each new layer of regulation has been added, whether in terms of rules and disciplines in new areas or tariff reductions and other concessions, these asymmetries in economic opportunity have been perpetuated and, more often than not, amplified. In this way the WTO's legal framework resembles a poorly layered cake.

With these preliminary remarks in mind, this chapter concerns itself with the likely contribution of the DDA to the development of the multilateral trading system. The chapter proceeds in two parts. The first part is concerned with establishing the character of the GATT/WTO system prior to the launch of the DDA. The aim here is to set out what the distribution of economic opportunity was before the launch of the Round, thereby establishing the foundations of the Doha negotiations. Set against this backdrop the second part of the chapter considers the likely outcome of the DDA and its impact on the overall shape of multilateral trade regulation. The argument pursued throughout is that the DDA is likely, at a minimum, to perpetuate, and, at a maximum, to amplify the inequalities of opportunity given rise to by the manner in which trade has been liberalised in the postwar era. To understand this, a bit of history is first in order.

The emergence and consolidation of asymmetry: trade liberalisation under the GATT[1]

The WTO's general purpose, core principles, legal framework, and operating procedures (what might be called its 'institutional characteristics') are all continuations, adaptations, variations, or developments of a trade institution designed to work in tandem with the International Monetary Fund (IMF) and the International Bank for Reconstruction and Development (IBRD and later, albeit slightly differently, World Bank) for the purposes of reconstructing a war-ravaged world economy – what was to have been the International Trade Organisation (ITO) but became, as we see below, the GATT. In this way the WTO's institutional characteristics reflect and have developed from an approach to reconstruction that had at its core a desire not only to rebuild a war-ravaged world economy but also to do so in such a way that enabled the US – as the principal architect of the postwar order – to take full advantage of the economic opportunities presented therein.

Forging multilateral trade liberalisation

At the cessation of hostilities the US found itself in a uniquely strong position. The impact of the First World War on the productive base of the dominant European powers and the reconstruction process that took place thereafter had already transformed the US into a major exporter of mass-produced goods. The impact of the Second World War on European industry further stimulated demand for US produce, and the postwar reconstruction process promised additional returns. It was thus in the US's interest to pursue a postwar international economic policy that would enable American industry to exploit these opportunities fully; and it was in the interests of the European powers to ensure that they had ready access to US goods to facilitate their reconstruction. What existed, then, was a convergence of interest in the removal of barriers to trade.

This was not, however, to be a blanket removal of trade barriers. Key areas of the US economy required – largely for reasons of domestic political popularity and national security – that significant forms of protection remain. This was most obvious in the case of agriculture (though later it was also to be the case with textiles and clothing). The depression of the 1930s hit the US agricultural sector particularly hard and had ushered in an array of production controls, price-support schemes, import quotas, and export subsidies, all of which made American agriculture distinctly ill-prepared for (and unwilling to accept) any exposure to global competition. As a result, the trade liberalisation process pursued by the US was to seek the opening of markets in those sectors in which it could accrue economic gain (and wherein the US faced little competition) but not in those areas of political and economic sensitivity.

US efforts to create a postwar economic architecture were thus guided by the desire to secure increasing market opportunities for its burgeoning industrial sector while at the same time protecting domestic agricultural production. Such a system could not, however, be achieved alone. It required, at the very least, the acquiescence of the remaining Allied powers. Yet despite the obvious material benefits of the US plan for the European powers – in terms of providing a machinery for, and assistance with, reconstruction – and the potential to carry through the wartime alliance, the American vision was far from a *fait accompli*. The crisis of the interwar years had severely damaged the idea of a liberal world economy. What emerged in its stead was a growing preference, among European policymakers and leading economists, for a measure of economic planning and government intervention to correct market failure. Europe, much more so than the US, also faced the very real spectre of mass unemployment arising from the postwar demobilisation of military personnel and the possibility for social unrest that this might create. The pressing concerns for Europe's political elites, then, were reconstruction *and* full employment to forestall any shift in public opinion towards a socialist alternative. As Klaus Knorr noted, this situation made the revival of 'multilateral trade a goal of something less than overriding concern to most nations or else render[ed] its implementation more difficult' (Knorr, 1948: 20).

The involvement of the UK proved particularly important in this regard. British involvement had a number of benefits. Not only did it build upon a wartime alliance and a common commercial *lingua franca*, but British involvement was strategically and economically beneficial to the US. By binding Britain to a wide-ranging commercial agreement based on a commitment to non-discrimination in trade, the US could prise open the UK's system of imperial preferences as well as ensure British domestic demand for its goods. Moreover, not only did a collaborative relationship with the UK open up new markets for American produce, it had a uniquely strategic dimension in the unfolding Cold War. Tying Britain into a comprehensive postwar economic programme would better enable the UK to manage the breakup of its empire, thus preventing the US from having to actively forestall any Soviet influence developing therein (Toynbee, 1947: 466).

Though they initially shared differing visions of the postwar order, British and American economic interests were congruous in other regards. Britain's economic complexion – as a nation and imperial power built on trade, and as a state lacking the necessary resources for self-sufficiency – ensured that its postwar economic growth was also contingent on a revitalisation of trade. Like the US, this was a trade-centred vision that gave particular importance to industrial products. Moreover, like the US, the UK was reluctant to open up its agriculture sector to full liberalisation. While imported foodstuffs would inevitably be cheaper than those produced domestically, it would create a level of agricultural dependence incompatible with Britain's national security objectives. It was thus also in Britain's interest to press for a revitalisation of world trade specifically targeted at stimulating demand for industrial goods while protecting its agricultural sector married to a comprehensive reconstruction programme.

It was on these foundations that a postwar economic architecture was to be created. However, the process of establishing an institutional apparatus to satisfy those interests proved more difficult than was at first imagined. Despite their agreement on the core of the reconstruction plan, British and American designs were initially quite different (see Gardner, 1956). Only after a process of negotiation did a draft Charter emerge for the creation of what was to become the ITO. Even then its refinement proved tortuous. And despite a two-month extension of the 1948 United Nations (UN) Havana Conference on Trade and Employment at which the final shape of the ITO was negotiated, and the concerted effort of all involved, the organisation's fate was sealed when, in December 1950, President Truman announced the decision to postpone indefinitely plans for US participation in the ITO (*New York Herald Tribune*, 7 December 1950; see Diebold 1952; Gardner, 1956). This was followed in February 1951 by similar announcements from the UK and the Netherlands. It was, in the end, an organisation that proved not to serve the interests of its principal architects, nor did it suit the political climate into which it was born. The GATT, however, did.

Establishing asymmetry

Even before the ITO's stillbirth, under US leadership 23 states engaged in a 'Round' of negotiations between April and October 1947. The result was an agreement to begin the liberalisation process and the negotiation of a legal framework designed to lock into place those concessions agreed. That legal framework was the GATT. The real significance of the GATT lay in its approach to liberalisation. Its format was largely derived from Chapter IV (Commercial Policy) of the ITO Charter but crucially it was without the additional provisions of its ill-fated sibling that had so frustrated the Havana negotiations (including the Charter's elaborate provisions for the maintenance of 'fair standards of labour', economic development, state trading, and inter-institutional linkages – see Wilkinson, 2002). This gave the emerging multilateral trade order an informality and flexibility that allowed the leading industrial powers to pursue their trade objectives without locking themselves into a rigid set of rules.

The first Round of negotiations out of which the GATT emerged saw discussions on some 45,000 items, the duties on all of which were bound against future increases until 1951, with a significant number being reduced (Gorter, 1954: 11); and plans for further bouts of liberalisation were quickly agreed. Crucially, however, the GATT was deployed to open markets of interest to its principal contracting parties (23 states may have signed the GATT but not all participated on an equal footing; the negotiations were very much an Anglo-American affair). No attempt was made to open up agricultural markets. What emerged from this first Round of negotiations, then, was not only a regulatory framework but also the beginnings of a deployment of that framework for the selective opening of markets. This was the first layer of multilateral trade regulation and it imbued the system with a distinct institutional bias towards the economic needs of its industrial contracting parties. It was, in short, an industrial nations club.

Three developments consolidated the GATT's emerging industrial character. First, slower-than-expected European reconstruction in the immediate postwar years reinforced an almost exclusive concentration on the liberalisation of industrial, manufactured, and some semi-manufactured goods. Second, agriculture was increasingly excluded from the GATT's remit. Third, in response to acute competition from East, South and South East Asia, measures were put in place to exclude textiles and clothing formally from the liberalisation process. In the first instance this consisted of extracting a series of voluntary quotas limiting imports from Japan, Hong Kong, Pakistan, and India. Thereafter these restrictions were codified, first during the Dillon Round (1960–61) with the negotiation of the *Short-Term Agreement on Cotton Textiles*. This, in turn, morphed into the 1962 *Long-Term Agreement Regarding Trade in Cotton Textiles* and subsequently the 1974 Multi-Fibre Agreement (MFA).

Taken together these three developments resulted in the emergence of an acutely asymmetrical system of trade regulation. Agricultural, and textile and clothing producers in the industrial states were protected from the growing competitiveness of developing and newly independent producers by the manner in which the GATT was deployed. Producers in industrial states were, nevertheless, able to benefit from negotiated reductions in barriers to trade in manufactured, semi-manufactured, low-, and high-technology goods. But for developing states the combination of the constraints of their own lack of development, the absence of substantive opportunity arising from the GATT, and their diminishing share of world trade served to amplify the value of the institutional advantages afforded to the industrial states.

Attempts were made to redress these imbalances; they were, however, few and far between and lacking in substance. In 1965 the contracting parties negotiated a protocol amending the GATT (effective 1966 and known as 'Part IV') in an effort to address some of the concerns of developing countries. It was, however, acutely inadequate. Part of the problem lay in its reliance upon the willingness of industrial states to consider adopting measures to assist developing countries in their commercial activities, rather than compelling them to put into place remedial measures. Thereafter, few attempts were forthcoming, though discussions during subsequent trade rounds on the problems facing developing countries did grow in intensity.

What is important for our purposes is that by the mid-1960s the character of multilateral trade regulation had been clearly established. At its base was a regulatory framework that had been designed to realise the opportunities afforded to the US in the wake of the Second World War and to facilitate Western European reconstruction as a reflection thereof. Upon that base a second layer of regulation was laid. This layer accentuated the extent to which GATT liberalisation concentrated on the opening of industrial and manufactured goods markets while excluding agriculture, and textiles and clothing.

The peculiar circumstances of the GATT's birth, however, ensured that, up until this point, the development of multilateral trade regulation had been largely informal. Few hard-and-fast rules were adopted and the General Agreement (and, more properly, its principal architects) demonstrated a distinct aversion to formal institutionalisation and bureaucratisation. Indeed, this had previously been seen as a strength. The narrow focus of the GATT and the absence of an extensive set of highly prescriptive rules lent it a streamlined, informal, and malleable quality (see Gorter, 1954: 7–8). It was perceived to be neither a tightly binding set of rules nor a constraint on the sovereign autonomy of the contracting parties (a feature that was particularly important to the US – see Pigman, 1998). Whilst this fluid character initially served the political and economic interests of the GATT's most economically significant contracting parties, and was far from beneficial to its smaller, more vulnerable, developing, primary, and agricultural-producing counterparts, it did so only in the early years. Thereafter, pressure was increasingly brought to bear for a formalisation of GATT disciplines.

The Tokyo Round (1973–79) witnessed a growth in the codification of international trade rules. With this codification came an extension, consolidation, and amplification of the inequalities of opportunity arising from the way in which GATT rules had been deployed. While the results of the Round may have produced a more visible and extensive system of international trade law, instead of attenuating existing asymmetries the shift away from what Sylvia Ostry terms 'broad statements of principle' to 'detailed legalisms' (Ostry, 1997: 89) simply made them worse. Needless to say, Tokyo failed to address many of the GATT's defects. Though progress was made on non-tariff barriers, it resulted in the negotiation of a clutch of side agreements (comprising, among others, the so-called Tokyo 'codes', the forerunners to the WTO's plurilateral agreements) that were binding for (and, as a result, beneficial to) only a handful of (largely) industrial signatories. Little movement was made in liberalising agricultural markets: the US continued to dish out lavish export subsidies to domestic producers and impose quotas on imports of dairy produce; and European discrimination in the sector was exacerbated by the further development of the CAP. Similarly, the Round oversaw the continued exclusion of textiles and clothing from the GATT's remit, first with the negotiation of the MFA and then with the extension of discrimination under MFA II. The result was a third layer that built upon and entrenched the asymmetry and inequity at the core of multilateral trade regulation.

Fashioning the WTO

It was not until the Uruguay Round (1986–94) that a concerted effort to broaden the GATT's commercial remit to include those areas of economic interest to developing countries took place. Yet rather than attending to the asymmetry of opportunity arising from the manner in which the GATT was deployed, the Uruguay Round actually presided over its perpetuation and amplification. The conclusion of the Uruguay Round saw the inclusion of agreements on agriculture, and textiles and clothing, within a wider suite of trade agreements administered by the soon-to-be-created WTO and the adoption of a range of provisions throughout the organisation's legal framework designed to ease some of the pressure for reform generated by the new rules. It also resulted in the adoption of agreements on services (the General Agreement on Trade in Services – GATS), intellectual property (the Agreement on Trade-Related Intellectual Property Rights – TRIPs), and investment measures (the Agreement on Trade-Related Investment Measures – TRIMs). Yet while the inclusion of agriculture, and textiles and clothing rectified an existing imbalance in the way in which the GATT had previously been deployed and the sprinkling of development-sensitive provisions represented a step forward from the GATT era, the introduction of new rules in services, intellectual property, and investment measures simply generated additional asymmetry. Whereas under Uruguay rules developing states could finally hope to benefit from the liberalisation of agricultural and textiles and clothing markets, their lack of capacity and resources ensured that this was not to be the case in the new areas. The potential fruits of Uruguay were, however, much larger for the industrial states. Not only were they existing beneficiaries of trade liberalisation in areas covered by GATT rules, but their economic make-up ensured they would be the principal beneficiaries of the market opportunities presented by the liberalisation of services and investment measures, and the codification of trade-related intellectual property rights.

What Uruguay clearly did, then, was to divide up further the arenas of economic activity in which member states could specialise and, in so doing, to accentuate the problems facing developing countries seeking to diversify their export portfolios. Moreover, not only were the industrial states better suited to taking advantage of these new rules, but their ability to utilise the market opportunities presented therein enabled them to develop a competitive advantage over future market entrants. The result was to carry across the transition in institutions from GATT to WTO an asymmetry of economic opportunity that would form the basis upon which future negotiations would ensue.

Perpetuating asymmetry

Almost from the outset the Uruguay agreements proved to be the source of much frustration; and efforts to further extend the trade agenda in the wake of the Uruguay Round were greeted with hostility from many developing countries. At the core of developing country concerns was the growing problem of implementation. It quickly became apparent that not only were a number of developing countries struggling with the requirements of the Uruguay Round agreements, but there was a good deal of foot-dragging and back-sliding on the part of their industrial counter-parts. Tensions were exacerbated by suggestions that the WTO's remit be extended to include investment, government procurement, competition policy, trade facilitation, environmental protection, and, most controversially, labour standards (see Hughes and Wilkinson, 1998; Wilkinson, 1999), and that the members embark on a further round of trade negotiations so soon after the conclusion of Uruguay. This tension played out over WTO ministerial meetings, each building on the last in terms of the degree of consternation involved. Most infamously, tensions came to a head during the November/December 1999 Seattle ministerial meeting when, amid mass demonstrations outside the convention centre, delegates failed to agree the launch of what was then touted as the 'millennium round'.

Crucially, the post-Seattle rehabilitation process saw a concerted effort to place development at the centre of a new trade round. This, combined with the sheer amount of effort put into building a consensus by key WTO officials (including the then Director-General, Mike Moore) and the tenderness of the political climate in which the Doha Ministerial meeting took place (just two months after the 11 September 2001 attacks on the US), proved enough for members to agree to a new Round – albeit named the 'Doha Development Agenda' rather than a Round, by way of a nod to its supposed focus. Yet despite its supposed focus, the DDA promised merely to address a handful of existing anomalies in return for an extension of the WTO's legal framework into new areas.

There were undoubted successes in tailoring the work programme towards areas of interest to the developing world: the Ministerial Declaration was steeped in the language of development; the Ministerial Decision on Implementation-Related Issues and Concerns (WTO, 2001b) and the Ministerial Declaration identified implementation issues as an integral part of the work programme – albeit that the former lacked real compunction; the agricultural negotiations set out to pursue substantial improvements in market access, and reduce (and eventually eliminate) export subsidies and trade-distorting domestic support systems; the negotiations on non-agricultural market access were structured such that the reduction and elimination of tariff peaks, high tariffs, tariff escalation, tariffs affecting the export interests of developing countries, and non-tariff barriers sat alongside a more traditional focus on the reduction of barriers to trade; the TRIPs negotiations included a commitment to extend the protection of geographical indicators to products other than wines and spirits; the Declaration on TRIPs and public health offered members greater flexibility in adhering to the TRIPs agreement in times of national health crises (WTO, 2001c); and the Ministerial Declaration promised to explore the relationship between trade, debt, and finance, the plight of small economies, the transfer of technology, technical co-operation and capacity-building, and a commitment to review and strengthen special and differential provisions.

However, the balance of potential gains from the work programme remained firmly with the industrial states. In addition to the benefits resulting from the full implementation of the Uruguay accords, improvements in NAMA, aspects of the negotiations on agriculture, and a further extension of the TRIPs, the DDA added a commitment to begin (albeit on the basis that an 'explicit consensus' should be forthcoming) negotiations in investment, government procurement, trade facilitation, and competition policy (the so-called Singapore issues, because they were first raised as desiderata during the 1996 Singapore Ministerial meeting) (and possibly a fifth: e-commerce) (WTO, 2001a). Moreover, the DDA put in place a specific timeframe in which negotiations would commence on the Singapore issues (subject to minor clarification, after the mid-term review of negotiations in Cancún) and stipulated that the results would form the basis of a second single undertaking. Unsurprisingly, the asymmetry in the DDA quickly became the source of developing country frustrations and resulted in a bout of alliance warfare that saw coalition upon coalition combine and consolidate to produce a deadlock. This resulted, in turn, in the collapse of the Cancún meeting (see Chapter 1 above for a more detailed account of the Cancún meeting; also Narlikar and Wilkinson, 2004). Indeed, the only common ground that emerged was that the DDA would not reach a conclusion before 1 January 2005 deadline.

After the initial period of reflection, and much like Seattle, the post-Cancún period saw renewed energy emerge among the WTO membership. Breaking the ice, in early 2004 both the US and EU signalled that they were ready to negotiate the elimination of all forms of agricultural export subsidies (including credits and food aid – US tools to promote exports – as well as more traditional means of subsidising exports) (Clapp, 2004: 1444). By June 2004 the then WTO DG, Supachai Panitchpakdi, was praising delegates for the progress that had been made in the agricultural negotiations (albeit peppered with the obligatory encouragement to keep moving forward). Each of the principal protagonists in the Cancún showdown had submitted papers outlining their preferred ways of moving forward – the G20, G10, and G33 – and the EU again stressed its willingness to phase out export subsidies on the condition that other (largely US) forms of subsidising exports were eliminated and that an 'acceptable' outcome could be reached on market access and domestic support (WTO, 2004). These developments nevertheless proved insufficient to enable members to agree upon formal negotiating modalities at the Hong Kong Ministerial. As is set out in more detail in Chapter 1, the result was a decision to scale back expectation ahead of the ministerial to ensure that some agreement was reached and to lock in the momentum that had been built into the negotiations since the collapse at Cancún.

That said, a modicum of agreement was forthcoming in Hong Kong. The meeting resulted in the production of a 59-paragraph, 11-page ministerial text with six accompanying annexes (relating to agriculture, market access for non-agricultural products, services, rules, trade facilitation, and special and differential treatment) altered slightly from the pre-meeting version. At its core the declaration saw members agree to: (in agriculture) the broad structure for reductions in domestic support and market access as well as to a date of the end of 2013 for the phase-out of export subsidies; (on cotton) the elimination of all forms of export subsidies 'in 2006' and duty-free and quota-free access for products from least developed members by the developed countries; (in NAMA) the adoption of the Swiss formula as the mechanism for cutting tariffs, though agreement on the respective coefficients for developed and developing members was not forthcoming; and (in services) movement forward in establishing the parameters of the negotiations without the pre-ministerial desiderata that countries engage in market access negotiations on a plurilateral basis should they be presented with a request to do so (see WTO, 2005). In addition, the Declaration set out five elements of a development package in the form of amendments to the special and differential treatment enjoyed by least developed members comprising (1) expediency in considering requests for waivers; (2) duty-free and quota-free market access on all 97 per cent of products originating in least developed countries (LDCs); (3) reaffirmation that LDCs need only undertake commitments and give concessions consistent with their level of development; (4) a provision empowering LDCs to deviate from their obligations under the TRIMs for seven years (for existing measures) and five years (for new measures); and (5) further technical and financial assistance to enable LDCs to meet their obligations and commitments as well as to better realise the opportunities presented by trade liberalisation (that is, provide Aid for Trade) (WTO, 2005: Annex F). Members also agreed to establish a task force on how Aid for Trade might contribute 'most effectively to the development dimension of the DDA' (WTO, 2005: paragraph 57).

The conclusion of the DDA and its likely consequences for multilateral trade regulation

The conclusion of the Hong Kong Ministerial proved to be a high point. The April 2006 deadline for the agreement of negotiating modalities agreed in Hong Kong was missed; little progress was made in the negotiations generally; and the Round came to an abrupt halt in July 2006. Inevitably this has led to a resurgence of speculation that the DDA was increasingly moribund. Moreover, the looming of the end of US fast-track authority in mid-2007 led to much debate about the capacity of the Round to be completed. Yet while the breakdown in the talks and the prospect of an expiry of fast-track authority is significant, the general pattern of Rounds to date (which since at least the Kennedy Round have been as tortuous as the DDA) suggests that in the long run missed deadlines and moments of heightened political contestation are merely punctuations in the general pattern of negotiations. The renewal of fast-track authority has so far not been a problem when it has run out during a Round (though, of course, this is not to claim that it will be unproblematic in this case); and nearly all of the previous eight Rounds have overrun, with the DDA's immediate predecessors – the Tokyo (1973–79) and Uruguay (1986–94) Rounds – doing so by some four years. What is significant is not when the Round will be concluded (2008 is probably the earliest date, with 2009 or 2010 being more likely) but what the consequences will be for the development of multilateral trade regulation and the distribution of economic opportunity arising therefrom once it has been concluded. Two points are noteworthy in this regard.

First, the balance of economic opportunity resulting from a conclusion to the DDA is likely to reside with the industrial states. Since the launch of the DDA the 'development' content of the Round has been progressively boiled down to a focus on agricultural liberalisation with a smattering of sweeteners for the least developed (Aid for Trade, best endeavour commitments, duty-free and quota-free access, and so on). However, a significant liberalisation of, particularly, US and EU agriculture markets is unlikely. That said, it is likely that the DDA will reach a conclusion only after some movement in agriculture has been seen to be made. The extent of the movement deemed to be sufficient is likely to be scaled back as the negotiations continue and negotiating fatigue sets in.[2] Moreover, the price for movement in agriculture demanded by the US and EU is likely to be disproportionately greater than the benefits that flow therefrom. This will most likely see significant gains being made in services and NAMA, among others. Inevitably, the Round's conclusion will also bring with it a greater number of sweeteners to ensure agreement. Furthermore, if the history of trade negotiations tells us anything about the general pattern of the conclusion of Rounds, the close of the DDA will not be just about the agreement of a bargain between the industrial and developing states. Since the Kennedy negotiations each Round has not been concluded without some kind of bilateral deal having to be negotiated between the US and EU (occasionally with other industrial states involved). For instance, the Uruguay Round negotiations were not to be concluded without the US and EU first agreeing to the infamous Blair House accord (and its renegotiation at the eleventh hour) on agriculture, or the US, EU, Japan, and Canada agreeing the July 1993 Tokyo accord.[3]

Second, that the DDA will probably result in an asymmetrical bargain is not, in itself, surprising; what are significant are the consequences of another asymmetrical bargain when that bargain is placed within the context of the overall development of postwar multilateral trade regulation. As we have seen, the development of multilateral trade regulation has been one of increasing asymmetry: the manner in which the GATT was first deployed saw the selective liberalisation of markets, establishing an asymmetry of economic opportunity; this was consolidated and amplified by the subsequent exclusion of agriculture, and textiles and clothing, from the GATT's purview and the concentration on the liberalisation of industrial, manufactured, and some semi-manufactured goods; and this pattern of asymmetry was further exacerbated and entrenched by the conclusion of the Tokyo negotiations and was institutionalised, consolidated, and extended by the bargain struck during the Uruguay Round. The problem here is that even a fraction of imbalance in favour of the industrial states in the final agreement of the DDA will result in the amplification of the economic opportunities afforded to the industrial members of the WTO. When understood in terms of the contribution of the DDA to multilateral trade regulation already laid, we can see that anything less than an agreement that markedly favours developing countries over their industrial counterparts (and even then, the most vulnerable of their number, not their largest, most notable constituents) will merely perpetuate existing imbalances. In the absence of such an outcome the consequences of adding a further layer on to the WTO's existing legal framework should the DDA be concluded will be significant. Many developing states will be able merely to consolidate their production of agricultural produce, textiles, and clothing, and some low-technology goods. Little industrial diversification will occur among the poorest or smallest economies as the costs of moving away from established industries and investing in new sectors will be prohibitive. This is irrespective of any increase in technical and other assistance that Aid for Trade packages may provide. The leading industrial states will nevertheless be able to consolidate their competitive advantages in sectors in which they are already dominant, thereby further crowding out the capacity of developing countries to be market entrants. Such an outcome will result in the DDA being significantly less than the development Round it was supposed to be. But then this has come to be the pattern of trade negotiations; little exists that suggests that the current or future Rounds will be any different.

Notes

1 This section draws on Wilkinson (2006).
2 In telephone interviews with the author in July 2006 LDC delegates were already expressing a desire to salvage something from their efforts in the round so far. This is likely to see LDCs revise their positions and agree to aspects of a wider bargain that they might otherwise have resisted, such is their need for a return for negotiating resources expended thus far.
3 The Tokyo Accord saw the US, EU, Japan, and Canada agree to eliminate tariff and non-tariff barriers in pharmaceuticals, construction equipment, medical equipment, steel, beer, furniture, farm equipment, and spirits; the harmonisation of tariffs among the group in chemical products; a target of 50 per cent on tariffs over 15 per cent (subject to exceptions); and tariff cuts of at least one-third in all other products (see Hoda, 2001: 37).

References

Bergsten, C. Fred (2005), 'Rescuing the Doha Round', *Foreign Affairs*, special edition (December).

Blair, Tony (2006), Address to the Australian Parliament, 27 March.

Clapp, Jennifer (2004), 'WTO Agricultural Trade Battles and Food Aid', *Third World Quarterly*, 25: 8.

de Jonquières, Guy (2006), 'Do-it-yourself Is Free Trade's Best "Plan B"', *Financial Times*, 23 August.

Diebold, William Jr (1952) 'The End of the ITO', *Essays in International Finance* No. 16, International Finance Section, Department of Economics, Princeton University.

Economist, The (2006), 'The Wrecking of the World Trade Talks Was Senseless and Short-sighted', 29 July.

Evans, John W. (1971), *The Kennedy Round in American Trade Policy: The Twilight of the GATT?* (Cambridge, Mass.: Harvard University Press).

Feis, Herbert (1948), 'The Geneva Proposal for an International Trade Charter', *International Organization*, 2: 1 (February).

Gardner, Richard N. (1956), *Sterling–Dollar Diplomacy: Anglo-American Collaboration in the Reconstruction of Multilateral Trade* (Oxford: Clarendon Press).

Gorter, Wytze (1954) 'GATT after Six Years: An Appraisal', *International Organization*, 8: 1 (February).

Hoda, Anwarul (2001), *Tariff Negotiations and Renegotiations under the GATT and WTO: Procedures and Practices* (Cambridge: Cambridge University Press).

Hughes, Steve, and Wilkinson, Rorden (1998), 'International Labour Standards and World Trade: No Role for the World Trade Organisation?', *New Political Economy*, 3: 3 (November).

Knorr, Klaus (1948) 'The Bretton Woods Institutions in Transition', *International Organization* 2: 1 (February).

Kock, Karin (1969), *International Trade Policy and the GATT, 1947–1967* (Stockholm: Almqvist and Wiksell).

Lamy, Pascal (2003), 'Trade Crisis', Speech to the European Institute, Washington, 4 November.

Narlikar, Amrita, and Wilkinson, Rorden (2004) 'Collapse at the WTO: A Cancún Post-mortem', *Third World Quarterly*, 25: 3.

Odell, John, and Eichengreen, Barry (1998), 'The United States, the ITO, and the WTO: Exit Options, Agent Slack, and Presidential Leadership', in Anne O. Krueger (ed.), *The WTO as an International Organization* (Chicago: University of Chicago Press).

Ostry, Sylvia (1997), *The Post-Cold War Trading System* (London: University of Chicago Press).

Pigman, Geoffrey Allen (1998), 'The Sovereignty Discourse and the US Debate on Joining the World Trade Organisation', *Global Society*, 12: 1.

Ruggie, John Gerard (1998), *Constructing the World Polity: Essays on International Institutionalization* (London: Routledge).

Toynbee, Arnold J. (1947), 'The International Economic Outlook', *International Affairs*, 23: 4 (October).

Wilkinson, Rorden (1999), 'Labour and Trade-Related Regulation: Beyond the Trade–Labour Standards Debate?', *British Journal of Politics and International Relations*, 1: 2 (June).

Wilkinson, Rorden (2002) 'Peripheralising Labour: The ILO, WTO and the Completion of the Bretton Woods Project', in Jeffery Harrod and Robert O'Brien (eds), *Globalized Unions? Theory and Strategies of Organized Labour in the Global Political Economy* (London: Routledge).

Wilkinson, Rorden (2004), 'Crisis in Cancún', *Global Governance*, 10: 2 (March).

Wilkinson, Rorden (2006), *The WTO: Crisis and the Governance of Global Trade* (London: Routledge).

Winham, Gilbert R. (1986), *International Trade and the Tokyo Round* (Princeton: Princeton University Press).

WTO (2001a), Doha Ministerial Declaration, WT/MIN(01)/DEC/1 (20 November).

WTO (2001b), Decision on Implementation-Related Issues and Concerns, WT/MIN(01)/17 (20 November).

WTO (2001c), Declaration on the TRIPs Agreement and Public Health, WT/MIN(01)/DEC/2 (20 November).

WTO (2004), 'Doha Work Programme: Decision adopted by the General Council on 1 August 2004', WT/L/579 (2 August).

WTO (2005), Hong Kong Ministerial Declaration, adopted 18 December, WT/MIN(05)/W/3/Rev.2.

Zoellick, Robert B. (2003), 'America Will Not Wait for the Won't Do Countries', *Financial Times*, 22 September.

Index